Travel Discount Coupon

This coupon entitles you to special discounts
when you book your trip through the

TRAVEL NETWORK®
RESERVATION SERVICE

Hotels ♦ Airlines ♦ Car Rentals ♦ Cruises
All Your Travel Needs

Here's what you get: *

♦ A discount of $50 USD on a booking of $1,000** or
  more for two or more people!

♦ A discount of $25 USD on a booking of $500** or more
  for one person!

♦ Free membership for three years, and 1,000 free miles
  on enrollment in the unique Travel Network Miles-to-
  Go® frequent-traveler program. Earn one mile for
  every dollar spent through the program. Redeem
  miles for free hotel stays starting at 5,000 miles. Earn
  free roundtrip airline tickets starting at 25,000 miles.

♦ Personal help in planning your own, customized trip.

♦ Fast, confirmed reservations at any property
  recommended in this guide, subject to availability.***

♦ Special discounts on bookings in the U.S. and around
  the world.

♦ Low-cost visa and passport service.

♦ Reduced-rate cruise packages and special car rental
  programs worldwide.

Visit our website at http://www.travelnetwork.com/Frommer
or call us globally at 201-567-8500, ext. 55. In the U.S., call
toll-free at 1-888-940-5000, or fax 201-567-1838. In Canada,
call at 1-905-707-7222, or fax 905-707-8108. In Asia, call
60-3-7191044, or fax 60-3-7185415.

* To qualify for these travel discounts, at least a portion of your trip must
  include destinations covered in this guide. No more than one coupon discount
  may be used in any 12-month period, for destinations covered in this guide.
  Cannot be combined with any other discount or promotion.
**These are U.S. dollars spent on commissionable bookings.
***A $10 USD fee, plus fax and/or phone charges, will be added to the cost of
  bookings at each hotel not linked to the reservation service. Customers must
  approve these fees in advance. If only hotels of this kind are booked, the traveler(s)
  must also purchase roundtrip air tickets from Travel Network for the trip.

Valid until December 31, 1998. Terms and conditions of the Miles-to-
Go® program are available on request by calling 201-567-8500, ext 55.

DGO234

Frommer's® 98

San Diego

by Elizabeth Hansen

Assisted by Suzanne Osborne

Macmillan • USA

ABOUT THE AUTHORS

Longtime San Diego resident **Elizabeth Hansen** is also the author of *Frommer's Australia, Frommer's Australia From $50 a Day, Frommer's New Zealand From $50 a Day,* and a contributor to *Frommer's California From $60 a Day, Frommer's California,* and *Frommer's USA.* Elizabeth regularly writes magazine articles and gives illustrated presentations on her hometown. When not traveling, the author and her husband, Richard Adams, live in La Jolla.

Suzanne Osborne has lived in San Diego since 1970. When she's not working on books with Elizabeth, she enjoys gardening, traveling, and spending time with friends, family, and "the boys" (her three big dogs).

MACMILLAN TRAVEL

A Simon & Schuster Macmillan Company
1633 Broadway
New York, NY 10019

Find us online at **www.frommers.com** or
on America Online at Keyword: **Frommers**.

ISBN 0-02-861671-5
ISSN 1047-787X

Editor: Vanessa Rosen
Production Editor: Chris Van Camp
Map Editor: Douglas Stallings
Design by Michele Laseau
Digital cartography by John Decamillis, Roberta Stockwell, and Ortelius Design

SPECIAL SALES

Bulk purchases (10+ copies) of Frommer's and selected Macmillan travel guides are available to corporations, organizations, mail-order catalogs, institutions, and charities at special discounts, and can be customized to suit individual needs. For more information, write to Special Sales, Macmillan General Reference, 1633 Broadway, New York, NY 10019.

Manufactured in the United States of America

Contents

List of Maps

For my mother, Katherine Nelson, with much love.

ACKNOWLEDGMENTS

I'm very grateful to the San Diego Convention & Visitors Bureau, the San Diego North County Convention & Visitors Bureau, and the Metropolitan Transit Development Board for the assistance they provided. I'd also like to thank my friends and family in San Diego who help me keep track of the latest changes in our dynamic hospitality industry, the readers who took the time to share their experiences with me, and my editor Vanessa Rosen. And most of all, I am indebted to my sister Jinny and niece Laurie who—3 decades ago—made the cross-country trek to San Diego with me and helped me begin to find my place here.

AN INVITATION TO THE READER

In researching this book, I discovered many wonderful places—hotels, restaurants, shops, and more. I'm sure you'll find others. Please tell me about them, so I can share the information with your fellow travelers in upcoming editions. If you were disappointed with a recommendation, I want to know that, too. Please write to:

Elizabeth Hansen,
Frommer's San Diego '98
c/o Macmillan Travel
1633 Broadway
New York, NY 10019

AN ADDITIONAL NOTE

Please be advised that travel information is subject to change at any time—and this is especially true of prices. We therefore suggest that you write or call ahead for confirmation when making your travel plans. The authors, editors, and publisher cannot be held responsible for the experiences of readers while traveling. Your safety is important to us, however, so we encourage you to stay alert and be aware of your surroundings. Keep a close eye on cameras, purses, and wallets, all favorite targets of thieves and pickpockets.

WHAT THE SYMBOL MEANS

✪ Frommer's Favorites

Our favorite places and experiences—outstanding for quality, value, or both.

The following abbreviations are used for credit cards:

AE	American Express	EU	Eurocard
CB	Carte Blanche	JCB	Japan Credit Bank
DC	Diners Club	MC	MasterCard
DISC	Discover	V	Visa
ER	enRoute		

FIND FROMMER'S ONLINE

Arthur Frommer's Outspoken Encyclopedia of Travel (**www.frommers.com**) offers more than 6,000 pages of up-to-the-minute travel information—including the latest bargains and candid, personal articles updated daily by Arthur Frommer himself. No other Web site offers such comprehensive and timely coverage of the world of travel.

Welcome to San Diego

If you've never been to San Diego or your last visit was more than a few years ago, my hometown holds some surprises for you. It's grown up. San Diego is no longer just a laid-back Navy town—its coming-of-age includes avant-garde architecture, sophisticated dining options, and world-class tourist facilities.

You'll notice the architecture right away. If you're driving to San Diego from the north, you'll pass the eye-catching Hyatt Regency La Jolla alongside Interstate 5. Near this striking neoclassical structure, the snow-white, multiturreted Mormon temple seems an unlikely neighbor. If you're flying in, look out the window as you approach Lindbergh Field to note the changes, such as high-rise office towers and hotels in the downtown area adjacent to San Diego Bay. Since the flight path goes right over downtown, you may sometimes feel that you're going to land on the rooftops.

Today, approximately 1.2 million people live in San Diego, making it the seventh-largest city in the United States (after New York, Los Angeles, Chicago, Houston, Philadelphia, and Phoenix) and the second-largest city in California. While the city's population keeps increasing, I'm happy to report that San Diego hasn't completely lost its small-town ambiance, and still retains a strong connection with its Hispanic heritage and culture.

1 Frommer's Favorite San Diego Experiences

- **Strolling Through the Gaslamp Quarter.** Victorian commercial buildings that fill a 16¹/₂-block area will make you think you've stepped back in time. The buildings, right in the heart of downtown, are beautifully restored and house some of the city's most popular shops, restaurants, and nightspots.
- **Shopping and Sipping Margaritas in Bazaar del Mundo.** Old Mexico is alive and well in San Diego's colorful Bazaar del Mundo. The lively strains of mariachi music add to the atmosphere.
- **Listening to Free Organ Recitals in Balboa Park on Sunday.** Even if you usually don't like organ music, you might enjoy these outdoor concerts and the crowds they draw—San Diegans with their parents, their children, their dogs. The music, enhanced with

commentary by the organist, runs the gamut from classical to contemporary. Concerts start at 2pm.

- **Relaxing with Afternoon Tea at the U.S. Grant Hotel or the Horton Grand.** A genteel tradition in San Diego, the custom of afternoon tea is at its most elegant at the U.S. Grant and quite cozy at the Horton Grand. Take your pick.
- **Taking the Ferry to Coronado.** This 15-minute ride gets you out onto San Diego Harbor and provides some of the best views of the city. The ferry runs every hour from the Broadway Pier, so you can tour Coronado on foot or by bike or trolley and return whenever you please.
- **Riding on the San Diego Trolley to Mexico.** The trip costs a mere $2.00 from downtown and only takes 40 minutes, and the clean, quick trolleys are fun in their own right.
- **Wandering Through Horton Plaza.** This place has a whimsy and an architectural appeal that blends many styles, colors, and myriad shops. It's conducive to wandering—created purposefully to keep you from getting directly from point A to point B.
- **Listening to Jazz at Croce's.** Ideally located in the center of downtown in a historic Gaslamp Quarter building, Croce's celebrates the life of musician Jim Croce and showcases the city's jazz musicians.
- **Watching the Sun Set Over the Ocean.** It's a free and memorable experience. My favorite sunset-watching spots include the Mission Beach and Pacific Beach boardwalks and the beach in Coronado in front of the Hotel del Coronado. At La Jolla's Windansea Beach, wandering down to the water at dusk, with wine glass in hand, is a nightly neighborhood event.
- **Drinking Coffee at a La Jolla Sidewalk Cafe.** San Diego offers a plethora of places to enjoy lattes, espressos, and cappuccinos, but the coffeehouses in La Jolla serve up a special panache. For my favorites, see the "Java Joints in La Jolla" box in chapter 6.
- **Enjoying Performing Arts Outdoors.** During the summer, dramas, comedies, and musicals take place on the Festival Stage at the Old Globe Theatre and in the Starlight bowl in Balboa Park, in the amphitheater atop Mount Helix in La Mesa, and at Moonlight Amphitheater in Vista.
- **Walking Along the Water.** The city offers walkers several great places to stroll. One of my favorites, along the waterfront from the Convention Center to the Maritime Museum, affords views of aircraft carriers, tuna seiners, and sailboats.
- **Visiting the "Lobster Lady" in Puerto Nuevo.** South of the border, they serve lobster with rice, beans, and tortillas, and it's delicious. (See chapter 11 for details.)
- **Purchasing Just-Picked Produce at a Farmers' Market.** On various days, markets throughout the area sell the bountiful harvest of San Diego County. For a complete schedule, see chapter 9.
- **Floating Up, Up, and Away Over North County.** Hot-air balloons carry passengers over the golf courses and luxury homes north of the city. These rides are especially enjoyable at sunset.
- **Going to the Movies San Diego–Style.** Imagine sitting on the deck of the world's oldest merchant ship afloat, watching a film projected on the "screen-sail," or floating on a raft in a huge indoor pool while a movie is shown on the wall. Only in San Diego!
- **Watching the Grunion Run.** These tiny sardine-shaped fish spawn on San Diego beaches between March and August, and the locals love to be there. To know the date of the next such event, pick up a free tide chart at a surf shop or consult the daily newspaper.

- **Picnicking in a Park.** San Diego's nearly perfect climate invites casual outdoor dining. Favorite spots include Balboa Park (I like the lawn next to the reflecting pool), Embarcadero Marina Park (near Seaport Village), and Ellen Browning Scripps Park overlooking the ocean in La Jolla.

2 The City Today

San Diego has always had great weather and beaches, but now it's got a lot more to offer beyond surf and sun. This change resulted in part from the influx of high-tech (especially biotech) industry to San Diego. The new arrivals contribute to the growth of the performing arts and support sophisticated dining, nightlife, and shopping.

Completion of the Convention Center, which took nearly 3 years to build, has also made a tremendous difference. The center attracts several hundred meetings, conventions, exhibits, and trade shows per year. Its proximity to the Gaslamp Quarter contributed to the Quarter's rebirth. Now when I wander past the chic restaurants and hot nightspots along Fourth and Fifth avenues, it's hard to remember how run-down this area used to be.

Some things about San Diego, however, haven't changed. The people who live here love to get out and enjoy their beautiful surroundings. San Diegans are often busy in-line skating, cycling, sailing, and surfing.

Our enthusiasm for active pursuits goes hand-in-hand with an interest in being healthy (and a very L.A.–style propensity toward vanity). It's not just a rumor that some of us embrace exotic herbs, holistic remedies, and nontraditional therapies at a rate unknown in other parts of the country. Large numbers also eschew red meat, and smokers are herded into smaller and smaller areas. It's not surprising that nationally renowned author Deepak Chopra makes his home here. Logically enough, San Diego County is also home to several health spas (I've described a few in chapter 11).

I'm not alone in my affection for San Diego. Since most people want to keep things just the way they are, it isn't hard to get "no growth" ballot issues passed. This doesn't help our economy, already weakened by cuts in defense spending, but it prevents something we all fear—"Los Angelization." Preventing Los Angelization means controlling smog and other forms of pollution and the sprawl of housing developments, which consume open space. A recent ballot issue dealt with setting aside a certain amount of open space for each residential tract so that the county won't become an endless sea of cookie-cutter houses.

For the moment we've tabled the debate on moving Lindbergh Field and are in the middle of a major (messy) expansion of the airport. Construction started before the Republican National Convention, which we hosted in August 1996 and is *supposed* to end before we host Super Bowl XXXII.

Other hot topics as this book went to press in late 1997 included the expansion of what was then known as Jack Murphy Stadium. The city council approved funds to increase the size of the structure prior to hosting Super Bowl XXXII, and the majority of local residents objected. The NFL stepped in and said if the stadium expansion wasn't completed, they'd move the January 1998 event to the Rose Bowl in Pasadena. The Chargers joined the melee and threatened to leave San Diego. This issue occupied the front page of the *San Diego Union-Tribune* for weeks until the president of Qualcomm, a local communications company, stepped in and offered to donate a portion of the additional funds needed for the expansion provided that the completed stadium would bear the company's name.

The year 1997 also saw the (apparently) final collapse of the San Diego Symphony. After being rescued by civic-minded angels on several occasions, the powers that be

San Diego Area at a Glance

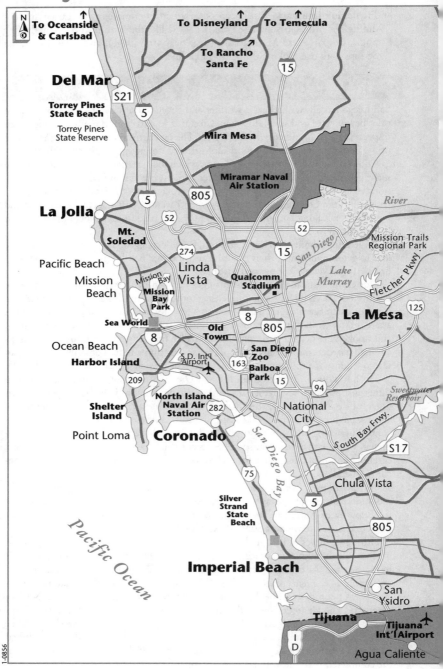

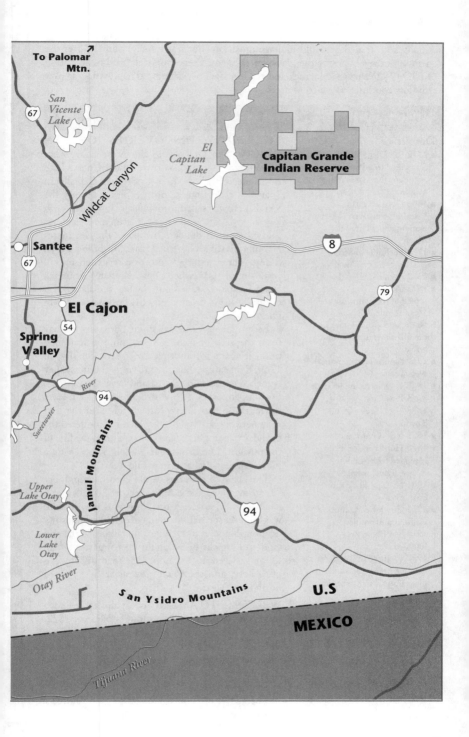

To Palomar Mtn.

San Vicente Lake

67

Wildcat Canyon

El Capitan Lake

Capitan Grande Indian Reserve

8

Santee

67

El Cajon

79

54

Spring Valley

River

94

Sweetwater

Jamul Mountains

Upper Lake Otay

94

Lower Lake Otay

Otay River

San Ysidro Mountains

U.S

MEXICO

Tijuana River

finally admitted they could manage musicians but not money. Shortly after the demise of the symphony the new owners of San Diego's only classical radio station KFSD (94.1) changed to a rock-and-roll format. The wailing and hand-wringing over this loss continues as we go to press.

3 History 101

Dateline

- **1542** San Diego Bay discovered by a Portuguese explorer, who names it San Miguel.
- **1602** Don Sebastián Vizcaíno rediscovers the bay, naming it San Diego de Alcala.
- **1769** Fr. Junípero Serra establishes first mission.
- **1822** Spanish rule ends.
- **1825–31** San Diego is the capital of California under Mexican rule.
- **1846** American flag flies for the first time; first Mormons arrive.
- **1867** Alonzo Horton founds New Town.
- **1868** 1,400 acres are set aside for Balboa Park.
- **1872** Great fire in Old Town.
- **1885** Railway arrives.
- **1888** Hotel del Coronado, equipped with "Edison electric light," opens.
- **1901** Naval military base established.
- **1915** City hosts Panama-California Exposition.
- **1916** San Diego Zoo founded.
- **1927** Charles Lindbergh tests the *Spirit of St. Louis* and plans historic transatlantic flight.
- **1935** City hosts California Pacific International Exposition; Old Globe Theatre built.
- **1941–45** Population in area doubles during World War II; military takes over Balboa Park.

continues

THE MANY DISCOVERIES OF SAN DIEGO San Diego is to the West Coast what Jamestown, Virginia, is to the East Coast. João Rodrigues Cabrilho (Juan Rodríguez Cabrillo in Spanish), a Portuguese-born explorer serving the Spanish crown, sailed into what is now San Diego Bay in 1542, 50 years after Christopher Columbus spotted land on the eastern side of the continent. Naming his discovery San Miguel, Cabrilho stayed 6 days, then departed. No one returned for 60 years—until 1602, when Don Sebastián Vizcaíno, a Spanish explorer, sailed into the bay and renamed it in honor of his flagship and his favorite saint, San Diego de Alcala.

Because the present day Point Loma hid the bay from the view of passing ships, no one stumbled upon it again for another 150 years. Finally, in 1769, the Spanish took steps to settle the area. They launched expeditions by sea and land: One arrival, Fr. Junípero Serra, a 58-year-old priest, would leave his mark on San Diego forever. He said the first mass here on July 16, 1769, which is considered the birthday of San Diego, and he established the first of the mission churches—a small adobe chapel—on a hill overlooking what is now Old Town.

The chain of missions would eventually number 21, strung along the California coast 30 miles, or a day's journey, apart. A fort known as the Presidio was built on the hilltop, and a fledgling community developed around it. Despite crop failures in the arid land and attacks by neighboring Kumeyaays, San Diego survived. In 1775, the first Spanish baby was born here, and the town grew as settlers moved north from Mexico.

WELCOME TO AMERICA Spanish rule ended in California the same year it did in Mexico: 1822. By then, the town had moved down the hill from the fort into the area now known as Old Town. A Mexican flag flew here until 1846, when the first American flag was raised in the plaza. California became a state in 1850.

The arrival of Alonzo Horton in 1867 started a new era of prosperity. Horton, who had profited in the California gold rush, was determined to turn San Diego into a great city. He recognized that the downtown area needed to be closer to the waterfront so goods could be easily shipped and received. He built a wharf (about where the Convention Center is now), bought up adjacent land (for about 27¢ an acre), sold off lots, and constructed commercial buildings. The city government moved to New Town in 1871. The arrival of the railroad in 1885 and the discovery of gold in the back country in 1869 further aided the community's growth. In 1888 San Diego's population hit 40,000; by 1890, Old Town was a thing of the past.

Two better-known entrepreneurs of this period were Elisha Babcock and H. L. Story, businessmen from the East who initially came to these parts for the curative climate and rabbit hunting. Once here, they decided to build a grand hotel, and in 1888, only 11 months after construction began, they opened the beautiful Hotel del Coronado, which to this day remains the largest wooden oceanside resort hotel in the world (see "A Hotel with History: Scenes from the Hotel del Coronado" in chapter 5). Thomas Edison himself had overseen the installation of the hotel's newfangled lighting system, and each room came with the notice that it was "equipped with Edison electric light" and the admonition "Do not attempt to light with a match. The use of electricity is in no way harmful to your health." The town of Coronado was incorporated in 1890 and still remains a municipality separate from San Diego.

In 1870, another successful businessman, George Marston, came to San Diego with his family from Wisconsin and started working in Alonzo Horton's hotel. He went on to found a successful department store, the Marston Company, which was a local landmark until it became part of the Broadway department stores in the 1960s.

Marston believed "people in this workaday world should not only have a living wage but opportunities for a great measure of health, comfort, and beauty," and he turned his enormous humanitarian and environmentalist energies, not to mention his money and clout, toward the creation of Balboa Park, Presidio Park, the Junípero Serra Museum, the San Diego Historical Society, and the Anza-Borrego Desert State Park.

In the late 1800s, San Francisco millionaire and sugar magnate John D. Spreckels became captivated by San Diego and Coronado and began investing in the area. In 1906, after the San Francisco earthquake, he made it his home. Spreckels, whose name is scattered on buildings throughout San Diego and Coronado to this day, soon owned most everything of value in both towns, including the Hotel del Coronado; two newspapers; a bank; a hotel; a railway; and the ferry, trolley, and water systems.

- **1948** Palomar Observatory opens.
- **1969** San Diego–Coronado Bay Bridge opens; seven women invade the "gentlemen only" Grant Grill.
- **1971** San Diego becomes California's second-largest city.
- **1982** First baby condor born at San Diego Zoo.
- **1987** San Diego Yacht Club wins the America's Cup (from Australia).
- **1989** San Diego Convention Center opens, sparking a rebirth of downtown.
- **1990** Economic recession hits.
- **1992** San Diego hosts (and retains) America's Cup.
- **1995** San Diego Chargers play in the Super Bowl; San Diego hosts and loses the America's Cup; first U.S. warm-weather Olympic training center opens in Chula Vista.
- **1996** San Diego hosts the Republican National Convention; two giant pandas from China arrive at the San Diego Zoo; the San Diego Symphony declares bankruptcy.
- **1997** The Navy's Top Gun school moves out of San Diego and Marine helicopters move in; public outcry over stadium expansion threatens future of Super Bowl XXXII. The local economy recovers.

His vast entrepreneurial skills, energy, and financial wherewithal contributed greatly to the cities' growth, beauty, and appeal over the next 20 years.

An architect who made his mark on the growing city, Irving Gill, arrived from Syracuse, New York, in 1893. Gill, influenced by the Spanish missions, built or remodeled more than 200 houses and buildings in San Diego County, and about 75 still exist; some can be seen in the Hillcrest section of San Diego and in La Jolla. At a time when ornamentation was the architectural mode, Gill set out to build houses that were "simple, plain, and substantial as a boulder," thinking it best to "leave the ornamentation to nature, who will tone it with lichens, chisel it with storms, make it gracious and friendly with vines and flower shapes as she does the stone in the meadow." He aligned himself with simplicity in an age of extravagance. Although he died in near obscurity in 1936, he is revered today.

THE 20TH CENTURY   In 1868, San Diego, with a population barely topping 2,000, set aside 1,400 acres for what would become this nation's second planned city park. Work began in 1903, and in 1910 the park was named Balboa, after the explorer who was the first European to venture through the Isthmus of Panama. In 1915 the city decided to host the Panama-California Exposition, similar to a world's fair, and Bertram Goodhue from New York was called in to design the buildings for it in Balboa Park. Goodhue, quite different from Irving Gill, imagined architecture that would provide "illusion rather than reality," and he created a fantasy city that blended Old Spain and Moorish, Aztec, Mexican, and even Asian influences.

The resulting highly ornamented buildings had a magical effect that left a lasting mark on San Diego architecture. Today the buildings house many of the museums in the park, which is the nation's second-largest museum complex (after the Smithsonian Institution in Washington, D.C.).

The world-famous San Diego Zoo was founded in Balboa Park in 1916 with animals that had been imported for the Panama-California Exposition. The director of the zoo, who happened to be the city health inspector, simply quarantined the animals and wouldn't let them leave.

The zoo would also become a botanical garden, which 20 years earlier would have seemed nonsense. Southern California had been called "the most undesirable, useless land in God's realm" for its barrenness. Not one tree was native to San Diego, but Kate Sessions, a teacher from San Francisco who was also a horticulturist, set about to change the nature of things in 1892. She had come to the area with the dream of opening a plant nursery (which still exists), and in exchange for the space to do so, she promised the city she would plant 100 trees a year in Balboa Park and 300 elsewhere in San Diego. To that end, she traveled around the world looking for species that would grow in a dry climate and so created one of the country's lushest cities.

Impressions

Thanks be to God, I have arrived at this Port of San Diego. It is beautiful to behold and does not belie its reputation.

—Father Serra, 1769

I thought San Diego must be a Heaven on Earth. . . . It seemed to me the best spot for building a city I ever saw.

—Alonzo Horton

In the 1920s, San Diego became known as an aviation center, and Charles Lindbergh chose the city's Ryan Corporation to manufacture the *Spirit of St. Louis,* in which he made his historic transatlantic solo flight.

In 1935, the city hosted the California Pacific International Exposition in Balboa Park. The internationally acclaimed Old Globe Theatre was built for the event, and each day shortened versions of 10 Shakespearean plays were presented. Among the exhibits, a new invention called television drew a lot of attention. Another exhibit was the Zoro Gardens nudist colony, staffed mainly by young women promoting healthful natural living. That may have had something to do with the fact that many of the people who came to the exposition were young naval recruits based in the area.

Home to the U.S. Navy since 1901, San Diego today contains the largest military complex in the world, claiming more than 80 major military shore commands and more than 100 ships—that's one-third of the U.S. Pacific Fleet. As they have since the turn of the century, U.S. Navy and Marine Corps recruits come here for training. From San Diego, they ship out to the far-flung corners of the world. Many return to San Diego: Coronado claims more retired admirals than any other city in the country.

4 Famous San Diegans

Deepak Chopra M.D. (b. 1956)   Born and raised in New Delhi, India, Chopra has taught at Tufts University and Boston Universtiy and was Chief of Staff at New England Memorial Hospital. He is the author of *Creating Health; Quantum Healing; Ageless Body, Timeless Mind;* and many other books. In 1992, Dr. Chopra was appointed to the National Institutes of Health ad hoc panel on alternative medicine. His Chopra Center for Well Being is located in La Jolla.

Dennis Conner (b. 1943)   An accomplished yachtsman, he has won the America's Cup four times and lost it twice—to Australia in 1983 and to New Zealand in 1995.

Jenny Craig (b. 1932)   The international headquarters of diet maven Jenny Craig overlooks Interstate 5 in Del Mar. Craig and her husband live in San Diego and are active in the community. The San Diego Hospice, United Way, and Children's Hospital are just a few of the organizations she supports.

Joan Embery (b. 1950)   As Goodwill Ambassador for the San Diego Zoo, Embery has appeared on numerous television shows with four-legged and winged friends. She lives on a ranch in Lakeside where she maintains her own collection of animals.

Theodor Seuss Geise (1904-1991)   "See Seuss on the Loose" on p. 10.

Françoise Gilot (b. 1921)   Born in France, Gilot has been a presence in the San Diego art community for many years. Her paintings and drawings fill *The Gods of Greece,* a collaboration with Arianna Huffington (Atlantic Monthly Press, 1993). Once the muse and model of Picasso, Gilot married Dr. Jonas Salk in 1970; he died in 1995.

Joan Kroc (b.1929)   Her late husband, **Ray,** founded the McDonald's Restaurant chain and owned the San Diego Padres baseball team. She lives in Fairbanks Ranch and contributes generously to the community.

Frankie Laine (b. 1913)   Laine became a star in 1947 with the popular recording "That's My Desire," followed by "Mule Train," "Jezebel," and many more, including the theme to the TV western *Rawhide* (1956–66). His autobiography, the name of another hit record, is *That Lucky Old Son* (1993). He has lived in Point Loma since 1968 where his next door neighbor is popular author **Joseph Wambaugh.**

Seuss on the Loose

In 1928, when he first visited San Diego, 24-year-old Theodor Seuss Geisel was working as a cartoonist in New York City. Enchanted by the balmy coastal village of La Jolla, he vowed to move there someday while he was "still young enough to enjoy it." He spent frequent summer holidays here, but it took 20 years before he and his wife built their pink Spanish-style stucco home around an old observation tower atop Mount Soledad. There, in his tile-roofed studio with sweeping coastal views, Geisel wrote and illustrated every Dr. Seuss book from *If I Ran the Zoo* (1950) through his last, *Oh, The Places You'll Go!* (1990).

Geisel was quite involved with the community, including Dr. Seuss art exhibits at the San Diego Museum of Art in Balboa Park and the Contemporary Art Museum on Prospect Street in La Jolla. When the San Diego Zoo's Wild Animal Park opened in the 1970s, he donated funds for a lion enclosure, which can be seen today from the Wgasa Bush Line monorail ride. However, Geisel was a shy and private man who did not want his name attached to buildings or monuments in his lifetime.

Charming Seussian memories cling to landmarks such as the Hotel del Coronado, site of the 1966 Charity Ball with a rollicking Dr. Seuss theme, and the Scripps Clinic and Research Foundation, where Geisel's multiple medical forays led to the 1984 best-seller *You're Only Old Once!* Following his death in 1991, nearly 70,000 children and their parents flocked to Balboa Park for a "Sunday in the Park with Seuss" memorial celebration.

Part of Dr. Seuss's San Diego legacy involves things you do not see. He fought against noise pollution and land destruction, an environmental concern that led to *The Lorax*. In the 1950s, he lobbied the La Jolla Town Council for a billboard ban and wrote and illustrated a pamphlet entitled *Signs of Civilizations*. It featured two Stone Age competitors, Guss and Zaxx, who hammer out signs for their businesses until their rocky wilderness is a litter of come-ons.

> *And thus between them, with impunity*
> *They loused up the entire community*
> *And even the dinosaurs moved away*
> *From that messed-up spot in the U.S.A.*
> *Which is why our business men never shall*
> *Allow such to happen in La Jolla, Cal.*

A sign code followed and became part of a San Diego ordinance.

His favorite hangout for more than 50 years was the Whaling Bar at La Valencia Hotel, where he often sat in the second booth on the right, laughing with other writers and conspiring to commit practical jokes. His memory lives on in two old-line La Jolla bookstores: John Cole's on Prospect Street and Warwick's on Girard Avenue.

Geisel's widow, Audrey Stone Geisel, recently stunned and pleased the community by donating $20 million to the library of the University of California, San Diego. In late 1995, the library was named The Geisel Library in honor of the man behind Dr. Seuss. It houses all of Dr. Seuss's manuscripts, sketches, and personal papers. Ted Geisel's birthday—March 2—has been declared Dr. Seuss Day at UCSD, and each year students crowd the library courtyard for readings, songs, and birthday cake, while a giant balloon of the Cat in the Hat keeps watch.

—by Judith and Neil Morgan,
authors of *Dr. Seuss & Mr. Geisel* (New York: Random House, 1995).

Greg Louganis (b. 1960)   An Olympic gold medalist in 1984, he earned medals for both springboard and platform diving, the first Olympic athlete to do so since 1928. In his 1995 book, *Breaking the Surface,* he discusses his traumatic childhood (in El Cajon), sexual orientation, and feelings about being HIV positive.

Gregory Peck (b. 1916)   The legendary actor was born in La Jolla, where his father owned a pharmacy on Prospect Street. He attended San Diego High School and San Diego State University. He cofounded the La Jolla Playhouse in 1947 with Dorothy McGuire and Mel Ferrer. Peck won a 1962 Academy Award for his performance in *To Kill a Mockingbird.*

Cliff Robertson (b. 1925)   The Academy Award-winning actor (*Charley,* 1968) was born in La Jolla and graduated from La Jolla High School. He still lives here in a house on the beach and participates in various community activities, including being the grand marshal of the Christmas parade.

Carl Rogers (1902–87)   Known as the father of humanistic psychology, he wrote *On Becoming a Person* (1961) and *A Way of Being* (1980) and founded the Center for Studies of the Person, based in La Jolla.

Dr. Jonas Salk (1914–95)   He developed the Salk polio vaccine in 1953 and founded the Salk Institute for Biological Studies in La Jolla in 1963. At the time of his death he was conducting AIDS research at his institute.

E. W. Scripps (1854–1926)   This newspaper publisher formed the Scripps-McRae League of Newspapers, which became Scripps-Howard Newspapers. He also developed United Press International (UPI). His half-sister, **Ellen Browning Scripps** (1836–1932), was a generous benefactor to Scripps Institution of Oceanography, Scripps Memorial Hospital, Scripps Clinic and Research Foundation, La Jolla Woman's Club, the Bishop's Schools, and many other causes.

2 Planning a Trip to San Diego

The Boy Scouts are right: It's a good idea to be prepared, so do your predeparture homework. It will help ensure that you will have the best possible time in San Diego.

1 Visitor Information

Before you leave home, contact the **International Visitor Information Center,** 11 Horton Plaza, San Diego, CA 92101 (☎ **619/ 236-1212;** fax 619/232-1707). Ask for the *San Diego Official Visitors Guide,* which includes information on accommodations, activities, and attractions, and has excellent maps. Also request the *Super Savings Coupon Book,* which is full of money-saving discount coupons. The staff at the center is multilingual, and brochures are available in English, French, German, Japanese, Portuguese, and Spanish. The center is open Monday through Saturday from 8:30am to 5pm year-round and Sunday from 11am to 5pm June through August.

If you're thinking of attending the theater while you're in town, contact the **San Diego Performing Arts League** (☎ **619/ 238-0700)** for a copy of *What's Playing?,* which contains information on upcoming performances in San Diego.

Another good source of information is the **San Diego North County Convention and Visitors Bureau.** Call ☎ **800/848-3336** to request their *Visitors Guide.*

Cybernaughts will find information on San Diego at the following Web sites:

- **gocalif.ca.gov/guidebook/SD** has helpful information on San Diego County, including maps that can be downloaded.
- **www.sandiego.org** is maintained by the San Diego Convention and Visitors Bureau and provides, among other things, up-to-date weather data.
- **www.infosandiego.com/visitor** is the Web site for The San Diego Visitor Center.
- **www.sannet.gov** is San Diego's home page.
- **www.sddt.com/newslibrary/art/artscaledar.html** features the Arts Calendar, which provides information on many San Diego performances.
- **members.aol.com/localspage/index.html** contains The Local Guy's Guide to San Diego, which gives lots of information on things to do and local history and facts.

What Things Cost in San Diego	U.S. $
Taxi from the airport to downtown	8.50
Bus from the airport to downtown	2.00
Local telephone call	.20 to .25
(depending on the phone you use)	
Double at the Marriott (expensive)	225.00
Double at the Best Western Bayside Inn (moderate)	85.00
Double at La Pensione (inexpensive)	50.00
Two-course lunch for one at The Vegetarian Zone (moderate)	13.00
Two-course lunch for one at Cafe Lulu (budget)	9.00
Three-course dinner for one at Café Pacifica (expensive)	32.00
Three-course dinner for one at Croce's (moderate)	28.00
Three-course dinner for one at the Old Spaghetti Factory (budget)	8.25
Bottle of beer	2.25
Coca-Cola	1.25
Cup of coffee	1.25
Roll of ASA 100 Kodacolor film, 36 exposures	5.20
San Diego Zoo adult admission	15.00
San Diego Zoo children's admission	6.00
Movie ticket	7.00
Theater ticket at Old Globe	36.00

- **www.iaco.com/features/lajolla/homepage.htm** features information about what's happening in La Jolla.
- **www.coronado.ca.us/Visitor** accesses the Coronado Visitors Bureau.
- **members.aol.com/localspage/Links.html** provides links to other pages with San Diego interest.
- **America Online** subscribers can access Digital City San Diego by using keyword "digital city san diego."

2 When to Go

San Diego is blessed with a mild climate, low humidity, good air quality, and skies that are a welcoming blue most of the year. In fact, *Pleasant Weather Rankings,* published by Consumer Travel, ranked San Diego's weather number two in the world (the number one spot is Las Palmas in the Canary Islands). Oceanside, the most northerly town in San Diego County, came in at number five.

Although the temperature can change 20°F to 30°F between the day and the evening, it doesn't usually reach a point of extreme heat. This means you should bring a jacket for cool evenings, even during the summer. But, since it rains very little in San Diego (in an average year there's only 9¹/₂ inches of rainfall), you probably won't need a raincoat. During the fall, you may encounter the local phenomenon known as a "Santa Ana"—a period of clear, dry weather brought about by winds blowing off the desert, from east to west. This hot, dry air often contributes to brush fires.

Impressions

What a change in weather! It was sleeting when I left St. Louis. Here, on the 23rd of February, palm leaves flutter in warm wind and sun.

—Charles Lindbergh, 1927

If you stay here for any length of time, you develop a low tolerance to change in the weather: If it's over 80°, it's too hot, and if it's under 70°, it's too cold.

—Overheard in Horton Plaza

Average Monthly Temperature & Rainfall (inches)

	Jan	Feb	Mar	Apr	May	June	July	Aug	Sept	Oct	Nov	Dec
High (°F)	65	66	66	68	70	71	75	77	76	74	70	66
(°C)	18	19	19	20	21	21	24	25	25	23	21	19
Low (°F)	46	47	50	54	57	60	64	66	63	58	52	47
(°C)	7	9	10	12	14	15	17	19	17	15	10	8
Rainfall	1.88	1.48	1.55	0.81	0.15	0.05	0.01	0.07	0.13	0.34	1.25	1.73

SAN DIEGO CALENDAR OF EVENTS

Below is a sample of annual events that take place in San Diego County and nearby in Temecula. For additional listings, you can purchase the *Official Major Events Calendar* from the San Diego Convention and Visitors Bureau for $15. The calendar is published in January and July. Make your check or money order payable to ConVis and send it to: **International Visitor Information Center,** 11 Horton Plaza, San Diego, CA 92101.

January

- **Maple Leaf Months.** San Diego honors their Canadian visitors up through February, with special discounts from merchants, hotels, restaurants, and attractions. Call ☎ **619/236-1212.**

- **Whale Watching.** The annual migration of California gray whales to the warmer waters of Baja California occurs through January and February. Visitors can watch through binoculars from the shore or go out on a boat for a closer look. For details, call ☎ **619/557-5450** or 619/236-1212.

- ✪ **Mercedes Championships,** La Costa Resort and Spa, Carlsbad. This Professional Golfers Association (PGA) tournament, held since 1952, has been played at the La Costa Resort and Spa since 1965. It features tour winners from the past 12 months, including the British Open, the Masters, the U.S. Open, and the PGA Regular and Senior Championships. The combined purse is $1.5 million. For information, call ☎ **800/918-4653** or 760/438-9111, ext. 4612, or write La Costa Resort and Spa, Costa del Mar Road, Carlsbad, CA 92009. Tickets go on sale in July. Early January.

- **San Diego Marathon.** The course begins at Plaza Camino Real in Carlsbad and stretches 26.2 miles, mainly along the coast. It's a gorgeous run, held the 3rd Sunday in January. For more information, call ☎ **619/792-2900.** For an entry application, send a self-addressed stamped envelope to In Motion, 511 S. Cedros, Suite B, Solana Beach, CA 92075. Spectators don't need tickets.

- **Martin Luther King Day Parade.** In 1998, this parade will take place on January 17. Continuing the tradition established in 1980 of honoring the civil rights

leader, the parade goes along Broadway from Eighth Avenue to State Street. Call
☎ **619/264-0542.**

- **Nations of San Diego International Dance Festival:** Founded in 1993, this festival focuses on San Diego's numerous ethnic dance groups and companies. Performances are at the Lyceum Theatre as well as free shows in public areas. Call ☎ **619/239-9255.** January 9 through January 18, 1998.

February

- **Wildflowers bloom in the desert,** usually February through April at Anza-Borrego Desert State Park. The timing varies from year to year, depending on the winter rainfall (see chapter 11). For details, call ☎ **760/767-4684** or 760/767-4205 (park information).

- ✪ **Buick Invitational,** Torrey Pines Golf Course, La Jolla. In existence since 1952, this annual PGA Tour men's gold tournament draws more than 100,000 spectators each year. It features 150 of the finest golf professionals in the world. For information, call ☎ **800/888-BUICK** or 619/281-4653, fax 619/281-7947, or write Buick Invitational, 3333 Camino Del Rio South, Suite 100, San Diego, CA 92108. Early to mid-February.

March

- **Ocean Beach Kite Festival.** At the Ocean Beach Recreation Center, you can build and decorate kites, as well as participate in a flying contest for all ages. The festival is held the first weekend of February at the **Ocean Beach Recreation Center,** 4726 Santa Monica Ave. (☎ **619/224-0189**).

- **St. Patrick's Day Parade.** A tradition here since 1980, the parade is held the Sunday before March 17. It starts at Sixth and Juniper and ends at Sixth and Laurel and is followed by an Irish Festival. For details, call ☎ **619/299-7812.**

- **Flower Fields at Carlsbad Ranch,** Carlsbad. Every March and April, the Flower Fields blossom into a spectacular sea of brightly colored ranunculus flowers. Visitors can view and tour the fields, which are located off Interstate 5 at the Palomar Airport Road exit. For more information, call ☎ **760/431-0352.**

April

- **Rosarito-Ensenada 50-Mile Fun Bicycle Ride,** Mexico. About 8,000 participants cycle from the Rosarito Beach Hotel along the two-lane free road to Ensenada and the Finish Line Fiesta, sometime in mid- to late April. For information, call ☎ **619/583-3001** (Web site: **www.adventuresports.com/asap/bike/rosarito/ensenada.htm**).

- **San Diego Crew Classic, Crown Point Shores,** Mission Bay. Since 1973, it has drawn collegiate teams of more than 2,000 athletes from the United States and Canada. It's held the 1st or 2nd weekend in April; call ☎ **619/488-0700.**

- **Del Mar National Horse Show,** Del Mar Fairgrounds. Olympic-caliber and national championship horse-and-rider teams compete here, from late April to mid-May. There are also western fashion boutiques and artists displays and demonstrations. For information, call ☎ **619/792-4288** or 619/755-1161.

- **Day at the Docks.** This sportfishing tournament and festival, held at Harbor Drive and Scott Street, Point Loma, features food, entertainment, and free boat rides. It's either the last weekend of April or the first weekend in May. Call ☎ **800/994-FISH.**

- **Lakeside Western Days and Annual Rodeo.** Mid-April is the time for western days in Lakeside. The celebration features arts and crafts, food, carnival, and a parade on Saturday at 10am. The rodeo features seven major rodeo events. It's held at the **Lakeside Rodeo Grounds,** Highway 67 and Mapleview Avenue, Lakeside (☎ **619/561-1031** or 619/561-4331).

May

- **Cinco de Mayo Festival,** Old Town. A tradition since 1983, this fiesta on May 5 includes mariachi music and margaritas galore. Call ☎ **619/296-3161** or 619/220-5422.

- **Wildflower Festival,** Julian Town Hall, Julian. A weeklong event held since 1926, it features displays of native plants. It's held early to mid-May; for details, call ☎ **760/765-1857.**

- **Balloon and Wine Festival,** Temecula. Even if you don't go up, up, and away, the sight of the balloons is spectacular. Call ☎ **909/676-4713.** The festival is usually held in either late April or early May.

- **The Mainly Mozart Festival** is held at different locations in San Diego and Tijuana from late May through mid-June. Call ☎ **619/558-1000.**

June

- **Indian Fair,** Museum of Man, Balboa Park. Native Americans from around the southwestern United States gather to demonstrate tribal dances and sell arts and crafts in mid-June. Call ☎ **619/239-2001.**

- **Twilight in the Park Concerts,** Spreckels Organ Pavilion, Balboa Park. These free concerts have been held since 1979 and run from late June through late August. For information, call ☎ **619/226-0819.**

- **Del Mar Fair.** San Diego's county fair, held from mid-June to about July 4, includes exhibits of farm animals and home arts and lots of rides. Concerts by top-name entertainers are free with admission. Call ☎ **619/793-5555.**

July

- ✪ **World Championship Over-the-Line Tournament,** Fiesta Island, Mission Bay. Very much a local tradition, San Diego's original beach softball event dates from 1953 and features 1,000 three-person teams competing in an elimination tournament. (*Warning:* This event gets pretty risqué and isn't appropriate for children and anyone who is easily offended.) For information, call ☎ **619/688-0817.** Spectators don't need tickets. Second and third weekends in July.

- **Festival of the Bells,** Mission San Diego de Alcala. This mid-July fiesta commemorates the founding of California's first church. Music, dancing, food, and the "blessing of the animals" are included. For details, call ☎ **619/281-8449.**

- **Annual San Diego Lesbian and Gay Pride Parade, Rally, and Festival.** The parade, either the 3rd or 4th weekend in July, begins at noon at University Avenue and Normal Street and proceeds west on University to Sixth Avenue. A festival follows on Saturday from 2 to 10pm and Sunday from noon to 10pm. For information, call ☎ **619/297-7683.**

- **Thoroughbred racing.** The "turf meets the surf" in Del Mar for daily races (except Tuesday), held late July through mid-September. Post time is 2pm for the nine-race program. Call ☎ **619/792-4242** or 619/755-1141.

August

- **Hillcrest Street Fair,** Fifth Avenue, between Ivy Lane and University Avenue. Held since 1983, the street fair features arts and crafts, food booths, a beer garden, and live entertainment. Call ☎ **619/299-3330.** This 1-day fair usually takes place in the beginning of the month.

- **U.S. Open Sandcastle Competition.** Held on the Imperial Beach Pier in mid-August, this annual event attracts international competitors. Call ☎ **619/424-6663.**

- **America's Finest City Week.** More than 70 events celebrate our city in mid-August, including a Midnight Madness Bike Ride and a volleyball festival. For details, call ☎ 619/437-0369.
- **Sunset Cinema Film Festival.** This free, open-air, weeklong film series is held at locations around San Diego. Classic movies are viewed from the beach as films are projected on a screen mounted on a floating barge. For details call ☎ 619/454-7373.
- **Julian Weed Show and Art Mart,** Julian. Held since 1959, this showcases the area's colorful weeds in myriad arrangements, from late August through September. Call ☎ 760/765-1857.
- **World Bodysurfing Championships.** U.S. and international bodysurfers compete at the Oceanside Pier. Call ☎ 760/966-4535.

September

- **San Diego Street Scene,** Gaslamp Quarter. California's largest, most diverse urban food and music festival occurs in early September. For tickets and information, call ☎ 619/557-8487.
- **Cabrillo Festival,** Cabrillo National Monument. This reenactment of Cabrillo's arrival in San Diego in 1542 is staged late September or early October. Call ☎ 619/557-5450.
- ✪ **La Jolla Rough-Water Swim,** La Jolla Cove. The country's largest rough-water swimming competition began in 1916 and features masters men's and women's swims, a junior swim, and an amateur swim. All events except the junior swim and gatorman 3-mile championship are 1 mile in distance. To register or receive more information, call ☎ 619/456-2100. For an entry form, send a self-addressed stamped envelope to Entries Chairman, La Jolla Rough-Water Swim, P.O. Box 46, La Jolla, CA 92038. Spectators don't need tickets. First Sunday after Labor Day (September 13, 1998).
- **Art Festival in the Village of La Jolla.** Held along Prospect and Girard Streets, usually the last weekend in September. This free festival includes quality juried artwork, live entertainment, gourmet food, and children's activities. For information, call ☎ 888/ART-FEST or 619/454-5718.
- **Apple Harvest and Back Country Arts Festival,** Julian. On weekends only, from mid-September through mid-November, enjoy autumn foliage, entertainment, and apple pie. Call ☎ 760/765-1857 for details.
- **Rosarito-Ensenada 50-Mile Fun Bicycle Ride,** Mexico. See April entry for details, or call ☎ 619/583-3001.

October

- **Zoo Founders Day.** It's free for everyone to go to the zoo on the 1st Monday of October, and it's free for children daily in October. Call ☎ 619/234-3153.
- **Columbus Day Parade.** Organized by the United Italian-American Association, it's been held in downtown San Diego since 1969. Call ☎ 619/698-0545 or 619/469-0795.
- **San Diego Concours d'Elegance.** The greatest assemblage of antique and classic cars exhibited in one Southern California location. Held annually in mid-October at the Torrey Pines Golf Course. The featured marque for 1997 was Mercedes Benz; Alfa Romeo will be honored in 1998. For more information, call ☎ 619/283-4221.

November

- **Veterans Day Parade,** along Pacific Highway in downtown San Diego. Call ☎ 619/239-2300.

- **Score Baja 1000.** This famous off-road race for cars, trucks, and motorcycles over Baja California's most challenging terrain has been held since 1969, in early to mid-November. Viewing is free; participants pay an entry fee. For details call ☎ **818/583-8068.**
- **Holiday Avenues of the Arts.** For one weekend only in mid- to late November, you'll find arts and crafts, gift items, food, and music in the Gaslamp Quarter. Call ☎ **619/239-1143.**

December

- **How the Grinch Stole Christmas,** at Lowes Coronado Bay Resort. Beginning the Friday after Thanksgiving through Christmas Eve, the Lowes lobby is transformed into *"Who-ville"* complete with *"Who."* This is where The Cat in the Hat reads Dr. Seuss's *How the Grinch Stole Christmas* to children of all ages. After each reading carolers perform and the audience is invited to enjoy punch and cookies. For more information on this free event, call ☎ **619/424-4416.**
- **Coronado Christmas Celebration and Parade.** On the first Friday of December, Santa's arrival by ferry is followed by a parade along Orange Avenue. Call ☎ **800/622-8300** or 619/437-8788.
- **Christmas on the Prado,** Balboa Park. The first weekend of December, a tradition since 1977 continues with a carol sing-along and food booths from 5 to 9pm on Friday and Saturday nights. Admission to all museums is free. For information, call ☎ **619/239-0512.**
- **Whale Watching.** It starts in mid-December; see the January listing above.
- **Port of San Diego Holiday Bowl Parade.** The marching bands of the two Holiday Bowl teams march with other bands through downtown San Diego. Call ☎ **619/234-0201.**
- **Holiday Bowl.** Collegiate football Bowl game held at **Qualcomm Stadium** (formerly Jack Murphy Stadium). Call ☎ **619/283-5808.**
- **Mission Bay Boat Parade of Lights,** from Quivira Basin in Mission Bay. Held on a mid-December Saturday, it concludes with the lighting of a 320-foot tower of Christmas lights at Sea World. Call ☎ **619/488-0501.**
- **San Diego Harbor Parade of Lights,** from Shelter Island to Harbor Island to Seaport Village. Decorated boats of all sizes and types participate, and spectators line the shore and cheer for their favorites. Held since 1971, it's on a Sunday in mid-December. Check the local newspaper for exact day and time.
- **First Night San Diego,** San Diego Concourse, downtown. Family-oriented activities, including dancers, clowns, mimes, and rock and roll, held from approximately 4pm to midnight on December 31. Call ☎ **619/280-7628.**

3 Tips for Travelers with Special Needs

FOR TRAVELERS WITH DISABILITIES   The **Accessible San Diego hot line** (☎ **619/279-0704;** fax 619/279-5118) helps travelers with disabilities link up with hotels, tours, attractions, and transportation accessible to them (if you call long distance and get the answering machine, leave a message and the staff will call you back collect). Or, for a useful 25-page access guide that lists local social-service agencies, send a $5 donation to Accessible San Diego, P.O. Box 124526, San Diego, CA 92112-4526.

In the *San Diego Convention and Visitors Bureau's Dining and Accommodations* guide, a wheelchair symbol designates places that are accessible to persons with disabilities.

On buses and trolleys, riders with disabilities pay a fixed fare of 75¢. Many MTS buses and all trolleys are equipped with wheelchair lifts; priority seating is available on both buses and trolleys. Bus stops served by accessible buses are marked with a wheelchair symbol. People with visual impairments benefit from the white reflecting ring that circles the bottom of the trolley door to increase its visibility.

Airport transportation for travelers with disabilities is available from **Cloud 9 Shuttle** (☎ **800/9-SHUTTLE** or 619/278-8877).

FOR GAY & LESBIAN TRAVELERS Gay or lesbian travelers will particularly enjoy the Hillcrest area near Balboa Park, where there are a number of popular meeting spots (see "The Bar & Coffeehouse Scene" in chapter 10).

The **Lesbian and Gay Men's Community Center** is at 3916 Normal St. (☎ **619/692-2077**). It's open Monday through Friday from 9am to 10pm and Saturday from 9am to 7pm. Community outreach and counseling is offered. The **Live and Let Live Alano Club,** 1730 Monroe Ave.(☎ **619/298-8008**), sponsors numerous alcohol-free activities and programs. Churches that welcome gay and lesbian visitors include the **Metropolitan Community Church,** 4333 30th St. (☎ **619/ 280-4333**), in North Park; **St. Francis Liberal Catholic Church,** 741 Cerro Gordo Ave. (☎ **619/239-0637**); and the metaphysical **Pacific Church of Religious Science,** 5333 Mission Center Rd. (☎ **619/294-9555**).

The **Annual San Diego Lesbian and Gay Pride Parade, Rally, and Festival** is held either the 3rd or 4th weekend in July. The parade begins at noon at University Avenue and Normal Street and proceeds west on University to Sixth Avenue. A festival follows on Saturday from 2 to 10pm and Sunday from noon to 10pm. For more information, call ☎ **619/297-7683.**

The free *San Diego Gay and Lesbian Times,* published every Thursday, is often available at the Blue Door Bookstore, in Hillcrest. Greg Louganis signed copies of his book *Breaking the Surface* at **Obelisk,** 1029 University Ave., Hillcrest (☎ **619/297-4171**).

FOR SENIORS When making an airline reservation, ask for the senior discount offered by many airlines on most fares. Just as you would on any trip, carry proof of age with you—your driver's license, passport, Medicare card, or membership card for an organization for seniors—so you can take advantage of senior discounts offered by some hotels and restaurants and by most attractions. Transport on the San Diego bus and trolley system is 75¢ one way for people 60 or older.

A delightful way to meet older San Diegans, many of whom are retired, is to join a free Saturday-morning stroll with **Downtown Sam,** a footloose retiree and guide with **Walkabout International** (see "Organized Tours" in chapter 7).

Finally, look into **Elderhostel educational programs** in the San Diego area. There is one at the Point Loma Youth Hostel. Those qualified to attend must be 55 years of age or older; companions must be adults. For more information, contact Elderhostel, 75 Federal St., Boston, MA 02110-1941 (☎ **617/426-7788;** fax 617/ 426-8351).

San Diego's special senior-citizens **referral and information line** is ☎ **619/ 560-2500.**

4 Getting There

BY PLANE
THE MAJOR AIRLINES

Incoming flights arrive at San Diego International Airport/Lindbergh Field (named after aviation hero Charles Lindbergh), served by many national and regional air carriers as well as Aeromexico and British Airways.

The following airlines arrive at the Commuter Terminal: **Alaska Commuter** (☎ 800/426-0333); **American Eagle** (☎ 800/433-7300); **Continental Connection** (☎ 800/525-0280); **Delta Connection** (☎ 800/221-1212); **Northwest AirLink** (☎ 800/225-2525); **Skywest Airlines** (☎ 800/453-9417); and **USAir Express** (☎ 800/428-4322).

East Terminal airlines include: **Aeromexico** (☎ 800/237-6639); **Alaska Airlines** (☎ 800/426-0333); **America West** (☎ 800/235-9292); **Continental Airlines** (☎ 800/525-0280); **Southwest Airlines** (☎ 800/435-9792); **Trans World Airlines** (☎ 800/221-2000); **United Airlines** (☎ 800/241-6522); and **US Airways** (☎ 800/428-4322).

West Terminal airlines include: **American Airlines** (☎ 800/433-7300); **British Airways** (☎ 800/247-9297); **Delta Airlines** (☎ 800/221-1212); **Frontier Airlines** (☎ 800/265-5505); **Midwest Express** (☎ 800/452-2022); **Northwest Airlines** (☎ 800/225-2525); **Reno Air** (☎ 800/736-6247); and **Western Pacific** (☎ 800/930-3030).

SAN DIEGO'S AIRPORT

San Diego International Airport/Lindbergh Field is located only slightly north of downtown. The landing approach is right over the central business district, creating a familiar sight of planes threading their way through high-rise buildings on their way to the airport. A curfew is enforced from 11:30pm to 6:30am to cut down on noise in the surrounding residential areas. Planes may land during the curfew period, but they can't take off.

Lindbergh Field consists of two adjacent airport terminals, "East" and "West," and the "Commuter Terminal," which is half a mile away. The "red bus" provides free service from the main airport to the Commuter Terminal.

At the airport you'll also find: car-rental desks, including Alamo, Avis, Budget, Dollar, Hertz, and National; a counter where you may purchase traveler's insurance; three Traveler's Aid booths with plenty of brochures; and hotel information and courtesy phones for making reservations and arranging airport pickup, which some hotels offer.

GETTING INTO TOWN FROM THE AIRPORT

BY BUS   New **Metropolitan Transit System (MTS)** Route 992 provides 10-minute weekday and 15-minute weekend service between the airport and downtown San Diego. Route 992 bus stops are located at each of the three terminals. The one-way fare is $2.00. The fare box accepts $1 bills and coins (no change made). Request a transfer if connecting to another bus or San Diego Trolley route downtown. Downtown, Route 992 stops on Broadway. The trip from the airport to downtown should take about 15 minutes.

The Transit Store, at Broadway and First Avenue (☎ **619/233-3004**), is where you can get information about greater San Diego's mass transit system (bus, rail, and ferry) and pick up free brochures, route maps, and timetables to get you where you're going.

BY TAXI   Taxis line up outside both terminals and charge $7 to $10 to take you to a downtown location, usually a 5- to 10-minute ride.

BY SHUTTLE   Several airport shuttles run regularly from the airport to downtown hotels and charge from $5 to $9 per person; you'll see designated areas outside each terminal. The shuttles are a good deal for single travelers; two or more people traveling together might as well take a taxi. Some of the shuttles providing service include **Cloud 9 Shuttle** (☎ **800/9-SHUTTLE** or 619/278-8877), **Coronado Livery**

(☎ **619/435-6310**), and **Peerless Shuttle** (☎ **619/554-1700**). All of these service the whole county, but Coronado Livery is the least expensive to Coronado, and Cloud 9 is the cheapest to downtown.

BY LIMO   Chauffeur service is available from **Luxury Transportation of La Jolla** (☎ **619/459-9090**) and **Luxury Transportation** (☎ **619/270-6666**) each of which will deliver you to your destination for about the same cost as a taxi. These companies don't use stretch limos, but do have a fleet of well-kept Mercedes sedans.

BY CAR   If you are driving the short distance into the city from the airport, follow Harbor Drive to Broadway, the main city street running east to west. Also refer to the "Getting Around" section in chapter 4.

BY CAR

Visitors arriving in San Diego by car from Los Angeles and points north do so via coastal route I-5; from points northeast, via I-15 (link up with I-8 West and Highway 163 South or Highway 94 West); and from the east, via I-8 (link up with Highway 163 South to drive into the downtown area; Highway 163 turns into 10th Avenue). If you arrive from the east on Highway 94, it turns into F Street. Try to avoid arriving during weekday rush hours, between 7 and 9am and 3 and 6pm. If you are heading to Coronado, take the Coronado Bridge via I-5. If there's a passenger in the car with you, stay in the far-right lanes to avoid paying the toll. Maximum speed in the San Diego area is 65 miles (105km) per hour, and many areas are limited to 55.

BY TRAIN

Trains from all points in the United States and Canada pass through Los Angeles to get to San Diego. Seven trains make the pretty Pacific-coast-hugging trip daily, a scenic 128-mile journey that lasts just under 3 hours and costs $20 one way. You'll arrive at the striking mission-style **Santa Fe Station,** built in 1914 and centrally located at Broadway and Kettner Boulevard, 1^1/$_2$ blocks from the Embarcadero, a block from the YMCA and Downtown Hostel, and within walking distance of some of the city's fine downtown hotels. For price and schedule information, call ☎ **800/ USA-RAIL** (☎ **800/523-6590** for people with hearing impairments).

BY BUS

Greyhound/Trailways (☎ **800/231-2222**) serves San Diego; the city's bus terminal has a central downtown location on Broadway between Front Street and First Avenue, within walking distance of major hotels, the YMCA, and the HI-AYH Hostel. Local buses and the trolley stop right outside. Lockers are available at $1 for 24 hours. If you leave belongings more than 24 hours, the charge is $3 per day. The bus station is open 24 hours, and security is provided from late evening to 7am.

BY SHIP

Renovated in 1985, the San Diego **Cruise Terminal,** at the B Street Pier, is awash with carnival colors inside and out. If you arrive in San Diego by sea, expect to be given a full day in port, from about 8am to 3 or 4pm.

Cruise companies whose ships regularly call into San Diego include **Royal Caribbean International** (☎ 800/327-6700), **Carnival Cruise Lines** (☎ 800/327-9501), **Seabourn Cruise Line** (☎ 800/929-9595), **Celebrity Cruises** (☎ 800/437-3111), **Princess Cruises** (☎ 800/421-0522), **Holland America Line** (☎ 206/281-3535), and **Cunard Line** (☎ 800/5-CUNARD). For more information about cruise ships that make San Diego their port of call, contact the **Port of San Diego** (☎ 619/686-6200).

When a ship is in port, **Traveler's Aid** staffs an information booth inside the terminal; outside, tour buses are waiting to take visitors around the city. You can also tour on your own by walking up Broadway eight blocks and wandering through Horton Plaza and the Gaslamp Quarter (see chapter 8). Or you can take the San Diego Trolley or MTS bus routes to get around. The **San Diego Trolley's** closest station is a short walk from the pier to the Santa Fe Depot. Across the street (southeast corner) of Broadway and Kettner you can catch the bus to several other popular destinations. The trolley's Blue Line will take you to Old Town and Mission Valley (to the north) or to the international border with Mexico to the south. The Orange Line will take you to Seaport Village or the Gaslamp Quarter. **MTS buses** provide frequent service to Sea World, Coronado, Balboa Park, and the San Diego Zoo. At the southeast corner of Broadway (at Kettner) catch Route 7, 7A, or 7B to Balboa Park and the zoo or Route 901 to Coronado. To visit Old Town State Park, take the Blue Line to Old Town Transit Center and transfer to Route 9 to Sea World. Bus and Trolley fares range up to $2.25, depending on distance traveled. Fare machines accept dollar bills and coins, but change is not given.

For Foreign Visitors

3

This chapter provides specific suggestions about getting to the United States as economically and effortlessly as possible, plus some helpful information about how things are done in San Diego—from receiving mail to making a local or long-distance telephone call.

1 Preparing for Your Trip

ENTRY REQUIREMENTS

DOCUMENT REGULATIONS   Citizens of Canada and Bermuda may enter the United States without visas, but they will need to show proof of nationality, the most common and hassle-free form of which is a passport.

The U.S. State Department has a visa-waiver pilot program allowing citizens of certain countries to enter the United States without a visa for stays of fewer than 90 days of holiday travel. At press time these included Andorra, Argentina, Australia, Austria, Belgium, Brunei, Denmark, Finland, France, Germany, Iceland, Ireland, Italy, Japan, Liechtenstein, Luxembourg, Monaco, the Netherlands, New Zealand, Norway, San Marino, Spain, Sweden, Switzerland, and the United Kingdom. (The program as applied to the United Kingdom refers to British citizens who have the "unrestricted right of permanent abode in the United Kingdom," that is, citizens from England, Scotland, Wales, Northern Ireland, the Channel Islands, and the Isle of Man, and not, for example, citizens of the British Commonwealth countries, such as Pakistan.

Citizens from these countries need only a valid passport and a round-trip air or cruise ticket in their possession upon arrival. If they first enter the United States, they may then visit Mexico, Canada, Bermuda, and/or the Caribbean islands and return to the United States without needing a visa. Further information is available from any U.S. embassy or consulate.

Citizens of countries other than those specified above, or those traveling to the United States for reasons or lengths of time outside the restrictions of the Visa-Waiver program, or those who require waivers of inadmissability, must have two documents:

- a valid passport, with an expiration date at least 6 months later than the scheduled end of the visit to the United States (some countries are exceptions to the 6-month validity rule; contact any U.S. embassy or consulate for complete information); and

- a tourist visa, available from the nearest U.S. consulate.

To obtain a visa, the traveler must submit a completed application form (either in person or by mail) with a 1¹/₂-inch square photo and the required application fee. There may also be an issuance fee, depending on the type of visa and other factors.

Usually you can obtain a visa right away or within 24 hours, but it may take longer during the summer rush period (June to August). If you cannot go in person, contact the nearest U.S. embassy or consulate for directions on applying by mail. Your travel agent or airline office may also be able to provide you with visa applications and instructions. The U.S. consulate or embassy that issues your visa will determine whether you will be issued a multiple- or single-entry visa. The Immigration and Naturalization Service officers at the port-of-entry in the United States will make an admission decision and determine your length of stay.

You may be asked to provide information about how you plan to finance your trip or show a letter of invitation from a friend with whom you plan to stay. Those applying for a business visa may be asked to show evidence that they will not receive a salary in the United States. Be sure to check the length of stay on your visa; usually it is 6 months. If you want to stay longer, you may file for an extension with the **Immigration and Naturalization Service** once you are in the country. If permission to stay is granted, a new visa is not required unless you leave the United States and want to reenter.

MEDICAL REQUIREMENTS   No inoculations are needed to enter the United States unless you are coming from, or have stopped over in, areas known to be suffering from epidemics, particularly cholera or yellow fever.

If you have a disease requiring treatment with medications containing narcotics or drugs requiring a syringe, carry a valid signed generic prescription from your physician to allay any suspicions that you are smuggling drugs. *Warning:* The prescription brands you are accustomed to buying in your country may not be available in the United States.

CUSTOMS REQUIREMENTS   Every adult visitor may bring in free of duty: 1 liter (1.1 qt.) of wine or hard liquor; 200 cigarettes or 100 cigars (but no cigars from Cuba) or 3 pounds of smoking tobacco; and $100 worth of gifts. These exemptions are offered to travelers who spend at least 72 hours in the United States and who have not claimed them within the preceding 6 months. It is altogether forbidden to bring foodstuffs (particularly cheese, fruit, cooked meats, and canned goods) and plants (vegetables, seeds, tropical plants, and so on) into the country. Foreign tourists may bring in or take out up to $10,000 in U.S. or foreign currency with no formalities; larger sums must be declared to customs upon entering or leaving.

INSURANCE

There is no national health system in the United States. Because the cost of medical care is extremely high, we strongly advise all travelers to secure health coverage before setting out on their trip.

You may want to take out a comprehensive travel policy that covers (for a relatively low premium) sickness or injury costs (medical, surgical, and hospital); loss or theft of your baggage; trip-cancellation costs; guarantee of bail in case you are arrested; and costs of accident, repatriation, or death. Automobile clubs sell packages (for example, "Europe Assistance" in Europe) at attractive rates; they are also offered by insurance companies, travel agencies, and some airports.

MONEY

CURRENCY   The U.S. monetary system has a decimal base: One American **dollar** ($1) = 100 **cents** (100¢). Dollar **bills** commonly come in $1 (a "buck"), $5, $10, $20, $50, and $100 denominations (the last two are not welcome when paying for small purchases and are not readily accepted in taxis). Two-dollar ($2) bills are also in circulation, but are less common than other denominations.

There are six **coin** denominations: 1¢ (one cent or "penny"); 5¢ (five cents or "nickel"); 10¢ (ten cents or "dime"); 25¢ (twenty-five cents or "quarter"); 50¢ (fifty cents or "half dollar"); and the $1 pieces (both the older, large silver dollar and the newer, quarter-sized Susan B. Anthony coin). The 50¢ and $1 coins, like the $2 bills mentioned above, are not commonly used.

ATM MACHINES   Automated teller machines are available throughout San Diego. Before you leave home, ask your bank for a directory of locations that will accept your card and how much the charge is for international withdrawals.

TRAVELER'S CHECKS   Traveler's checks in U.S. dollars are accepted at most hotels, motels, restaurants, and large stores. Sometimes picture identification is required. American Express, Citibank, Thomas Cook, and Barclay's Bank traveler's checks are readily accepted in the United States.

CREDIT CARDS   The most widely used method of payment is the credit card: Visa (BarclayCard in Britain), MasterCard (Eurocard in Europe, Access in Britain, Diamond in Japan), American Express, Discover, Diners Club, enRoute, Japan Credit Bank, and Carte Blanche, in descending order of acceptance. You can save yourself trouble by using "plastic" rather than cash or traveler's checks in 95% of all hotels, motels, restaurants, and retail stores. A credit card can also serve as a deposit for renting a car, as proof of identity, or as a "cash card," enabling you to draw money from automatic-teller machines (ATMs) that accept them.

You can telegraph money or have it telegraphed to you very quickly using the **Western Union system** (☎ **800/325-6000**).

SAFETY

While tourist areas are generally safe, crime is on the increase everywhere, and U.S. urban areas tend to be less safe than those in Europe or Japan. Visitors should always stay alert. This is particularly true of large U.S. cities. It is wise to ask the city's or area's tourist office if you're in doubt about which neighborhoods are safe. Avoid deserted areas, especially at night. Don't go into any city park at night unless there is an event that attracts crowds.

In Balboa Park, stay on designated walkways and away from secluded areas day and night. In the Gaslamp Quarter, don't go east of Fifth Avenue. San Diego's proximity to the international border contributes to its high rate of auto theft.

Remember also that hotels are open to the public, and in a large hotel, security may not be able to screen everyone entering. Always lock your room door—don't assume that once inside your hotel you are automatically safe and no longer need be aware of your surroundings.

DRIVING   Safety while driving is particularly important. Question your rental agency about personal safety, or ask for a brochure of traveler safety tips. Obtain written directions, or a map with the route marked in red, from the agency, showing how to get to your destination. And, if possible, arrive and depart during daylight hours.

Recently more and more crime has involved cars and drivers. If you drive off a highway into a doubtful neighborhood, leave the area as quickly as possible. If you have an accident, even on the highway, stay in your car with the doors locked until you assess the situation or until the police arrive. If you are bumped from behind on the street or are involved in a minor accident with no injuries and the situation appears to be suspicious, motion to the other driver to follow you. Never get out of your car in such situations. Go directly to the nearest police precinct, well-lighted service station, or all-night store.

If you see someone on the road who indicates a need for help, do not stop. Take note of the location, drive to a well-lighted area, and telephone the police by dialing ☎ **911.**

Park in well-lighted, well-traveled areas if possible. Always keep your car doors locked, whether attended or unattended. Look around you before you get out of your car, and never leave any packages or valuables in sight. If someone attempts to rob you or steal your car, do not try to resist the thief/carjacker—report the incident to the police department immediately.

2 Getting to the U.S.

Travelers from overseas can take advantage of the **APEX** (advance purchase excursion) fares that all the major U.S. and European carriers offer. Aside from these, attractive values are offered by **Virgin Atlantic** (☎ 0293/747-747 in London) to Los Angeles.

The only international flights direct to San Diego are from Mexico and England. Other overseas travelers bound for San Diego will need to change planes at another U.S. gateway. If your port of entry is Los Angeles, you can either fly to San Diego or take a train or bus. Unfortunately, the Los Angeles train and bus stations are a long way from Los Angeles International Airport (LAX), so it isn't convenient to use these modes of transportation to get to San Diego. However, if you're flying into L.A. and staying there a few days, you could get to San Diego by train or bus. Seven trains daily make the 2-hour 58-minute trip for a $20 one-way fare. The train station in Los Angeles, Union Station, is located at 800 Alameda. The Los Angeles bus terminal is located at Seventh and Alameda, and buses depart on the hour from 6am to 6pm daily with some later departures; check with Greyhound for current schedules. The trip takes 2 hours and 45 minutes, and the one-way fare is $11.

In addition to the domestic U.S. airlines listed in chapter 2, many international carriers serve LAX and other U.S. gateways. These include: **Aer Lingus** (☎ 01-844-4777 in Dublin), **Air Canada** (☎ 800/268-7240 in Canada), **Air New Zealand** (☎ 0800/737-000 in New Zealand), **British Airways** (☎ 0345/222-111 in London), **Japan Airlines** (☎ 0354/89-1111 in Tokyo), **Qantas** (☎ 13-13-13 in Australia), and **Swissair** (☎ 01/258-3434 in Zurich, or 022/799-5999 in Geneva).

3 Getting Around the U.S.

On their transatlantic or transpacific flights, some large U.S. airlines offer special discount tickets for any of their U.S. destinations (American Airline's **Visit USA** program and Delta's **Discover America** program, for example). The tickets or coupons are not on sale in the United States and must be purchased before you leave your point of departure. This system is the best, easiest, and fastest way to see the United States at low cost. You should obtain information well in advance from your travel agent or the office of the airline concerned, since the conditions attached to these discount tickets can be changed without advance notice.

The visitor arriving by air, no matter what the port of entry, should cultivate patience and resignation before setting foot on U.S. soil. Getting through immigration control may take as long as 2 hours on some days, especially summer weekends, so have your guidebook or something else to read handy. Add the time it takes to clear customs, and you will see you should make a very generous allowance for delay in planning connections between international and domestic flights—figure on 2 to 3 hours at least.

In contrast, for the traveler arriving by car or by rail from Canada, the border-crossing formalities have been streamlined to the vanishing point. And for the traveler by air from Canada, Bermuda, and some places in the Caribbean, you can sometimes go through customs and immigration at the point of departure, which is much quicker and less painful.

International visitors can also buy a **USA Railpass,** good for 15 or 30 days of unlimited travel anywhere in the United States on Amtrak. The pass is available through many foreign travel agents and in the United States. Prices in 1997 for a 15-day pass were $260 off-peak, $375 peak; a 30-day pass costs $350 off-peak, $480 peak (peak season is June 1 to September 1). In addition to this pass which allows nationwide travel, there are less expensive regional passes for the far west, western, eastern, and northeast areas of the country. Children 2 to 15 are charged half price. With a foreign passport, you can also buy passes at any staffed train station in the United States. Reservations are generally required and should be made for each part of your trip as early as possible. Contact Amtrak at ☎ **800/USA-RAIL.** Amtrak also offers tours which include accommodations and sightseeing. For information on this option, call ☎ **800/321-8684.**

Although ticket prices for short bus trips between cities are often the most economical form of public transit, at this writing, bus passes are priced slightly higher than similar train passes. **Greyhound,** the nationwide bus line, offers an **Ameripass** for unlimited travel for 7 days (for $189), 15 days (for $299), 30 days (for $409), and 60 days (for $599). Bus travel in the United States can be both slow and uncomfortable, so this option is not for everyone. In addition, bus stations are often located in undesirable neighborhoods. To contact Greyhound call ☎ **800/231-2222.** For further information specific to San Diego, see "Getting Around" in chapter 4.

FAST FACTS: For the Foreign Traveler

Automobile Organizations   Auto clubs will supply maps, suggested routes, guidebooks, accident and bail-bond insurance, and emergency road service. The major auto club in the United States, with 983 offices nationwide, is the **American Automobile Association (AAA).** Members of some foreign auto clubs have reciprocal arrangements with the AAA and enjoy its services at no charge—inquire about AAA reciprocity before you leave. The AAA can provide you with an **International Driving Permit** validating your foreign license, although drivers with valid licenses from most home countries don't really need this permit. You may be able to join the AAA even if you are not a member of a reciprocal club. To inquire, call ☎ **619/233-1000.** In addition, some automobile-rental agencies now provide these services, so ask when you rent your car.

Business Hours   **Banks** are open weekdays from 9am to 4pm or later and sometimes Saturday morning. In San Diego, **Wells Fargo Bank** has the most locations. To find a handy one for your use call ☎ **800/869-3557,** available 24 hours a day. Two of the most convenient locations are in Ralph's Supermarket on Via La Jolla Drive and on Mission Boulevard in Pacific Beach. These are open Monday to Saturday from 10am to 7pm and Sunday from 11am to 5pm. **Post Offices** are generally open weekdays from 8:30am to 5pm and Saturday from 8:30am to noon.

However, the branch on Midway Drive has extended hours from 3:30pm to 1am. To find the post office nearest you, call ☎ **800/275-8777. Shops,** especially those in shopping malls, tend to stay open until about 9pm weekdays and until 6pm on weekends.

Climate   See "When to Go" in chapter 2.

Currency   See "Preparing for Your Trip" above.

Currency Exchange   Thomas Cook Currency Services (☎ **800/287-7362**) offers a wide variety of services: more than 100 currencies, commission-free traveler's checks, drafts and wire transfers, check collections, and precious-metal bars and coins. Rates are competitive and service is excellent. They are located downtown at 177 Horton Plaza, within walking distance of the train station, and at 4525 La Jolla Village Drive, in University Towne Centre near La Jolla. Both are open Monday to Friday from 10am to 6pm and Saturday from 10am to 4pm. An **American Express Travel Services office** with a currency-exchange desk is at 258 Broadway (☎ **619/234-4455**), also within walking distance of the train station.

Drinking Laws   The legal age to drink alcohol in San Diego is 21. Alcohol can only be purchased between the hours of 6am and 2am, 365 days a year.

Electricity   The United States uses 110 to 120 volts, 60 cycles, compared to 220 to 240 volts, 50 cycles, as in most of Europe. Besides a 100-volt converter, small appliances of non-American manufacture, such as hair dryers or shavers, will require a plug adapter, with two flat, parallel pins. The easiest solution is to purchase dual-voltage appliances that operate on both 110 and 220 volts; then all that is required is a U.S. adapter plug.

Embassies and Consulates   All embassies are located in the national capital, Washington, D.C.; some consulates are located in major cities. Listed here are the embassies and West Coast consulates of the major English-speaking countries. Travelers from other countries can get telephone numbers for their embassies and consulates by calling **"Information"** in Washington, D.C. (☎ **202/555-1212**).

The **Australian Embassy** is at 1601 Massachusetts Ave. NW, Washington, DC 20036 (☎ **202/797-3000**). The **Consulate** in Los Angeles is located at Century Park Towers, 19th Floor, 2049 Century Park E., Los Angeles, CA 90067 (☎ **310/229-4800;** fax 310/277-2258).

The **Canadian Embassy** is at 501 Pennsylvania Ave. NW, Washington, DC 20001 (☎ **202/682-1740**). The **Consulate** in Los Angeles is located at 300 S. Grand Ave., Suite 1000, Los Angeles, CA 90071 (☎ **213/346-2700**).

The **Irish Embassy** is at 2234 Massachusetts Ave. NW, Washington, DC 20008 (☎ **202/462-3939**). The **Consulate** in San Francisco is located at 44 Montgomery St., Suite 3830, San Francisco, CA 94104 (☎ **415/392-4214;** fax 415/392-0885).

The **New Zealand Embassy** is at 37 Observatory Circle NW, Washington, DC 20008 (☎ **202/328-4800**). The **Consulate** in Los Angeles is located at 12400 Wilshire Blvd., Los Angeles, CA 90025 (☎ **310/207-1605**).

The **U.K. Embassy** is at 3100 Massachusetts Ave. NW, Washington, DC 20008 (☎ **202/462-1340**). The **Consulate** in Los Angeles is located at 11766 Wilshire Blvd., Suite 400, Los Angeles, CA 90025 (☎ **310/477-3322**).

Emergencies   Call ☎ **911** for fire, police, and ambulance. If you encounter such travelers' problems as sickness, accident, or lost or stolen baggage, call **Traveler's Aid,** an organization that specializes in helping distressed travelers. It has offices at the airport's East Terminal (☎ **619/231-7361**) and West Terminal (☎ **619/231-5230**) and at the Santa Fe (train) Station (☎ **619/234-5191**).

The main police station is located downtown at 1401 Broadway at 14th Street (☎ **619/531-2000**).

U.S. hospitals have emergency rooms, with a special entrance where you will be admitted for quick attention. In Hillcrest, near downtown San Diego, **UCSD Medical Center-Hillcrest,** 200 W. Arbor Dr. (☎ **619/543-6400**) has the best-located emergency room. In La Jolla, **Thornton Hospital,** 9300 Campus Point Dr. (☎ **619/657-7600**) has a good emergency room, and you'll find another in Coronado, at **Coronado Hospital,** 250 Prospect Place, opposite Le Meridien Hotel (☎ **619/435-6251**).

Gasoline (Petrol)   One U.S. gallon equals 3.75 liters, while 1.2 U.S. gallons equals 1 imperial gallon. A gallon of unleaded gas (short for gasoline), which most rental cars accept, costs about $1.38 if you fill your own tank (it's called "self-serve"); 10¢ more if the station attendant does it (called "full-service").

Holidays   On the following national legal holidays, banks, government offices, post offices, and many stores, restaurants, and museums are closed: January 1 (New Year's Day), 3rd Monday in January (Martin Luther King Day), 3rd Monday in February (Presidents' Day), last Monday in May (Memorial Day), July 4 (Independence Day), 1st Monday in September (Labor Day), 2nd Monday in October (Columbus Day), November 11 (Veterans Day/Armistice Day), 4th Thursday in November (Thanksgiving Day), and December 25 (Christmas Day). The Tuesday following the 1st Monday in November is Election Day. Presidential elections are held every 4 years (the next is in 2000).

Mail   You may receive mail c/o General Delivery, San Diego Post Office, 2535 Midway Dr., San Diego, CA 92138-999, USA. Pick up your mail there by taking bus no. 8 from downtown San Diego to Midway Drive at Barnett Avenue. Call ☎ **800/275-8777** for more information. The addressee must pick it up in person and must produce proof of identity (driver's license, credit card, passport, and so on). Mailboxes are blue with a red-and-white logo and carry the inscription U.S. MAIL.

Medical Emergencies   See "Emergencies" above.

Newspapers/Magazines   The *San Diego Union-Tribune, Los Angeles Times,* and the magazines *Newsweek* and *Time* cover world news and are available at newsstands. For newspapers from Europe and elsewhere, try **Seventh Near "B" Coffee and News,** 1146 Seventh Ave. near B Street (☎ **619/696-7071**) or **Paras Newsstand and Cigar Shop,** 3911 30th St. at University (☎ **619/296-2859**).

Postage   Within the United States, it costs 20¢ to mail a standard-size postcard and 32¢ to send an oversize postcard (larger than $4^1/_4$ by 6 in., or 10.8 by 15.4cm). Letters that weigh up to 1 ounce (that's about five 8-by-11-in., or 20.5-by-28.2cm, pages) cost 32¢, plus 23¢ for each additional ounce. A postcard to Mexico costs 35¢, a half-ounce letter 40¢; a postcard to Canada costs 40¢, a half-ounce letter 46¢. A postcard to Europe, Australia, New Zealand, the Far East, South America, and elsewhere costs 50¢ for the first half ounce and 40¢ for each additional half ounce; and first-class letters cost 60¢ for the first half ounce and 40¢ for each additional half ounce. An Aerogramme to anywhere in the world costs 50¢.

Post Offices   See "Mail" above.

Safety   No matter what country you're in, when you're in an unfamiliar city, stay alert. Be aware of your immediate surroundings. Wear a money belt and don't flash expensive jewelry and cameras in public. Pay attention even in heavily touristed areas. If you're traveling in a rental car, never leave any belongings in the trunk. For more specific information, see "Fast Facts: San Diego" in chapter 4.

San Diego is generally a safe city, but deserted areas downtown and elsewhere should be avoided at night.

Taxes If you bring gifts into the United States with a value of over $100, you will be required to pay a duty tax. In the United States there is no VAT (value-added tax) or other indirect tax at a national level.

Sales tax is levied on goods and services by state and local governments, however, and is not included in the price tabs you'll see on merchandise. These taxes are not refundable. Sales tax in San Diego is 7.75%. Tax on hotel rooms is 10.5%.

Telephone and Fax Pay phones can be found on street corners, as well as in bars, restaurants, public buildings, stores, and at service stations. Some accept 20¢, most are 25¢.

For local directory assistance ("information"), dial ☎ **411;** for long-distance information within the United States and Canada, dial 1, then the appropriate area code and **555-1212.**

For long-distance or international calls, it's most economical to charge the call to a telephone charge card or a credit card; or you can use a lot of change. The pay phone will instruct you on how much to deposit and when to deposit it into the slot on the top of the telephone box.

For long-distance calls within the United States, dial 1 followed by the area code and number you want. For direct overseas calls, first dial 011, followed by the country code (Australia, 61; Republic of Ireland, 353; New Zealand, 64; United Kingdom, 44), and then by the city code (for example, 71 or 81 for London, 21 for Birmingham, 1 for Dublin) and the number of the person you wish to call.

Before calling from a hotel room, always ask the hotel phone operator if there are any telephone surcharges. There almost always are, often as much as 75¢ or $1, even for a local call. Avoid these charges by using a public phone, calling collect, or using a telephone charge card.

For reversed-charge or collect calls and for person-to-person calls, dial 0 (zero, not the letter "O") followed by the area code and number you want; an operator will then come on the line, and you should specify that you are calling collect, or person-to-person, or both. If your operator-assisted call is international, immediately ask to speak with an overseas operator.

Most hotels have fax machines available for their customers and usually charge to send or receive a facsimile. You will also see signs for public faxes in the windows of small shops.

Time San Diego is on Pacific time, which is 3 hours earlier than on the U.S. East Coast. For instance, when it is noon in San Diego, it is 3pm in New York and Miami; 2pm in Chicago, in the midwestern part of the country; and 1pm in Denver, Colorado, in the central part of the country. San Diego, like most of the United States, observes daylight saving time during the summer; in late spring, clocks are moved ahead 1 hour and then are turned back again in the fall. This results in lovely long summer evenings, when the sun sets as late as 8:30 or 9pm. To verify the correct time, call ☎ **619/853-1212.**

Tipping Some rules of thumb: bartenders, 10% to 15%; bellhops, at least 50¢ per bag, or $2 to $3 for a lot of luggage; cab drivers, 10% of the fare; cafeterias and fast-food restaurants, no tip; chambermaids, $1 per day; checkroom attendants, $1 per garment; theater ushers, no tip; gas-station attendants, no tip; hairdressers and barbers, 15% to 20%; waiters and waitresses, 15% to 20% of the check; valet parking attendants, $1.

Toilets   Rest rooms are easy to come by in San Diego, although you won't find public facilities on street corners. Instead, expect to find them in hotel lobbies and in public places, such as Horton Plaza and Seaport Village. If there's a rest-room attendant (unusual in San Diego), leave a coin—10¢ or 25¢. Rest rooms in cafes and restaurants are for patrons only, but in an emergency you can just order a cup of coffee or simply ask to use the pay phone, usually conveniently positioned beside the rest rooms.

4 Getting to Know San Diego

San Diego is laid out in an easy-to-decipher manner, so learning the lay of the land is neither confusing nor daunting. Besides being easy to get around, most San Diegans welcome visitors and are eager to answer questions and provide assistance. Chances are good that you'll feel like a local before you know it.

1 Orientation

VISITOR INFORMATION

There are **Traveler's Aid booths** at the East and West airport terminals, one at the train station, and (as mentioned in chapter 2) one at the cruise-ship terminal. Volunteers can answer questions and provide helpful brochures and maps (☎ **619/231-7361,** or use the courtesy phone at the airport).

In downtown San Diego, the **International Visitor Information Center** is on First Avenue at F Street, near Horton Plaza. The multilingual staff offers brochures in English, French, German, Japanese, Portuguese, and Spanish. They also provide the *San Diego Official Visitors Planning Guide,* which includes information on accommodations, dining, activities and attractions, tours, and transportation, and also has excellent maps. You should also ask for the *Super Savings Coupon Book,* which is full of money-saving discount coupons. The center also sells telephone calling cards in $10 and $20 denominations. These cards can be used from any telephone in the United States. The center is open Monday through Saturday from 8:30am to 5pm year-round and Sunday from 11am to 5pm June through August; it is closed Thanksgiving, Christmas, and New Year's Day. For more information, call ☎ **619/236-1212** (fax 619/230-7084; E-mail **sdinfo@sandiego.org**).

Additional visitor information is available from **Balboa Park Visitors Center,** 1549 El Prado, San Diego, CA 92101 (☎ **619/ 239-0512**); the **Coronado Visitors Bureau,** 1047 "B" Ave., Coronado, CA 92118 (☎ **800/622-8300** or 619/437-8788; fax 619/437-6006; E-mail **corcvb@aol.com**); the **San Diego Visitor Information Center,** 2688 E. Mission Bay Dr., San Diego, CA 92109 (☎ **619/276-8200,** ext. 3; fax 619/276-6041; E-mail **visitor@infosandiego.com**; Web site: **www.infosandiego.com/ visitor**); **North County Convention & Visitors Bureau** (covers from La Jolla to Escondido and includes Julian and Anza-Borrego) 720 N. Broadway, Escondido, CA 92025 (☎ **800/848-3336** or 760/745-4741); **Old Town State Historic Park Headquarters,** 4002 Wallace St. (☎ **619/220-5422**); and the **La Jolla Town Council,** Box 1101, La Jolla, CA 92038 (☎ **619/454-1444**).

For the latest on San Diego nightlife and entertainment, pick up the *Reader,* a free newspaper which comes out on Thursday and is available at locations all over the city. Also check "Night and Day," the Thursday supplement in the *San Diego Union-Tribune.*

CITY LAYOUT
MAIN ARTERIES & STREETS

It's not hard to find your way around downtown San Diego. Most streets run one way: First through Twelfth avenues alternate running north and south (Fifth Avenue is two-way in the Gaslamp Quarter only); A through K streets alternate running east and west. Broadway, the equivalent of D Street, is a two-way street, as are Market Street and Harbor Drive. East-west streets (north of A Street) bear the names of trees, in alphabetical order: Ash, Beech, Cedar, Date, etc. Harbor Drive runs past the airport and along the waterfront known as the Embarcadero. The Coronado Bay Bridge leading to Coronado is accessed from I-5; Ash Street and Broadway are the downtown arteries that connect with Harbor Drive. I-5 north leads to Old Town, Mission Bay, La Jolla, and North County. Balboa Park, home of the San Diego Zoo, and the Hillcrest and Uptown areas lie northeast of downtown San Diego. The park and zoo are easily reached via Twelfth Avenue, which becomes Park Boulevard and leads up to their respective parking lots. Fifth Avenue leads to Hillcrest and Uptown (turn right onto University to get to the latter).

In Coronado   In Coronado, the main streets are Orange Avenue, where most of the hotels and restaurants are clustered, and Ocean Drive, which hugs Coronado Beach.

In Downtown San Diego   The major thoroughfares in downtown San Diego are Broadway (a major bus artery), Fourth and Fifth avenues (running south and north, respectively), C Street (the trolley line), and Harbor Drive, which hugs the waterfront and passes the Maritime Museum, Seaport Village, and the Convention Center.

In Hillcrest Area   In the Hillcrest area near Balboa Park, the main streets are University and Washington, both two-way running east and west, and Fourth and Fifth avenues.

In La Jolla   In La Jolla, the main avenues are Prospect and Girard, which are perpendicular to one another.

In Pacific Beach   In Pacific Beach, Mission Boulevard is the main drag, and perpendicular to it are Grand and Garnet avenues and Pacific Beach Drive; East and West Mission Bay drives and Ingraham Street enable you to zip around the periphery of the bay or bisect it.

FINDING AN ADDRESS

It's easy to find an address on a street running east-west when you're downtown. If the address is 411 Market St., for example, you'll find it between Fourth and Fifth avenues on Market; if it's 326 Broadway, it's between Third and Fourth avenues; if it's 1051 University, it's between 10th and 11th avenues. Even numbers are located on the north or west sides of streets; odd numbers are located on the south or east sides of streets.

STREET MAPS

The **International Visitor Information Center,** located at First Avenue and F Street (☎ **619/236-1212**), provides excellent, free maps inside the *Official Visitors Guide,* which has five easy-to-read maps: downtown San Diego and Coronado (with arrows pointing which way each street runs), Old Town, Balboa Park, La Jolla and Mission Bay, and San Diego County and vicinity.

The **Automobile Club of Southern California,** which has several locations, including 815 Date St. (☎ **619/233-1000**) also has great maps, which are free to its members and members of international auto clubs. The **Transit Store,** at 102 Broadway (at First Avenue) (☎ **619/233-3004**), is a storehouse of bus and trolley maps, with a friendly staff on duty to answer specific questions.

Hotel receptionists can provide complimentary maps of the downtown area. You can buy maps of the city and vicinity at **Le Travel Store** at 745 Fourth Ave. or the **Upstart Crow** bookstore in Seaport Village.

If you're moving to San Diego or plan to spend a long time here, I suggest you buy a copy of the *Thomas Bros. Guide,* available at bookstores, drugstores, and large supermarkets throughout San Diego. This all-encompassing book of maps deciphers San Diego for you, street by street.

NEIGHBORHOODS IN BRIEF

In this guidebook San Diego is divided into six areas, each with its own hotel and restaurant listings (see chapters 5 and 6).

Coronado   Actually an incorporated city in its own right, but included as a neighborhood here because of its close proximity to downtown San Diego by car and ferry, Coronado is a sedate place: home of the revered Hotel del Coronado and of more retired admirals than any other community in the country. It has a lovely duned beach (one of the area's most popular), fine restaurants, and a downtown area that reminds me of the small town in the Midwest where I grew up.

Downtown   The business, shopping, dining, and entertainment heart of the city, it includes Horton Plaza, the Gaslamp Quarter, the Embarcadero (waterfront), Seaport Village, and the distinctive Convention Center. The Maritime Museum, the downtown branch of the Museum of Contemporary Art, and the Children's Museum are also located here. Visitors with business to conduct in the city center would be wise to stay downtown. This is also the best area for those attending meetings at the Convention Center. The Gaslamp Quarter offers great dining and nightlife, but is surrounded by areas of questionable safety. Little Italy, a small neighborhood along India Street between Cedar and Fir at the northern edge of downtown, is the best place to find gelato, espresso, pizza, and pasta.

Hillcrest/Uptown   These two adjacent inner-city neighborhoods offer interesting dining and alternative entertainment options. Considered the city's gay area, they lie near Balboa Park, which is home to the San Diego Zoo and numerous museums, including the Museum of Art, the Museum of Photographic Arts, and the Reuben H. Fleet Space Theater and Science Center. Hillcrest and Uptown are centrally located and accommodations here are less expensive than other parts of the city.

Impressions

People in other places work hard to get somewhere, but in San Diego you're already there.

—Neil Morgan, Associate Editor, *San Diego Union-Tribune*

La Jolla   With an atmosphere that is a cross between Rodeo Drive and a Mediterranean village, this seaside community is home to an inordinate number of wealthy folks who could live anywhere, but choose to live here surrounded by the beach, the University of California San Diego, outstanding restaurants, excellent (albeit pricey) shops, and some of the world's best medical facilities. It is the wise tourist who beds down here, thereby taking advantage of the community's attributes without having to buy a piece of its high-priced real estate. The name is a compromise between Spanish and American Indian, as is the pronunciation—La-*hoy*-ya—and it has come to mean "the jewel."

Mission Bay/Pacific Beach   Here's where they took the picture on the postcard you'll send home. Mission Bay is a watery playground perfect for waterskiing, sailing, and windsurfing. The adjacent communities of Mission Beach and Pacific Beach are known for their wide stretches of sand fronting the Pacific, active nightlife, and California-casual dining. Many San Diego singles choose to live here, and once you've visited you'll understand why. The boardwalk, which runs from South Mission Beach through North Mission Beach to Pacific Beach, is a popular place for in-line skating, bike riding, and watching sunsets. This is the place to stay if you are traveling with beach-loving children or want to walk barefoot on the beach.

Old Town/Hotel Circle   This area encompasses the Old Town State Historic Park, Presidio Park, Heritage Park, and numerous museums harking back to the turn of the century and the city's beginnings. There's shopping and dining here, too, all aimed at tourists. Not far from Old Town, **Hotel Circle** offers midprice and budget accommodation options on either side of I-8.

2 Getting Around

San Diego has many walkable neighborhoods, from the historic downtown area, to Hillcrest and nearby Balboa Park, to the Embarcadero, to Mission Bay Park. You get yourself there by car, bus, or trolley, and your feet will do the rest. For inspiration, turn to the city strolls in chapter 8. Always remember to cross the street at corners or in crosswalks; there's a $54 fine for jaywalking.

BY PUBLIC TRANSPORTATION

BY BUS   San Diego has an adequate, but not remarkable, bus system that will get you to where you're going—eventually. Most drivers are friendly and helpful. The system encompasses over 100 routes in the greater San Diego area. The **Transit Store,** at 102 Broadway (at First Avenue) dispenses passes, tokens, timetables, maps, brochures, ID cards for seniors 60 and older as well as travelers with disabilities (these two categories pay only 75¢ per ride), and lost-and-found information. Request a copy of the useful brochure *Your Open Door to San Diego,* which details the city's most popular tourist attractions and the buses that will take you to them. You may also call ☎ **619/233-3004** (TTY/TDD 619/234-5005 for the hearing impaired) and tell them where you are and where you want to go; Transit Store staff will tell you the nearest bus stop and what time the next couple of buses will pass by. If you know your route and just need schedule information call ☎ **619/685-4900** from any touch-tone phone. That's service. You can call between 5:30am and 8:30pm daily except Thanksgiving and Christmas. The line is often busy, and the best times to call are noon to 3pm and on weekends. The Transit Store office is open Monday through Friday from 8:30am to 5:30pm and Saturday through Sunday noon to 4pm.

Bus stops are marked by rectangular blue signs every other block or so on local routes, longer distances on express routes. More than 20 bus routes pass through the

Of all the dilapidated, miserable-looking places I've ever seen, this was the worst . . . an altogether dreary, sunblasted point of departure for nowhere. . . .
    —Mary Chase Walker (San Diego's first schoolteacher), 1865

A little land and a living, surely, is better than a desperate struggle and wealth, possibly.
    —William E. Smythe (Utopian founder of the Little Landers Movement), 1908

---

downtown area, among them Routes 2, 3, 4, 5, and 7 (to Balboa Park); 20, 29, 30, and 34 (to Mission Beach, Pacific Beach, and La Jolla); Route 901 (to Coronado via the bridge); and Route 992 (to the airport). Most bus fares range from $1.75 to $2.25 depending on distance and type of service (local or express).

You can request a **transfer** at no extra charge as long as you continue on a bus or trolley with an equal or lower fare (if it's higher, you simply pay the difference). Transfers must be used within two hours, and you can actually return to where you started.

A particular saving is the **Day Tripper** pass, which allows unlimited rides on MTS and trolley routes. Passes are sold for 1, 2, 3, and 4 consecutive days, and cost $5, $8, $10, and $12, respectively. Day Trippers are sold at The Transit Store and all Trolley Station automatic ticket vending machines.

Some of the most popular tourist attractions served by bus and rail routes are Balboa Park (Routes 1, 3, 7, 7A, 7B, and 25); the San Diego Zoo (Routes 7, 7A, and 7B); the Children's Museum, the Convention Center, and the Gaslamp Quarter (San Diego Trolley Orange Line); Coronado (Route 901); Horton Plaza (most downtown bus routes and the San Diego Trolley's Blue and Orange lines pass through here); Old Town (San Diego Trolley's Blue Line); Cabrillo National Monument (Route 26 from Old Town Transit Center); Seaport Village (Routes 7, 7A, 7B, and the San Diego Trolley's Orange Line); Sea World (Route 9 from the Old Town Transit Center); Qualcomm Stadium (San Diego Trolley Blue Line); and Tijuana (San Diego Trolley Blue Line to San Ysidro).

The **Coronado Shuttle,** bus Route 904, runs between the Le Meridien Hotel and the Old Ferry Landing and then continues along Orange Avenue to the Hotel del Coronado, Glorietta Bay, Lowes, and back again. It costs only 50¢ per person. Route 901 goes all the way to Coronado from San Diego and costs $1.75 for adults and 75¢ for seniors and children. Call ☎ **619/233-3004** for more information about this and other bus routes.

When planning your route, please note that schedules vary and buses do not run all night. Some buses stop running at 6pm while other lines continue to 9pm, midnight, and 2am—ask your bus driver for more specific information; on Saturdays some routes run all night long.

Organized bus tours are a good way to explore San Diego beyond the local bus routes with an expert in whatever area may interest you. Both **San Diego Mini Tours** (☎ **619/477-8687**) and **Gray Line Tours** (☎ **691/491-0011**) offer city tours and will take you to see all the highlights of the San Diego area including Cabrillo National Monument, Tijuana, Disneyland, the Wine Country, and Baja California.

BY TRAIN San Diego's express rail commuter service, **The Coaster,** travels between the downtown Santa Fe Depot station and the Oceanside Transit Center, with stops en route at Old Town, Sorrento Valley, Solana Beach, Encinitas, and Carlsbad. Fares range from $2.75 to $3.50 each way, depending how far you go

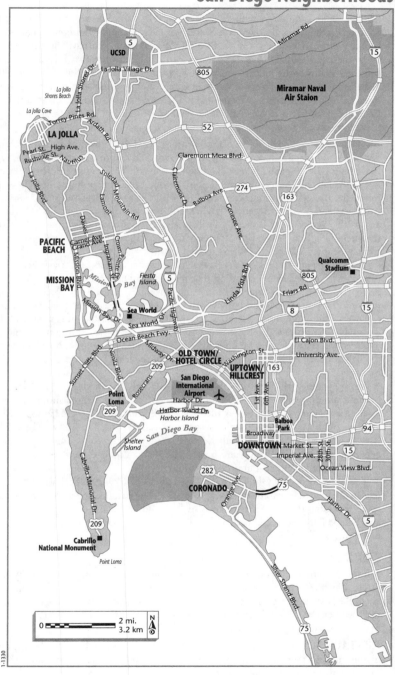

San Diego Neighborhoods

UCSD

La Jolla Village Dr.

Miramar Rd.

Miramar Naval
Air Staion

La Jolla
Shores Beach

La Jolla Cove

Torrey Pines Rd.

Ardath Rd.

LA JOLLA

Claremont Mesa Blvd.

Pearl St.   High Ave.

Rushville St.   Nautilus

Soledad Mountain Rd.

Claremont Dr.

Balboa Ave.

Genesee Ave.

Linda Vista Rd.

PACIFIC
BEACH

Garnet Ave.

Grand Ave.

Ingraham Dr.

Crown Point Dr.

MISSION
BAY

Mission Bay

Fiesta
Island

Mission Bay Dr.

Sea World

Sea World Dr.

Ocean Beach Fwy.

Pacific Highway

Qualcomm
Stadium

Friars Rd.

El Cajon Blvd.

University Ave.

OLD TOWN/
HOTEL CIRCLE

Washington St.

UPTOWN/
HILLCREST

Sunset Cliffs Blvd.

Nimitz Blvd.

Midway Dr.

Rosecrans

San Diego
International
Airport

Point
Loma

Harbor Dr.

Harbor Island Dr.

Harbor Island

1st Ave.

6th Ave.

Balboa
Park

San Diego Bay

Shelter
Island

Broadway

DOWNTOWN   Market St.

Imperial Ave.

Ocean View Blvd.

28th St.

30th St.

Cabrillo Memorial Dr.

CORONADO

Orange Ave.

Silver Strand Blvd.

Cabrillo
National Monument

Point Loma

0   2 mi.
      3.2 km

N

1-1330

(eligible seniors and riders with disabilities pay a half-price discount fare). The trip between Oceanside and downtown San Diego takes just under an hour. Trains run Monday through Saturday; call ☎ **800/COASTER** for the current schedule.

Amtrak (☎ **800/USA-RAIL**) trains run daily between San Diego and Los Angeles. Trains to LA depart the Santa Fe Depot and stop at Solana Beach and Oceanside. Some trains stop at San Juan Capistrano. A round-trip ticket to Solana Beach is $10, round-trip to Oceanside is $15, round-trip to San Juan Capistrano is $24, and round-trip to Los Angeles is $40. Visitors can also get to Disneyland (Anaheim) on the train.

BY TROLLEY   The San Diego Trolley routes serve downtown, the Mexican border (a 40-min. trip from downtown), Old Town, and east to the city of Santee. On November 23, 1997 the Trolley's extension to Mission Valley was completed. It carries sports fans to Qualcomm Stadium, major hotels, and shopping centers. Downtown, the trolleys run along C Street (one block north of Broadway) and stop at Broadway and Kettner (America Plaza), Third Avenue (Civic Center), Fifth Avenue, and 12th Avenue (City College). Trolleys also circle around downtown's Bayside (parallel to Harbor Drive), with stops serving the Gaslamp Quarter, the Convention Center, Seaport Village, and the Santa Fe Depot.

Trolleys operate on a self-service fare-collection system; riders purchase tickets from machines in stations before boarding. The machines list fares for each destination and dispense change. Tickets are valid for 3 hours from the time of purchase, in any direction. Fare inspectors board trains at random to check tickets. The bright-red trains run every 15 minutes during the day (every 10 min. on the Blue Line, between Old Town and the Border, during weekday rush hours) and every 30 minutes at night. Trolleys stop at each station for only 30 seconds. To open the door for boarding, push the lighted green button; to open the door to exit the trolley, push the lighted white button.

Trolley travel within the downtown area costs only $1; the fare to the Mexican border from downtown is $2.00. Children under 5 ride free; seniors and riders with disabilities pay only 75¢. For recorded transit information call ☎ **619/685-4900.** To speak with a customer service representative, call ☎ **619/233-3004** (TTY/TDD 619/234-5005 for the hearing impaired) daily from 5:30am to 8:30pm. The trolley generally operates daily from 5am to about 12:30am, although the Blue line, which goes to the border, runs 24 hours on Saturday.

The privately owned **Old Town Trolley Tours** (☎ **619/298-TOUR** (**8687**)) offers an alternative way to tour the city by trolley. The narrated tours cover a 30-mile route including the highlights of areas such as Old Town, Downtown, Coronado, and Balboa Park. You can board and reboard the trolley at over a dozen stops every half hour.

BY CAR

San Diegans complain of increasing traffic, but the city is still easy to navigate by car. Streets downtown tend to run one way, which may frustrate you until you learn the lay of the land (the International Visitor Information Center map is a big help, complete with arrows). Finding a parking space can be tricky, but some reasonably priced parking lots are fairly centrally located.

RENTALS   If you don't arrive by car in San Diego, you should probably rent one if your budget allows. While it's possible to get around by public transportation, having your own wheels is a big advantage.

All the major car-rental agencies have offices at the airport and in the larger hotels. **Avis,** like several other car-rental companies in San Diego, will allow its cars

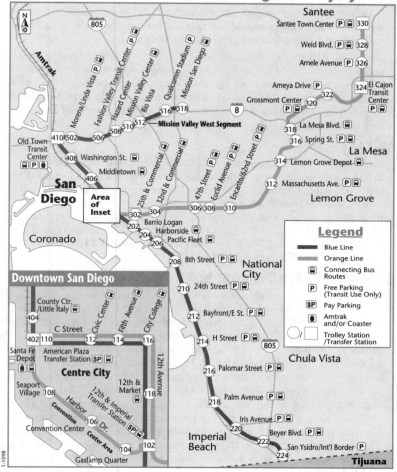

San Diego Trolley System

Santee
Santee Town Center 330
Weld Blvd. 328
Arnele Avenue 326
Ameya Drive
324 El Cajon Transit Center
Grossmont Center 320
322
La Mesa Blvd. 318
Spring St. 316
La Mesa
Lemon Grove Depot 314
Massachusetts Ave. 312
Lemon Grove

Santee
805
Morena/Linda Vista
Fashion Valley Transit Center
Hazard Center
Mission Valley Center
Rio Vista
Qualcomm Stadium
Mission San Diego
516 518
8
Mission Valley West Segment
508 510 512
410 502 506
Old Town Transit Center
408 Washington St.
406 Middletown
Barrio Logan
302 304
202 204 206
Harborside
Pacific Fleet

San Diego
Area of Inset
Coronado

23th & Commercial
32nd & Commercial
47th Street
Euclid Avenue
Encanto/62nd Street
306 308 310

208 8th Street
National City
210 24th Street
212 Bayfront/E St.
214 H Street
805
216 Palomar Street **Chula Vista**
218 Palm Avenue
220 Iris Avenue
222 Beyer Blvd.
224 San Ysidro/Int'l Border
Imperial Beach
Tijuana

Legend

— Blue Line
— Orange Line
Connecting Bus Routes
P Free Parking (Transit Use Only)
SP Pay Parking
Amtrak and/or Coaster
○/□ Trolley Station /Transfer Station

Downtown San Diego
County Ctr. /Little Italy
404
C Street
402 110 112 114 116
Santa Fe Depot
American Plaza Transfer Station **SP**
Centre City
Seaport Village 108
12th & Market 118
106 Convention Center
Convention Center Dr.
104 102
Gaslamp Quarter
Civic Center
Fifth Avenue
City College
12th Avenue
12th & Imperial Transfer Station **SP**
Harbor Center Area

Amtrak

1-1098

into Mexico as far as Ensenada. Beyond Ensenada, the roads aren't as well maintained, and it's more difficult to get to the car should there be a breakdown or other problem (see "Tijuana: Going South of the Border" and "Baja California: Exploring More of Mexico" in chapter 11).

PARKING   The garage at Horton Plaza, at G Street and Fourth Avenue, is free to shoppers for the first 3 hours (the parking ticket must be validated by a merchant or you must show your cinema or theater stub from Horton Plaza). After the first 3 hours, you have to pay $1 per half hour. A quick way to zip into Horton Plaza and avoid the ever-upward spiral until you find a parking spot is to enter the back way, via Third Avenue. The fenced-in lot adjacent to the Embarcadero, called **Allright Parking,** at 900 Broadway and Harbor Drive (☎ 619/298-6944), charges $3 to park between 5:30am and midnight. More convenient to downtown shopping and the Children's Museum is the open-air lot on Market Street between Front and First streets, where you can park all day weekdays for $3, and weekends for $2. Three-hour meters line Harbor Drive opposite the ticket offices for harbor tours; even on weekends, you have to feed them.

Parking meters are plentiful in downtown San Diego; trouble is, the spaces belonging to them are usually taken. Meters take quarters, up to a 2-hour limit; you have to feed them between 8am and 6pm, even on weekends.

DRIVING RULES California has a seat-belt law, so buckle up before you venture out. You may turn right at a red light after stopping unless a sign says otherwise. Likewise, you can turn left on a red light from a one-way street onto another one-way street after coming to a full stop. Most freeway exits are to the right. Keep in mind when driving in San Diego that pedestrians have the right-of-way at all times, so stop for pedestrians who have stepped off the curb.

BY TAXI

Half a dozen taxi companies serve the San Diego area, and they do not have standardized rates, except from the airport into downtown, which will cost about $8.50 with tip. Taxis don't cruise the streets here like they do in other cities, so you'll have to call one of the companies for quick pickup. If you are at a hotel or restaurant, the front-desk attendant or maître d' will call for you. Among the local companies are **Orange Cab** (☎ 619/291-3333), **San Diego Cab** (☎ 619/226-TAXI), and **Yellow Cab** (☎ 619/234-6161). The **Coronado Cab Company** (☎ 619/435-6211) serves Coronado. In La Jolla, use **La Jolla Cab** (☎ 619/453-4222).

BY FERRY, WATER TAXI, OR BOAT

BY FERRY There's regularly scheduled ferry service between San Diego and Coronado (☎ **619/234-4111** for information). Ferries leave from the Broadway Pier on the hour from 9am to 9pm Sunday through Thursday and from 9am to 10pm Friday and Saturday. They return from the Old Ferry Landing in Coronado to the Broadway Pier every hour on the 42-minute mark from 9:42am to 9:42pm Sunday through Thursday and from 9:42am to 10:42pm Friday and Saturday. The ride to and from Coronado takes 15 minutes. Ferries also run from the Fifth Avenue Landing near the Convention Center to the Old Ferry Landing every hour on the half hour from 9:30am to 9:30pm Sunday through Thursday and from 9:30am to 10:30pm Friday and Saturday; the trip from Coronado to the Fifth Avenue Landing is every hour at the 18-minute mark from 9:18am to 9:18pm Sunday through Thursday and from 9:18am to 10:18pm Friday and Saturday. The fare is $2 for each leg of the journey (50¢ extra if you bring your bike). Purchase tickets in advance at the Harbor Excursion kiosk on Broadway Pier or the Fifth Avenue Landing in San Diego or at the Old Ferry Landing in Coronado.

BY WATER TAXI Water taxis (☎ **619/235-TAXI**) will take you around most of San Diego Bay for $5. If you want to go to the southern part of the bay (to Loews Coronado Bay Resort, for example) you will be charged a flat fee of $25.

You can either call a taxi to pick you up from any landing in the bay or you can go to the Harbor Excursion Dock at the foot of Broadway Pier, where taxis wait for passengers.

BY BOAT Boat tours provide a great way to explore San Diego from one of its many bays including Mission Bay and San Diego Bay. **Bahia Belle** (☎ 619/539-7779), **Hornblower Invader Cruises** (☎ 691/234-8687), and **San Diego Harbor Excursions** (☎ 691/234-4111) all offer narrated cruises of the local bays and drop off and pick up passengers at the various hotels along the bays.

BY BICYCLE

San Diego is flat enough for easy exploration by bicycle, and many roads have designated bike lanes. Bikes are readily rentable. Downtown, you can try

Pennyfarthing's, 314 G St., in the Gaslamp Quarter (☎ **619/233-7696**), or **Seaport Cycling & Surreys,** 565 Harbor Lane (☎ **619/238-3842**). In Mission Bay there's **Hamel's Action Sports Center,** 704 Ventura Place, off Mission Boulevard at Ocean Front Walk (☎ **619/488-5050**), and **Hilton Beach and Tennis Resort,** 1775 E. Mission Bay Dr. (☎ **619/276-4010**). In La Jolla there's **La Jolla Sports and Photo,** 2199 Avenida de la Playa (☎ **619/459-1114**). In Coronado are **Holland's Bicycles,** 977 Orange Ave. (☎ **619/435-3153;** fax 619/435-2586; E-mail **hollands@mill.net**), and **Bikes and Beyond,** 1201 First St. at the Ferry Landing Marketplace (☎ **619/435-7180**). Free pickup and delivery in San Diego for a day's rental is available through **Rent A Bike,** at First Avenue and Harbor Drive (☎ **619/232-4700**). Bike rentals average about $10. You can also rent by the week or month, and two-seaters for couples are available.

Any bus stops that have bike-route signs attached alert you that buses stopping here have a bike rack attached and will take your trusty two-wheeler for free. Just let the driver know you want to use it. Once you have stowed the bike on the back of the bus, board and pay your regular fare. When you get off, remind the bus driver that you need to get your bike. With this service, you can bus the bike to an area you'd like to explore, do your biking there, then return by bus with your wheels in tow. Not all routes are served by buses with bike racks; call ☎ **619/233-3004** for information.

The San Diego Trolley has a **Bike-N-Ride** program that lets you bring your bike on the trolley for free. You'll need to get a bike permit and display it on the bike before you board. Permits to bikers who are 16 and older cost $4 and are issued through the **Transit Store,** 102 Broadway (☎ **619/234-1060**). Bikers must board at the back end of a trolley car, which is where the bike-storage area is located; cars carry two bikes except during weekday rush hour when the limit is one bike per car. Several trolley stops connect with routes for buses that are conveniently equipped with bike racks. For more information, call the **Transit Information Line** at ☎ **619/233-3004.**

Bikes are also welcome on the ferry connecting San Diego and Coronado, which has 15 miles of dedicated bike paths.

FAST FACTS: San Diego

Airport   See "Getting There," in chapter 2.

American Express   A full-service American Express office in downtown is at 258 Broadway (☎ **619/234-4455**).

Area Code   Dial **619** to call most towns in San Diego County. Use **760** to reach Encinitas, Carlsbad, Oceanside, Escondido, Ramona, Julian, and Anza-Borrego.

Baby-Sitters   A number of hotels will secure a bonded sitter for guests, or you can call **Marion's Child** (☎ **619/582-5029**), whose sitters are bonded.

Business Hours   **Banks** are open weekdays from 9am to 4pm or later, and sometimes Saturday morning. **Shops** in shopping malls tend to stay open until about 9pm weekdays and until 6pm weekends.

Camera Repair   Both **George's Camera & Video,** 3827 30th St., (☎ **619/297-3544**), and **Professional Photographic Repair,** 7910 Raytheon Rd. (☎ **619/277-3700**) provide cameras and repair services.

Car Rentals   See "Getting Around," earlier in this chapter.

Climate   See "When to Go," in chapter 2.

Dentists   See "Doctors," below.

Doctors   For dental referrals, contact the **San Diego County Dental Society** at ☎ **800/201-0244** or call 800/DENTIST. **Hotel Docs** (☎ **800/468-3537** or 619/275-2663) is a 24-hour network of physicians, dentists, and chiropractors who claim they'll come to your hotel room within 35 minutes of your call. They accept credit cards, and their services are covered by most insurance policies. In a life-threatening situation, dial ☎ **911.**

Driving Rules   See "Getting Around," earlier in this chapter.

Drugstores   See "Pharmacies," below.

Embassies/Consulates   See chapter 3, "For Foreign Visitors."

Emergencies   Call ☎ **911** for fire, police, and ambulance. The main police station is located at 1401 Broadway at 14th Street (☎ **619/531-2065;** 619/531-2000 for hearing impaired).

Eyeglass Repair   **Optometric Expressions,** 55 Horton Plaza, (☎ **619/544-9000**) is located at street level near the Westin Hotel; it's open Monday, Wednesday, and Friday from 8am to 6pm and Tuesday, Thursday, and Saturday from 9:30am to 6pm. **Optometry on the Plaza,** 287 Horton Plaza (☎ **619/239-1716**) is open daily from 10am to 6pm (later during summer). Both can fill eyeglass prescriptions, repair glasses, replace contact lenses, and sell you some jazzy new shades.

Hospitals   In Hillcrest, near downtown San Diego, **UCSD Medical Center-Hillcrest,** 200 W. Arbor Dr. (☎ **619/543-6400**) has the best-located emergency room. In La Jolla, **Thornton Hospital,** 9300 Campus Point Dr. (☎ **619/657-7600**) has a good emergency room, and you'll find another in Coronado, at **Coronado Hospital,** 250 Prospect Place, opposite Le Meridien Hotel (☎ **619/435-6251**).

Hot Lines   Adult Children of Alcoholics: ☎ 619/276-6232; HIV Hot Line: ☎ 800/922-2437 (English) or 800/922-7432 (multilingual); Alcoholics Anonymous: ☎ 619/265-8762; Debtors Anonymous: ☎ 619/525-3065; Mental Health Crisis Line: ☎ 619/236-3339; Overeaters Anonymous: ☎ 619/563-4606; Traveler's Aid Society: ☎ 619/231-7361.

Information   See "Visitor Information," earlier in this chapter.

Libraries   The public library, at 820 E St. (☎ **619/236-5800**), is open Monday through Thursday from 10am to 9pm, Friday and Saturday from 9:30am to 5:30pm, and Sunday from 1 to 5pm; it's closed on holidays.

Liquor Laws   The drinking age in California is 21. Beer, wine, and hard liquor are sold daily from 6am to 2am and are available in grocery stores.

Lost Property   To report an item lost or found on the trolley or bus, call **619/234-1060.** Anything that has been on a bus may be retrieved the following day after 10am at the Transit Store at 102 Broadway (at First Avenue). Items found on trolleys may be picked up at the Transit Store on Monday, Wednesday, or Friday after 11:30am. Lost articles are held for 30 days. The airport has a lost-and-found department, as does each airline. For items left in hotel rooms, check with housekeeping.

Luggage Storage/Lockers   The Greyhound Bus Station, on Broadway between First and Front streets, has locker space available for $1 for 24 hours. Most hotels will store luggage on a short-term basis at no charge. There are no lockers at the airport, and only limited storage at the Amtrak Station.

Maps   See "City Layout," earlier in this chapter.

Newspapers/Magazines   The *San Diego Union-Tribune* is published daily, and its informative entertainment section, "Night & Day," is in the Thursday edition. For the irreverent alternative press, check the *Reader,* published weekly (on Thursday) with dining and entertainment sections. *San Diego* magazine is filled with extensive entertainment and dining listings (and more ads for face-lifts and tummy tucks than you could ever imagine), while *San Diego Home-Garden Lifestyles* magazine highlights the city's homes and gardens and provides a monthly calendar of events, including garden tours and talks and family-oriented outings. Both magazines are published monthly and sold at newsstands. The free *San Diego This Week* has restaurant listings and information about shopping, attractions, nightlife, and the latest goings-on about town, as does the *Guest Quick Guide* (for coverage of San Diego, La Jolla, and North County), published quarterly by Guest Informant.

Pharmacies   Long's, Sav-On, and **Thrifty** sell pharmaceuticals and nonprescription products. Look in the phone book to find the one nearest you. If you need a pharmacy after normal business hours, Sav-On Drugs, 8831 Villa La Jolla Dr., La Jolla (☎ **619/457-4390**) is open 24 hours; other Sav-On locations include 1652 Garnet Ave., Pacific Beach (☎ **619/273-7810**) and 3327 Rosecrans St., San Diego (☎ **619/222-0434**). Longs Drugs Stores' locations include 7525 Eads Ave. (corner Pearl St.), La Jolla (☎ **619/551-0699**); 4445 Mission Blvd., Pacific Beach (☎ **619/273-0440**); and 71 Horton Plaza in downtown San Diego (☎ **619/231-9135**). Thrifty Drugs Stores has locations at 402 Broadway (near Fourth) in downtown San Diego (☎ **619/233-6545**) and at 535 Robinson Ave. in Hillcrest (☎ **619/291-3703**). Local hospitals also sell prescription drugs.

Police   The downtown police station is at 1401 Broadway (☎ **619/531-2000**). Call ☎ **911** in an emergency.

Post Office   The **downtown branch** of the post office, at 815 E St., between Eighth and Ninth avenues, is open Monday through Friday from 8:30am to 5pm and on Saturday from 8:30am to noon. The more centrally located **51 Horton Plaza branch,** beside the Westin Hotel, is open Monday through Friday from 8am to 6pm and Saturday from 9am to 5pm. The **Midway Drive** branch has extended hours until 1am. For post-office information, call ☎ **800/275-8777.** See also "Business Hours" and "Mail" under "Fast Facts: For the Foreign Traveler," in chapter 3.

Rest Rooms   Horton Plaza and Seaport Village downtown, Balboa Park, Old Town State Historic Park in Old Town, and the Ferry Landing Marketplace in Coronado all have well-marked rest rooms. In general, you won't have a problem finding one.

Safety   San Diego is a safe city, but parts of it tend to become deserted after 9pm, when most people have eaten and are headed home. The best nights for walking in the city are Friday and Saturday, when everybody is out. It is best to avoid deserted or sparsely populated beaches after dark, even though they may appear to be romantic. In Balboa Park, stay on designated walkways and away from secluded areas day and night. In the Gaslamp Quarter, don't go east of Fifth Avenue. It's always a good idea to stay alert and aware of your surroundings when you're in any unfamiliar city, even in the most heavily touristed areas. Take particular care to lock your car and park in well-lit areas. San Diego's proximity to the border contributes to its high rate of auto theft.

Taxes   Sales tax in restaurants and shops is 7.75%. Hotel tax is 10.5%.

Taxis   See "Getting Around," earlier in this chapter.

Television   The main stations in San Diego are 6 (Fox), 8 (CBS), 10 (ABC), 39 (NBC), 15 (PBS), and independent stations include channels 51 and 69. Channels 12, 19, and 52 offer programming in Spanish. Many hotels have cable TV, including HBO for movies.

Time Zone   San Diego, like the entire West Coast, is in the Pacific standard time zone, which is 8 hours behind Greenwich mean time. Daylight saving time is observed. To find out what time it is, call ☎ **619/853-1212.**

Tipping   See "Fast Facts: For the Foreign Traveler," in chapter 3.

Transit Information   Call ☎ **619/233-3004** (TTY/TDD 619/234-5005 for the hearing impaired). If you know your route and just need schedule information, call ☎ **619/685-4900** from any touch-tone phone.

Useful Telephone Numbers   For the latest San Diego arts and entertainment information, call ☎ **619/238-0700;** for half-price day-of-performance tickets, call ☎ **619/497-5000;** for a beach and surf report, call ☎ **619/221-8884.**

Weather   Call ☎ 619/289-1212.

Accommodations

San Diego offers a wide variety of places to stay that range from pricey high-rise hostelries to inexpensive low-rise motels and some out-of-the-ordinary B&Bs. By using this book, you'll have the option of sleeping over the water, on the water, in historic surroundings, facing the bay, or with ocean views.

Rates given here do not include hotel tax, which is an additional 10.5%. I've noted when the price includes breakfast. Rates, of course, are subject to change. You will find that weekend rates are often less expensive at downtown hotels and higher in resort areas. Accordingly, tariffs are higher from Memorial Day through Labor Day—especially in the beach areas. San Diego hoteliers also sometimes raise rates during periods when the city is hosting more conventions than usual. You'll notice that some listings mention a free airport shuttle. This is common in San Diego hotels, so, before you take a taxi from the airport, check to see what your hotel can offer.

For the lowest available prices in all accommodations categories, including motels and other properties that charge $39 and up, contact **San Diego Hotel Reservations,** 7380 Clairemont Mesa Blvd., Suite 218, San Diego, CA 92111, (☎ **800/SAVE-CASH** or 619/627-9300; fax 619/627-9405; Web site: **www.savecash.com**) or **California Reservations,** 165 Eighth St., Suite 201, San Francisco, CA 94103 (☎ **800/576-0003** or 415/252-1107; fax 415/252-1483; E-mail **hotel@cal-res.com**). For information on 30 bed-and-breakfasts in the San Diego area, send $3.95 for a 20-page directory to **B&B Resources,** P.O. Box 3292, San Diego, CA 92163 (☎ **800/619-ROOM** [7666] or 619/297-3130).

For those who prefer to stay as close as possible to the airport, here are two good choices: the 1,045-room **Sheraton San Diego Hotel and Marina,** 1380 Harbor Island Dr. (☎ **800/325-3535** or 619/291-2900), offers rooms from $150 to $280 and the 208-room **Travelodge Hotel–Harbor Island,** 1960 Harbour Island Dr. (☎ **800/255-3050** or 619/291-6700), which costs $129 to $149. Both of these hotels offer guests marina views, a health club, a pool, and close proximity to downtown San Diego.

Readers who want to improve their minds and/or their bodies while they are in San Diego should be sure to read the "Select Spas" box in chapter 11. Places to stay outside of San Diego and its suburbs are listed in chapter 11.

San Diego Accommodations

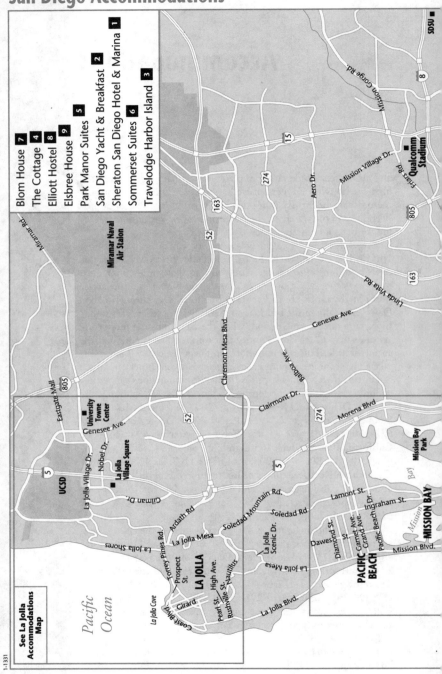

Blom House **7**
The Cottage **4**
Elliott Hostel **8**
Elsbree House **9**
Park Manor Suites **5**
San Diego Yacht & Breakfast **2**
Sheraton San Diego Hotel & Marina **1**
Sommerset Suites **6**
Travelodge Harbor Island **3**

See La Jolla
Accommodations
Map

1:1331

Pacific
Ocean

UCSD

Eastgate Mall

University
Towne
Center

Genesee Ave.

Nobel Dr.

La Jolla Village Dr.

La Jolla
Village Square

Gilman Dr.

Ardath Rd

La Jolla Mesa

La Jolla Shores

Torrey Pines Rd.

Prospect St.

LA JOLLA

High Ave.

Pearl St.

Rushville St.

Nautilus

Girard

Coast Blvd

La Jolla Cove

La Jolla Blvd.

Soledad Mountain Rd.

Soledad Rd

La Jolla Scenic Dr.

La Jolla Mesa

Lamont St.

Dawesn St.

Diamond St.

Garnet Ave.

Grand Ave.

Ingraham St.

Pacific Beach Dr.

PACIFIC
BEACH

Mission Blvd.

MISSION BAY

Mission Bay
Park

Mission Bay

Morena Blvd

Clairmont Dr.

Claremont Mesa Blvd.

Balboa Ave.

Genesee Ave.

Linda Vista Rd.

Miramar Rd.

Miramar Naval
Air Staion

Mission Village Dr.

Friars Rd.

Qualcomm
Stadium

Mission Gorge Rd.

SDSU ■

5
805
52
163
15
274
8
805
163
274
5

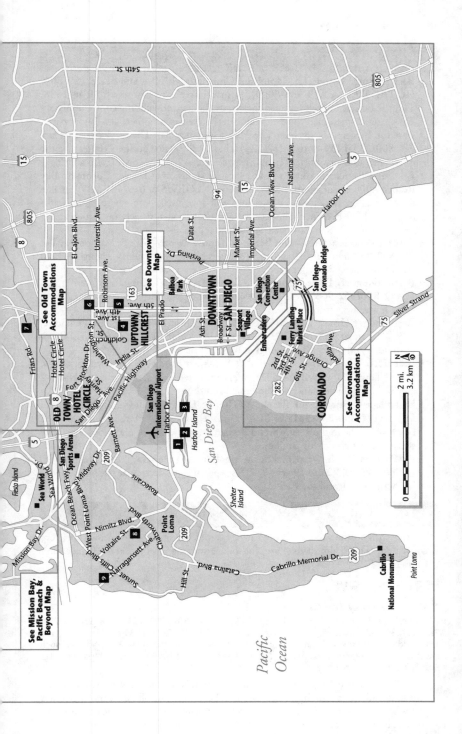

1 Best Bets

- **Best Historic Hotel:** The **Hotel del Coronado,** 1500 Orange Ave. (☎ **800/HOTEL-DEL** or 619/435-8000), positively reeks of history. Built in 1888, Thomas Edison himself installed the electric lights, and later the course of history was changed when the Prince of Wales met Wallis Simpson here at a dinner party.
- **Best for Business Travelers: The Hyatt Regency San Diego,** 1 Market Place (☎ **800/233-1234** or 619/232-1234), has a full-service business center and the other amenities that businesspeople expect. Access to downtown is also a plus.
- **Best for a Romantic Getaway:** The sense of seclusion at **Loew's Coronado Bay Resort,** 4000 Coronado Bay Rd. (☎ **800/23-LOEWS** or 619/424-4000), makes it a good choice for a tryst. The spacious well-appointed rooms, large marble bathrooms, and fine bed linens also set the stage. (For a romantic getaway farther afield, see the listing for Rancho Valencia in chapter 11.)
- **Best for Families:** The **Hilton Beach & Tennis Resort,** 1775 E. Mission Bay Dr. (☎ **800/962-6307** or 619/276-4010), offers plenty of activities—enough to keep family members of all ages happy.
- **Best Moderately Priced Hotel:** The **Sommerset Suites Hotel,** 606 Washington St. (☎ **800/962-9665** or 619/692-5200), one of San Diego's best bargains, feels like a home away from home.
- **Best Budget Hotel:** Located in San Diego's Little Italy, **Hotel La Pensione,** 606 W. Date St. (☎ **800/232-4683** or 619/236-8000), feels like a small European hotel and offers tidy lodgings at bargain prices.
- **Best B&B:** The **Heritage Park Bed & Breakfast Inn,** 2470 Heritage Park Row, at Old Town (☎ **619/299-6832**), offers attractive rooms, delicious breakfasts— all within walking distance of restaurants and shops.
- **Best Place to Stay on the Beach:** At **The Sea Lodge,** 8110 Camino del Oro, in La Jolla (☎ **800/237-5211** or 619/459-8271), you can walk right onto the wide beach and frolic in the great waves. Lifeguards and the lack of undertow here make this a popular choice for families.
- **Best Hotel Pool:** What makes the pool at **La Valencia,** 1132 Prospect St. (☎ **800/451-0772** or 619/454-0771), so special is its spectacular setting overlooking Scripps Park and the Pacific.

2 Downtown

Visitors with business to conduct in the city center will find the downtown area very convenient. This is also the best area for those attending meetings at the Convention Center.

VERY EXPENSIVE

✪ Hyatt Regency San Diego

1 Market Place (at Harbor Dr.), San Diego, CA 92101. ☎ **800/233-1234** or 619/232-1234. Fax 619/239-5678. 819 rms, 56 suites. A/C MINIBAR TV TEL. $235–$280 double; from $400 suite. Additional person $25. Children under 12 stay free in parents' room. Packages and much lower weekend rates available. AE, CB, DC, DISC, MC, V. Valet parking $13; self-parking $10. Bus: 1. Trolley: Seaport Village.

The 40-story Hyatt Regency, the tallest waterfront hotel on the West Coast, offers visitors a choice of ocean, bay, or city views. The friendly, helpful desk staff welcomes you when you enter the light, airy lobby adorned with Italian limestone columns and touches of marble and embellished with two 27-foot-high paintings of country scenes by San Diegan Richard Babriel Chase. The quiet and restful rooms are done in a

Downtown San Diego Accommodations

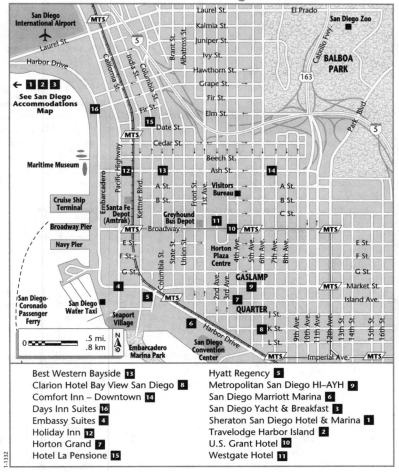

Best Western Bayside **13**	Hyatt Regency **5**
Clarion Hotel Bay View San Diego **8**	Metropolitan San Diego HI–AYH **9**
Comfort Inn – Downtown **14**	San Diego Marriott Marina **6**
Days Inn Suites **16**	San Diego Yacht & Breakfast **3**
Embassy Suites **4**	Sheraton San Diego Hotel & Marina **1**
Holiday Inn **12**	Travelodge Harbor Island **2**
Horton Grand **7**	U.S. Grant Hotel **10**
Hotel La Pensione **15**	Westgate Hotel **11**

variety of fabrics, textures, and colors, each with a floral chintz bedspread, a plaid armchair, 18th-century English furniture, custom-designed lamps, and impressionist-style paintings. Baths have ample counter space, and hallways have picture windows at either end. The Hyatt Regency, which opened in 1992, is adjacent to Seaport Village and within walking distance of the Convention Center and the Gaslamp Quarter. There's a club floor which provides upgraded service to guests, and more than 80% of the rooms are designated nonsmoking.

Dining/Entertainment: Sally's, a rather formal seafood restaurant, attracts locals as well as guests. There are two other less formal spots (all three offer alfresco dining) and two bars (including one with a spectacular 40th-floor view).

Services: Concierge, 24-hour room service, dry cleaning, laundry, shoe-shine, newspaper delivery, in-room massage, twice-daily maid service, baby-sitting, express checkout, valet parking, courtesy car.

Facilities: State-of-the-art health club/spa, whirlpool, four tennis courts, boat/bicycle rental, water-sports rental, business center, conference rooms, car-rental desk, beauty salon, gift shop.

✪ San Diego Marriott Marina

333 W. Harbor Dr. (at Front St.), San Diego, CA 92101-7700. ☎ **800/228-9290** or 619/234-1500. Fax 619/234-8678. 1,354 rms, 54 suites. A/C MINIBAR TV TEL. $225–$245 double; from $375 suite. Children under 18 stay free in parents' room. AARP discount and honeymoon and other packages available. AE, CB, DC, DISC, MC, V. Valet parking $13; self-parking $9. Bus: 1. Trolley: Convention Center.

San Diego's most striking modern hotel dominates the waterfront with two graceful, curving towers and a 446-slip marina, lush grounds, and waterfall-accented outdoor pool. Many rooms have balconies with breathtaking bay-and-beyond views. The well-situated hotel is a short stroll from Seaport Village, Embarcadero Marina Park, the Convention Center, and the restaurants and nightspots of the Gaslamp Quarter.

Dining/Entertainment: There are several restaurants; my favorite is the Yacht Club, a popular place for informal dining and dancing on the waterfront.

Services: Concierge, 24-hour room service, dry cleaning/laundry, newspaper delivery, secretarial services, express checkout, valet parking.

Facilities: VCR, in-room movies, two outdoor pools (including one with a waterfall), fitness center, daily aerobics classes, two whirlpools, sauna, six lighted tennis courts, bicycle and boat rentals, game room, spa, business center with secretarial services, conference rooms, self-service Laundromat, car-rental desk, tour desk, hair salon, shops.

✪ San Diego Yacht & Breakfast Company

Marina Cortez, 1880 Harbor Island Dr., Dockside G-Dock, San Diego, CA 92101. ☎ **800/YACHT-DO**, 800/922-4836, or 619/297-9484. Fax 619/295-9182. E-mail yachtdo@yachtdo.com. Web site: www.yachtdo.com. 3 floating villas, 2 power yachts, and 3 sailboats. TV TEL. $245 double; $25 extra person. Lower rate for multinight stay. Rates include buffet breakfast. AE, DISC, MC, V.

Here's an unusual opportunity to sleep on the water in your own yacht or floating villa. On the floating villas, you won't leave the dock (unless you make special arrangements), but you will have a great view over the Marina Cortez on Harbor Island and a wonderful sea breeze. However, on the yachts, a cruise is included in the price.

The floating villas are 650 square feet and feel like modern condos. Each has one bedroom and $1^1/_2$ bathrooms and sleeps up to four. They have full kitchens, laundry facilities, very nice furnishings, two TVs, a VCR, a stereo, and many other comforts of home. The well-kept 41-foot power yacht has two staterooms, two heads, a full galley, a VCR, a stereo system, and TV. Serious sailors may prefer to sleep on one of the 38-foot sailboats. The sailboats accommodate two to four people, but are best suited for one couple. If you have a sailor's license, you can take the sailboats out for a spin. All guests receive a 20% discount at Harbor Island restaurants, can rent sailboats and water toys (such as kayaks) at discounted rates, and can use the pool at the marina. The location is handy to the airport and downtown, and the rate includes a voucher for the large breakfast buffet served at the nearby Travelodge.

U. S. Grant Hotel

326 Broadway (between Third and Fourth aves.), San Diego, CA 92101. ☎ **800/334-6957** or 619/232-3121 in California, 800/237-5029 elsewhere. Fax 619/232-3626. 280 rms, 60 suites. A/C MINIBAR TV TEL. $165–$185 double; from $265 suite. Children under 12 stay free in parents' room. AE, CB, DC, MC, V. Parking $13. Bus: 1, 2, 3, or 25. Trolley: Civic Center (C St. and Third Ave.)

In 1910, Ulysses S. Grant, Jr. opened this stately hotel, now on the National Register of Historic Places, in honor of his father. The younger Grant lived in a suite here from 1919 until his death in 1929; his wife stayed until her death in 1942. Famous guests have included Albert Einstein, Charles Lindbergh, FDR, and JFK. The elegant lobby has a luxurious, specially designed rug and, as its centerpiece, a giant floral arrangement. Rooms and baths are spacious and furnished with 18th-century reproductions and mahogany two-poster beds. Terry-cloth robes hang in the closet. The hotel is right across the street from Horton Plaza.

Note: This is one of the few top-class hotels that permits pets to stay in guest rooms. Rumor has it that pooches even get their own personalized pillows.

Dining/Entertainment: The prestigious Grant Grill is a lunchtime favorite that resembles an exclusive private club. In fact, in 1969, eight determined female San Diegans defied the "gentlemen only" lunch restriction, and a plaque in the restaurant honors their successful effort. You can watch your meal being prepared in the unique rotisserie kitchen. The Grant Grill Lounge, with a working fireplace and wood-paneled walls, offers light lunches (carved sandwiches, meat and seafood pies, and salads), cocktails, and live blues and jazz, usually Thursday through Saturday nights. Afternoon tea, served in the lobby Tuesday through Saturday, with soft piano music as a backdrop, is a highlight of a stay here.

Services: Concierge, 24-hour room service, same-day laundry/dry cleaning (except Sunday), turndown service, baby-sitting, courtesy shuttle to and from the airport and to downtown attractions, limousine service.

Facilities: In-room movies, 24-hour fitness center with panoramic view of downtown, in-room exercise bike and rowing-machine rentals, access to San Diego Athletic Club, meeting rooms, business services, safe-deposit boxes, terry-cloth robes.

The Westgate Hotel

1055 Second Ave. (between Broadway and C St.), San Diego, CA 92101. ☎ **800/221-3802** or 619/238-1818. Fax 619/557-3604. 212 rms, 10 suites. A/C MINIBAR TV TEL. $164–$194 double; from $400 suite. Extra adult $10. Children 18 and under stay free in parents' room. Honeymoon and other packages available. AE, DC, DISC, MC, V. Underground valet parking $10. Bus: 1, 2, 3, or 25. Trolley: Civic Center (C St. and Third Ave.).

This lavish hotel, built in 1970, exemplifies European style. No two rooms are alike, and antiques have full reign. The lobby, lit with a half-dozen Baccarat crystal chandeliers, is right out of 18th-century France. French tapestries and Persian carpets complete the picture. Not surprisingly, the Westgate is a member of the Leading Hotels of the World and is popular with foreign dignitaries. Its complimentary shuttle service to downtown appointments and attractions is an added bonus. A number of airline booking offices, among them those for United, Delta, American, and Aeromexico, are conveniently located in the building's base, with entrances on Broadway.

Dining/Entertainment: The Fontainebleau Room offers candlelight dining; the Westgate Room, casual dining; and the Plaza Bar, cocktails and live entertainment. There's also a deli with international foods and wines.

Services: Concierge; 24-hour room service; valet service; complimentary transportation to airport, downtown appointments, Sea World, and the zoo.

Facilities: Workout room, sundeck, meeting rooms, barbershop, gift shop.

EXPENSIVE

Clarion Hotel Bay View San Diego

660 K St. (at Sixth), San Diego, CA 92101. ☎ **800/766-0234** or 619/696-0234. Fax 619/231-8199. 312 rms and suites. A/C TV TEL. $109–$139 double; $149–$169 suites. Children under 18 stay free in parents' room. Additional person $10. AE, DC, DISC, MC, V. Parking $8 per day. Bus: 1. Trolley: Gaslamp/Convention Center.

This relatively new entry on the San Diego hotel scene provides an economical alternative for those attending meetings at the Convention Center—it's almost as close as the Marriott and the Hyatt, but considerably less expensive. Its location near the Gaslamp Quarter makes it an excellent choice for those who plan to enjoy the nightlife and want to avoid walking far late at night. All quarters are spacious, bright, and modern, and more than half offer views of San Diego Bay and the Coronado Bridge. All rooms have sliding glass doors that provide ample fresh air, and many have minibars. In-room safes are standard, as are tub/shower combinations; 80% of the rooms are reserved for nonsmokers. The carpeted rooftop sundeck offers a great view as well as a Jacuzzi, sauna, workout room, and video arcade.

Dining/Entertainment: Just off the marble-floored lobby is the Gallery Cafe, serving breakfast, lunch, and dinner daily. There's a big-screen TV in the bar, and Joey & Maria's Comedy Italian Wedding Dinner Theatre is popular on Friday and Saturday nights.

Services: Concierge, room service (6am to 10pm), dry cleaning/laundry, express checkout.

Facilities: In-room pay-per-view movies; workout room with Nautilus equipment; Jacuzzi; sauna; sundeck; video-game room; coin-operated washer and dryer; in-room touch-screen TVs can be used for express checkout, ordering breakfast, and retrieving voice-mail messages.

Embassy Suites

601 Pacific Hwy. (at N. Harbor Dr.), San Diego, CA 92101. ☎ **800/EMBASSY** or 619/ 239-2400. Fax 619/239-1520. 337 suites. A/C MINIBAR TV TEL. $150–$275 suite (including full breakfast and afternoon cocktail). Children under 12 stay free in parents' room. AE, DC, DISC, MC, V. Valet parking $12; indoor self-parking $8. Bus: 2. Trolley: Seaport Village.

Built in 1988, this sand-colored building with green trim is topped with a neon design that looks like a stylized clock with the minute hand gone awry. The comfortable suites have sofa beds in the living/dining areas and a microwave and coffeemaker. The 12-story atrium, with lush plants, bridges, waterways with giant goldfish, and a bubbling fountain, is the hotel's focal point. Glass-enclosed elevators provide a good view. The hotel is one block from Seaport Village and five blocks from downtown.

Dining/Entertainment: Barnett's Grand Café, serving continental cuisine, looks onto the atrium and offers patio seating. Winning Streak Sports and Games Bar, serving lunch and dinner, has a large video screen, sports memorabilia, and video interactive trivia.

Services: Complimentary breakfast and beverages, airport pickup, laundry.

Facilities: Seven nonsmoking floors, microwave, coffeemaker, in-room movies, indoor pool (open long hours), sauna, weight room, Jacuzzi, sundeck, meeting rooms, gift shop.

Holiday Inn on the Bay

1355 N. Harbor Dr. (at Ash St.), San Diego, CA 92101-3385. ☎ **800/HOLIDAY** or 619/ 232-3861. Fax 619/232-4924. 563 rms, 17 suites. A/C TV TEL. $135–$155 single or double; from $400 suite. Children under 18 stay free in parents' room. B&B packages available. AE, DC, MC, V. Parking $10. Bus: 2, 9, 29, 34, 34A, or 35.

Renovated in 1992, this hotel is ideally located on the harbor, overlooking the Maritime Museum, the cruise-ship pier, and Harbor Island. It's only 1 1/2 miles from the airport (you can watch the planes landing and taking off) and two blocks from the train station and trolley. The rooms are decorated in a California contemporary style; some offer harbor views. In general, the hotel's baths are small, but they have separate sinks with a lot of counter space.

Dining/Entertainment: The Elephant and Castle Restaurant, the San Diego branch of the world famous Ruth's Chris Steakhouse, and Hazelwoods serve lunch and dinner.

Services: Room service (6 to 11am and 5 to 11pm), baby-sitting, laundry, valet.

Facilities: Cable TV and in-room movies, nonsmoking rooms, outdoor pool, self-service laundry, meeting rooms, voice-mail.

Horton Grand

311 Island Ave. (at Fourth Ave.), San Diego, CA 92101. ☎ **800/542-1886** or 619/544-1886. Fax 619/544-0058. 108 rms, 24 minisuites. TV TEL. $109–$149 double; $129–$189 minisuite. Weekend and special packages available. Children under 12 stay free in parents' room. AE, DC, DISC, MC, V. Valet parking $8 overnight with unlimited in/out privileges. Bus: 1. Trolley: Convention Center.

A cross between an elegant hotel and a charming B&B, the Horton Grand combines two hotels dating from 1886—the Horton Grand and the Brooklyn Hotel, which for a time was the Kahle Saddlery Shop. Both were saved from demolition, moved to this spot, and connected by an airy atrium lobby filled with white wicker. The facade, with its graceful bay windows, is original.

Each room is unique and contains antiques and a gas fireplace (on a timer so you can fall asleep in front of it); even the baths, complete with WC and pedestal sink, are genteel. Rooms overlook either the city or the fig tree–filled courtyard. Suites have a microwave, a minibar, two TVs and telephones, a sofa bed, and computer modem hookup. This is an old hotel, and sounds carry more than they might in a modern one, so if you're a light sleeper, request a room with no neighbors.

Dining/Entertainment: Ida Bailey's restaurant, named for the well-loved madam whose establishment used to stand on this spot, is open for breakfast, lunch, and dinner. It opens onto the hotel's courtyard, which is used for Sunday brunch on warm days. Afternoon tea is served in the Palace Bar, Tuesday through Saturday from 2:30 to 5pm; live music is featured Thursday through Saturday evenings and Sunday afternoons.

Services: Concierge, room service (7am to 10pm).

Facilities: Access to nearby pool and weight room.

MODERATE

Best Western Bayside Inn

555 W. Ash St. (at Columbia St.), San Diego, CA 92101. ☎ **800/341-1818** or 619/233-7500. Fax 619/239-8060. 122 rms. A/C TV TEL. $85–$105 double. Harbor view $10 extra. Children under 12 stay free in parents' room. All rates include continental breakfast. Weekend rates (except in summer) and packages available. AE, AM (Amoco), CB, DC, DISC, ER, MC, V. Free covered parking. Bus: 5 or 105. Trolley: C Street and Kettner.

You'll be pleased with this quiet, unassuming hotel with a friendly, accommodating staff and stunning city and harbor views. It's an easy walk to the Embarcadero (it should be called Bayview rather than Bayside), a bit farther to Horton Plaza, four blocks to the trolley stop, and five blocks to the train station. The comfortable rooms, all remodeled in 1993, have balconies overlooking the bay or downtown.

The hotel's restaurant, the Bayside Bar and Grill, serves breakfast, lunch, and dinner; the bar has a 50-inch TV. Good restaurants and bars are nearby, and meals are available from room service. Complimentary airport transportation and in-room movies are provided. You can relax by the outdoor pool or in the Jacuzzi.

INEXPENSIVE

Inexpensive motels line Pacific Highway between the airport and downtown. The **Days Inn Suites** ($49 to $69), 1919 Pacific Hwy. at Grape Street (☎ **800/325-2525** or 619/232-1077) is within walking distance of the Embarcadero, the Maritime Museum, and the Harbor Excursion.

🚸 Family-Friendly Hotels

Hilton Beach & Tennis Resort *(see p. 59)* This bay-front property has a kids' wading pool and playground plus plenty of space for them to run around.

The Beach Cottages *(see p. 62)* Kids enjoy the informal atmosphere and the location near the beach.

Catamaran Resort Hotel *(see p. 60)* Myriad sports facilities and a safe swimming beach make this resort an ideal place for families. Accommodations are comfortable, but not so posh that Mom and Dad need to worry.

Elliott Hostel *(see p. 65)* A short drive from the beach, this hostel has four family rooms, a TV room, a big kitchen, and a patio with picnic tables.

The Sea Lodge *(see p. 68)* Right smack on the beach, kids can choose between the pool and ocean. They can even eat in their swimsuits on the patio.

Loew's Coronado Bay Resort *(see p. 72)* Its Commodore Kids Club, for children ages 4 to 12, provides year-round supervised indoor/outdoor activities during the day and some evenings, too.

Comfort Inn-Downtown

719 Ash St. (at Seventh Ave.), San Diego, CA 92101. ☎ **800/228-5150** or 619/232-2525. Fax 619/687-3024. 67 rms. AC, TV, TEL. $79–$84 double. Extra person $5. Children 17 and under stay free in parents' room. Dine-A-Mate discount available. Lower weekly rates. Rates include continental breakfast. AE, DISC, MC, V. Free parking. Free shuttle to train, bus, and airport. Bus: 1, 3, 25, 5, 105.

Located across the street from the landmark El Cortez Hotel (sadly closed for several years now), this three-story Comfort Inn has an eye-catching butterscotch-and-teal exterior. The rooms are modern, bright, spacious, and surprisingly quiet—given the central location just four blocks north of Broadway. Guests have the choice of one queen bed or two doubles, and nonsmoking rooms are available. Room doors open onto exterior walkways—which is nice, except for the top floor which seemed a little precarious to me, in spite of the sturdy, window-box–sporting railings. This dollar-wise property also offers free coffee in the lobby and a heated spa.

✪ Hotel La Pensione

606 W. Date St. (at India St.), San Diego, CA 92101. ☎ **800/232-4683** or 619/236-8000. Fax 619/236-8088. E-mail lapensione@sdic.net. 80 rms. TV TEL. $44–$64 double. Packages available. AE, CB, DC, MC, V. Underground parking, free on a daily basis or $10 per week. Bus: 2. Trolley: County Center/Little Italy.

This place has a lot going for it: modern amenities, cleanliness, remarkable value, a quiet location within walking distance of the central business district, a friendly staff, and parking, which is a premium for small hotels in San Diego. La Pensione is built around a courtyard and feels like a small European hotel. The lobby is small but inviting, and the rooms, while not overly large, make the most of their space and leave you with area to move around. Each room offers a tub/shower combination, ceiling fan, wet bar, microwave, and small refrigerator. Quarters are cleaned once a week for weekly guests, daily for those who stay a shorter period. It has two restaurants: Caffè Italia, which offers sandwiches and salads, as well as Sunday brunch and jazz on Friday and Saturday, and Vicino Mare, which serves Italian seafood. The fourth floor is for nonsmoking guests. La Pensione is located in San Diego's Little Italy neighborhood and within walking distance of eateries (mostly Italian) and nightspots.

The Metropolitan–San Diego, HI–AYH

521 Market St. (at Fifth Ave.), San Diego, CA 92101. ☎ **619/525-1531.** Fax 619/338-0129. 98 beds in 24 rms, 8 with private bath. In dorm, $16 members, $19 nonmembers; couple's room, $18 per person members, $21 per person nonmembers. Half-price for children under 18. There is a $5 key deposit. MC, V. Limited metered parking available on street. Bus: 2. Trolley: Convention Center.

San Diego's downtown hostel is conveniently located in the Gaslamp Quarter, surrounded by cafes, nightclubs, restaurants, and shops. There are 3 double rooms, 20 4- or 6-bed dorms, and one 10-bed dorm. Linen is provided free of charge, and guests may use the TV/VCR room, lounge, and the large kitchen with dining area. There are also plenty of books for swapping. Vending machines and coin-op laundry are on the premises. Guests have 24-hour access to the hostel; the front desk is staffed between 7am and midnight. Two-hour metered street parking and pay-to-park lots are nearby. You can reserve a bed or room with a credit card.

3 Hillcrest/Uptown

This area is convenient to many sights and good restaurants and offers less expensive accommodations than other parts of town.

MODERATE

Park Manor Suites

525 Spruce St. (at Fifth and Sixth aves.), San Diego, CA 92103. ☎ **800/874-2649** or 619/291-0999. Fax 619/291-8844. 80 rms. TV TEL. $55–$95 studio for 1 or 2; $75–$125 one-bedroom unit for 1 or 2; $120–$165 two-bedroom unit for up to 4. Children under 12 stay free in parents' room. Weekly rates available. Rates include continental breakfast. AE, DC, MC, V. Free parking. Bus: 1 or 3.

The stately Park Manor Suites is a good, convenient choice for a longer stay in the area. Built across the street from Balboa Park in 1926, it has a welcoming lobby with a hand-painted ceiling and a glittering chandelier, a young enthusiastic staff, old-fashioned rooms (that means big, with high ceilings and ample closet space), and separate kitchen and dining areas. (A market is one block away.) Some rooms are modern, and those facing the park are quietest. Baths include tubs and showers. There's a restaurant on the ground floor, open for lunch and dinner, and many others are within walking distance. The bus stops a block away. The hotel attracts visiting actors in local productions, especially those at the nearby Old Globe Theatre. The main entrance to Balboa Park is six blocks away. Laundry and dry cleaning services are offered. There's no air-conditioning, but it's rarely needed; there's steam heat for chilly days.

✪ Sommerset Suites Hotel

606 Washington St. (at Fifth Ave.), San Diego, CA 92103. ☎ **800/962-9665** or 619/692-5200; 800/356-1787 in California. Fax 619/692-5299. 80 suites. A/C TV TEL. $95 studio suite; $170 one-bedroom suite; $200 executive suite. Children under 12 stay free in parents' room. Rates include large continental breakfast. AE, CB, DC, DISC, MC, V. Free covered parking. Courtesy shuttle. Take Washington St. exit off I-5. Bus: 16 or 25.

This is one of San Diego's best bargains and the first choice for those who prefer a home away from home rather than a hotel. The staff is friendly and helpful, and in the late afternoon they serve complimentary snacks, soda, beer, and wine in the cozy guest lounge. The poolside patio, set up for barbecues, encourages impromptu gatherings and picnics among guests. Accommodations include studio, one-bedroom, and executive suites. All are tastefully furnished and have in-room safes and fully equipped modern kitchens (including dishwashers in the executive suites), large closets, and balconies. Even the studios are spacious. Services include a concierge; laundry and dry cleaning; courtesy van service (7am to 9pm) to the airport, Sea World, the zoo, and other attractions within a 5-mile radius; video rentals; and two-line phones and voice mail. Rollaway beds and cribs are available. Facilities include a small outdoor pool, a Jacuzzi, a rooftop sundeck, gas barbecue grills, a snack room, and a coin-operated laundry. No restaurants are on-site, but many are within walking distance. Nonsmoking rooms are available.

INEXPENSIVE

The Cottage

3829 Albatross St. (off Robinson), San Diego, CA 92103. ☎ **619/299-1564.** Fax 619/299-6213. 1 rm, 1 cottage. TV TEL. $59–$65 Garden Room for 2; $85–$95 cottage for 2. Extra person in cottage $10. Rates include continental breakfast. AE, MC, V. Bus: 1, 3, 8, 11, or 25.

Built in 1913, the two-room Cottage exists in a secret garden, a private hideaway tucked behind a homestead-style house, at the end of a residential cul-de-sac. There's an herb garden out front, birdbaths, and a flower-lined walkway to the back. Owner Carol Emerick used to run an antique shop, and her house has inherited its treasures. You can stay in either the cottage or the Garden Room. The cottage has a living room with a working wood-burning stove and a queen-size sofa bed, and a charming kitchen. The bedroom features a king-size bed and a hidden TV. The Garden Room is in the main house. Both accommodations are filled with fresh flowers and antiques put to clever uses, and both feature a private entrance and bath. Carol serves a scrumptious breakfast, complete with the morning newspaper. Guests are welcome to use the dining room and parlor in the main house, where they sometimes light a fire and rev up the 19th-century player piano. In this haven, expect to wake up to the gentle chirping of birds. The Cottage is a block from Front Street, 1 1/2 miles from the zoo, and only 4 miles from the airport.

4 Old Town, Hotel Circle & Beyond

Old Town is a popular area for families because of its proximity to Old Town State Historic Park and other attractions in the area. Hotel Circle offers easy freeway access, budget prices, and is popular with sports fans who come to San Diego to watch a game at Qualcomm Stadium.

EXPENSIVE

Hacienda Hotel

4041 Harney St. (just east of San Diego Ave.), San Diego, CA 92110. ☎ **800/888-1991** or 619/298-4707. Fax 619/298-4771. 150 suites. A/C TV TEL. $109–$119 suite. Children under 16 stay free in parents' room. AE, CB, DC, DISC, ER, MC, V. Free underground parking. Bus: 4 or 5/105. From I-5 take Old Town Ave. exit; turn left onto San Diego Ave. and right onto Harney St.

Perched above Old Town, this Best Western all-suite hotel is brightly lit and creates an impressive sight at night. The outdoor pool and patio offer excellent views of Old Town. The comfortable suites have 20-foot-high ceilings, ceiling fans, refrigerators, microwave ovens, coffeemakers, VCRs, and furnishings right out of the American Southwest. The one-room units have either one or two queen-size beds. Walkways thread through courtyards with bubbling fountains, palm trees, lampposts, and bougainvillea-trimmed balconies.

Dining/Entertainment: The Acapulco restaurant (yes, it's Mexican) serves breakfast, lunch, and dinner daily from its perch atop the hotel. Guests also have signing

Accommodations in Old Town, Hotel Circle & Beyond

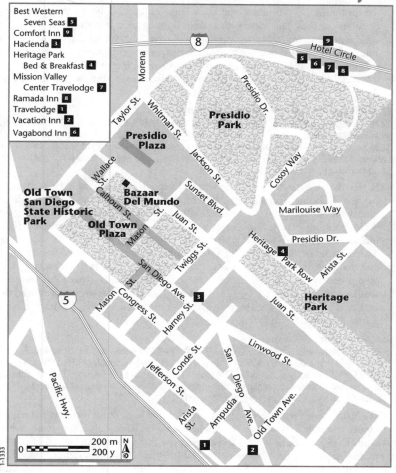

Best Western
  Seven Seas **5**
Comfort Inn **9**
Hacienda **3**
Heritage Park
  Bed & Breakfast **4**
Mission Valley
  Center Travelodge **7**
Ramada Inn **8**
Travelodge **1**
Vacation Inn **2**
Vagabond Inn **6**

privileges next door at the Brigantine Restaurant and down the street at Cafe Pacifica (see "Old Town, Hotel Circle & Beyond," in chapter 6).

Services: Concierge (Monday through Friday), room service (6:30am to 2pm and 4 to 10pm), hosted manager's social Monday through Thursday, complimentary airport/train transportation.

Facilities: Movie rentals with complimentary bag of microwave popcorn, pool, Jacuzzi, spa, fitness center, conference suites, meeting rooms, coin-operated laundry.

MODERATE

Comfort Inn & Suites

2485 Hotel Circle Place, San Diego, CA 92108. ☎ **800/647-1903** or 619/291-7700. Fax 619/297-6179. 200 rms. A/C TV TEL. $69–$99 double. Extra person $10. Children under 18 stay free in parents' room. Rates include continental breakfast. AE, CB, DC, DISC, MC, V. Free parking.

This well-priced modern motel at the western end of Hotel Circle is a high-rise, complete with box balconies and a small free-form pool. It underwent a complete refurbishment in 1996, and all rooms are large and comfortably furnished with king- or queen-size beds, plus baths with separate dressing areas. Higher-priced rooms have whirlpool baths, individual refrigerators, and terraces. Nonsmoking rooms are available. There's a heated outdoor pool and Jacuzzi, a car-rental desk, a game room, and a washer/dryer. Tennis courts are across the street, as is an 11-hole golf course (yes, *11* holes). The hotel doesn't have a restaurant, but there's a Hungry Hunter right next door.

○ Heritage Park Bed & Breakfast Inn

2470 Heritage Park Row, San Diego, CA 92110. ☎ **619/299-6832.** Fax 619/299-9465. E-mail innkeeper@heritageparkinn.com. 10 rms (all with bath), 1 suite. $90–$150 single or double; $205 suite. Extra person $20. Rates include full breakfast and afternoon tea. AE, MC, V. Free parking. Take I-5 to Old Town Ave., turn left onto San Diego Ave., then turn right onto Harney St. to Heritage Park. Bus: 4 or 5/105.

In this 1889 Queen Anne mansion set in a Victorian park, you can arrange for champagne or sparkling cider and chocolates on arrival, as well as a five-course candlelight dinner for two served in your room. Particularly enticing is the large Manor Suite, with a fainting couch, four-poster bed, and Jacuzzi bath. Other alluring rooms include the Victorian Rose Room, with its iron-and-brass bed; the sunny, secluded Turret Room in the tower of the house; the award-winning Forget-Me-Not Room; and the small and thoroughly Early American Country Heart Room, where an old school desk serves as a bedside table. Any antiques that are replaceable, as well as smaller remembrances, are for sale. Amenities include turndown service, the services of a concierge, and a housekeeping staff of four. In the evenings, vintage films are shown in the Victorian parlor.

Vacation Inn

3900 Old Town Ave., San Diego, CA 92110. ☎ **800/451-9846** or 619/299-7400. Fax 619/299-1619. 119 rms, 6 suites. A/C TV TEL. Sept–May $79.50–$95 double; $110–$160 suite. June–Aug $95.50–$110.50 double; $125–$170 suite. Extra person $10. Children 17 and under stay free in parents' room. Rates include continental breakfast and afternoon refreshments. AE, CB, DC, DISC, ER, MC, V. Free parking. Bus: 4 or 5/105.

It's Spanish on the outside, conforming with the Old Town architectural requirements, and pure European on the inside. Rooms are beautifully appointed—even the baths have artwork in them—and practical, with a coffeemaker, microwave, and a writing table. Drapes, bedspreads, and tablecloths have a floral design. Second and third floor rooms that face the courtyard have balconies. The lobby, surrounded by five sets of French doors, features a large fireplace, several sitting areas, and a TV. Dry cleaning and laundry services are offered; the hotel also has an outdoor pool and Jacuzzi. The hotel entrance, on Jefferson Street, is hard to find but definitely worth the search.

INEXPENSIVE

Room rates at properties on Hotel Circle, about 2 miles from Old Town, are significantly cheaper than those in Old Town itself. There you'll find a cluster of inexpensive hotels and motels, including **Best Western Seven Seas** (☎ **800/421-6662** or 619/291-1300), **Mission Valley Center Travelodge** (☎ **800/255-3050** or 619/297-2271), **Ramada Inn** (☎ **800/532-4241** or 619/291-6500), and **Vagabond Inn** (☎ **800/522-1555** or 619/297-1691).

The Blom House

1372 Minden Dr., San Diego, CA 92104. ☎ **800/797-BLOM** (2566) or 619/467-0890. Fax 619/467-0890. 4 rms (all with bath). A/C, TV, TEL. $85–$100 double. Lower weekly, monthly, senior, cash, and midweek winter rates. Rates include full breakfast. Packages also available.

DISC, MC, V. Take 163 to Friars Rd. west to Ulrich St. and turn right. Take next 3 rights, on Linbrook, Babette, and Minden.

Bette Blom is the consummate B&B hostess, offering her guests extensive breakfasts served on Bavarian china, homemade cookies, a video library, and rooms with robes, small refrigerators, coffee- and tea-making facilities, VCRs, and hair dryers. Guests feel at home in her home and enjoy sitting in the hot tub on the deck, which overlooks Mission Valley. Some visitors even use the kitchen to prepare evening meals. Breakfast fare ranges from huevos rancheros to blueberry pancakes, and guests "eat at their time." The house is a little cluttered, but if you stay here, this former schoolteacher's kind heart will be your lasting impression. No smoking inside.

Travelodge
2380 Moore St., San Diego, CA 92110. ☎ **800/292-9928** or 619/291-9100. Fax 619/291-4717. 70 rms, 9 suites. A/C TV TEL. Sun–Thurs $49–$59 double; $84–$89 suite. Fri–Sat $59–$64 double; $89–$94 suite. Children under 18 stay free in parents' room. Lower off-season prices. Rates include continental breakfast. AE, DC, DISC, MC, V. Free underground parking. Follow I-5 North and take Old Town exit; go straight at traffic light; hotel is on the right. Bus: 1 or 5.

A friendly staff offers a warm welcome at this small, inviting Travelodge. Rooms are comfortable and furnished in the bright colors of the American Southwest. Suites, which are somewhat small, have skylights, Jacuzzis, microwaves, sitting areas, refrigerators, and wet bars. About 80% of the rooms are reserved for nonsmokers. The property is a 5-minute walk from Old Town attractions. Reserve in advance for Friday and Saturday nights, when the parents of naval graduates are likely to be in town. Movie rentals, irons, and 24-hour coffee/tea in the lobby are available; also offered are an outdoor pool and a Jacuzzi.

5 Mission Bay, Pacific Beach & Beyond

This is the place to stay if you are traveling with beach-loving children or want to walk barefoot on the beach.

VERY EXPENSIVE

✪ Hilton Beach & Tennis Resort
1775 E. Mission Bay Dr., San Diego, CA 92109. ☎ **800/445-8667** or 619/276-4010; 800/962-6307 in Calif. and Ariz. Fax 619/275-7991. 357 rms, 8 suites. A/C MINIBAR TV TEL. $145–$230 double; from $325 suite. Extra person $20. Children under 18 stay free in parents' room. Lower off-season rates. AE, CB, DC, DISC, JCB, MC, V. Valet parking $6; free self-parking. Take I-5 to Sea World Dr. exit and turn north on E. Mission Bay Dr.

Completely renovated in 1995, this Mediterranean-style resort with terra-cotta roofs occupies 18 acres on the east side of Mission Bay and is a handy one-quarter mile from the Visitor Information Center. All rooms (contained in one eight-story tower and several low-rise buildings) have ceiling fans, a balcony or terrace, a refrigerator, a coffeemaker, an iron and ironing board, a hair dryer, and a makeup mirror. The baths are elegant, with shells surrounding the sconce-flanked mirrors. Even the standard rooms are spacious, and many rooms interconnect. The staff is friendly and helpful here, and the shops are fun for browsing in-between lolling by the pool, biking along the bay, and taking tennis lessons. Sea World is across the bay, and the ocean is 5 miles to the west.

Dining/Entertainment: Cafe Picante, open daily for all meals, offers casual fare and atmosphere. The Cavatappi restaurant serves Italian cuisine nightly. You can dine and drink at Fundidos, which overlooks Mission Bay. Cocktails are also served in the Lobby Bar and at the poolside Banana Cabana.

Services: Concierge, room service (7am to 11pm), dry cleaning/laundry service, baby-sitting, supervision for children on the weekends and in the summer, free airport transportation.

Facilities: In-room movies, Olympic-size pool, children's wading pool, four Jacuzzis, sauna, weight-training room, five lighted tennis courts, pro shop, water sports, scuba diving, bike and jogging trails, putting green, arts and crafts for kids, children's playground, business center, bike and boat rental, yacht charters, massage, game arcade, meeting rooms, laundry facilities, hair salon, shops, voice-mail messages.

EXPENSIVE

Blue Sea Lodge

707 Pacific Beach Dr., San Diego, CA 92109-5094. ☎ **800/BLUE-SEA** or 619/488-4700. Fax 619/488-7276. 100 rms. TV TEL. Mid-Sept to mid-June $125–$159 double; from $225 suite. Mid-June to mid-Sept $140–$170 double; from $250 suite. Children under 13 stay free in parents' room. AAA and AARP discounts. Rates include continental breakfast. AE, CB, DC, DISC, MC, V. Free underground and outdoor parking. Take I-5 to Grand/Garnet exit, follow Grand Ave. to Mission Blvd. and turn left, then turn right onto Pacific Beach Dr. Bus: 34.

The entrance here is a little strange: A stairway leads up to the lobby from an alleylike lane. Travelers with disabilities access the building from the elevator in the underground garage. Most rooms have recently been renovated, and about half have kitchens. The oceanfront accommodations have great views. The lobby offers coffee, tea, and a microwave for guests, and outside you'll find a heated pool and Jacuzzi just steps away from the beach. This is a Best Western property, within walking distance of the fun spots.

Services: Dry cleaning/laundry service, free coffee in the lobby.

Facilities: Kitchenettes, outdoor heated pool, beach, Jacuzzi, sundeck, self-service Laundromat.

Catamaran Resort Hotel

3999 Mission Blvd. (4 blocks south of Grand Ave.), San Diego, CA 92109. ☎ **800/288-0770** or 619/488-1081; 800/233-8172 in Canada. Fax 619/488-1387. 160 rms, 100 studios, 50 suites. A/C TV TEL. $160–$205 double; from $265 suite; $170–$225 studio. Children under 18 stay free in parents' room. AE, DISC, MC, V. Valet parking $7; self-parking $5. Take Grand/Garnet exit off I-5 and go west on Grand Ave., then south on Mission Blvd. Bus: 34 or 34A.

Ideally situated right on Mission Bay, the Catamaran enjoys its own beach and water-sports facilities. Polynesia blossoms here, with a 15-foot waterfall and full-size dugout canoe in the atrium lobby. After dark, torches blaze throughout the grounds, which burgeon with numerous varieties of bamboo and palm. Each room—located in either the 13-story building or one of the six 2-story buildings—is decorated in soft tropical colors and has a balcony or patio. Tower rooms have commanding views of the entire bay, the San Diego skyline, La Jolla, and Point Loma. The staff is among the nicest I've encountered anywhere. The hotel's bars are popular with both locals and visitors. The Catamaran is also within walking distance of many fine restaurants and nightspots and a block from the ocean. The grounds are beautifully maintained.

Dining/Entertainment: The Atoll restaurant, which offers both indoor and bayside seating, serves light fare along with its regular dinner menu, as well as nightly specials and Sunday brunch. The large, lively Cannibal Bar hosts bands and videos. Its counterpoint, Moray's (named for the moray eels that inhabited its large aquarium until they became too aggressive), is an intimate piano bar.

Services: Concierge, room service (6:30am to 11pm), dry cleaning/laundry service, nightly turndown, baby-sitting, secretarial services, express checkout, lifeguard in summer only, valet parking, supervised children's programs.

Accommodations in Mission Bay, Pacific Beach & Beyond

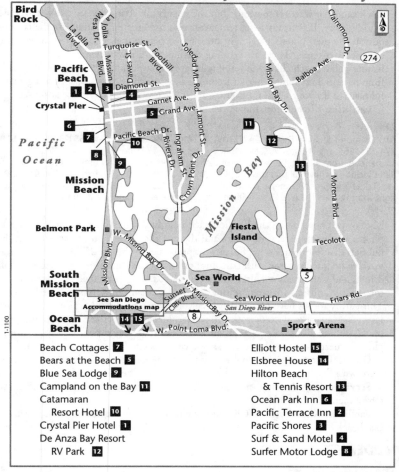

Beach Cottages **7**
Bears at the Beach **5**
Blue Sea Lodge **9**
Campland on the Bay **11**
Catamaran
   Resort Hotel **10**
Crystal Pier Hotel **1**
De Anza Bay Resort
   RV Park **12**

Elliott Hostel **15**
Elsbree House **14**
Hilton Beach
   & Tennis Resort **13**
Ocean Park Inn **6**
Pacific Terrace Inn **2**
Pacific Shores **3**
Surf & Sand Motel **4**
Surfer Motor Lodge **8**

Facilities: Kitchenettes, movie channels, outdoor heated pool, whirlpool spa, beach, sundeck, health club, water-sports concessions, jogging track, stroller joggers, bike rental, children's program during the summer, business center, conference rooms, car-rental desk, tour desk, gift shop.

✪ Crystal Pier Hotel

4500 Ocean Blvd. (at Garnet), San Diego, CA 92109. ☎ **800/748-5894** or 619/483-6983. 26 cottages. TV. Cottages for up to 4 people, $145–$250 mid-June to mid-Sept; $95–$200 rest of the year. 3-day minimum in summer. Weekly and monthly rates available. DISC, MC, V. Free parking. Take I-5 to Grand/Garnet exit; follow Garnet to the pier. Bus: 34 or 34A.

This historic property, which dates from 1927, offers a unique opportunity to sleep over the water. Built on a pier over the Pacific Ocean, the hotel offers self-contained cottages with breathtaking beach views. Twenty older cottages date from 1936; six newer ones from 1992. Fourteen of the older cottages have been renovated. The remodeled units are really lovely, the older ones slightly down-at-the-heels. My favorite units are upstairs. Each comes with a private patio, living room, bedroom, and kitchen, and has welcoming blue shutters and window boxes. The around-the-clock sound of waves is soothing, but the boardwalk action is only a few steps (and worlds) away. If you stay here, remember that the quietest quarters are the farthest out on the pier. Guests park right on the pier beside their cottage, a real boon on crowded weekends. There are vending machines and movie rentals. Boogie boards, fishing poles, beach chairs, and umbrellas are also available. The office is open daily from 8am to 8pm. These unique accommodations book up fast. Besides being a restful place to lay your head, the pier is a great place to watch the surfers at sunset.

Facilities: Kitchenettes, movie channels.

○ Pacific Terrace Inn

610 Diamond St., San Diego, CA 92109. ☎ **800/344-3370** or 619/581-3500. Fax 619/ 274-3341. 65 rms, 8 suites. A/C MINIBAR TV TEL. $185–$225 double; $195–$225 double with kitchenette; from $285 suite. Rates about $20 higher per person in summer. Extra person $10. Rates include continental breakfast. AE, CB, DC, DISC, MC, V. Free underground-secured parking. Take I-5 to Grand/Garnet exit and follow either Grand or Garnet west to Mission Blvd., turn right (north), then left (west) onto Diamond; it's at the end of the street on the right. Bus: 34 or 34A.

My favorite hotel along the Pacific Beach boardwalk, this place is both pretty and pink. I like its upscale atmosphere and the fact that it's slightly removed from the hubbub that dominates other beachfront properties in this area. The large and comfortable bedrooms come with balconies or terraces, refrigerators stocked with soft drinks, and wall safes. Amenities include *USA Today* delivered daily, hair dryers, cotton robes, vanities with separate sinks, and voice mail. Forty rooms have kitchens. Third-story rooms have particularly nice views, and the suites have large baths with Jacuzzis. Management keeps popcorn, coffee, and lemonade in the snack room, called the Caribbean Room. There is an attractive outdoor heated pool facing the ocean, plus a Jacuzzi, valet laundry service, and a coin-operated laundry.

Dining/Entertainment: No restaurant on the premises, but the hotel has an agreement with five local restaurants with which meals can be billed to the hotel.

Services: Dry cleaning, nightly turndown, express checkout, free coffee and refreshments in the lobby.

Facilities: Kitchenettes, VCRs, movie channels, outdoor heated pool, whirlpool spa, beach.

MODERATE

The Beach Cottages

4255 Ocean Blvd. (a block south of Grand Ave.), San Diego, CA 92109-3995. ☎ **619/ 483-7440.** Fax 619/273-9365. 28 rms, 12 studios, 18 apts, 17 cottages, 3 suites. TV TEL. Summer $95–$115 double; $125 studio for up to 4; $145–$190 apt for up to 6; $155–$180 cottage for up to 6; $220–$240 two-bedroom suite for up to 6. Lower rates rest of year. Weekly rates available except in summer. AE, CB, DC, DISC, MC, V. Free parking. Take I-5 to Grand/ Garnet exit, go west on Grand Ave. and right on Mission Blvd.; it's a block south of Grand Ave. Bus: 34 or 34A.

I just love this place. Even though I live nearby, I've often been tempted to check in. If I did, I'd request cottage no. 506 which is 12 steps from the sand (look both ways for speeding cyclists before crossing the boardwalk). There's a wide variety of accommodations, and they all come with country-flavor decor. All rooms except the motel rooms have fully equipped kitchens. The balcony/walkway on the third floor offers a great ocean view. The Beach Cottages are particularly suited for young couples (especially honeymooners) and families who want to stay directly on the beach. It's also within walking distance of shops and restaurants and has barbecue grills, shuffleboard courts, table tennis, and a laundry. The rustic cottages contain either one or two bedrooms and sleep up to six; each has a patio with tables and chairs.

To make a reservation, call between 9am and 9pm, when the office is open. It's advisable to reserve the most popular cottages well in advance.

Bears at the Beach

1047 Grand Ave. (Between Cass and Dawes), San Diego (Pacific Beach), CA 92109. ☎ **619/ 272-2578.** No fax. 2 rms (shared or private bath—see below). TV. $88 double shared bath ($82 double for each room when booked together). $92 double private bath. Rates include breakfast. No credit cards. Parking only on street. Bus: 30 or 34.

Doña Denson just loves bears—cute little stuffed ones, others flying on kites, even the one on the California state flag—and they abound in her pretty little two-bedroom unit at the rear of a neat-and-tidy four-plex located just $2^1/_2$ blocks from the beach. This dainty decor may not appeal to everyone, but I think it's great. Guests get as much mollycoddling or privacy as they want—Doña lives around the corner and comes in every morning to cook breakfast, which she serves on the patio, and is available to answer questions throughout the day. Both rooms have TVs, ceiling fans, and robes. One has an oversize double bed, the other a queen. If you are two people and don't want to share the house with someone else, you can reserve the whole house for $92. You'll have the hotel to yourself, but you can only use one bed (you can, however, put your bags in the closet of the other room to give you more space). As Bears is immaculate, it's no wonder that smoking is not permitted. Doña also has a vacation rental apartment which sleeps four on the same property (a 4-day minimum applies).

Ocean Park Inn

710 Grand Ave., San Diego, CA 92109. ☎ **800/231-7735** or 619/483-5858. Fax 619/ 274-0823. Web site: go-explore.com/opinn. A/C TV TEL. 73 rms, 4 suites. A/C TV TEL. Summer $104–$154 double; $179–$189 suite. Rates include continental breakfast. AE, DC, DISC, MC, V. Free indoor parking. Take Grand/Garnet exit off of I-5; follow Grand Ave. to ocean.

This modern oceanfront motor hotel offers attractive, spacious rooms with well-coordinated contemporary furnishings. King suites are extra large and have an additional sofa bed and a Roman tub. Two-room suites are the most spacious. Rates vary with the view; oceanfront rooms are the more dear. However, these high-priced digs could be noisy, so you might be wise to take a quieter pool-view room. All quarters have terraces and refrigerators. Some are set aside for nonsmokers. The Ocean Park Inn doesn't have it's own restaurant, but there are many nearby.

Surfer Motor Lodge

711 Pacific Beach Dr. (at Mission Blvd.), San Diego, CA 92109. ☎ **800/787-3373** or 619/ 483-7070. Fax 619/274-1670. 52 units. TV TEL. Summer $89–$122; winter $69–$90. Weekly rates available off-season. AE, DC, MC, V. Free parking. Take I-5 to Grand/Garnet, then Grand Ave. to Mission Blvd.; turn left, then right onto Pacific Beach Dr. Bus: 34 or 34A.

Frankly this property is a little tired, but it's still often booked solid during the summer because it offers moderately priced digs right on the boardwalk at the beach, as well as a heated pool. Most rooms in this four-story property have balconies and views and are cooled by ocean breezes. Fans are also available. On the premises is a coin-operated laundry. A popular restaurant serving three meals a day is adjacent. The staff can arrange bike rentals and fishing or golf outings.

INEXPENSIVE

Pacific Shores Inn

4802 Mission Blvd. (between Law and Chalcedony), San Diego (Pacific Beach), CA 92109. ☎ **800/826-0715** or 619/483-6300. Fax 619/483-9276. 55 rms. TV, TEL. $58–$78 double in winter. Extra person $5. Higher rates June 15–Sept 15. Super Savings Coupon Book discount offered. Children under 16 stay free in parents' room. Rates include continental breakfast. AE, DC, DISC, MC, V. Free parking. Bus: 30 or 34.

If the beach is going to be a major feature of your San Diego vacation, you couldn't stay in a better location than the one enjoyed by this two-story motel located at the north (quiet) end of Pacific Beach. The sand starts about 100 yards to the west, and there's also a nice heated pool. They don't advertise "beach views," but I happen to know that rooms 23, 29, 31, 33, and 35 have them. Half the units have kitchens; the others offer small refrigerators. There's a little deferred maintenance, but the modern furnishings are in good condition. Nonsmoking rooms are available, and there's free HBO and a coin-op laundry. All but three rooms are air-conditioned. Pets (not huge ones) are accepted for a small extra charge. Ask for a room away from the street.

Surf & Sand Motel

4666 Mission Blvd. (at Diamond St.), San Diego, CA 92109. ☎ **619/483-7420.** Fax 619/237-9940. 23 rms, 1 three-bedroom house, 2 one-bedroom apts. TV TEL. Memorial Day to Labor Day: $89–$109 double room; $1,050/week for house; $750/week one-bedroom apt. Much lower off-season rates and lower long-stay rates off-season. AE, DISC, MC, V. Free off-street parking. Take I-5 to Grand/Garnet exit; go west on Garnet Ave. to Mission Blvd. and turn right. Bus: 34 or 34A.

This modest motel, a half block from the beach, has a small pleasant lobby and clean basic units with modern furnishings. Rooms in the back aren't as susceptible to the noise from Mission Boulevard as the ones in the front. Some bathrooms have tub/shower combinations, others just showers. One room has a queen bed and a Jacuzzi. All quarters come with minirefrigerators, six have kitchenettes, and some are air-conditioned. The three-bedroom house has two bathrooms and sleeps up to eight people; the one-bedroom apartments sleep four. There's a small, heated pool on the property.

PLACES TO CAMP

Campland on the Bay

2211 Pacific Beach Dr., San Diego, CA 92109-5699. ☎ **800/4-BAY-FUN,** 619/581-4200, or 619/581-4212 (24 hours). E-mail reservation@campland.com. Web site: www.campland.com. 600 hookup sites. Summer, $26–$52 for up to 4 people. Off-season, $19–$37 for up to 4 people. Lowest-priced sites do not have hookups. Senior rates available. Weekly and monthly rates available off-season. Extra (small) charge for dogs. Day use of facilities $5. MC, V. Take I-5 to Grand/Garnet exit, follow Grand to Olney and turn left; turn left again onto Pacific Beach Dr.

This bay-side retreat is popular with a mixed crowd: RVers, campers (with or without van), boaters, and their children and pets. At their fingertips are parks, a beach, a bird sanctuary, and a dog walk. Other facilities include pools, a Jacuzzi, catamaran and Windsurfer rentals and lessons, bike and boat rentals, a game room, a cafe that's open for three meals a day, a market, and laundry. Planned activities include games and crafts for children; Sea World is 5 minutes away.

De Anza Bay Resort RV Park

2727 De Anza Rd., San Diego, CA 92109. ☎ **800/924-PLAY** or 619/273-3211. Fax 619/274-0362. 250 hookup sites. Summer $36–$41 per night. Off-season $25–$30 per night. Lower-priced sites do not have hookups. Weekly and monthly rates available off-season. MC, V. Take I-5 to the Clairemont Dr. exit, go west and turn right onto E. Mission Bay Dr. at the Visitor Information Center; follow E. Mission Bay Dr. for about a mile to the north end of the bay. Bus: 34 or 34A.

Directly across an inlet from Campland on the Bay and under the same management, this serenely situated park caters only to RV vacationers, offering them a market, laundry, private beach, floating dock and diving platform, fishing, boating, water sports, bike rental, auto rental, free movies, potluck dinners, dancing, beach parties, and bingo. Small pets are welcome. A plus for golfers: It's adjacent to an executive 18-hole course that's open day and night.

A NEARBY HOSTEL

Hostelling International—Elliott Hostel

3790 Udall St., San Diego, CA 92107. ☎ **619/223-4778.** Fax 619/223-5217. 62 beds. $12 dorm; $14 semiprivate (2-person room); $14 double bed. Rates are per person, per night for members; nonmembers add $3. MC, V. Free parking. From Los Angeles, take I-5 south to Sea World Dr. exit and go west. Follow signs to Sunset Cliffs Blvd. Turn left on Voltaire, continue for 1 mile; make a right on Worden. Hostel is on the corner of Worden and Udall. From downtown San Diego or airport, follow N. Harbor Dr.; turn right on Nimitz and follow it to Chatsworth and turn right, left on Poinsettia, left on Udall; the hostel will be on the right. Bus: 35 (to Ocean Beach); catch it on Broadway (downtown) and get off at Voltaire (in front of subway) about a 20-min. ride. Cross the street to Worden. Hostel is on the corner of Worden and Udall sts.

Officially known as the Elliott (Point Loma) Hostel, these budget digs are 6 miles from downtown San Diego and 3 miles from the airport. It's a short drive, or figure 30 minutes to get there by city bus from downtown San Diego. Rooms sleep two to eight people, and there are five couples rooms (with double beds) and four family rooms. Facilities include showers, an impressive kitchen, a large common room, a TV room, Ping-Pong table, and a patio with picnic tables. The hostel is a short distance to the beach and Sea World. Reception is open from 8am to 10pm every day.

A NEARBY BED & BREAKFAST

Elsbree House

5054 Narragansett Ave., San Diego, CA 92107. ☎ **619/226-4133.** E-mail Ktelsbree@juno.com. Web site: www.oceanbeach-online.com/elsbree/b&b. 6 rms and 1 three-bedroom condo. $95 double room/night; $1,250 condo/week. Room rate includes breakfast. MC, V. Buses 35 and 23 stop 1½ blocks away on Narragansett at Cable St. Driving directions from the airport: take Harbor Dr. west to Nimitz Blvd. to Lowell St., which becomes Narragansett Ave.

Located in Ocean Beach, just 500 feet from the Pacific and the longest pier on the West Coast, Elsbree House offers six immaculate B&B rooms—each with country-English decors, ensuite bathrooms with tub/shower combinations, large closets, and either a patio or balcony. (I prefer the balconies, which come with the upstairs rooms.) Most quarters have queen-size beds, but one has twins that can be made into a king. Guests share a lounge where there is a TV and fireplace, a cheerful breakfast room, and a patio surrounded by attractive landscaping. Hosts Katie and Phil Elsbree couldn't be nicer—he bakes the morning muffins and scones; she enjoys putting together special packages for honeymooners, family reunions, and anniversaries. The spacious three-bedroom/three-bathroom condo, which has a fully furnished kitchen and laundry facilities, is available only by the week. This very appealing property is in a mixed residential area—so, don't leave valuables in your car and be prepared for some airport noise. There are several good restaurants in the area. No smoking inside.

6 La Jolla

I've recommended La Jolla's most centrally located places to stay. Chain hotels outside of the village include a **Hyatt Regency,** at 3777 La Jolla Village Dr. (☎ **800/233-1234** or 619/552-1234), which is a glitzy place where the contemporary decor includes lots of marble. The architect, Michael Graves, received an American Institute of Architects Onion Award for the design (an Onion Award recognizes architectural flops); and a **Marriott Residence Inn,** at 8901 Gilman Dr. (☎ **800/ 331-3131** or 619/587-1770), a good choice for those who want a fully equipped kitchen and more space. The **Sheraton Grande Torrey Pines,** at 10950 N. Torrey Pines Rd. (☎ **800/762-6160** or 619/558-1500; fax 619/597-6962), is perched on a bluff above the Pacific Ocean adjacent to the famed Torrey Pines Golf Course. All are near the University of California San Diego.

VERY EXPENSIVE

✪ La Valencia Hotel

1132 Prospect St. (at Herschel Ave.), La Jolla, CA 92037. ☎ **800/451-0772** or 619/454-0771. Fax 619/456-3921. 90 rms, 13 suites. A/C MINIBAR TV TEL. $190–$230 standard double; $385–$400 full ocean-view double; from $500 suite. AE, DC, DISC, MC, V. Valet parking $8. Take Ardath Rd. exit off I-5 north or the La Jolla Village Dr. west exit off I-5 south. Take Torrey Pines Rd. to Prospect Place and turn right. Prospect Place becomes Prospect St.

La Valencia is a gracious Spanish-colonial hotel that delights the senses at every turn. Overlooking the ocean, beauty flows from the colonnaded entrance with a vine-covered trellis to the lush gardens surrounding the large pool to the exquisite mosaic tile work within. A haven for celebrities dating back to the days of Greta Garbo and Charlie Chaplin, you can still experience the old-world charm, outstanding personal service, and the impressive location. At the back of the hotel, garden terraces open toward the ocean.

The guest rooms are decorated with European antique reproductions and offer fine-quality linens. Amenities include terry-cloth robes, oversize towels, and bathroom phones. The ocean-view rooms have fantastic vistas.

Dining/Entertainment: The elegant rooftop Sky Room serves French cuisine in an intimate setting; the Mediterranean Room and Patio serves California cuisine either indoors or on a patio. There's also the legendary Whaling Bar & Grill (where Ginger Rogers and Charlton Heston once hung out) and the adjoining Café La Rue. Piano music is offered in the lobby lounge Monday through Saturday evenings and refreshments are served on the adjoining ocean-view terrace on request.

Services: Concierge, 24-hour room service, dry cleaning/laundry service, morning newspaper, nightly turndown, in-room massage, daily maid service, baby-sitting, secretarial services, express checkout, valet parking.

Facilities: Kitchenettes, VCR, video rental, a free-form heated pool edged with a lawn, flowering trees, shrubs, and a flagstone sundeck. There's also a mini–health club, Jacuzzi, sauna, massage room, shuffleboard, access to tennis courts, and three conference rooms.

EXPENSIVE

✪ Colonial Inn

910 Prospect St. (Between Fay and Girard), La Jolla, CA 92037. ☎ **800/826-1278** or 619/ 454-2181. Fax 619/454-5679. 64 rms, 11 suites. TV TEL. $165 double with village view, $185–$210 double with ocean view; from $230 suite. Lower off-season rates. Children under 18 stay free in parents' room. AE, CB, DC, MC, V. Valet parking $5. Take Ardath Rd. exit off I-5 north or the La Jolla Village Dr. west exit off I-5 south. Take Torrey Pines Rd. to Prospect Place and turn right. Prospect Place becomes Prospect St.

The Colonial Inn is one of my favorite places in La Jolla. I like the old-world atmosphere, the tasteful decor, and the spacious rooms enhanced by traditional furnishings and elegant fabrics. The property was built in 1913, and its Putnam's Restaurant now occupies the site of a drugstore by the same name. The hotel is one block from the ocean and just down the street from the more expensive La Valencia. Guests who

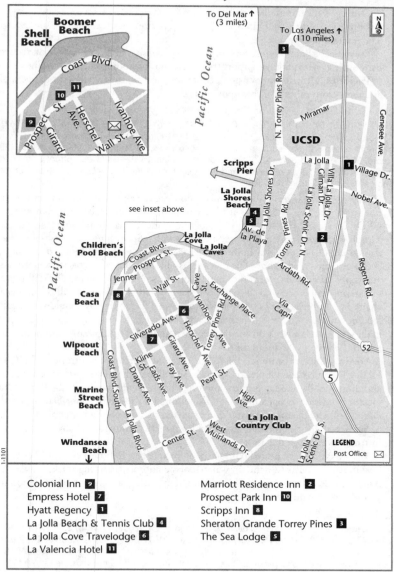

La Jolla Accommodations

To Del Mar ↑
(3 miles)

To Los Angeles ↑
(110 miles)

3

Boomer Beach

Shell Beach

Coast Blvd.

11

10

9

Prospect St.
Girard
Herschel Ave.
Ivanhoe Ave.
Wall St.

✉

Pacific Ocean

N. Torrey Pines Rd.

Miramar

UCSD

La Jolla

1 Village Dr.

Villa La Jolla Dr.
Gilman Dr.

Nobel Ave.

2

Genesee Ave.

Regents Rd.

Scripps Pier

La Jolla Shores Beach

La Jolla Shores Dr.

Torrey Pines Rd.

La Jolla Scenic Dr. N.

see inset above

4

5

Av. de la Playa

La Jolla Cove

La Jolla Caves

Children's Pool Beach

Pacific Ocean

Coast Blvd.
Prospect St.

Jenner

Cave St.

Exchange Place

Ardath Rd.

Via Capri

Casa Beach

8

Wall St.

6

Silverado Ave.

Ivanhoe Ave.

Torrey Pines Rd.

7

Girard Ave.

Herschel Ave.

Wipeout Beach

Kline St.
Eads Ave.
Fay Ave.
Draper Ave.

Pearl St.

52

5

Marine Street Beach

Coast Blvd. South

La Jolla Blvd.

Center St.

West Muirlands Dr.

High Ave.

La Jolla Country Club

La Jolla Scenic Dr. S.

Windansea Beach
↓

1-1101

LEGEND
Post Office ✉

Colonial Inn **9**	Marriott Residence Inn **2**
Empress Hotel **7**	Prospect Park Inn **10**
Hyatt Regency **1**	Scripps Inn **8**
La Jolla Beach & Tennis Club **4**	Sheraton Grande Torrey Pines **3**
La Jolla Cove Travelodge **6**	The Sea Lodge **5**
La Valencia Hotel **11**	

choose to stay here instead of at La Valencia will sacrifice air-conditioning for a ceiling fan in each room, but will gain elbow room (and save money). The inn, originally an apartment hotel, has oversized closets and feels more homey. A large spray of fresh flowers is the focal point in the lounge, where guests gather in front of the fireplace. The outdoor heated pool, set in a landscaped garden, is open from sunup to sundown. Walking tours of La Jolla depart from the hotel at 11am on Thursday through Saturday or other times by appointment. Airport transportation is available for $9 one way.

Dining/Entertainment: The bar in Putnam's was once a soda fountain; today it's a popular watering hole. Drinks are also served in front of the fireplace in the lounge. The restaurant serves excellent California cuisine.

Services: 24-hour room service, dry cleaning/laundry, turndown service on request, baby-sitting, valet parking, airport transportation, complimentary shoe-shine.

Facilities: Heated outdoor pool, conference rooms, car-rental desk, refrigerators and terry-cloth robes available upon request.

✪ La Jolla Beach & Tennis Club

2000 Spindrift Dr., La Jolla, CA 92037. ☎ **800/624-CLUB** or 619/454-7126. Fax 619/456-3805. Web site: www.ljbtc.com. 15 rms, 18 studios, 20 two-bedroom suites, 32 one-bedroom suites, 3 three-bedroom suites, and 2 cottages. TV TEL. $75 double rm, $139–$235 studio, $169 one-bedroom, $279 two-bedroom cottage, $309–$475 oceanfront suite. Additional person $15. Lower off-season and mid-season rates. AE, DC, MC, V. Located in La Jolla Shores about a mile from the village.

It may come as a surprise that La Jolla's most exclusive private club also rents rooms to the public. The "B&T," as it's known locally, has a membership comprised of CEOs, MDs, and JDs, and this is where they come to relax—and now you can, too. Although the two-story pink-stucco building with a Spanish tile roof sits right smack dab on La Jolla Shores Beach, this place has a very private feel. Rooms overlook the ocean or plant-filled patios. The property is old, but rooms are spacious, clean, and attractive. All quarters except the "hotel rooms" come with kitchens. The staff is used to catering to people who like things just right: The beach crew will set up beach chairs and umbrellas for guests and will give you a flag to display should you require food or beverage service. Boogie boards and kayaks can be rented. There's a kids' program several days a week during the summer, and baby-sitting can be arranged year-round. Reserve a year ahead for summer.

Dining/Entertainment: There are three oceanfront restaurants: The Club Dining Room is open for breakfast, lunch, and dinner; the Marine Room serves lunch and dinner daily, Sunday brunch, and often has live entertainment; the Beach Hut, located beachside, is open daily from Memorial Day through Labor Day for breakfast and lunch. There's also patio dining adjacent to the swimming pool.

Services: Dry cleaning/laundry, turndown service on request, baby-sitting, swim instruction, massage therapist.

Facilities: 25-yard heated outdoor pool, private beach, fitness center, 12 championship tennis courts (8 lighted), water-sports equipment, jogging track, 9-hole par-3 golf course, table tennis, children's program during summer, conference rooms, Laundromat, tennis shop.

✪ The Sea Lodge

8110 Camino del Oro (at Avenida de la Playa), La Jolla, CA 92037. ☎ **800/237-5211** or 619/459-8271. Fax 619/456-9346. 128 rms and suites. TV TEL. $175–$379 double; $409 suite. Children under 12 stay free in parents' room. Lower off-season and long-stay rates. AE, DC, DISC, MC, V. Free covered parking. Take the Ardath Rd. exit off I-5 north or the La Jolla Village Dr. west exit off I-5 south. Take La Jolla Shores Dr., turn left onto Avenida de la Playa, turn right on Camino del Oro.

The Sea Lodge is a great location for those who want to be right on the beach instead of in the village near shops and restaurants. This low-rise property, with its early-California decor, has a nice pool, but my guess is that most people will prefer the Pacific. Nonsmoking rooms are available, and all units offer a terrace or balcony and a refrigerator; 19 rooms come with kitchens. A nice restaurant and bar overlook the water. Baby-sitting and valet service are provided, and a car-rental desk, sauna, and tennis courts are on the premises.

MODERATE

Empress Hotel of La Jolla

7766 Fay Ave. (at Silverado), La Jolla, CA 92037. ☎ **888/369-6387** or 619/454-3001. Fax 619/454-6387. 73 rms and suites. A/C TV TEL. $109–$135 double; $325 Jacuzzi suite. Extra person $10. Children under 18 stay free in parents' room. Rates include continental breakfast. Lower off-season and long-stay rates. AE, DC, DISC, MC, V. Valet parking $5. Take the Ardath Rd. exit off I-5 north or the La Jolla Village Dr. west exit off I-5 south. Take Torrey Pines Rd. to Girard, turn right, then left on Silverado St.

The Empress Hotel offers spacious quarters with traditional furnishings a block or two away from La Jolla's "main drag" and the ocean. It's definitely quieter here than at the Colonial Inn or the Prospect Park Inn. All rooms come equipped with refrigerators, hair dryers, coffeemakers, and terry-cloth robes. The four Empress Rooms have sitting areas with full-size sleeper-sofas. While these rooms only have microwaves, four suites have complete cooking facilities. Two suites come equipped with grand pianos. The top two floors in this five-story building have partial ocean views. I like the European ambiance, marble bathrooms with large mirrors, and tasteful decor. Room service comes from the award-winning Manhattan Restaurant located on the ground floor.

✪ Prospect Park Inn

1110 Prospect St. (at Coast Blvd.), La Jolla, CA 92037. ☎ **800/433-1609** or 619/454-0133. Fax 619/454-2056. 23 rms and suites. A/C TV TEL. $105–$165 double rm., $250 village-view suite, $300 oceanview suite. Lower off-season rates. Rates include continental breakfast. AE, DC, DISC, MC, V. Free off-site indoor parking. Take the Ardath Rd. exit off I-5 north or the La Jolla Village Dr. west exit off I-5 south. Take Torrey Pines Rd. to Prospect Place and turn right. Prospect Place becomes Prospect St.

This place is a real gem. It's a small property—next door to La Valencia—that offers charming rooms, some with ocean views. Built in 1947 as a boarding house for women, this spotless boutique hotel feels more European than Californian—there isn't even an elevator in the three-story building. Fruit, cookies, and beverages are offered in the library area every afternoon and breakfast is served on the sundeck, which has a great ocean view. Prospect Park Inn enjoys essentially the same location as La Valencia and the Colonial Inn—the beach, park, shops, and myriad restaurants are within steps—at much lower prices. The Cove Suite is extra large and has an outstanding ocean view; other units have balconies or terraces. Beach towels and chairs are provided free of charge for guests. This is a nonsmoking establishment.

Scripps Inn

555 Coast Blvd. S. (at Cuvier), La Jolla, CA 92037. ☎ **619/454-3391.** Fax 619/456-0389. 8 rms, 5 suites. TV TEL. Summer $120–$205 double, $205 suites. Off-season, $105–$185 single or double, $185 suites. Extra person $10. Children under 5 stay free in parents' room. Weekly and monthly rates available off-season. Rates include continental breakfast. AE, DISC, MC, V. Free parking. Take the Ardath Rd. exit off I-5 north or the La Jolla Village Dr. west exit off I-5 south. Take Torrey Pines Rd., turn right on Prospect Place, veer right (downhill) onto Coast Blvd. (if you miss the turn, drive through town and turn right at the museum).

Only a small, grassy park comes between this cozy inn and the beach, cliffs, and tide pools. All the guest rooms have ocean views and Early American furnishings; two have working fireplaces (Room 12 has a fireplace, wet bar, and a particularly fine view, rivaled only by Room 14). The four suites have separate bedrooms and kitchenettes. The view from the second-story deck seems to hypnotize guests, who gaze out to sea indefinitely. The inn supplies beach towels, as well as wood for fireplaces. The Museum of Contemporary Art, San Diego, is next door, and Prospect Street shops and restaurants are a short walk away.

INEXPENSIVE

La Jolla Cove Travelodge

1141 Silverado St. (at Herschel)., La Jolla, CA 92037. ☎ **800/578-7878** or 619/454-0791. Fax 619/459-8534. 30 rms. A/C TV TEL. $59–$89 double. AE, DC, MC, V. Rates are seasonal and subject to availability. Free off-street parking.

Located at the corner of Silverado and Herschel, this three-story motel is good value and convenient to shops, nightlife, and restaurants. The rooms are clean and basic and come with coffeemakers and free HBO. Rooms have queen-size, king-size, or two double beds. There isn't a pool, but there is a modest sundeck on the third floor with a view to the ocean, which is about three-quarters of a mile away. Nonsmoking rooms are available.

7 Coronado

The great beach and small-town atmosphere of Coronado attract families who want a more laid-back setting.

VERY EXPENSIVE

✪ Hotel del Coronado

1500 Orange Ave., Coronado, CA 92118. ☎ **800/468-3533** or 619/435-8000. Fax 619/ 522-8238. 700 rms. MINIBAR TV TEL. From $195 standard; from $235 deluxe; from $295 ocean view; from $385 oceanfront; from $600 suite. Packages available. Children under 18 stay free in parents' room. AE, CB, DC, DISC, MC, V. Parking $10. From I-5 take the Coronado Bridge; turn left onto Orange Ave. Bus: 901. Ferry: From Broadway Pier.

The "Hotel Del," as it is affectionately called, turned 109 years old in 1997. Built in a scant 11 months by Chinese laborers and Scandinavian wood-carvers, this National Historic Landmark is one of the world's largest wooden buildings. Its famous red roofs and turrets, white facade, rows of prim windows, and graceful verandas are instantly recognizable. Inside, the woodwork is impressive, especially in the Crown Room, where the 30-foot-high sugar-pine ceiling is put together solely with wooden pegs. The ceiling, which has never been stained, is hand-polished twice a year. The large room also has no pillar support—not surprising, since the hotel's architects had a background building railroad stations. The rooms in the original building have ceiling fans; only those in the Ocean Towers and poolside have air-conditioning. The rooms in the original building tend to be small, but the larger (preferable) ones evoke an earlier era.

Dining/Entertainment: Several dining areas include the Crown Room and the smaller Coronet Room for California cuisine with a French accent; the Prince of Wales Grill for fine dining; the Ocean Terrace for alfresco bistro fare; the Del Deli for matzo-ball soup, potato and meat knishes, and lox and bagels (24 hours); and the Palm Court in the lobby for continental breakfast. There's music and dancing nightly in the Ocean Terrace Lounge, piano music in the Palm Court bar, and Sunday-buffet dinner dances in the Crown Room. The Ocean Terrace Bar has dewdrop chande-liers, a wood ceiling, and round tables that beg for a card game.

Services: Concierge, 24-hour room service, laundry/dry cleaning, valet, baby-sitting, beauty salon, limousine service, self-guided tour of hotel with audiocassette, $10 guided tours of the hotel, 24-hour deli, special activities for children, airport shuttle ($9).

Facilities: Two outdoor pools, beach, health spa, massage, six tennis courts, car-rental desk, electronic games, meeting rooms, shopping arcade, lobby shop.

A Hotel with History: Scenes from the Hotel del Coronado

Welcome to the Hotel del Coronado, romantic, unmistakable, and filled with enchanting and colorful memories.

Several familiar names helped shape the hotel. Thomas Edison personally installed the electricity in 1887; the building had its own electrical power plant, which also supplied the entire city of Coronado until 1922. Author L. Frank Baum, a frequent guest, designed the Crown Dining Room's elegant crown-shaped chandeliers. Since Baum wrote several of his beloved *Wizard of Oz* series in Coronado, many believe he modeled the Emerald City's geometric spires after the Del's conical turrets.

The hotel has hosted royalty and celebrities as well. The first visiting monarch was Kalakaua, Hawaii's last king, who spent Christmases here in the 1890s. But the best-known royal guest would be Edward, Prince of Wales (later Edward VIII and then duke of Windsor), who came to the hotel in April 1920, the first British royal to visit California. Of the many lavish social affairs held during his stay, at least two were attended by Wallis Simpson (then Navy wife Wallis Warfield), 15 years before her official introduction to the prince in London. Speculation continues as to whether their love affair, which culminated in his abdication of the throne in order to marry her, might have begun right here.

America's own "royalty" also often visited the hotel. In 1927, San Diego's beloved son, Charles Lindbergh, was honored here following his historic 33 1/2-hour solo flight across the Atlantic. Hollywood stars, including Mary Pickford, Greta Garbo, Charlie Chaplin, and Esther Williams, have flocked to the Del. Director Billy Wilder filmed *Some Like It Hot* at the hotel; longtime hotel staffers remember seeing stars Marilyn Monroe, Tony Curtis, and Jack Lemmon romping on the beach during filming. The hotel has also hosted 14 U.S. presidents. And some guests have never left: the ghost of Kate Morgan, whose body was found in 1892 where the tennis courts are today, still allegedly roams the halls today.

Visitors and guests intrigued by the hotel's past should stroll through the lower level History Gallery, a minimuseum of hotel memorabilia.

—by Stephanie Avnet

Le Meridien

2000 Second St. (At Glorietta Blvd.), Coronado, CA 92118. ☎ **800/543-4300** or 619/435-3000. Fax 619/435-3032. 265 rms, 7 suites, 28 oceanfront villas. A/C MINIBAR TV TEL. $205–$255 double; from $375 suite; from $475 oceanfront villa. Children under 12 stay free in parents' room. AE, CB, DC, MC, V. Valet parking $9; self-parking $7. Airport transfers $6 each way. From I-5 take the Coronado Bridge, turn right onto Glorietta Blvd., take first right to hotel. Bus: 901. Ferry: From Broadway Pier.

I find it confusing that they answer the phone *"bonjour"* here, because the French name and the restaurant cuisine are the only evidence of a Gallic connection. However, this is still one of the area's loveliest hotels, with a waterfront location, clean lines, open architecture, and an airy lobby with a rough-hewn ceiling, oversize rattan chairs, and a beige limestone floor. The rooms have thick carpeting, overstuffed chairs, pale-wood paneling and bright striped wallpaper, desks, and vanities; bathrooms with oversize bathtubs and adjustable shower heads are nicely lit and have fresh flowers, hair dryers, and terry-cloth robes. All rooms feature either balconies or patios; suites have Jacuzzis and safes. On the grounds are plenty of plants, a boardwalk to the base of the Coronado Bridge, preening pink flamingos, white and black swans, and even a walk-in aviary. From here, you feel you can almost reach across the bay and touch the San Diego Convention Center. Guests have the option of splurging and taking a 1-day rejuvenator at the hotel spa: A facial, massage, herbal wrap, and spa lunch costs about $170.

Dining/Entertainment: Marius, the hotel's much-acclaimed French restaurant features French gourmet cuisine and is open for dinner only, Tuesday through Sunday. The more informal L'Escale, a brasserie restaurant, serves breakfast, lunch, and dinner daily, a Saturday jazz brunch, a Sunday champagne brunch, and provides bay views from its dining terrace; outdoor refreshments are served at La Riviera Pool. La Provence, the hotel cocktail lounge, is open daily from 4pm to 1am and features live piano music Friday and Saturday.

Services: Concierge, 24-hour room service, laundry/valet, turndown service, twice-daily maid service, baby-sitting, bicycle rental, currency exchange, valet parking, complimentary shuttle to Horton Plaza.

Facilities: Three outdoor heated pools (including lap pool), two outdoor whirlpools, European health club and spa, yoga and exercise sessions, massage, six lighted tennis courts, tennis clinic, bicycle rental, water sports, jogging trail and bike path, private dock, business center with fax and secretarial services, meeting rooms, shopping arcade.

✪ Loew's Coronado Bay Resort

4000 Coronado Bay Rd., Coronado, CA 92118. ☎ **800/23-LOEWS** or 619/424-4000. Fax 619/424-4400. 400 rms, 37 suites. A/C MINIBAR TV TEL. $195–$245 double; $395–$595 executive suite; $595–$1,500 bay-side villa. Additional person $20. Children under 18 stay free in parents' room. "Romance" and tennis packages available. AE, CB, DC, DISC, MC, V. Valet parking $13; self-parking (under cover) $10. Take I-5 to the Coronado Bridge, go left onto Orange Avenue, continue 8 miles down Silver Strand Hwy., turn left at Coronado Bay Rd., entrance to the resort.

This lovely luxury resort opened in 1991 and lounges on a secluded 15-acre peninsula, slightly removed from both downtown Coronado and San Diego. It's perfect for those who prefer a self-contained resort in a get-away-from-it-all location. All quarters offer terraces that look onto the hotel's private 80-slip marina, the Coronado Bay Bridge, or the San Diego Bay. Each room is very well appointed with the finest furnishings and large marble bathrooms. The resort is 30 minutes from the airport, 3 miles from downtown Coronado, and a short drive from Tijuana. A private pedestrian underpass leads to nearby Silver Strand Beach. The hotel features the Commodore Kids Club, an outstanding program for children 4 to 12, with activities daily from 9am to 4pm and Thursday through Saturday from 6:30 to 9:30pm (additional charge). It's available year-round, with a two-child minimum.

Dining/Entertainment: Azzura Point serves up California cuisine and a memorable view, while the more casual RRR's American Cafe has both indoor and outdoor seating. Guests also enjoy a lounge, a poolside bar and grill, and a specialty food market.

Services: Concierge, 24-hour room service, laundry/valet, newspaper delivery, turndown service, in-room massage, twice-daily maid service, baby-sitting, secretarial service, express checkout, valet parking. The hotel's Commodore Kids Club, for children 4 to 12, offers supervised half-day, full-day, and evening programs with meals.

Facilities: VCRs; video rentals; 3 outdoor swimming pools; fitness center with equipment, saunas, steam room, and whirlpools; massage; large sundeck; hydro spas; five night-lit tennis courts and pro shop; water sports; bicycle, in-line skate and water-sports rentals; marina; business center, fax machines in suites; meeting space; washer and dryer; car-rental desk; beauty salon; boutiques.

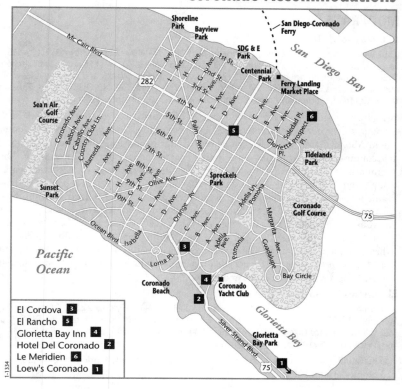

Coronado Accommodations

Map labels:
Shoreline Park
Bayview Park
SDG & E Park
San Diego-Coronado Ferry
San Diego Bay
McCain Blvd
282
Centennial Park
Ferry Landing Market Place
Sea'n Air Golf Course
Coronado Ave
Balboa Ave
Cabrillo Ave
Country Club Ln.
Alameda Ave
1st St
2nd St.
3rd St.
4th St.
5th St.
6th St.
7th St.
8th St.
9th Ave.
10th St.
H Ave.
G Ave.
F Ave.
Palm Ave.
D Ave.
C Ave.
B Ave.
A Ave.
Soledad Pl.
Glorietta prospect Pl.
Tidelands Park
Sunset Park
Olive Ave.
Spreckels Park
Orange Av.
Adella Ln.
Pomona
Margarita Ave.
Guadalupe
Coronado Golf Course
75
Pacific Ocean
Ocean Blvd.
Isabella
Loma Pl.
Coronado Beach
Coronado Yacht Club
Bay Circle
Glorietta Bay
Silver Strand Blvd.
Glorietta Bay Park
75

El Cordova **3**
El Rancho **5**
Glorietta Bay Inn **4**
Hotel Del Coronado **2**
Le Meridien **6**
Loew's Coronado **1**

1-1334

EXPENSIVE

Glorietta Bay Inn

1630 Glorietta Blvd. (near Orange Ave.), Coronado, CA 92118. ☎ **800/283-9383** or 619/435-3101. Fax 619/435-6182. E-mail rooms@gloriettabayinn.com. Web site: www.gloriettabayinn.com. 81 rms, 17 suites. A/C TV TEL. Mansion $145–$155 double; $165–$200 suite; $300 penthouse. Annex $115–$155 double; suites from $189. AE, DC, DISC, MC, V. Free parking. Take I-5 to the Coronado Bridge, and turn left on Orange Ave. After 2 miles, turn left onto Glorietta Blvd.; it's across the street from the Hotel del Coronado.

Right across the street and somewhat in the shadow of the Hotel del Coronado, this pretty white hotel incorporates the John D. Spreckels mansion (1908) with original fixtures and marble-and-brass staircase. The lobby is inviting: wicker furniture, lush hanging ferns, and an adjoining music room and outdoor patio. Rooms in the mansion are Victorian in style, while those in the annex are modern. They all have refrigerators. The grounds are beautifully landscaped and tended, and the hotel is within walking distance of the beach, golf, tennis, water sports, shopping, and dining.

Services: In-room movies, laundry/dry cleaning, baby-sitting, complimentary morning coffee, continental breakfast available for a charge.

Facilities: Kitchenettes available, heated pool and spa pool, bicycle rental, conference rooms, guest laundry.

MODERATE

El Cordova Hotel

1351 Orange Ave. (at Adella Ave.), Coronado, CA 92118. ☎ **800/229-2032** or 619/435-4131. Fax 619/435-0632. 14 rms, 26 suites. TV TEL. $85–$95 double; $105–$115 studio with kitchen; $130–$145 one-bedroom suite; $155–$175 two-bedroom suite. Weekly and monthly rates available off-season. Children under 12 stay free in parent's room. AE, DC, DISC, MC, V. Take I-5 to the Coronado Bridge, and turn left onto Orange Ave. No off-street parking.

Built as a Spanish-style mansion in 1902, El Cordova became a hotel in 1930. Each room, a little different from the next, features a ceiling fan, brightly tiled bathroom, and Mexican and native American furnishings in soothing earth tones. A suite, accommodating four to six people, has a separate living room and kitchenette. The grounds are filled with flowers and shrubs; unfortunately there's no off-street parking or air-conditioning. This inviting place welcomes children and pets. It's advisable to reserve at least 6 months in advance, and a year ahead for the month of August. The hotel, well located near the beach and the Hotel del Coronado, attracts a young clientele and probably isn't a good choice for those who like to go to bed early. Services include a laundry room and vending machines. Facilities include a heated pool, a patio, a barbecue area with a picnic table, an arcade with shops, and a Mexican restaurant. This venerable property is gradually being upgraded. I suggest requesting a room in the renovated section.

El Rancho Motel

370 Orange Ave. (at Fourth St.), Coronado, CA 92118. ☎ **619/435-2251.** 6 rms. A/C TV. Summer $45–$90 single or double. Winter $65–$75 single or double. AE, CB, DC, DISC, JCB, MC, V. Free parking. Take I-5 to the Coronado Bridge, and turn left onto Orange Ave. Bus: 901. Ferry: From Broadway Pier.

This small, pretty, Spanish-style place is owned and lovingly tended by Cecilia Leith. The modern and clean rooms feature walk-in closets, tiled baths with Jacuzzis, sitting areas, loft-style beamed ceilings, and plush carpets. They come equipped with refrigerator, coffeemaker, and microwave, and overlook a small garden filled with azaleas, roses, camellias, and flowering jasmine. The motel's reception area is tiny, but Ms. Leith will supply you with brochures that you can take back to your room. The services include ice and soda machines and in-room coffee, tea, and cocoa. Guests can relax outside on the brick patio. The beach is a block and a half away.

Dining 6

Restaurants here win kudos all the time for cuisine, service, ambiance, and romantic bay and ocean views. A rich mix of ethnic restaurants exists, along with local restaurants (and restaurateurs) that are unique to San Diego.

It's a town that's famous for huge salads, and the locals usually prefer seafood over beef. Wood-fired pizza is much more popular than the traditional sausage and pepperoni. "Wrapps," the latest craze to hit the streets of San Diego, are gourmet tortillas filled with various international ingredients. For instance, one restaurant might offer a Thai chicken wrapp while another might serve a wrapp filled with tuna.

Given the city's history and location, it's not surprising that Mexican fare consistently ranks as a favorite ethnic cuisine. Actually, it's more accurate to say *Americanized Mexican* food since, like Tex Mex, what you'll savor in San Diego is not what you'll be served south of the border. Some of the best Mexican restaurants are located in Old Town. The three in the Bazaar del Mundo (Casa de Pico, Rancho el Nopal, and Casa de Bandini) and the Old Town Mexican Cafe on San Diego Avenue are the most popular. Diners on the run head for Rubios, a Mexican fast-food emporium with locations throughout the city. And if you enjoy a margarita with your meal, remember that some believe the drink has local origins: Legend has it that a bartender at La Jolla's La Valencia Hotel was the first person to concoct this now world-famous drink.

In this chapter, I've indexed restaurants by cuisine as well as by location and price category. For diners on a budget, the more expensive San Diego restaurants are very accommodating if you want to order a few appetizers instead of a main course. Dress tends to be pretty casual, even in pricey places. (Some restaurateurs post the local law—"Shoes and shirt required"—to discourage those who would be *too* laid-back.) California law mandates no smoking. However, smoking is allowed in the bar areas of restaurants.

Note: Don't forget to look at the dining listings in chapter 11. Many places listed as day trips or excursions farther afield might make a great lunch or dinner destination.

1 Best Bets

- **Best Spot for a Business Lunch: Dakota Grill and Spirits,** at 901 Fifth Ave., in the Gaslamp Quarter (☎ **619/234-5554**), has the three important ingredients of a business lunch locale: great location, appropriate atmosphere, and excellent food.

- **Best View:** In San Diego, many restaurants overlook the ocean, but only from **Brockton Villa,** at 1235 Coast Blvd., La Jolla (☎ **619/454-7393**), can you see the La Jolla Cove. Diners with a window seat feel like they're looking out on a gigantic picture postcard.
- **Best Value:** The food at the **Grand Central Cafe,** located in the downtown YMCA at 500 W. Broadway (☎ **619/234-CAFE**), isn't fancy, but its prices can't be beat.
- **Best for Kids:** At the **Old Spaghetti Factory,** located at Fifth Avenue and K Street, in the Gaslamp Quarter (☎ **619/233-4323**), family dining is the name of the game—so if your kids are noisy, nobody will notice.
- **Best Chinese Cuisine:** The Szechuan fare at **Mandarin House,** at 2604 Fifth Ave., Downtown (☎ **619/232-1101**), and in Pacific Beach and La Jolla, is exceptional—and there's a selection of spicy dishes if you want to turn up the heat a notch.
- **Best Italian Cuisine: Fio's,** 801 Fifth Ave., in the Gaslamp Quarter (☎ **619/234-3467**), offers fine northern Italian food, in chic surroundings.
- **Best Seafood:** Not only does **The Fish Market/Top of the Market** offer the city's best fish, at 750 N. Harbor Dr. (☎ **619/232-FISH** or 619/234-4TOP), it also offers a memorable view out across San Diego Bay.
- **Best American Cuisine: Croce's** menu cleverly includes dishes from a half-dozen different countries—all adapted to American tastes. The results are delicious and can be found at 802 Fifth Ave., in the Gaslamp Quarter (☎ **619/233-4355**).
- **Best Mexican Cuisine:** The women making tortillas in the front window catch the attention of passersby, but it's the great food that keeps the locals coming back to the **Old Town Mexican Cafe,** at 2489 San Diego Ave., Old Town (☎ **619/297-4330**).
- **Best Vegetarian: The Vegetarian Zone,** at 2949 Fifth Ave., in Hillcrest (☎ **619/298-7302**), offers tasty meat-free dishes from a variety of ethnic cuisine.
- **Best Pizza:** For an imaginative pizza, such as the "Greek Grilled Chicken" with marinated chicken, mozzarella, sliced tomatoes, red onion, feta cheese, and Kalamata olives, head for **D'Lish,** at 7514 Girard Ave., La Jolla (☎ **619/459-8118**), or 386 East H Street, Chula Vista (☎ **619/585-1371**), which also offers great salads and pasta dishes.
- **Best Desserts:** You'll forget your diet at **Extraordinary Desserts,** at 2929 Fifth Ave., in Hillcrest (☎ **619/294-7001**). Proprietor Karen Krasne has a Certificate de Patisserie from the Cordon Bleu in Paris, and she makes everything fresh on the premises daily.
- **Best Late-Night Dining:** Open later than any place else downtown, **Cafe Lulu,** at 419 F St. (☎ **619/238-0114**), serves until 2am during the week, 4am on weekends.
- **Best Fast Food:** Fish tacos from **Rubios,** at 901 Fourth Ave., in the Gaslamp Quarter (☎ **619/231-7731**) and other locations, are legendary in San Diego. Taste one and you'll know why.
- **Best Picnic Fare:** Pack a humongous sandwich from the **Cheese Shop** for a picnic lunch and you won't be hungry for dinner. There's one downtown at 401 G St. (☎ **619/232-2303**) and another in La Jolla Shores at 2165 Avenida de la Playa (☎ **619/459-3921**).

2 Restaurants by Cuisine

AMERICAN

Bay Beach Cafe (Coronado, *M*)
Chart House (Coronado,
La Jolla, *E*)
Corvette Diner (Hillcrest/
Uptown, *I*)
Croce's Restaurant (Downtown, *E*)
Dakota Grill and Spirits
(Downtown, *M*)
Firehouse Beach Cafe (Mission Bay,
Pacific Beach & Beyond, *I*)
Galaxy Grill (Downtown, *I*)
Grand Central Cafe (Downtown, *I*)
Hard Rock Cafe (La Jolla, *I*)
Hob Nob Hill (Hillcrest/
Uptown, *M*)
Kansas City Barbecue
(Downtown, *I*)
Karl Strauss Brewery & Grill
(Downtown, La Jolla, *I*)
Planet Hollywood (Downtown, *M*)
Rhinoceros Cafe & Grill
(Coronado, *M*)
T. D. Hays (Mission Bay, Pacific
Beach & Beyond, *M*)

CALIFORNIA

The Atoll (Mission Bay, Pacific
Beach & Beyond, *E*)
Brockton Villa (La Jolla, *I*)
Cafe Pacifica (Expensive, Old
Town, *E*)
George's at the Cove (La Jolla, *VE*)
George's Ocean Terrace and Café/
Bar (La Jolla, *M*)
Planet Hollywood (Downtown, *M*)
Putnam's Restaurant & Bar
(La Jolla, *E*)
The Whaling Bar/Tropical Patio
(La Jolla, *I*)

CHINESE

Mandarin Cafe (Coronado, *I*)
Mandarin House (Downtown,
Pacific Beach, La Jolla, *I*)
Panda Inn (Downtown, *M*)

COFFEE AND TEA

Garden House Coffee & Tea
(Old Town, *I*)
Pannikin Hillcrest (Hillcrest/
Uptown, *I*)
Pannikin La Jolla (See "Java Joints
in La Jolla" box)
The Secret Garden (See "Java Joints
in La Jolla" box)
Wall Street Cafe (See "Java Joints in
La Jolla" box)

CONTINENTAL

Dobson's (Downtown, *VE*)
Top O' the Cove (La Jolla, *VE*)

DESSERTS

Extraordinary Desserts (Hillcrest/
Uptown, *I*)

ENGLISH

The Princess Pub & Grille
(Downtown, *I*)

FRENCH

Chez Loma (Coronado, *E*)
Laurel (Hillcrest/Uptown, *I*)
Liaison (Hillcrest/Uptown, *M*)

INTERNATIONAL

Cafe Lulu (Downtown, *I*)
The Green Flash (Mission Bay,
Pacific Beach & Beyond, *M*)

IRISH

Hennessey's Tavern (Mission Bay,
Pacific Beach & Beyond, *I*)
McP's Irish Pub (Coronado, *I*)

ITALIAN

Arrivederci Italian Restaurant
(Hillcrest/Uptown, *M*)
D'Lish (La Jolla, Chula Vista, *I*)
Filippi's Pizza Grotto (Downtown,
Mission Bay/Pacific Beach, and
other locations, *I*)
Fio's (Downtown, *M*)

Key to abbreviations: *E* = Expensive; *I* = Inexpensive; *M* = Moderate; *VE* = Very Expensive

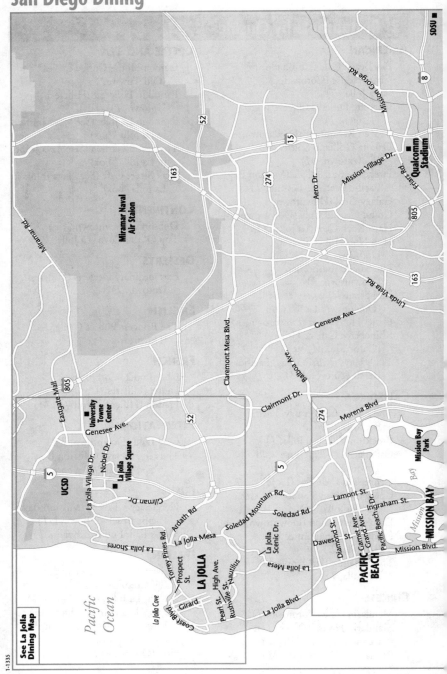

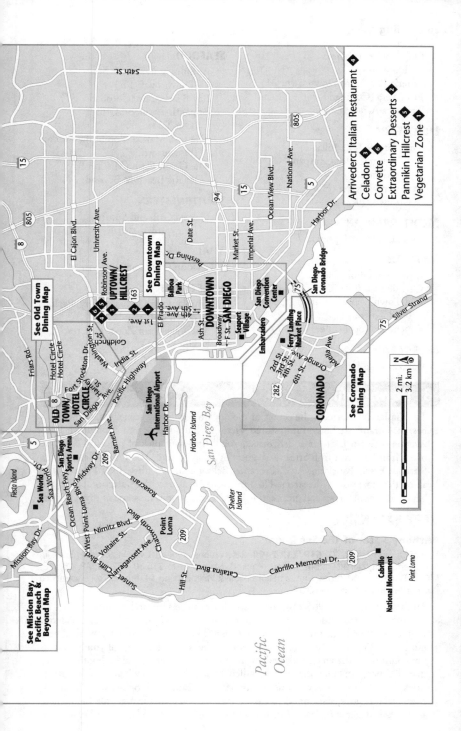

See Mission Bay, Pacific Beach & Beyond Map

See Old Town Dining Map

See Downtown Dining Map

See Coronado Dining Map

UPTOWN/HILLCREST

OLD TOWN/HOTEL CIRCLE

DOWNTOWN
SAN DIEGO

CORONADO

Arrivederci Italian Restaurant **4**
Celadon **3**
Corvette **6**
Extraordinary Desserts **2**
Pannikin Hillcrest **5**
Vegetarian Zone **1**

San Diego International Airport

San Diego Convention Center

Seaport Village

Embarcadero

Ferry Landing Market Place

San Diego-Coronado Bridge

Balboa Park

San Diego Sports Arena

Sea World

Fiesta Island

Mission Bay Dr.

Point Loma

Shelter Island

Harbor Island

San Diego Bay

Pacific Ocean

Cabrillo National Monument

Point Loma

Silver Strand

Friars Rd.

Hotel Circle

Fort Stockton Dr.
Washington St.
Goldfinch St.
India St.
Pacific Highway
San Diego Ave.
Fort Stockton Dr.

El Cajon Blvd.
University Ave.
Robinson Ave.
Date St.

1st Ave.
4th Ave.
5th Ave.
El Prado
Ash St.
Broadway
F St.
Market St.
Imperial Ave.
Pershing Dr.
Ocean View Blvd.
National Ave.
Harbor Dr.

2nd St.
3rd St.
4th St.
6th St.
Orange Ave.
Adella Ave.

Harbor Dr.

Barnett Ave.
Rosecrans
Midway Dr.
West Point Loma Blvd.
Ocean Beach Fwy.
Sunset Cliffs Blvd.
Narragansett Ave.
Voltaire St.
Chatsworth Blvd.
Nimitz Blvd.
Catalina Blvd.
Hill St.
Cabrillo Memorial Dr.

54th St.

15
805
8
805
8
5
163
94
15
5
282
75
75
209
209
209

N

0   2 mi.
0   3.2 km

79

Old Spaghetti Factory
   (Downtown, *I*)
Osteria Panevino (Downtown, *M*)
Primavera (Coronado, *E*)
Trattoria Acqua (La Jolla, *E*)

LIGHT FARE
The Cottage (, La Jolla, *I*)
Kensington Coffee Company
   (Coronado, *I*)
Pannikin Hillcrest (Hillcrest/
   Uptown, *I*)

MEDITERRANEAN
Laurel (Hillcrest/Uptown, *E*)

MEXICAN
Casa de Bandini (Old Town, *M*)
Casa de Pico (Old Town, *I*)
Old Town Mexican Cafe
   (Old Town, *I*)
Rancho el Nopal (Old Town, *I*)

MOROCCAN
Marakesh (La Jolla, *E*)

SEAFOOD
Anthony's Star of the Sea
   (Downtown, *VE*)
Bay Beach Cafe (Coronado, *M*)
Brigantine Seafood Grill
   (Old Town, *E*)
The Fish Market/Top of the Market
   (Downtown, *E*)
The Green Flash (Mission Bay,
   Pacific Beach & Beyond, *M*)

SOUTHWESTERN
Dakota Grill and Spirits
   (Downtown, *M*)

THAI
Celadon (Hillcrest/Uptown, *M*)

VEGETARIAN
Souplantation (Mission Bay, Pacific
   Beach & Beyond, *I*)
The Vegetarian Zone (Hillcrest/
   Uptown, *I*)

3 Downtown

The Gaslamp Quarter is the center of the downtown dining scene, where the city's best restaurants are housed in restored Victorian buildings. If you stroll down Fifth Avenue between E Street and K Street, you'll find your pick of places to eat. The block from G Street to F Street is the best hunting ground. You'll find Trattoria La Strada, Osteria Panevino, Asti Ristorante, Bella Luna, and Little Joe's Pizza House all on the same side of the street. The Embarcadero, a stretch of waterfront along the bay, is also home to several great eating spots. Listed below are some of my favorites.

VERY EXPENSIVE

Anthony's Star of the Sea Room
Harbor Dr. and Ash St. ☎ **619/232-7408.** Reservations required 1 wk. in advance, 3 wk. in advance for Sat; call after 2pm. Jackets required. Main courses $16.50–$32.50. AE, CB, DC, MC, V. Daily 5:30–10:30pm. Closed major holidays. Valet parking $4. Bus: 2. Trolley: America Plaza or Seaport Village. SEAFOOD.

An institution since 1965, Anthony's specializes in service, style, and seafood—all superbly delivered under the attentive eye of manager and maître d' Mario Valerio, who has been with the restaurant since it began. The "newest" waiter has worked here more than 25 years. The restaurant is set over the water on pilings (if you look, you can count more than a dozen), and its arched window wall and raised booths ensure that all diners can enjoy the view. Candlelight adds to the glow here. Popular appetizers are the clams Genovese tossed with béchamel sauce and topped with Parmesan cheese and the lobster scampi della casa. Other seafood dishes that get top billing here are the baked sole *à l'admiral* (stuffed with lobster, shrimp, and crab) and swordfish,

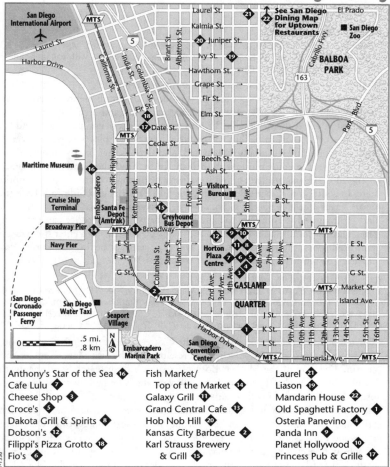

Anthony's Star of the Sea 16
Cafe Lulu 7
Cheese Shop 3
Croce's 5
Dakota Grill & Spirits 8
Dobson's 12
Filippi's Pizza Grotto 18
Fio's 6

Fish Market/
   Top of the Market 14
Galaxy Grill 11
Grand Central Cafe 13
Hob Nob Hill 20
Kansas City Barbecue 2
Karl Strauss Brewery
   & Grill 15

Laurel 21
Liason 19
Mandarin House 22
Old Spaghetti Factory 1
Osteria Panevino 4
Panda Inn 9
Planet Hollywood 10
Princess Pub & Grille 17

both prepared for two. Come with a hearty appetite, as the portions here are quite large.

Dobson's

956 Broadway Circle (between Broadway and Horton Plaza). ☎ **619/231-6771.** Reservations recommended. Main courses $15–$24. AE, CB, DC, MC, V. Mon–Wed 11:30am–10pm, Thurs–Fri 11:30am–11pm, Sat 5:30–11pm. Valet parking (after 5pm) $3. CONTINENTAL.

This has long been a local in place, especially for politicians and those who observe them. Personable owner Paul Dobson, or his wife, Carol, is likely to greet you at the door. Dobson's menu features veal, lamb, fish, duckling, quail, and venison. Popular dishes include mussel bisque, veal chops, and, for lunch, Dobson's famous hamburger or Cobb salad. Jackets aren't required here, but something about the place—beginning with the etched-glass front door and green awning—makes you want to dress up. The tables overlooking the bar are the most fun. The bar is open until midnight.

EXPENSIVE

○ Croce's Restaurant

802 Fifth Ave. (at F St.). ☎ **619/233-4355.** Reservations recommended. Main courses $13.50–$22.95. AE, DC, DISC, MC, V. Daily 5pm–midnight. Valet parking $6 with validation. Bus: 1, 3, 25, or 945. Trolley: Gaslamp Quarter. AMERICAN.

Diners who choose this spot are in for a surprise if they think, as I did, that Croce's is a popular jazz and blues spot that serves food as an afterthought. My recent meal here, which began with a wonderful grilled lamb salad and included the salmon in puff pastry, was truly memorable. Prawns wrapped in basil and prosciutto and Chef Fay Nakanishi's Alaskan halibut with sautéed prawn and spicy *nasi goreng* cream are also tempting. The restaurant is separated from Croce's Jazz Bar by an open divider so that diners can enjoy music with their meals. Seating is both indoors and out.

Ingrid Croce has created an inviting cluster of dining and entertainment options here. In addition to Croce's Restaurant, **Ingrid's Cantina and Sidewalk Cafe** (next door) serves excellent Southwestern cuisine. **Upstairs at Croce's,** open only Friday and Saturday nights from 7pm to 2am, is a wonderful cocktail/coffee bar serving light fare. Those who dine at either of the full-service restaurants can enter the two adjacent nightspots, the Jazz Bar and the Top Hat, without paying the normal cover charge. The music venues are described in chapter 10, "San Diego After Dark."

The Fish Market/Top of the Market

750 N. Harbor Dr. ☎ **619/232-FISH** (Fish Market), or 619/234-4TOP (Top of the Market). Reservations recommended for Top of the Market. Reservations not accepted at The Fish Market. Main courses $8.65–$25 (Fish Market); $15–$31.50 (Top of the Market). AE, CB, DC, MC, V. Daily 11am–10pm. Valet parking $4. Bus: 7/7B. Trolley: Seaport Village. SEAFOOD.

The red building perched on the end of the G Street Pier at the Embarcadero houses two of San Diego's most popular seafood restaurants: The Fish Market and its pricier cousin, The Top of the Market. Both offer superb fresh seafood and menus that change daily. The chalkboard out front tells you what's freshest, be it Mississippi catfish, Maine lobster, Canadian salmon, or Mexican yellowtail. At ground level, the Fish Market, a market and casual restaurant, has oyster and sushi bars and a cocktail lounge. Upstairs, the elegant Top of the Market looks like a private club, with teakwood touches, mounted fish trophies, and historic photographs. The panoramic view from here encompasses the bay, the Coronado Bay Bridge, and, sometimes, aircraft carriers (the restaurant thoughtfully provides binoculars). Besides seafood, you can get homemade pasta and choose from a wine list as extensive as the menu. This lofty place inspires some to dress up and make a reservation, but you're also welcome to drop by just for a drink and enjoy the view. Outdoor seating is directly above the water. You can spend a moderate amount downstairs here—a lot more upstairs. There is another **Fish Market** Restaurant in Del Mar at 640 Via de la Valle (☎ **619/755-2277**).

MODERATE

○ Dakota Grill and Spirits

901 Fifth Ave. (at E St.). ☎ **619/234-5554.** Reservations recommended. Main courses $9–$18. AE, DC, DISC, MC, V. Mon–Fri 11:30am–2:30pm; Mon–Thurs 5–10pm, Fri–Sat 5–11pm, Sun 5–9pm. Valet parking (after 5pm) $5; self-parking in the area $7. Bus: 1, 3, 25, or 945. Trolley: Gaslamp Quarter. AMERICAN/SOUTHWESTERN.

If you like art and artifacts from the American Southwest, you'll find the interior decor of Dakota's very appealing. Dried flower arrangements in pint-size black leather cowboy boots grace every table, and a large painting of cowgirls hangs on the second floor. Since its opening, Dakota's has been a nonsmoking restaurant and bar. Little

To See . . . Perchance to Eat

Incredible ocean views, a sweeping skyline, and sailboats fluttering along the shore-line—it's the classic backdrop for a memorable meal. So where can you find the best views? Downtown, the **Fish Market** and its pricier cousin **Top of the Market** overlook San Diego Bay, and the management provides binoculars for getting a good look at aircraft carriers and other vessels. Across the harbor in Coronado, the **Bay Beach Cafe** offers a panoramic view of the San Diego skyline. In Pacific Beach, **The Green Flash** is just steps from the sand, and the **Firehouse Beach Cafe's** lofty dining deck provides another perspective of the same scene. Nearby, **The Atoll** in the Catamaran Resort Hotel faces tranquil Mission Bay. In La Jolla, **George's at the Cove** and **Top O' the Cove** are near the water, but **Brockton Villa** actually offers the La Jolla Cove as advertised on every postcard stand in town.

handguns on the menu indicate the most popular items, which include shrimp *tasso* (sautéed with Tasso Cajun ham and sweet peas in an ancho chili cream), spit-roasted chicken with orange chipotle glaze or Dakota barbecue sauce, and the mixed grill served with roasted garlic and grilled red potatoes. Dakota won the 1994 and 1995 Gold Medallion Award for Best American Cuisine. A pianist plays weekend nights.

○ Fio's

801 Fifth Ave. (at F St.). ☎ **619/234-3467.** Reservations recommended for dinner. Main courses $8.95–$21.95. AE, DC, DISC, MC, V. Mon–Fri 11:30am–3pm; Mon–Thurs 5–11pm, Fri–Sat 5pm–midnight, Sun 5–10pm. Valet parking (after 5pm) $6 with validation. Trolley: Gaslamp Quarter. NORTHERN ITALIAN.

Elegant and usually filled to overflowing, this see-and-be-seen spot is best known for its *tutto mare* black linguine with seafood. For lunch, which is geared to business folk in a hurry, choices include antipasti, pizza, calzones, and *panini* (Italian sandwiches)—those who arrive after 1pm won't have to wait as long to get seated. The dinner menu features pasta, meat, and seafood dishes, and the bar and cocktail areas serve a full menu. All pastas may be ordered in half portions. This is the Gaslamp's hottest spot, but unlike most trendy hangouts, it offers great value. Highly recommended.

Osteria Panevino

722 Fifth Ave. (between F and G sts.). ☎ **619/595-7959.** Reservations recommended. Main courses $8.95–$19.95. AE, CB, DC, DISC, MC, V. Sun–Thurs 11:30am–10pm, Fri–Sat 11:30am–11:30pm. ITALIAN.

This is still one of the most popular Italian restaurants in town, but on my last visit the Chianti was warm and the TV was blaring over the bar. Many locals are still loyal—they probably had better luck than I did. The decidedly unself-conscious atmosphere is reminiscent of a Tuscan farmhouse, with ceramics and large terra-cotta tiles from Italy; old wine barrels are stacked in a rear alcove. Other nice touches include a mural of Florence opposite the bar, picture windows looking onto the street, high ceilings, good lighting (you can actually see your food), and a brick oven that turns out pizzas. For antipasto, consider the assorted marinated vegetables with prosciutto, fresh mozzarella, and tomatoes; fried squid and parsley; or bite-size mozzarella in prosciutto, baked over sautéed spinach. More than a dozen dishes feature homemade pasta. Fish and meat dishes include veal medaillons topped with French string beans, smoked mozzarella, and tomato bruschetta; grilled boneless chicken with diced vegetables, crushed red pepper, and drizzled with olive oil and rosemary; and poached salmon fillet with wild mushrooms, carrots, and pine nuts in white-wine sauce. My favorite dish is the spinach ravioli. The atmosphere is very cozy, or crowded, depending on how close you like to be to your fellow diners.

Panda Inn

Horton Plaza (top floor). ☎ **619/233-7800.** Reservations recommended. Main courses $7.75–$18.25. AE, DC, DISC, JCB, MC, V. Sun–Thurs 11am–10pm, Fri–Sat 11am–10:30pm. Bus: 1, 2, 3, 25, 34, or 34A. Trolley: America Plaza. CHINESE.

Elegant and sophisticated, this restaurant beautifully displays modern art, Chinese pottery, and other interesting forms of Chinese art. The back dining area (one of three) looks out onto the city; a lounge offers a full bar. The varied menu features seasonal specials and Mandarin and Szechuan dishes, including sweet-and-pungent shrimp, lemon scallops, honey walnut shrimp, and enoki-mushroom chicken. Complete dinners, a real bargain at about $10, include soup, fried rice, an egg roll, fried shrimp, a main course, tea, and cookies.

Planet Hollywood

197 Horton Plaza. ☎ **619/702-STAR** (7827). Reservations not accepted. Main courses $6.50–$17.95. AE, DC, JCB, MC, V. Daily 11am–1am. Horton Plaza Garage parking; 3 hr. free with validation. Bus: 1, 2, 3, 25, 34, or 34A. Trolley: America Plaza. CALIFORNIA/AMERICAN.

Twenty thousand gawkers gathered here in March 1995, when this Planet Hollywood—number 19 in the chain—opened. They came to see the celebrity shareholders—Arnold Schwarzenegger, Bruce Willis, Sylvester Stallone, and Demi Moore—frolic with their celebrity friends. Today, folks stand in line for a turn to eat here and ogle the movie memorabilia. Glass cases contain more than 300 objects, including an Animatronic owl from *Indiana Jones and the Temple of Doom,* Roddy McDowell's costume from *Planet of the Apes,* and a submachine gun from *Die Hard.* This noisy, friendly, thoroughly enjoyable place is understandably popular with families. Menu items include pizza, pasta, burgers, sandwiches, salads, and a handful of light California cuisine choices—on a recent visit I thoroughly enjoyed grilled salmon served on a bed of trendy salad greens, atop a crisp pizza crust. Kids can drink a "Home Alone" (an ice-cold combination of strawberry, banana, and grenadine), an "E.T." (grapefruit and orange juice topped with soda), or a "Predator" (pineapple, ginger ale, and grenadine). The wait staff regularly hands out free movie posters and passes. If you don't relish standing in line, be there at 11am when they open, between 2 and 5pm, or after 9pm. There's an adjacent retail outlet.

INEXPENSIVE

✪ Cafe Lulu

419 F St. (near Fourth Ave.). ☎ **619/238-0114.** Main courses $2.95–$6.75. No credit cards. Sun–Thurs 9am–2am, Fri and Sat 9am–4am. Trolley: Gaslamp Quarter. INTERNATIONAL.

Light fare at this sparsely decorated coffeehouse runs the gamut from Brie or pizza baguettes to bagels to croissants to quiche to lasagne. Look for the chalkboard specials and soup of the day. With regard to drinks, the emphasis is on coffee, but you can also get tea, natural soda, Aqua Libra, sarsaparilla, and beer or wine by the glass or bottle. Imported and microbrewery beers are also served here. Open quite late, Cafe Lulu is centrally located and particularly popular with students.

Filippi's Pizza Grotto

1747 India St. (between Date and Fir sts. in Little Italy). ☎ **619/232-5095.** Fax 619/695-8591. Main courses $4.75–$12.50. AE, DC, DISC, MC, V. Mon–Sat 11am–11pm, Sun 11am–10pm. Free parking. Bus: 5. Trolley: County Center/Little Italy. ITALIAN.

🅜 Family-Friendly Restaurants

Planet Hollywood *(see p. 84)* Your kids can sip a "Home Alone" while they drink in the decor, which includes more than 300 pieces of movie memorabilia.

Galaxy Grill *(see p. 85)* The waitresses make a big deal out of small fry, and the menu items, a throwback to soda fountain days, are fun.

Old Spaghetti Factory *(see p. 86)* Kids get special attention, even their own toys. There's a special play area for them, too.

Hard Rock Cafe *(see p. 100)* Besides the great burgers, salads, and sandwiches, the family can also enjoy the wide range of rock memorabilia exhibited here. The casual atmosphere, blaring music, and friendly staff will make the kids feel right at home.

Corvette Diner *(see p. 88)* Resembling a 1950s diner, this place appeals to teens and preteens. Parents will have fun reminiscing about *their* teen years, and the kids will enjoy the burgers and fries or other short-order fare, served in sock-hop surroundings.

Souplantation *(see p. 94)* Kids can build their own salad, choose from a selection of soups, get slices of pizza, add various toppings to baked potatoes and nachos, and create their own dessert.

Filippi's Pizza Grotto *(see p. 84)* Children's portions are available, and kids will feel right at home here. There are 15 pizza varieties to choose from.

To get to one of the half-dozen dining areas decorated with Chianti bottles, you have to walk through an Italian grocery store/deli strewn with cheeses, pastas, wines, bottles of olive oil, and salamis. You might even end up eating behind shelves of canned olives, but don't feel bad—this has been the tradition since 1950, when the place opened. Choose from more than 15 pizzas (including a vegetarian variety) and the requisite pasta dishes. Children's portions are available, and kids will feel right at home here. The original of a dozen stores, this Filippi's has free parking; other locations are in Pacific Beach, Kearny Mesa, East Mission Valley, and Escondido, among others.

Galaxy Grill

Horton Plaza (top level). ☎ **619/234-7211.** Main courses $3.50–$6.50. AE, DISC, MC, V. Sun 11am–8pm, Mon–Thurs 11am–9pm, Fri–Sat 11am–10pm. Bus: 2, 7, 9, 29, 34, or 35. 3-hr. free parking with validation. Trolley: America Plaza. AMERICAN/DINER.

The freewheeling atmosphere and waitresses make you feel most welcome. You can still get two songs for a quarter on the jukebox, and the menu is pure soda-fountain. Remember the last time you had a cherry Coke or a malted? Fare includes burgers, supersonic chili, grilled-cheese sandwiches, tuna melts, shakes, and sundaes. Coffee comes leaded or unleaded, and they serve beer.

✪ Grand Central Cafe

500 W. Broadway (in YMCA building). ☎ **619/234-CAFE** (2233). Main courses $5.25–$6.95. AE, DISC, MC, V. Mon–Fri 7am–2pm, Sat–Sun 7am–1pm. Closed Thanksgiving and Christmas. Bus: 2, 7, 9, 29, 34, or 35. Trolley: America Plaza. AMERICAN.

This good-value spot located around the corner from the Santa Fe Station has a train theme: The "Main Line" fare includes Philly steak & cheese, Cape Cod battered fish, and roasted eggplant with grilled herbs and peppers. The "Soup Station" offers beef stew, chili, and clam chowder. The "Caboose" includes homemade cobblers and strawberry shortcake. The cafe serves wine and beer, and it's an inviting spot to read the paper or write home. You might also pick up a picnic here to enjoy on the train to LA. The dining room is sunny and cheerful, with high ceilings and tall arched windows looking onto Broadway. The Grand Central Cafe is popular with families because portions are large and prices low. When it gets busy, especially at lunch, service can slow down.

Kansas City Barbecue

610 W. Market St. ☎ **619/231-9680.** Reservations taken only for large parties. Main courses $8.75–$11.50. MC, V. Daily 11am–1am. Trolley: Seaport Village. AMERICAN.

Part of Kansas City Barbecue's honky-tonk mystique derives from the fact that the bar scene in the movie *Top Gun* was filmed here. The walls are covered with county-fair memorabilia, old car tags from Kansas, *Top Gun* posters, and a photograph of official bar wench Carry Nation. The star of the menu is the barbecue, slow-cooked over an open fire and served with sliced white bread and your choice of coleslaw, beans, fries, onion rings, potato salad, or corn on the cob. The food is okay, but the atmosphere is the real draw. It's kitty-corner to the Hyatt Regency Hotel.

Karl Strauss Brewery & Grill, Downtown

1157 Columbia St. (between B and C sts.). ☎ **619/234-BREW** (2739). Main courses $7–$15. MC, V. Sun–Wed 11:30am–10pm (beer and wine until 11pm), Thurs–Sat 11:30am–midnight (beer and wine until 1am). Bus: 5. Trolley: America Plaza. AMERICAN.

This is an actual brewery where you can see the stainless-steel vats from your seat at the bar and taste some of the outstanding beers, lagers, and ales made on the premises. (They're best known for the amber lager.) Five-ounce samplers are 85¢ each, and eight to nine choices are available on any given day. The "Taster Eight" costs $5.95. There's also nonalcoholic beer and wine by the glass. The menu includes Creole sausage gumbo, beer-battered fish-and-chips, and a pesto turkey sandwich served warm on focaccia, as well as old favorites such as burgers and salads. Beer-related memorabilia and brewery tours are available (for more information, see "Pitcher This: San Diego's Microbreweries," in chapter 10).

✪ Mandarin House

2604 Fifth Ave. (at Maple). ☎ **619/232-1101.** Reservations accepted. Most main courses $6.50–$10. AE, DC, MC, V. Mon–Thurs 11am–10pm, Fri 11am–11pm, Sat noon–11pm, Sun 2–10pm. CHINESE.

San Diego's most popular Chinese restaurant, Mandarin House has won many awards. My favorite dish is the kung pao chicken; not spicy, but just as delicious, is the moo-shu pork. If you expect the usual Chinese-red decor, you'll be surprised by the pleasant sea-foam-and-peach color scheme. Mandarin House also has locations in La Jolla (6765 La Jolla Blvd.) and Pacific Beach (1820 Garnet Ave.).

✪ Old Spaghetti Factory

275 Fifth Ave. (at K St.). ☎ **619/233-4323.** Main courses $4.25–$8.10. DISC, MC, V. Mon–Thurs 11:30am–10pm, Fri 11:30am–10pm, Sat–Sun noon–10pm. Bus: 1. Trolley: Gaslamp Quarter. ITALIAN.

It's lively and it's a great deal—no wonder folks are always waiting on the overstuffed divans inside or the benches outside for their names to be called. For the price of a main course, you also get salad, sourdough bread, ice cream, and coffee or tea with refills. Wine is available by the glass or decanter. The restaurant, housed in what used to be a printing company, has creative seating; some people even dine inside a 1917 trolley car. The decor is lavish early bordello, and the service is cordial. There's a small play area for kids.

The Princess Pub & Grille

1675 India St. (at Date St.). ☎ **619/702-3021.** Main courses $8.95. DISC, MC, V. Daily 11:30am–1am. Bus: 5. Trolley: Santa Fe Depot. ENGLISH.

This local haunt is great for Anglophiles and others hungry for a ploughman's plate, Cornish pasty, steak-and-kidney pie, fish-and-chips, and bangers in hefty portions. Photos and commemorative plates of Princess Diana hang everywhere, along with flags from the motherland, a well-worn dart board, and a photo of the Queen Mother downing a pint; you can usually find a copy of the *Union Jack* (a newspaper published in the U.S. for British expatriates), too. Among the English beers available are Bass and Watney's. For a taste of Ireland, they also serve Guinness. They have hard Devon cider, too. Friday and Saturday nights are particularly busy. There's takeout during the day.

4 Hillcrest/Uptown

Hillcrest and Uptown are filled with reasonably priced ethnic restaurants and inexpensive mom-and-pop spots offering down-home cooking. Many are within walking distance of Balboa Park, and plans are in the works for a new restaurant called **Terrace on the Prado,** which will be located in the park itself in the House of Hospitality (☎ **619/236-1935**), to open by the end of 1997. For some reason, their management is being quite secretive prior to opening, but rumor has it that a Southwestern menu is in the works.

EXPENSIVE

✪ Laurel

505 Laurel St. (at Fifth Ave.). ☎ **619/239-2222.** Reservations recommended. Main courses $14–$19. AE, DISC, MC, V. Sun–Thurs 5–10pm, Fri–Sat 5–11pm. SOUTHERN FRENCH AND MEDITERRANEAN.

This relatively new restaurant is especially popular with theatergoers: it's close to the Old Globe and offers shuttle service. Diners park at Laurel, enjoy their main meal, take the shuttle to the theater, and then come back for an after-performance dessert. (The $2.50 per person for the shuttle is applied to the cost of the dessert.) I've also dined here after an especially long opera when most other options were closed.

   The sophisticated decor is gorgeous. The food is also wonderful. The plethora of appetizers is a godsend to people like me who love to graze. Some of the more popular petite portions include eggplant ravioli in a roasted-tomato-and-black-olive jus, house-cured duck-breast prosciutto, and warm caramelized onion and Roquefort tart. Main courses include crisp Muscovy duck confit, pan-roasted veal sweetbreads in black-olive sauce, and grilled salmon with herb-crusted fingerling potatoes.

MODERATE

✪ Arrivederci Italian Restaurant

3845 Fourth Ave. (between Robinson and University). ☎ **619/299-6282.** Reservations recommended. Main courses $7.50–$14.50. AE, MC, V. Mon–Fri 11:30am–2:30pm, Sat noon–2:30pm; Mon–Thurs 5–10pm, Fri–Sat 5–11pm, Sun noon–10pm. Bus: 1 or 3. ITALIAN.

Rough plaster and exposed brick walls, tile floors, wooden tables, and numerous wine racks give Arrivederci an authentic Italian feel. The food is wonderful, and my assistant, Suzanne, personally recommends the La Divina Ceasare (Caesar Salad), Fettuccine Bel Paese (fettuccine, tossed with a wild-mushroom-and-brandy sauce), and Penne Arrabbiate (penne pasta with julienne chicken breast in spicy tomato sauce). The ravioli, lasagne, and gnocchi change daily and are all solid choices. The portions here are quite large, making Arrivederci a good value, as well. But be sure to save room for the tiramisu, which was the best Suzanne has had this side of the Atlantic. You'll also find a great cup of cappuccino or espresso here. They have a full bar and also offer outdoor seating.

Celadon

3628 Fifth Ave. (between Brooks and Pennsylvania). ☎ **619/295-8800.** Reservations recommended on weekends. Main courses $8.50–$14.50. AE, MC, V. Mon–Fri 11:30am–1pm, Sat 5–10pm. Bus: 1 or 3. THAI.

A modern place decorated in hues of pink and rose, Celadon serves specialties such as shrimp in a spicy, creamy coconut sauce; sautéed scallops in "burnt" sauce with a touch of garlic; a pineapple boat filled with rice, chicken, pineapple, and Chinese sausage; and Bua Sawan, shrimp, chicken, and cashews served in lotus-shaped leaves. Popular appetizers include Poo Ja, deep-fried pork and crabmeat; Goong Sarong, shrimp wrapped in noodles and deep-fried; and satay, meat on a skewer. Statues and pots from Thailand are displayed throughout the restaurant. The gold, red, and green outfit displayed in the entrance is the costume of a Thai classical dancer. Service is friendly, and there are plenty of eating nooks from which to choose.

Hob Nob Hill

2271 First Ave. (at Juniper). ☎ **619/239-8176.** Breakfast and lunch $3.25–$8.25; dinner $8–$14. AE, DISC, MC, V. Daily 7am–9pm. Bus: 1 or 3. AMERICAN.

Consider this your kitchen away from home, as do many professional and retired San Diegans. It's been serving up home-style cooking since 1944, and some of the waitresses have been greeting patrons here for 30 years. Everything is made from scratch, and the rolls are tops. The large breakfast menu includes eggs (from fried to Florentine), pancakes, waffles, and heartier fare like beef hash; there's even champagne by the glass (pretty fancy for a mom-and-pop place). Lunch features sandwiches, salads, and meat or fish meals; dinner, old-fashioned chicken and dumplings, roast turkey, prime rib, turkey croquettes, and a vegetarian plate. A children's menu is available.

Liaison

2202 Fourth Ave. (at Ivy). ☎ **619/234-5540.** Main courses $10.75–$19.75. AE, CB, DC, DISC, MC, V. Tues–Sun 5–10:30pm. Bus: 1 or 3. FRENCH.

The cuisine and decor hark back to the French countryside in this cozy little cafe with stone walls, blue-and-white tablecloths, candles on the tables, and copper pots hanging from the rafters. The fixed-price dinner is a great deal, since the meal includes pâté, salad or soup, a main course, and dessert. The lunch menu features salads, including warm duck salad with balsamic vinaigrette and shrimp-and-avocado salad; pastas such as homemade crab ravioli in lobster sauce; and three fresh-fish dishes daily. At dinner you can choose from lamb curry, medaillons of pork or beef, coquilles St. Jacques, roast duckling à l'orange, salmon with crayfish butter, and more. The house specialty dessert costs extra: a Grand Marnier chocolate or amaretto soufflé for two, at $5 per person. Ooh la la!

INEXPENSIVE

Corvette Diner

3946 Fifth Ave. (between Washington and University). ☎ **619/542-1001.** Reservations not accepted. Main courses $4.50–$9.95. AE, DC, DISC, MC, V. Sun–Thurs 11am–10pm, Fri–Sat 11am–midnight. Free weekday valet parking; evening and weekend valet $4. Bus: 1 or 3. AMERICAN.

The slightly faded facade lets you know you're in for something a little unusual: a trompe l'oeil painting of a cafe with a giant female strolling across the roof. Inside, the decor is art deco, with a sleek Corvette as the centerpiece. Portraits of popular singers by local artist Gina Falk—from the Beatles to Connie Francis—fill the walls. Do pay your respects to Norma Jean. The menu features burgers, sandwiches, and other diner fare. Besides the old-fashioned soda fountain, there's a full bar. At night, a DJ plays your requests; on Tuesday and Wednesday evenings, a magician performs, an 8-year tradition. This is a fun place with a young crowd, and it's great for kids; expect a line on weekends.

✪ Extraordinary Desserts

2929 Fifth Ave. (between Palm and Quince). ☎ **619/294-7001.** Desserts $1.75–$4.95. MC, V. Mon–Thurs 8:30am–11pm, Fri 8:30am–midnight, Sat 11am–midnight, Sun 2–11pm. DESSERTS.

This cute place is one of the only dessert shops in town. Fresh flowers top small tables in a contemporary gardenlike setting. More seating is available on the outdoor patio. Owner and chef Karen Krasne earned a Certificate de Patisserie from the Cordon Bleu School in Paris. Everything is made fresh on the premises daily. Passion fruit ricotta torte, cherry chocolate-chip cookies, and 24kt chocolate praline *daquoise* are especially popular. Daquoise consists of crunchy chocolate praline mousse between chocolate cakes and hazelnut meringues, soaked with frangelico and covered in dark chocolate.

Pannikin Hillcrest

523 University Ave. ☎ **619/295-1600.** Menu items $1.25–$5. AE, MC, V. Sun–Thurs 7:30am–11pm, Fri–Sat 7:30am–midnight. Bus: 1 or 3. COFFEEHOUSE/LIGHT FARE.

This no-smoking-inside coffeehouse, with monthly exhibits by local artists, is strewn with newspapers and people at leisure. Coffee is always on tap, even iced cappuccino, along with muffins, English scones, and desserts. There's also light fare such as lasagne, quiche, curry rolls, and cheeses. There's a cozy upstairs seating area. Note the subtle door decor. Smoking is permitted on the patio.

✪ The Vegetarian Zone

2949 Fifth Ave. (between Palm and Quince). ☎ **619/298-7302** (deli/takeout 619/298-9232). Reservations not accepted. Main courses $6.50–$9.50. DISC, MC, V. Mon–Thurs 11:30am–9pm, Fri 11:30am–10pm, Sat 8:30am–10pm, Sun 8:30am–9pm; deli, daily 10am–10pm. Bus: 34 or 34A. VEGETARIAN.

Around since 1975, San Diego's top vegetarian spot offers an extensive menu, from stuffed grape leaves and tofu dishes to quesadillas and garden burgers. Drinks include iced sun tea, fruit smoothies, and wine by the glass. On Saturdays and Sundays, brunch is served until 1pm. There is indoor and outdoor seating, and the adjacent vegetarian deli provides take-out service. This peaceful place is filled with plants and soothing music. Parking is available.

5 Old Town, Hotel Circle & Beyond

Visitors to San Diego should try to experience at least one meal in the Old Town area—Mexican food and bathtub-size margaritas are the big draw, as are mariachi music and the colorful decor.

EXPENSIVE

Brigantine Seafood Grill

2444 San Diego Ave. ☎ **619/298-9840.** Reservations recommended on weekends. Main courses $7.95–29.95; early-bird special $10–$14. AE, CB, DC, MC, V. Mon–Thurs 11am–10:30pm, Fri–Sat 11am–11pm, Sun 10am–10:30pm. Bus: 4 or 5/105. SEAFOOD.

The Brigantine is best known for its oyster-bar happy hour from 4 to 7pm (until 9:30pm on Mondays), when beer, margaritas, and food are heavily discounted, and you can expect standing-room only. Early-bird specials are offered on Sunday through Thursday from 5 to 7pm; the dinners include seafood, steak, or chicken served with several side dishes and baked bread. Inside, the decor is upscale and nautical; outside, there's a pleasant patio with a fireplace to take the chill off the night air. At lunch, you can get everything from crab cakes or fish-and-chips to fresh fish or pasta. Lunch specials come with sourdough bread and two side dishes. The bar and oyster bar are open daily until midnight.

Cafe Pacifica

2414 San Diego Ave. ☎ **619/291-6666.** Reservations recommended. Main courses $15–$26. AE, DC, MC, V. Mon–Fri 11:30am–2pm; Mon–Sat 5:30–10pm, Sun 5:30–9:30pm. Bus: 4 or 5/105. CALIFORNIA.

The framework of an old house provides a unique backdrop here; the walls and rafters are painted white and the beams are accented with tiny white lights. Mirrors add more twinkle, and latticework and candles on the tables add to the charm. Among the temptations on the menu are grilled shrimp cocktail with spicy Chinese mustard; oysters on the half shell; and Dungeness-crab salad with papaya, avocado, and endive—and these are just for starters. Main courses include saffron linguine with rock shrimp, clams, mussels, and calamari; herb-crusted sea bass; and lamb chops with tomatoes, sweet garlic, and mint pesto. The signature dish is Hawaiian ahi with shiitake mushrooms and ginger butter. Patrons tend to dress up, though it's not required. To avoid the crowds, arrive in the early evening. A two-course "Prix" Theater Dinner is served between 5:30 and 6:30pm and costs $16.40.

MODERATE

Casa de Bandini

Opposite Old Town Plaza, Old Town. ☎ **619/297-8211.** Reservations not accepted. Main courses $5.50–$14. AE, DC, MC, V. Daily 11am–9pm. Bus: 4 or 5/105. MEXICAN.

An Old Town tradition complete with mariachi music on weekends, this lively restaurant—with its appealing balcony and courtyard—fills the nooks and crannies of an adobe hacienda. The house was built in 1823 for Juan Bandini, once a merchant and politician in these parts; later, with a second floor added, it became a hotel. Today it's the scene of many a happy repast over dishes like crab enchiladas, chicken-and-avocado salad, crab brochette with mild green chilies, and jumbo cod fillet with sautéed vegetables. Some of the dishes are gourmet Mexican, others simple south-of-the-border fare; you'll never run short of refried beans, guacamole, or jumbo margaritas. The history attached to the actual house makes the restaurant extra special.

INEXPENSIVE

Casa de Pico

Bazaar del Mundo, Old Town. ☎ **619/296-3267.** Reservations not accepted. Main courses $5–$14. AE, DC, MC, V. Sun–Thurs 10am–9pm, Fri–Sat 10am–9:30pm. Bus: 4 or 5/105. MEXICAN.

The heartbeat of Bazaar del Mundo, Casa de Pico has a carnival atmosphere and a colorful courtyard complete with fountain, flags and umbrellas, and mariachis and guitarists who will serenade your table on request. The restaurant sits on the original site of the home of General Pío Pico, the last governor of Mexican California. Flowers and birds are stenciled in primary colors on the white walls, and ceiling beams

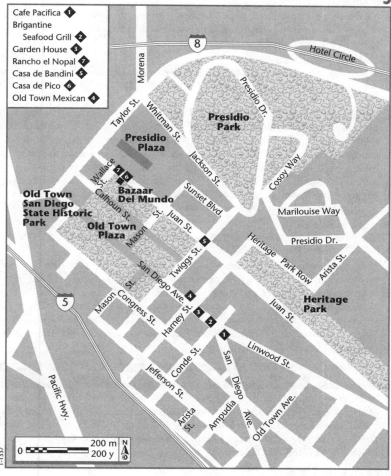

Cafe Pacifica ❶
Brigantine
  Seafood Grill ❷
Garden House ❸
Rancho el Nopal ❼
Casa de Bandini ❺
Casa de Pico ❻
Old Town Mexican ❹

Presidio Park

Hotel Circle

Morena

Taylor St.

Whitman St.

Presidio Dr.

Presidio Plaza

Jackson St.

Cosoy Way

Old Town
San Diego
State Historic
Park

Wallace St.

Calhoun St.

Bazaar
Del Mundo

Sunset Blvd.

Marilouise Way

Old Town
Plaza

Mason St.

Juan St.

Presidio Dr.

Heritage Park Row

Arista St.

Twiggs St.

San Diego Ave.

Heritage
Park

Mason St.

Congress St.

Harney St.

Juan St.

Conde St.

Linwood St.

San Diego Ave.

Old Town Ave.

Pacific Hwy.

Jefferson St.

Arista St.

Ampudia St.

0   200 m
      200 y   N

1-1337

are bright yellow and orange. The extensive and daunting menu includes a diagrammed explanation of the Mexican dishes. A popular selection is the Mexican sampler, called La Especial de Juan, with chimichangas, enchiladas, and fajitas. You can also get some health-conscious choices like chicken fajita salad or black-bean burritos. The guacamole is good, but the chips can be greasy. Breakfast is served all day. To avoid standing in line for a table, try coming here before 5pm or after 8pm Sunday through Thursday.

Garden House Coffee & Tea

2480 San Diego Ave. ☎ **619/220-0723.** Menu items $1–$3. No credit cards. Mon–Thurs 7am–6pm, Fri–Sat 7am–9pm, Sun 7am–7:30pm (shorter hours in winter). Bus: 4 or 5/105. COFFEE SHOP.

Set off San Diego Avenue along a brick walkway beside the Whaley House, this gourmet coffee-and-tea shop in an old wooden house is always good for a cup of fresh-brewed coffee (any variation or size). You get 10¢ off if you bring your own cup the way the locals do; refills are half price. Muffins and pastries are also available. While it's mostly a take-out place, there are a few chairs on the porch and some benches nearby. This is a great place to rest in the shade of the wizened pepper trees. It's next to the Old Town Drug Store Museum.

✪ Old Town Mexican Cafe

2489 San Diego Ave. ☎ **619/297-4330.** Reservations accepted for groups of 10 or more. Main courses $7.50–$11.50. AE, DISC, MC, V. Sun–Thurs 7am–11pm, Fri–Sat 7am–midnight; bar service until 2am. Bus: 4 or 5/105. MEXICAN.

This place is so popular it's almost an Old Town tourist attraction in its own right. Most folks are lured by the sight of tortillas being handmade and whole chickens roasting right in the window. Inside is a maze of booths and tables, as well as a patio and banquet room. There are two bars, one inside and one on the patio. The most popular dishes are *carnitas*—the traditional Mexican dish of deep-fried pork served with tortillas, guacamole, sour cream, beans and rice, and rotisserie chicken, but you'll also find all your Mexican favorites. Patrons usually wait a half hour to be seated at lunch and up to an hour at dinner, but nobody seems to mind.

Rancho el Nopal

Bazaar del Mundo, Old Town. ☎ **619/295-0584.** Main courses $5–$9. AE, DC, DISC, MC, V. Daily 11am–9pm. Bus: 4 or 5/105. MEXICAN.

This place is saturated with color—from the swirling skirts of the waitresses, to the tiny sparkling lights in the ivy hanging over the bar. A glass of iced tea is big enough to serve the whole family, and you get chips and salsa with every meal. Of the many Mexican dishes to choose from, the chicken fajita salad is popular. The decor is pure south-of-the-border, with indoor and outdoor dining. There's also a kids' menu. "We're here to catch the spillover from Pico," my waitress told me. And spill over they do. It's next door to park headquarters.

6 Mission Bay, Pacific Beach & Beyond

This is a popular area for diners who want a view of the water. Additional locations of several restaurants described elsewhere in this chapter are also in the Mission Bay/Pacific Beach area: **Mandarin House,** at 1820 Garnet St., in Pacific Plaza, Pacific Beach (☎ **619/273-2288**); and **Filippi's Pizza Grotto,** at 962 Garnet St., Pacific Beach (☎ **619/483-6222**).

EXPENSIVE

The Atoll

3999 Mission Blvd. (in the Catamaran Resort Hotel), Pacific Beach. ☎ **619/488-1081.** Reservations recommended for Sun brunch. Main courses $16–$20; Sun brunch $22.95. AE, CB, DC, DISC, MC, V. Sun–Thurs 6:30am–10pm, Fri–Sat 6:30am–11pm. Valet parking $7; free self-parking with validation. Bus: 34 or 34A. CALIFORNIA.

While the food is gourmet, you can always count on a burger or sandwich here. Among the appetizers are spicy crab cakes with lime and ginger-butter sauce; lamb ravioli on ratatouille or spinach salad; and vine-ripened tomatoes with mozzarella, olive oil, and basil. Main courses include grilled sea bass, salmon, tenderloin, veal chops, and broiled lamb chops or swordfish. To add to the restaurant's pleasant yet casual ambiance, fresh flowers grace the linen tablecloths. There are nightly specials, and the wine list features selections from France, Italy, Germany, and California. Sunday brunch, served from 10am to 2pm, comes with unlimited champagne. The service is friendly. You can dine on the bay-front patio (weather permitting).

Dining in Mission Bay, Pacific Beach & Beyond

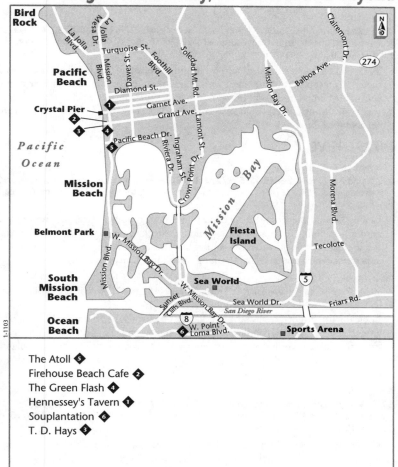

The Atoll **5**
Firehouse Beach Cafe **2**
The Green Flash **4**
Hennessey's Tavern **1**
Souplantation **6**
T. D. Hays **3**

MODERATE

The Green Flash

701 Thomas Ave. (at Mission Blvd.), Pacific Beach. ☎ **619/270-7715.** Reservations recommended. Main courses $10–$20. AE, DC, DISC, MC, V. Mon–Thurs 8am–9:30pm, Fri 8am–10pm, Sat 7:30am–10pm, Sun 7:30am–9:30pm. Bus: 34 or 34A. SEAFOOD/INTERNATIONAL.

You can spend as much or as little as you choose in this place; the menu caters to a variety of budgets and hankerings. It's known for its fresh fish, but you may also order steaks and prime rib, steak-and-seafood combos, chicken dishes, or burgers. Or simply make a meal of appetizers: fresh oysters, steamed clams, shrimp cocktail, and ceviche. Salads and sandwiches are available at lunch, and there are $9.95 sunset dinner specials Sunday through Thursday from 5 to 7pm. The outdoor tables here are prime real estate, especially when the sky begins to blush. The ambiance couldn't be livelier. Ask your waitperson to explain how the restaurant got its name.

T. D. Hays

4315 Ocean Blvd. (at Grand Ave.), 2nd floor, Pacific Beach. ☎ **619/270-6850.** Reservations recommended on weekends. Main courses $10–$20. AE, DISC, MC, V. Mon–Thurs 5–10pm, Fri–Sat 4:30–10pm, Sun 4–9pm. Bus: 34 or 34A. AMERICAN.

T. D. Hays is popular among locals for its prime rib and picture windows overlooking the sea. You can start off the meal with potato skins, sautéed mushrooms, or shrimp cocktail. Main courses—the prime rib, mesquite-broiled steaks and chicken, and a variety of shrimp dishes—come with bread and rice or a baked potato. You can also get a whole lobster.

INEXPENSIVE

Firehouse Beach Cafe

722 Grand Ave., Pacific Beach. ☎ **619/272-1999.** Reservations recommended on weekends. Main courses $8–$12. AE, DISC, MC, V. Sun–Thurs 7am–9pm, Fri–Sat 7am–10pm. Free parking. Bus: 34 or 34A. AMERICAN.

Ceiling fans stir the air in this cheerful, comfortably crowded place, and there's pleasant rooftop dining with an ocean view if you're lucky enough to snag a seat. Specialties are black-bean burritos, fish-and-chips, and lasagne. You can make a meal of appetizers, which are served all day long. A children's menu is available.

Hennessey's Tavern

4650 Mission Blvd. (at Emerald), Pacific Beach. ☎ **619/483-8847.** Menu items $5–$8. AE, MC, V. Daily 7am–2am. Bus: 34 or 34A. IRISH.

Look for the bright green and brick facade of this neighborhood pub that's been around since 1976. It's Irish through and through, even serving corned beef hash and eggs for breakfast. For lunch, try the hamburgers, steaks, and deli sandwiches; nightly specials include corned beef and cabbage, a homemade turkey dinner, and fish and chicken entrees.

Souplantation

3960 W. Point Loma Blvd., Point Loma. ☎ **619/222-7404.** Reservations not accepted. All-you-can-eat buffet $7.19. DC, DISC, MC, V. Sun–Thurs 11am–9pm, Fri–Sat 11am–10pm. VEGETARIAN.

Understandably popular with families, the Souplantation seems to have something for everyone. You can make your own salad from a huge assortment of ingredients, and there's a selection of serve-yourself soups. In addition to assorted rolls and breads, you can also help yourself to slices of pizza, baked potatoes with various toppings, and nachos. If you still have room, waddle up to the dessert bar where the serve-yourself frozen yogurt is a popular item. The atmosphere is light, bright, modern, and abuzz with chatter from boisterous families.

There is a similar restaurant, **The Soup Exchange,** at 1840 Garnet Ave., Pacific Beach (☎ **619/272-7766**).

7 La Jolla

Most of La Jolla's top restaurants are clustered along Prospect Street and Pearl Street in the village. However, a great Greek restaurant, **Aesop's Tables,** is located at 8650 Genesee Ave. in the Costa Verde shopping center near La Jolla Village Drive (☎ **619/455-1535**). "Sisters" of dining places described elsewhere in this chapter include **Mandarin House,** at 6765 La Jolla Blvd. (☎ **619/454-2555**) (bad rest rooms; get takeout) and the **Chart House,** at 1270 Prospect (☎ **619/459-8201**).

La Jolla Dining

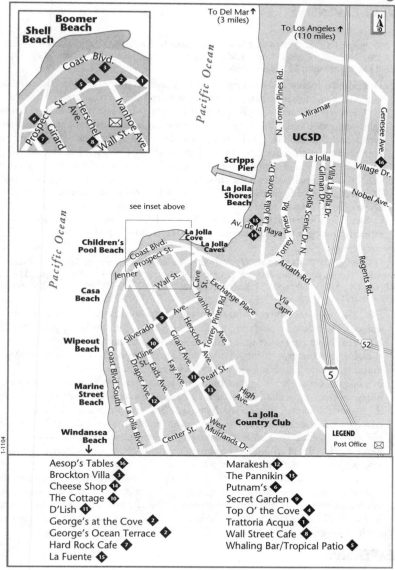

Aesop's Tables 16
Brockton Villa 3
Cheese Shop 14
The Cottage 10
D'Lish 11
George's at the Cove 2
George's Ocean Terrace 2
Hard Rock Cafe 7
La Fuente 15

Marakesh 12
The Pannikin 13
Putnam's 6
Secret Garden 9
Top O' the Cove 4
Trattoria Acqua 1
Wall Street Cafe 8
Whaling Bar/Tropical Patio 5

La Jolla also has a McDonald's, so small that it's named McSnack, on Prospect Street in the heart of town.

La Jolla restaurants don't serve very late. If you get hungry after the traditional dinner hour, head for **Karl Strauss Brewery & Grill** on Fay Street, where the kitchen stays open until 9pm Monday through Wednesday, 10pm on Thursday and Sunday, and 11pm on Friday and Saturday (see "Pitcher This: San Diego's Microbreweries" in chapter 10, for more information). The Hard Rock (see below) also serves late.

VERY EXPENSIVE

George's at the Cove

1250 Prospect St. ☎ **619/454-4244.** Reservations recommended. Main courses $17–$39.
AE, DC, DISC, MC, V. Mon–Thurs 11:30am–10pm, Fri–Sat 11:30am–11pm, Sun 11am–10pm.
Valet parking at night, $5. CALIFORNIA.

This popular local restaurant gets raves for its seafood dishes, creative pastas, ocean view, and great sunsets in summer. There are several seating areas in this lively place; the Garden Room and Wine Room are the quietest choices. For lunch, you can go light with a soup and salad or have one of the many seafood dishes. For dinner, start with steamed mussels or pâté de foie gras and proceed to the rack of lamb; sautéed venison chops with yam cakes; or mixed grill of shrimp, king salmon, and swordfish with three sauces. I absolutely adore the smoked chicken soup here, but on a recent visit I was disappointed with the chocolate soufflé-cake dessert (Chocoholics might do better getting a fix across the street at the Rocky Mountain Chocolate Factory). Owner George Hauer started out as a waiter in Pacific Beach and became a legend in San Diego's restaurant business. See below for the listing of George's less-expensive eating enterprise, George's Ocean Terrace and Café/Bar.

✪ Top O' the Cove

1216 Prospect St. ☎ **619/454-7779.** Web site: www.topofthecove.com. Reservations recommended. Jackets suggested for men at dinner. Main courses $25–$32; Sun brunch $18.50.
AE, CB, DC, MC, V. Mon–Sat 11:30am–10:30pm, Sun 10:30am–10:30pm. Valet parking $5.
CONTINENTAL.

San Diego magazine has voted this restaurant "the most romantic" for the past 9 years; Table 6, the most frequently requested table, is booked through the year 2000 for New Year's Eve. Any other time, call 2 to 3 weeks in advance to reserve it. If it's not available, don't worry—plenty of other tables have created their own share of magic in this restaurant, which opened in 1955. One of the prettiest restaurants anywhere, in a historic cottage with fig trees out front, it has fireplaces glowing on chilly evenings, an elegant circular bar upstairs, and a gazebo and patio for dining on balmy days—perfect, in fact, for Sunday champagne brunch. Lunch is on the light side—creative salads, pasta dishes, or a burger or club sandwich—while dinner is more lavish, with fish, duck, veal, lamb, and venison prepared and served quite elegantly. The house coffee is laced with Grand Marnier, crème de cacao, and amaretto. The dessert specialty, a bittersweet chocolate box filled with cream and fruit in a raspberry sauce, goes very nicely with the coffee. A computerized wine list keeps track of the 10,000 bottles in the cellar. Proprietor and community dynamo Ron Zappardino heads a stellar staff. If you're deciding between here and George's, both have excellent food. The difference is in the ambiance: Top O' the Cove is very cozy and old-world; George's is slicker.

EXPENSIVE

✪ Marakesh

634 Pearl St. (at Draper). ☎ **619/454-2500.** Main courses $15–$19.95; 5-course "feasts" $16.50–$23. AE, DC, DISC, MC, V. Sun–Thurs 5–10pm, Fri–Sat 5–11pm. MOROCCAN.

Diners get more than a meal here—they get a total experience. It starts when you're seated on cushions around a low table and your server washes your hands in traditional Moroccan style. The decor consists of colorful North African fabrics and objets d'art. I recommend ordering one of the feasts, a multicourse meal that starts with soup, salad, and *bastilla* (a wonderful pastry), and includes a choice of lemon chicken, lamb in honey sauce, or—my favorite—lamb couscous, the national Moroccan dish.

Java Joints in La Jolla

While cafes specializing in espresso, latte, and cappuccino have sprung up all over San Diego, no other area in the city caters to java hounds like La Jolla does. Here are descriptions of a few area coffeehouses that serve up caffeine as well as charm (they are plotted on the "La Jolla Dining" map).

My personal favorite is the **Wall Street Cafe,** at 1044 Wall St., between Girard and Herschel avenues (☎ 619/551-1044). I used to bank here, before the Security Pacific turned into a coffeehouse. Today the rest rooms are located in the old vault, so patrons who use the facilities must pass through the huge door that once secured much of La Jolla's money. I like this cafe for its visual appeal, friendly staff, and really good fare. The local businesspeople pop in for cups to go or for lunch, while the midmorning and afternoon crowd lingers a little longer and has time to sit and read the newspaper. Live entertainment, such as light jazz or a mellow guitar, makes this a particularly popular place on Friday and Saturday nights between 8pm and midnight. They serve beer and wine here also.

When it opened in 1968, the **Pannikin,** at 7467 Girard Ave., near Pearl (☎ 619/454-5453), was La Jolla's first coffeehouse, and, in some ways, it still seems like 1968 inside here. Long-haired men ponder chess moves on the porch, and the notice board tells of the next meditation seminar. This is a favored hangout of UCSD students and faculty. Inside the old house, the fireplace and communal seating are conducive to impromptu intellectual discussions. Some customers wander next door to D. G. Wills bookstore. The Pannikin's retail store across the street draws loyal locals.

At **The Secret Garden,** at 928 Silverado Ave., between Fay and Girard avenues (☎ 619/551-0928), the weekday customers are almost all regulars. Many work or work out nearby and, whether they're wearing ties or tights, the staff knows their names and their preferred drinks—it's like the "Cheers" of the local coffeehouse scene. This is a good choice for early risers: The official opening time is 7am, but locals know that they can get a fresh hot cup anytime after 6:15am. The weekend crowd consists mainly of shoppers taking a coffee break. (Stairs into the cottage may hinder access for travelers with disabilities.)

No matter where you enjoy your java, mind the time limit for your parking spot. La Jolla doesn't have meters, but street parking in the village is restricted to either 1 or 2 hours, and zealous parking-enforcement officers dole out tickets with great regularity.

Your feast concludes with fruit, pastry, and mint tea poured from a height of 3 feet. If you aren't up for all that, you can order a dinner, accompanied only by soup or salad and bastilla. Did I mention that Moroccan meals are eaten with your fingers, not knives and forks?

Putnam's Restaurant & Bar

In the Colonial Inn, 910 Prospect St. ☎ **619/454-2181.** Reservations recommended. Main courses $18–$23; early-bird specials $12.95 (daily 5–8pm). AE, CB, DC, MC, V. Mon–Fri 7–10am and 11am–2:30pm, Sat–Sun 7am–2:30pm; Sun–Thurs 5–10pm, Fri–Sat 5–11pm. Free valet parking. CALIFORNIA.

When the Colonial Inn was completed in 1928 it housed a drugstore named Putnam's, known in La Jolla as "Putty's." Gregory Peck's father was the pharmacist, and locals flocked there to buy their sundries and enjoy a soda. Today, that corner of the hotel is the site of Putnam's Restaurant, which retains an elegant, old-world atmosphere, complete with polished terrazzo floors, gleaming woodwork, brass fixtures, crisp white tablecloths, and fresh flowers. The dinner menu changes seasonally, but often contains grilled farm-raised chicken with honey-onion marmalade, grilled marinated duck breast with golden tomato-curry sauce, grilled Atlantic salmon fillet, and roasted rack of lamb with mustard herb crust. I always order the tasty lamb shanks when they're offered and have learned to avoid the salmon because the hot mustard is a little too spicy for my taste. This is also a popular spot for breakfast and weekend brunch.

○ Trattoria Acqua

1298 Prospect St., in Coast Walk, La Jolla. ☎ **619/454-0709.** Reservations recommended. Main courses $13–$22. AE, MC, V. Daily 11:30am–2:30pm; Sun–Thurs 5–9:30pm, Fri–Sat 5–10:30pm. ITALIAN.

Both the atmosphere and the food at this popular spot are reminiscent of the Mediterranean. Trattoria Acqua overlooks the Pacific, but doesn't offer the full view found farther down the street at places like George's. The menu here includes 10 different pastas and about half a dozen creative pizzas, but the real stars are the main courses. These include *saltimboca con funghi* (veal scaloppini with sage, prosciutto, and a forest-mushroom sauce), *cassoulet à la Toulousaine* (traditional Toulouse style cassoulet with duck confit, sausage, and braised lamb baked with white beans, tomato, and fresh thyme), and *salmone al pepe* (roasted peppercorn-crusted Atlantic salmon served over lentils with a sherry-and-shallot vinaigrette). The Mediterranean ambiance is created by the quarry tile patio, rough plaster walls, crisp white tablecloths—and, of course, the sea breeze. Seating is available both indoors and out.

The Whaling Bar/Tropical Patio

In La Valencia Hotel, 1132 Prospect St. (at Herschel Ave.). ☎ **619/454-0771.** Reservations recommended. Main courses $10–$15 at lunch, $11–$25 at dinner. AE, CB, DC, MC, V. Daily 11:30am–5pm and 6–10:30pm. CALIFORNIA.

In 1947, 21 years after the founding of La Valencia Hotel, the Whaling Bar became a permanent fixture here. For several decades, it was the haunt of movie stars such as Ginger Rogers and Charlton Heston, who came down from Los Angeles to perform at the La Jolla Playhouse. The bar feels like a club, filled with authentic New Bedford harpoons and lanterns, pewter candleholders, wooden shutters, scrimshaw displays, and whale murals by artist Wing Howard. The barrel clock behind the bar and the full-rigged sailing ship model were gifts from hotel devotees. At lunchtime, the Tropical Patio, at the hotel's entrance, is popular. The Mandarin chicken salad, duck quesadilla, and *carne asada* (grilled steak) are old standbys; and whatever you order, you can expect generous portions.

MODERATE

○ Brockton Villa

1235 Coast Blvd. (across from La Jolla Cove). ☎ **619/454-7393.** Reservations accepted (call by Thurs for Sun brunch). Breakfast $4–$7.25; dinner main courses $10–$18. AE, DISC, MC, V. Mon–Wed 8am–5pm, Thurs–Sun 8am–9pm (later in summer). Validated parking in Coast Walk Center. CALIFORNIA.

Located in a beach cottage that dates from 1894, Brockton Villa offers good food, a great view of the La Jolla Cove, and charming historic surroundings. The blue-and-white bungalow has a wooden floor that's appropriately worn and perhaps not entirely level. Diners can sit inside, outside on the patio, or on a semienclosed porch. My favorite lunch choice is Shari's turkey meat-loaf sandwich on toasted sourdough bread with spicy tomato-mint chutney. Interesting breakfast items include homemade granola, "coast toast" (French toast that resembles a soufflé), and Greek steamers (three eggs steamed and scrambled using the espresso machine and mixed with feta, tomato, and basil). The dinner menu consists of dishes such as a five-pepper filet mignon and grilled salmon. Or, you can simply enjoy one of their many coffee drinks, with or without a baked goody. *Tip:* If you're thinking of having dessert, ask them to take it out of the refrigerator case ahead of time. I've eaten some chilly sweets that would have been more enjoyable at room temperature. There's no access for people with disabilities.

✪ George's Ocean Terrace and Café/Bar

1250 Prospect St. ☎ **619/454-4244.** Reservations not accepted. Lunch main courses $7.50–$10.75; dinner main courses $9.50–$14.95. AE, DC, DISC, MC, V. Sun–Thurs 11am–10pm, Fri–Sat 11am–11pm. Valet parking $5. CALIFORNIA.

The main dining room on level one at George's (see listing above) is legendary and has won numerous awards for its haute cuisine. But George's also accommodates those seeking good food and a spectacular setting with a more reasonable price tag—the level-three Ocean Terrace and the level-two Café/Bar prepare similar dishes as well as new creations in the same kitchen as the high-priced fare. These two areas offer indoor and outdoor seating overlooking La Jolla Cove and the same great service as the main dining room. For dinner, you can choose from one of several seafood or pasta dishes, or have something out-of-the-ordinary like George's meat loaf served with mushroom-and-corn mashed potatoes. The smoked chicken soup is to die for. Valet parking is available, but if you drive around long enough, you'll find a place on the street.

INEXPENSIVE

✪ The Cottage

7702 Fay Ave. (at Kline). ☎ **619/454-8409.** Reservations accepted for dinner only. Breakfast and lunch $5–$7; dinner main courses $7–$12. AE, DISC, MC, V. Aug–June, daily 7:30am–3pm; July, daily 7:30am–3pm and 4–9pm. LIGHT FARE.

The turn-of-the-century Cottage, on a sunny corner in downtown La Jolla, is light and airy inside—with booths and tables under a skylight and a welcoming white fence, trellis, and large brick patio outside. You can get farm-fresh eggs most any style, granola and fresh fruit, oatmeal pancakes, Belgian waffles, or vegetable frittata, or a filling continental breakfast, each for just $4.75. For lunch, my favorite soup is the Mexican chicken and rice, served with baked tortilla chips and grated cheddar cheese, and the hot tuna is my favorite sandwich. For dinner, I like the chicken Jerusalem, tender chicken breast sautéed in a light cream sauce with garlic white wine, artichoke hearts, and fresh mushrooms, served on a bed of steamed and wild rice. The Cottage bakery makes all the *wonderful* desserts, pastries, and bread (with the exception of focaccia). There's no smoking inside or out.

✪ D'Lish

7514 Girard Ave. (at Pearl St.). ☎ **619/459-8118.** Reservations accepted. Main courses $5.95–$15. AE, DC, DISC, MC, V. Sun–Thurs 11:30am–10pm, Fri–Sat 11:30am–11pm. Free underground parking. Bus: 34 or 34A. CONTEMPORARY ITALIAN.

I confess to having a passion for pizza—not the traditional style, but the trendy wood-fired kind with toppings you wouldn't have imagined a decade ago. So it's not surprising that I've checked out all the places in La Jolla that serve such fare and, while there are other candidates within a few blocks, D'Lish definitely gets my vote for the best pizza in San Diego. My favorite is the Greek grilled chicken (described earlier in this chapter, under "Best Bets"), but I also like the pizza with shrimp, mozzarella, Roma tomatoes, Kalamata olives, sun-dried tomatoes, pesto sauce, and pine nuts. My husband loves the pasta dishes, especially the shrimp-scallop angel-hair, one of many heart-healthy choices. They also have a wonderful Caesar salad. *Here's a hot tip:* Don't sit upstairs when the weather's warm because it gets extremely hot and stuffy up there. There's another D'Lish in Chula Vista at 386 E. H Street in the Terra Nova Plaza (☎ **619/585-1371**).

Hard Rock Cafe

909 Prospect St. (at Fay Ave.). ☎ **619/454-5101.** Reservations not accepted. Main courses $5.50–$15. AE, DC, MC, V. Sun–Thurs 11:30am–11pm, Fri–Sat 11:30am–midnight. Bus: 34, 34A. AMERICAN.

San Diego's branch of "the Smithsonian of rock 'n' roll," as Andy Warhol described the Hard Rock Cafe, is a great spot for families. Preteens, teens, and tourists pack the place. It isn't *just* the huge inventory of music memorabilia on display—the Hard Rock also serves generous portions of really good food, with most main courses costing about $6.95. Burgers are the house specialty; salads and sandwiches are also served. The service isn't swift, but there's plenty to listen to and look at in the interim, such as Madonna's bustier from the "Who's That Girl" tour, a vintage Cher doll, and one of John Lennon's band-leader coats from the Sergeant Pepper era. If the line is long and you're really starving, see if there's a place at the counter. You can also eat in the bar—the only place where smoking is allowed. Browsing through the small retail-sales shop at the entrance is a good way to kill some time until your name is called. The bar stays open until midnight Sunday through Thursday and 1am on Friday and Saturday.

8 Coronado

Coronado has some wonderful hotels and each presents a variety of dining options. You may wish to consider **Marius** in Le Meridien, **Azzura Point** in Loew's Coronado Bay Resort, and the **Crown Room** or **Prince of Wales Grill,** among others, at the Hotel del Coronado.

EXPENSIVE

Chart House

1701 Strand Way. ☎ **619/435-0155.** Reservations recommended. Main courses $6.95–$24.95. AE, CB, DC, DISC, MC, V. Daily 5–11pm. AMERICAN.

Perched at the edge of Glorietta Bay and resembling a cupola that must have escaped from the Hotel del Coronado up the hill, this restaurant has been here in the Del's former boathouse since 1968. Inside, you'll find 38 antique tables and the largest collection of Tiffany lamps in southern California (about 20 at last count). Enjoy dinner on the deck in summer or in the upstairs lounge; the mahogany, teak, and stained-glass bar came from Atlanta and dates from 1880. The fare here is straightforward—seafood, steaks, or prime rib, with plenty of fresh-fish specials daily. The view from the restaurant encompasses Glorietta Bay, the Coronado Yacht Club, and the Coronado Bay Bridge.

Chez Loma

1132 Loma (off Orange Ave.). ☎ **619/435-0661.** Reservations recommended. Main courses $19–$26. AE, DC, MC, V. Daily 5–10pm; Sun 10am–2pm. FRENCH.

In a house dating from 1889, Chez Loma has been welcoming diners since 1975. Plenty of windows, ceiling fans, and soft lighting complement the Victorian decor.

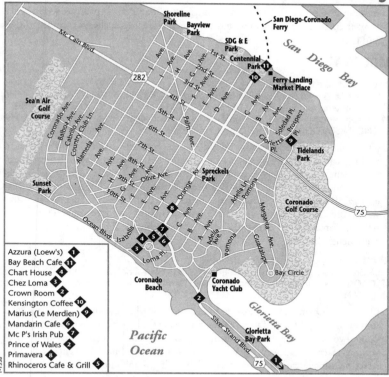

Azzura (Loew's) **1**
Bay Beach Cafe **11**
Chart House **4**
Chez Loma **3**
Crown Room **2**
Kensington Coffee **10**
Marius (Le Merdien) **9**
Mandarin Cafe **6**
Mc P's Irish Pub **7**
Prince of Wales **2**
Primavera **8**
Rhinoceros Cafe & Grill **5**

1-1338

The upstairs salon, reminiscent of a Victorian parlor, is a cozy spot for sipping wine or coffee and nibbling on appetizers or dessert. Among the creative entrees are salmon with smoked-tomato vinaigrette and duck with cherry-and-lingonberry sauce. The duck, which is tender and not at all oily, has been on the menu since the restaurant opened. All main courses are served with soup or salad, rice or potatoes, and fresh vegetables. California wines and American microbrewery beers are available. Follow dinner with a creamy crème caramel or Kahlúa crème brûlée. Chez Loma's service is attentive, and the herb rolls are absolutely addictive.

✪ Primavera

932 Orange Ave. ☎ **619/435-0454.** Reservations recommended. Main courses $11.95–$21.95. AE, CB, DC, DISC, MC, V. Mon–Fri 11am–2:30pm; daily 5–10:30pm. NORTHERN ITALIAN.

Primavera serves tasty northern-Italian dishes and pays remarkable attention to detail. The bar is as pretty as the long, narrow dining room; an elevated seating area is set off by wood panels with etched glass. Besides pasta, meat, and fish dishes at lunch, you can order a variety of Italian salads and sandwiches, which are quite satisfying as a meal unto themselves. At dinner, popular appetizers are *bagna caoda primavera* (grilled eggplant, roasted red peppers, sun-dried tomatoes, Montrachet, and Parmesan cheese, with bagna caoda sauce [white wine, lemon, garlic, and anchovies]), or you might be tempted to try the Caesar salad for two. Main courses include angel-hair pasta with mushrooms, garlic, prosciutto, capers, anchovies, and herbs; filet mignon in Cognac sauce with fresh mushrooms; and chicken breast with eggplant, mozzarella cheese, mushrooms, and wine sauce. The menu always includes fish, veal, and lamb specials.

MODERATE

Bay Beach Cafe
1201 First St. (in the Ferry Landing Marketplace). ☎ **619/435-4900.** Reservations recommended for dinner on weekends. Main courses $9–$17. AE, DISC, MC, V. Mon–Fri 7–10:30am, 11am–4pm, and 5–10:30pm; Sat–Sun 7–11:30am, noon–4pm, and 5–10:30pm. Free parking. AMERICAN/SEAFOOD.

The setting here is positively wonderful. Diners gaze across San Diego Bay to the city skyline, which is pretty by day and even more enticing at night. The ferry docks at a wooden pier, discharging passengers into the Ferry Landing Marketplace where shops and eateries await. At the Bay Beach Cafe, there's a congenial bar for drinks, and meals are served indoors and alfresco. Several fresh-fish specials are offered daily, and rack of lamb, vegetarian pasta, and roasted free-range chicken with wild-mushroom sauce are other popular dinner items. The pub menu consists of sandwiches and burgers.

Rhinoceros Cafe & Grill
1166 Orange Ave. (between 10th and 11th). ☎ **619/435-2121.** Main courses $8.95–$17.95. AE, DISC, MC, V. Sun 8am–12:30pm, Mon–Sat 11am–3pm; Fri–Sat 5–10pm, Sun–Thurs 5–9pm. AMERICAN.

Owner Scott Hanlon won't explain to the wait staff why he named this place as he did, so they made up a story. If they tell you it refers to the large portions served here, they're pulling your leg. This light, bright bistro is a good place for people-watching, as large windows face the sidewalk outside. Inside, white walls, hung with large, colorful abstract paintings, reach up to the very high ceiling. Lunch possibilities include salads, burgers, sandwiches, and pasta. Favorite dinner specials are charbroiled swordfish with citrus glaze, halibut with cucumber dill sauce, and live Maine lobster. There's a good wine list, or you might decide to try Rhino Chaser's American Ale. This is a good choice for a pretheater dinner, as Lamb's Players Theatre is next door.

INEXPENSIVE

Kensington Coffee Company
1106 First St. ☎ **619/437-8506.** Menu items $1.50–$4.50. AE, DISC, MC, V. Daily 6am–11pm. LIGHT FARE.

Dropping by here is a great way to start or end the day—or take a break during it. Choose an international coffee from one of five giant thermoses; top it with a little cinnamon or chocolate; then complement it with a bagel, croissant, filled pastry, muffin, or scone—or if it's dessert time, with cheesecake, gelato, brownies, or chocolate truffles. The creamy cappuccinos and double mochas can substitute for dessert. Light fare, such as burritos and salad, is served at lunchtime. You can buy the *Coronado Journal*, the *San Diego Union-Tribune*, the *Los Angeles Times*, and postcards here. Indoor and outdoor seating is available.

Mandarin Cafe
1330 Orange Ave., #280, (in Coronado Plaza, 2nd floor). ☎ **619/435-2771.** Reservations suggested. Main courses $6.25–$12.95. AE, MC, V. Mon–Thurs 11am–10pm, Fri 11am–11pm, Sat–Sun 1–10pm. Free underground parking. MANDARIN/SZECHUAN CHINESE.

This modern-looking restaurant serves early-bird combination dinners until 6:30pm; gourmet dinners are available for two or more. House favorites are the honey shrimp and the sizzling seafood noodles. Conscientious waiters bring sherbet and cookies at the end of the meal, and the kitchen will hold the MSG, sugar, and salt on request. Despite its address, the restaurant is actually on Churchill Street, within steps of the beach.

McP's Irish Pub

1107 Orange Ave. ☎ **619/435-5280.** Main courses $5–$18. AE, DC, MC, V. Daily 11am–9pm; Sun brunch 10am–2pm. IRISH.

The "Cheers" of Coronado is authentic down to the aroma of stale beer. You'll assume most customers have been darkening its door for years to socialize and enjoy the hearty fare that includes mulligan stew, corned beef and cabbage, and fish-and-chips. The varied menu also features homemade soups, deli-style sandwiches, burgers, and daily specials. The nightly live entertainment, jazz or rock 'n' roll, draws a large blue-jeans–clad crowd, especially on Thursdays.

9 Only in San Diego

Southern California's car culture is alive and well in San Diego. So is "car cuisine," a.k.a. fast food. How can we live in our vehicles if we can't eat in them? A local favorite is **Rubios,** home of the fish taco, mahimahi burrito, and other Cali-Mex specialties. You'll find these emporia scattered around the city. Some convenient locations are 901 Fourth Ave., at E Street (☎ **619/231-7731**); in Pacific Beach at 910 Grand Ave. (☎ **619/270-4800**); and at 3555 Rosecrans St., near Midway Drive (☎ **619/223-2631**). While most San Diegans swear by Rubios, my personal favorite dive for cheap Mexican food is **La Fuente Restaurante,** 2171 Avenida de la Playa, La Jolla Shores (☎ **619/454-8955**).

You might also try **In-N-Out Burgers.** Some of my most highbrow friends admit to a private passion for these thin meat patties, doused in secret sauce, and served with fresh lettuce and tomato on toasted buns. I've even found some wrappers from here left in the car by none other than my very own husband! There is an In-N-Out just off I-5 in Pacific Beach at 2910 Damon Ave., near E. Mission Bay Drive (no phone). Other locations include 3102 Sports Arena Blvd. (at Rosecrans) and 4375 Kearny Mesa Rd.

Because San Diego's benign climate lends itself to dining alfresco, picnics have become a popular and relaxing form of portable meals. My favorite spot to pick up sandwiches is **The Cheese Shop,** downtown at 401 G St. (☎ **619/232-2303**), or in La Jolla Shores at 2165 Avenida de la Playa (☎ **619/459-3921**). Other places to buy picnic fare include **D. Z. Akins Deli** at 6930 Alvarado Rd. (☎ **619/265-0218**); **Boudin Sourdough Bakery and Cafe** and **The Farmer's Market,** both in Horton Plaza; and **Old Town Liquor and Deli,** at 2304 San Diego Ave. (☎ **619/ 291-4888**). Another spot that's very popular with San Diegans is **Point Loma Seafoods,** located on the water's edge in front of the Municipal Sportfishing Pier, at 2805 Emerson, near Scott Street, south of Rosecrans and west of Harbor Drive (☎ **619/223-1109**). There's a fish market here, and they sell seafood sandwiches and salads to go. If you decide to make your own sandwiches, the best bread in the county comes from **Charlie's Best Bread,** 1808 Garnet Ave., in Pacific Beach (☎ **619/ 272-3521**), and 640 University Ave., in Hillcrest/Uptown (☎ **619/574-6446**).

San Diegans also are reputed to consume large amounts of sushi. If you like it, you'll love **Cafe Japengo,** adjacent to the Hyatt Regency La Jolla at 8960 University Center Lane, just off La Jolla Village Drive (☎ **619/450-3355**).

7

Exploring San Diego

You won't run out of things to see and do in San Diego. The San Diego Zoo, Sea World, and the Wild Animal Park are the three top drawing cards, but many other activities—a substantial number of them free—also await. And with San Diego's near-perfect climate, chances are good that the sun will shine while you're here, making everything you do just that much more fun.

SUGGESTED ITINERARIES

If You Have 1 Day

Visit the zoo in the morning and have lunch at Albert's in the Treehouse in Gorilla Tropics. In the afternoon, walk along the Embarcadero, stopping to tour the vessels that comprise the Maritime Museum, or shop until you drop in Horton Plaza. Either way, finish off the day with a meal in the Gaslamp Quarter at Fio's.

If You Have 2 Days

Spend the 1st day wandering around the zoo and Embarcadero. On Day 2, visit Sea World during the day. In the evening, enjoy a play at one of San Diego's outstanding theaters.

If You Have 3 Days

Continue meeting the animals of San Diego, as described above. Visit the Wild Animal Park during the day. When you return to the city, ferry over to Coronado for a look at the Hotel del Coronado and dinner. A walk on the beach would be lovely before or after dinner.

If You Have 4 Days or More

On your 4th day, plan a visit to the Cabrillo National Monument in the morning and spend the rest of the day browsing in the shops or enjoying the beach in La Jolla or Del Mar.

For ventures farther afield, consider Temecula, Julian, the Anza-Borrego Desert, or Tijuana (see chapter 11).

1 The Three Major Animal Parks

Looking for wild times? San Diego supplies them like no other city can. Its world-famous zoo is home to more than 4,000 animals, many of them rare and exotic. A sister attraction, the San Diego

Wild Animal Park, offers another 2,500 creatures representing 275 species in an *au naturel* setting. And Shamu and his friends form a veritable chorus line at Sea World—waving their flippers, waddling across an ersatz Antarctica, and blowing killer-whale kisses—in more than a dozen shows a day.

✪ San Diego Zoo

Park Blvd. and Zoo Place, Balboa Park. ☎ **619/234-3153.** TDD 619/233-9639. Web site: www.sandiegozoo.org. Admission $15 adults, $6 children 3–11, free for children under 3 and military in uniform. Deluxe package which includes admission, guided bus tour, and round-trip skyfari aerial tram, $21 adults, $18.90 seniors 60 and over, $11 children, free for children 2 and under. Combination Zoo/Wild Animal Park Package, $31.95 adults, $18.35 children; includes deluxe package at zoo and admission to the WAP and is valid for 5 days from date of purchase. DISC, MC, V. Open daily year-round 9am–4pm, grounds close at 5pm; extended summer hours, 9am–9pm, grounds close at 10pm. Bus: 7/7B.

More than 4,000 animals reside at this world-famous zoo, which was founded in 1916 with a handful of animals originally brought here for the 1915–16 Panama-California International Exposition. Many of the buildings you see in surrounding Balboa Park were built for the exposition. The zoo's founder, Dr. Harry Wegeforth, a local physician and lifelong animal lover, once braved the fury of an injured tiger to toss medicine into its roaring mouth.

In the early days of the zoo, "Dr. Harry" would travel around the world and barter native Southwestern animals such as rattlesnakes and sea lions for more exotic species. The loan of two giant pandas from The People's Republic of China is a twist on this long-standing tradition—instead of exchanging exotic species, the San Diego Zoo agreed to pay $1 million each year that the pandas are here to aid the conservation effort in China. (See "Panda-monium" feature below.)

The zoo is also an accredited botanical garden, representing over 6,000 species of flora from many climate zones, all installed to help simulate native environments for the animals who live here.

Today, the giant pandas are the big attention-getters, but the zoo has many other rare and exotic species: cuddly koalas from Australia, long-billed kiwis from New Zealand, wild Przewalski's horses from Mongolia, lowland gorillas from Africa, and giant tortoises from the Galapagos. Of course, the zoo's regulars—lions, elephants, giraffes, tigers, and bears—prowl around the zoo as well, not to mention a great number of tropical birds. Most of the animals are housed in barless, moated enclosures that resemble their natural habitats. These habitats include Australasia, Tiger River, Sun Bear Forest, two of the world's largest walk-through bird aviaries, Flamingo Lagoon, Gorilla Tropics (my personal favorite), Hippo Beach, and Polar Bear Plunge.

The zoo offers two types of bus tours daily—both provide a narrated overview and allow you to see 75% of the park. You can choose the 35-minute guided bus tour in which you get on the bus and complete a circuit around the zoo (the cost is $4 for adults and $3 for kids 3 to 11, but is included in the deluxe package). Or, you might opt for the Kangaroo Bus Tour, which costs $8 for adults and $5 for children—you can get on and off the bus as many times as you want at any of the eight stops—you can even go around more than once. In general, it's better to take the tour early in the morning or late in the afternoon, when the animals are more active. The last tour starts an hour before closing—it's not as crowded as the others, but you won't see the elephants because it's their feeding time. Call the **Bus Tour Hot Line** (☎ **619/685-3264**) for information about these tours, as well as Spanish-language tours, a comedy tour, and signed tours for the hearing impaired. Alternatively, you can get an aerial perspective via the Skyfari, which costs $1 per person each way. The ride lasts about 5 minutes—but, as it doesn't get particularly close to the animals, it's better for a bird's-eye view of Balboa Park and an overview of the zoo.

San Diego Attractions

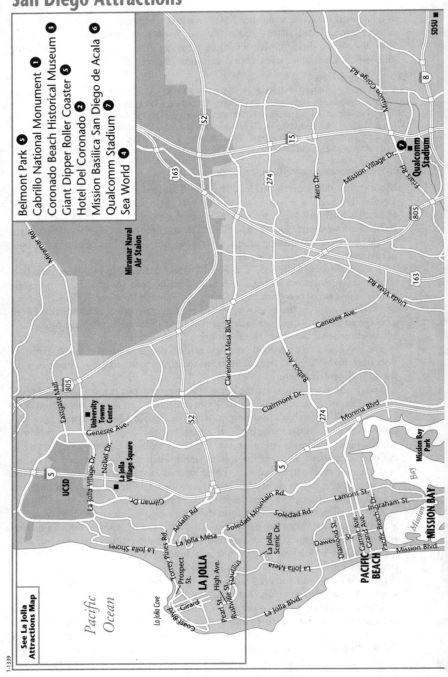

Belmont Park **5**
Cabrillo National Monument **1**
Coronado Beach Historical Museum **3**
Giant Dipper Roller Coaster **5**
Hotel Del Coronado **2**
Mission Basilica San Diego de Acala **6**
Qualcomm Stadium **7**
Sea World **4**

See La Jolla Attractions Map

Pacific Ocean

Miramar Naval Air Station

UCSD
University Towne Center
La Jolla Village Square

LA JOLLA

PACIFIC BEACH

MISSION BAY

Mission Bay Park

Qualcomm Stadium **7**

SDSU

1-1339

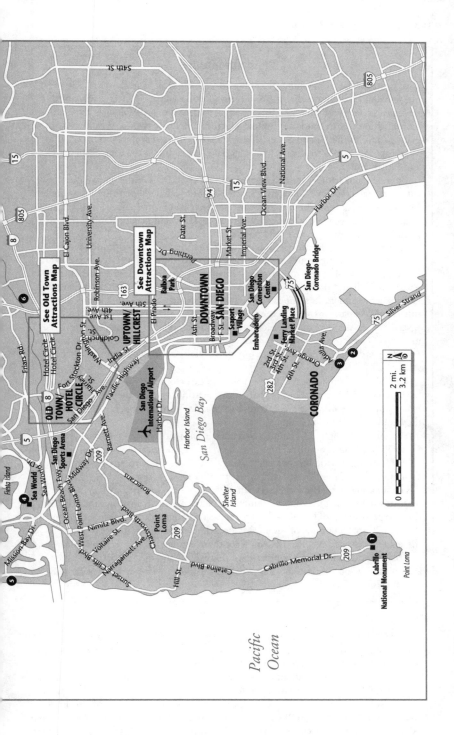

See Old Town Attractions Map

See Downtown Attractions Map

OLD TOWN/HILL CREST

UPTOWN/HILLCREST

HOTEL CIRCLE

Hotel Circle
Hotel Circle

Friars Rd.

University Ave.

Robinson Ave.

El Cajon Blvd.

54th St.

Washington St.

Goldfinch St.

India St.

Pacific Highway

Fort Stockton Dr.

Jefferson St.

San Diego Ave.

San Diego International Airport

Harbor Dr.

Harbor Island

San Diego Bay

Shelter Island

DOWNTOWN SAN DIEGO

Balboa Park

Pershing Dr.

Date St.

Market St.

Imperial Ave.

Ocean-View Blvd.

National Ave.

Harbor Dr.

1st Ave.
4th Ave.
5th Ave.

El Prado

Broadway

Ash St.

E St.

Seaport Village

Embarcadero

San Diego Convention Center

Ferry Landing Market Place

2nd St.
3rd St.
4th St.
6th St.

Orange Ave.
Adella Ave.

CORONADO

San Diego-Coronado Bridge

75

Silver Strand

75

Point Loma

Catalina Blvd.

Cabrillo Memorial Dr.

Sunset
Narragansett Ave.
Voltaire St.
Nimitz Blvd.
Chatsworth Blvd.

Hill St.

Rosecrans

West Point Loma Blvd.
Ocean Beach Fwy.
Midway Dr.

Barnett Ave.

San Diego Sports Arena

Sea World
Sea World Dr.

Mission Bay Dr.

Fiesta Island

Pacific Ocean

Cabrillo National Monument

Point Loma

209

282

75

5

8

805

15

94

163

N

0   2 mi.
    3.2 km

1
2
3
4
5
6

107

Panda-monium

Two giant pandas from China, Shi Shi (a 13-year-old male) and Bai Yun (a 3-year-old female), finally arrived at the San Diego Zoo in late 1996 after 3 years of intense negotiation with the U.S. Department of the Interior, the Wolong Giant Panda Conservation Centre, and the Chinese government. These two are the only pair of giant pandas in the United States. A single male is housed at the National Zoo in Washington, D.C. In total, only about 15 giant pandas live in zoos outside of China and North Korea.

Because giant pandas are endangered and protected under the Convention on International Trade in Endangered Species (CITES) a federal permit was required for their importation. The zoo's previous requests had been denied, but this time the powers-that-be were convinced that this project would make a significant contribution to the effort to save wild pandas.

Giant pandas live in dense bamboo and coniferous forests at altitudes of 5,000 to 10,000 feet and are among the rarest mammals in the world—fewer than 1,000 remain in the wild. Their numbers have dwindled due to the destruction of their natural habitat and poaching—which is still a problem in spite of the fact that the Chinese government has imposed life-in-prison sentences for those convicted of this crime. As part of the agreement to get the pandas here, the San Diego Zoo agreed to contribute $1 million each year to wild-panda habitat protection projects in China. These projects were established in order to help double the number of existing panda preserves and create protected wildlife corridors connecting these areas.

You needn't worry that the pandas will be gone before you get here: The loan is for a period of 12 years. During that time, scientific study of their breeding and behavior patterns will take place. (Any baby pandas born at the zoo will belong to the People's Republic of China.)

Shi Shi, who weighs 230 pounds, was born in the wild and taken to the Wolong Giant Panda Conservation Centre after he was found critically wounded—probably from a fight with another male panda. Bai Yun was born at that center on September 7, 1991 and was raised by her mother Dong Dong.

Giant pandas are related to both bears and raccoons. They are bearlike in shape, with striking black and white markings, and have unique front paws that enable them to grasp stalks of bamboo. This plant makes up about 95% of their diet, and they eat 20 to 40 pounds of food every day. This takes them 10 to 16 hours, so there's a pretty good chance that you'll see them eating.

Because of the enormous popularity of this exhibit and the fact that the pandas are not always on display, the zoo provides a panda-viewing hot line (☎ **888/MY-PANDA**). Call before you go.

The Children's Zoo is scaled to a youngster's viewpoint. There's a nursery with baby animals and a petting area where kids can cuddle up to sheep, goats, and the like. The resident wombat is a special favorite here.

The zoo offers wheelchair and stroller rentals and numerous food outlets, including a delightful restaurant called Albert's.

Tip: Refer to the money saving coupons for the Zoo in the back of this book if you're planning on going to the zoo and Wild Animal Park, you might want to consider buying a **Zoological Society Membership,** which costs $68 a year for two adults living in the same household. The adult/couple membership gives each cardholder unlimited entrance to the zoo and Wild Animal Park, plus two adult-admission passes, six discounted admission passes, and four twofer bus tickets, plus a subscription to *Zoo News* magazine. A Koala Club membership for a child costs $15 and provides unlimited entry for a year. If you don't buy the annual pass, the best discount is the one for AAA members. The next best deal is using the coupons in the *Super Savings Coupon Book* available from the International Visitor Center.

Wild Animal Park

15500 San Pasqual Valley Rd., Escondido. ☎ **760/747-8702.** TDD 760/738-5067. Web site: www.sandiegozoo.org. Admission $18.95 adults, $17.05 seniors 60 and over, $11.95 children 3–11, free for children 2 and under and military in uniform. Combination Zoo/Wild Animal Park Package, $31.95 adults, $18.35 children; includes deluxe package at zoo and admission to WAP and is valid for 5 days from date of purchase. DISC, MC, V. Daily 9am–4pm (grounds close at 5pm); extended hours during the summer and the Festival of Lights in December. Parking costs $3 per car. See "Tip" under San Diego Zoo above. Take I-15 to Via Rancho Pkwy.; follow signs from here for about 3 miles.

Just 30 miles north of San Diego, in the San Pasqual Valley, the Wild Animal Park transports you to the African plains and other landscapes where 3,200 animals, many of them endangered species, roam freely over 1,800 acres. In a reversal of roles, the humans are the creatures enclosed here instead of the animals. This living arrangement encourages breeding colonies, so it's not surprising that more than 80 white rhinoceroses have been born here. Several species of rare animals that had vanished from the wild, such as cheetahs and Przewalski's wild horses, have been reintroduced to their natural habitats from stocks bred by the park. Approximately 650 baby animals are born every year in the park, which also serves as a botanical preserve with more than 2 million plants, including 300 endangered species.

The best way to see the animals is by riding the 5-mile monorail (included in the price of admission); for the best views, sit on the right-hand side. During the 50-minute ride, you'll pass through areas resembling Africa and Asia, and you'll learn interesting tidbits—did you know that rhinos are susceptible to sunburn and mosquito bites? Trains leave every 20 minutes; you can watch informative videos while you wait in the stations.

If you'd like to get a little closer to the animals, the park offers several alternative ways to explore the area. On the 1³/₄-mile Kilimanjaro self-guided safari walk, you'll see tigers, elephants, and cheetahs close up, as well as the Australian rain forest and views of East Africa. You can also journey into the Heart of Africa (the park's newest feature) via a three-quarter-mile self-guided trail which leads walkers through dense forest, flourishing wetlands, sprawling savannas, and open plains to discover Africa's biodiversity. It encompasses 30 acres and is home to about 300 animals representing nearly 30 species. Photo caravan tours venture into the field enclosures. The photo tours run Wednesday through Sunday, and they cost $65 or $90 depending on the tour. Stroller and wheelchair rentals are available. Take a jacket along; it can get cold in the open-air monorail.

Local public transportation will get you here, but it takes three buses and 3¹/₂ hours. **Gray Line** offers a 7-hour tour for about $41 for adults and $25 for kids, including admission and shows. For more information, call ☎ **619/491-0011.**

See the San Diego Zoo listing above for details on discounted admission.

Sea World

1720 S. Shores Rd., Mission Bay. ☎ **619/226-3901;** 714/939-6212 in Los Angeles; TDD for the deaf 619/226-3907. Admission $32.95 adults, $29.65 seniors 55 and older, $24.95 children 3–11, free for children 2 and under. DISC, JCB, MC, V. Parking $5 per car, $2 per motorcycle, and $7 per RV. Guided 90-min. behind-the-scenes tours, $6 adults, $5 children 3–11 and seniors. Ticket sales stop 1^1/$_2$ hr. before closing. June–Aug daily 9am–10pm; Sept–May daily 10am–5pm. Bus: 9 or 81. By car, exit I-5 west onto Sea World Dr. or from I-8 onto W. Mission Bay Dr. to Sea World Dr. E.

Sea World is one of the best-promoted attractions in California and may be your main reason for coming to San Diego. The 150-acre, multimillion-dollar aquatic playground is a showplace for marine life, made politically correct with a nominally "educational" atmosphere. Several successive 4-ton black-and-white killer whales have functioned as the park's mascot, all named Shamu. At its heart, Sea World is a family entertainment center where the performers are dolphins, otters, sea lions, walruses, and seals. Shows are presented continuously throughout the day, while visitors rotate through various theaters watching the performances.

The 2-acre hands-on area called **Shamu's Happy Harbor** encourages kids to handle everything—and features everything from a pretend pirate ship, with plenty of netted towers, to tube crawls, slides, and chances to get wet. The newest attraction is **Wild Arctic,** a virtual-reality trip to the frozen north complete with polar bears, beluga whales, walruses, and harbor seals. Other draws include **Baywatch at Sea World,** a water-ski show named for the popular TV show, and **Shamu Backstage,** which makes it possible for visitors to get up close and personal with killer whales.

The Dolphin Interaction Program creates an opportunity for people to interact with bottlenose dolphins. Although this program does not allow swimming with the dolphins, it gives you the opportunity to wade waist-deep into the water and plenty of time to stroke the mammals and give commands like the trainers. This 2-hour program (1 hr. of education and instruction, 15 min. of wet-suit fitting, and 45 min. of interaction in the water with the dolphins) costs $125 per person ($95 per person for Sea World members), which includes admission to Sea World on the day of your program plus a 2nd day within a week. Space is limited to eight people per day, so advance reservations are required. Participants must be 13 years old or older.

Although Sea World is best known as Shamu's home, the facility also plays an important role in rescuing and rehabilitating beached animals found along the West Coast—including more than 300 seals, sea lions, marine birds, and dolphins in 1 year. The staff recently rescued a baby California gray whale, which is now on display.

2 San Diego Beaches

San Diego County is blessed with 70 miles of sandy coastline and more than 30 beaches that attract surfers, snorkelers, swimmers, and sunbathers. In summer, the beaches teem with locals and visitors alike. The rest of the year, they are popular places to walk and jog, and surfers don wet suits to pursue their passion.

Here I've listed some of San Diego's most accessible beaches, each with its own personality and devotees. They are listed geographically from south to north. If you are interested in others, *The California Coastal Access Handbook,* published by the California Coastal Commission, is helpful; it's available locally at Bookstar for $18.95, or you can order it through your local bookseller. All California beaches are public to the mean high-tide line, and this publication tells you how to get to each one. Exploring tide pools—areas which retain water after the tide has gone out providing homes for a plethora of sea creatures—can be a lot fun. You can get a tide chart, available free or for a nominal charge from many surf and diving shops, including **Emerald City Surf & Sport,** at 1118 Orange Ave., Coronado, and **San Diego Divers Supply,** at 5701 La Jolla Blvd., La Jolla.

San Diego Beaches

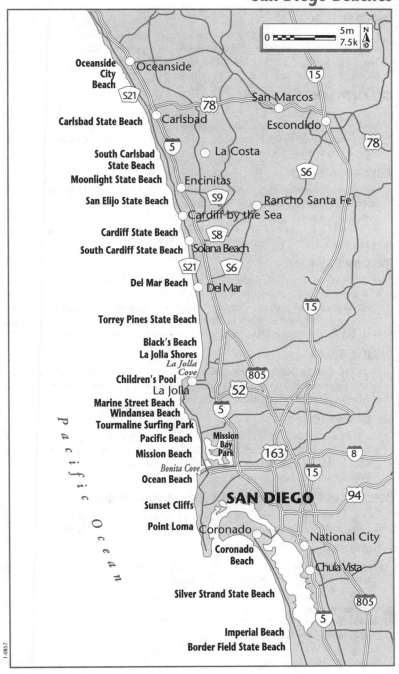

Oceanside City Beach
Oceanside

S21

Carlsbad State Beach
Carlsbad

San Marcos

15

78

Escondido

South Carlsbad State Beach
La Costa

5

Moonlight State Beach

S6

San Elijo State Beach
Encinitas

S9

Rancho Santa Fe

Cardiff by the Sea

Cardiff State Beach

S8

South Cardiff State Beach
Solana Beach

S21 S6

Del Mar Beach
Del Mar

15

Torrey Pines State Beach

Black's Beach
La Jolla Shores
La Jolla Cove
Children's Pool
La Jolla

805

52

Marine Street Beach
Windansea Beach
Tourmaline Surfing Park
Pacific Beach
Mission Beach

5

Mission Bay Park

163

8

Bonita Cove
Ocean Beach

15

SAN DIEGO

94

Sunset Cliffs

Point Loma
Coronado

National City

Coronado Beach

Chula Vista

805

Silver Strand State Beach

5

Imperial Beach
Border Field State Beach

Pacific Ocean

0   5m
    7.5k

N

1-0857

IMPERIAL BEACH

Half an hour south of San Diego by car or trolley, and only a few minutes from the Mexican border, lies **Imperial Beach.** Besides being popular with surfers, it hosts the Annual U.S. Open Sandcastle Competition in July, with world-class sand creations ranging from sea scenes to dragons to dinosaurs.

OCEAN BEACH

Near the pier off I-8 and Sunset Cliffs Boulevard, this is surfers' and sunset-lovers' heaven and the stuff Beach Boys songs are made of. Not far away are **Dog Beach,** where four-legged beach lovers roam unleashed, and **Garbage Beach,** another surfing spot (fortunately, it smells better than it sounds).

CORONADO BEACH

Lovely, wide, and sparkling white, this beach is conducive to strolling and lingering, especially in the late afternoon. It fronts Ocean Boulevard and is especially pretty in front of the Hotel del Coronado. The islands visible from here, but 18 miles away, are named "Los Coronados," and they belong to Mexico. It's an ideal spot for a marriage proposal.

MISSION BAY PARK

In this 4,600-acre aquatic playground, you'll discover 27 miles of bay front, 17 miles of oceanfront beaches, picnic areas, children's playgrounds, and paths for biking, roller-skating, and jogging. The bay lends itself to windsurfing, sailing, jet-skiing, waterskiing, and fishing. There are dozens of access points; one of the most popular is off I-5 at Clairemont Drive, where there's a visitor information center.

PACIFIC BEACH

Here you'll find a popular beach and boardwalk for meeting friends, grabbing a bite to eat, jogging, biking, or in-line skating. It runs along Ocean Boulevard (just west of Mission Boulevard), north of Pacific Beach Drive.

MISSION BEACH

While Mission Bay Park is a body of salt water surrounded by land and bridges, Mission Beach is actually a beach on the Pacific Ocean. Surfing is popular year-round here. The long beach and boardwalk extend from Pacific Beach Drive south to Belmont Park and beyond to the jetty.

BONITA COVE/MARINER'S POINT AND MISSION POINT

Facing Mission Bay in South Mission Beach, with calm waters, grassy areas for picnicking, and playground equipment, these spots are perfect for families.

WINDANSEA

One of California's finest surfing beaches, this area along Neptune Street in La Jolla achieved cult status in 1968, when the serious surfers who rode its waves were the

---

Impressions

Let Coronado wear her crown
As Empress of the Sea;
Nor need she fear her earthly peer
Will e'er discovered be.

—L. Frank Baum, 1905

subject of Tom Wolfe's book *The Pumphouse Gang.* This is a great place for watching the sun set.

✪ LA JOLLA COVE

The protected, calm waters—praised as the clearest along the California coast—attract swimmers, snorkelers, scuba divers, and families alike. There's a small sandy beach, and on the cliffs above, the Ellen Browning Scripps Park. The cove's "look but don't touch" policy protects the colorful Garibaldi, California's state fish, plus other marine life, including abalone, octopus, and lobster. The unique **Underwater Park** stretches from here to the northern end of Torrey Pines State Reserve and incorporates kelp forests, artificial reefs, two deep submarine canyons, and tidal pools. La Jolla Cove can be accessed from Coast Boulevard.

LA JOLLA SHORES BEACH

A mile-long flat stretch of beach, it's popular for jogging, swimming, and body- and board surfing for beginners. Families often come here, where lifeguards are on duty year-round.

BLACK'S BEACH

The area's unofficial (and illegal) nude beach, it lies between La Jolla Shores Beach and Torrey Pines State Beach. Located below some steep cliffs, it is out of the way and not easy to reach. To get here, take North Torrey Pines Road, park at the Glider Port, and walk from there. *Note:* Although the water is shallow and pleasant for wading, this area is known for its rip currents.

DEL MAR

After a visit to the famous fairgrounds that host the Del Mar Thoroughbred Club, you may want to make tracks for the beach, a long stretch of sand backed by grassy cliffs and a playground area. Del Mar is about 15 miles from downtown San Diego (see chapter 11).

NORTHERN SAN DIEGO COUNTY

Those inclined to venture even farther north in San Diego County won't be disappointed. Pacific Coast Highway leads to some inviting beaches, such as these in Encinitas: peaceful **Boneyards Beach, Swami's Beach** for surfing, and **Moonlight Beach,** popular with families and volleyball buffs. Farthest north in this beach-blessed county is **Oceanside,** which has one of the West Coast's longest wooden piers, wide sandy beaches, and several popular surfing areas.

3 Attractions in Balboa Park

Balboa Park's 1,174 acres encompass walkways, gardens, historical buildings, a few restaurants, an ornate pavilion with the world's largest outdoor organ, a high-spouting fountain, an OMNIMAX theater, a nationally acclaimed theater, and a world-famous zoo. The park's most distinctive features are the architectural beauty of the Spanish-Moorish buildings lining **El Prado,** its main street, and the group of outstanding and diverse museums contained within it.

Free tram transportation within the park is provided Monday through Friday from 8am to 5pm and Saturday and Sunday from 11am to 4pm. Ask at the Visitor Center about free walking and museum tours. I've also mapped out a stroll in chapter 8.

Many Balboa Park attractions are free on certain days; refer to "Free of Charge & Full of Fun" below for specifics. If you plan on visiting all or most of the museums in the park, you may be interested in purchasing the **Passport to Balboa Park** for $19. The passport, which represents a $56 value, is a coupon booklet that allows one entrance to each of 11 museums and is valid for a week. The passport can be purchased at any participating museum, the Balboa Park Visitor Center, and the Times Arts Tix Booth in Horton Plaza.

✪ San Diego Aerospace Museum

Pan-American Plaza, Balboa Park. ☎ **619/234-8291.** Admission $6 adults, $2 children 6–17, free for active military with ID and children under 6. Free 4th Tues of each month. Sept–May daily 10am–4:30pm; June–Aug daily 10am–5:30pm (last admission 1/2 hour before closing). Bus: 7/7B, 16, or 25.

The Aerospace Museum, with its International Aerospace Hall of Fame, provides an overview of the nation's air and space history, from the days of hot-air balloons to the space age. There is special emphasis on local aviation history, including the construction here of the *Spirit of St. Louis.* The museum is housed in the cylindrically shaped Ford Building, built by the Ford Motor Company for the California Pacific International Exposition of 1935. Behind-the-scenes restoration tours are available.

Museum of Art

1450 El Prado, Balboa Park. ☎ **619/232-7931.** Admission to permanent collection Mon–Thurs $7 adults, $5 seniors 65 and over and students with ID, $4 military with ID, $2 children 6–17, free for children 5 and under; Fri–Sun $8 adults, $6 seniors and students, $5 military, $3 children 6–17, free for children 5 and under. Permanent collection free 3rd Tues of each month. Tues–Sun 10am–4:30pm. Bus: 7/7B, 16, or 25.

The museum has outstanding collections of Italian Renaissance and Dutch and Spanish baroque art, along with contemporary paintings and sculptures. The Grant-Munger Gallery on the ground floor features works by Monet, Toulouse-Lautrec, Renoir, Pissarro, van Gogh, and Dufy. Bouguereau's arresting *Young Shepherdess* commands Gallery 9. Upstairs in the Fitch Gallery is El Greco's *Penitent St. Peter* and in the Gluck Gallery, Modigliani's *Boy with Blue Eyes* and Braque's *Coquelicots.* The museum has a shop, sculpture garden, and cafe with outdoor seating. Its rotunda features a striking Spanish-style tile staircase.

Museum of Photographic Arts

1649 El Prado, Balboa Park. ☎ **619/238-7559.** Admission $3.50 adults, free for children 12 and under with adult. Free 2nd Tues of each month. Daily 10am–5pm. Bus: 7/7B, 16, or 25.

This is one of the few museums in the country dedicated exclusively to photographic arts, and the work they show spans the entire 150-year history of the medium. Their extensive permanent collection of 3,600 images includes work by Edward Weston, Duane Michals, Ansel Adams, Max Yavno, Manual Alvarez Bravo, Mary Ellen Mark, Margaret Bourke-White, Sebastiao Salgado, and many others. They also have six to eight changing exhibitions every year.

Natural History Museum

1788 El Prado, Balboa Park. ☎ **619/232-3821.** Web site: www.sdnhm.org. Admission $7 adults, $6 seniors and active-duty military, $5 students 6–17, free for children under 6. Free 1st Tues of each month. Daily 9am–6pm. Bus: 7/7B, 16, or 25.

The museum focuses on the flora, fauna, and mineralogy of the Southwest. Kids marvel at the animals they find here and enjoy exploring the Desert Lab downstairs, home to live snakes and tarantulas.

Reuben H. Fleet Space Theater and Science Center

1875 El Prado, Balboa Park. ☎ **619/238-1233.** Web site: www.rhfleet.org. Space Theater, for IMAX/OMNIMAX shows, $6.50 adults, $3.50 juniors 5–15, $5 seniors 65 and over (to include Science Center, add $1 for adults and seniors, 50¢ for juniors). Science Center, $2.50 adults and

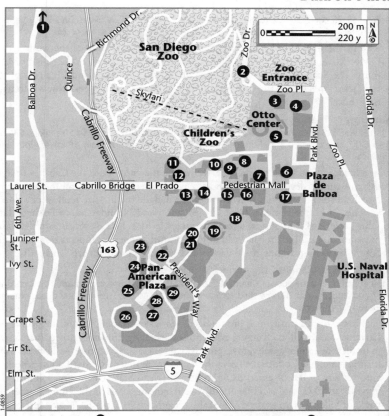

seniors, $1.25 children, free to all 1st Tues of each month. MC, V. Mon–Tues 9:30am–6pm, Wed–Thurs and Sun 9:30am–9pm, Fri–Sat 9:30am–10pm. Bus: 7/7B, 16, or 25.

The Reuben H. Fleet Space Theater and Science Center houses the world's first OMNIMAX theater, a 76-foot tilted-dome screen that shows IMAX/OMNIMAX films. The Science Center features more than 50 hands-on exhibits. It's possible to buy tickets in advance to avoid waiting in line, especially on weekends, which tend to be busy.

Museum of Man

1350 El Prado, Balboa Park. ☎ **619/239-2001.** Admission $5 adults, $4.50 seniors, $3 children 6–17, free children 5 and under. Free 3rd Tue of the month. Daily 10am–4:30pm. Bus: 16 or 25.

In a landmark building in the park, just inside the entrance at the Cabrillo Bridge, this museum is devoted to anthropology with a special emphasis on the peoples of North and South America. Favorite exhibits include the life-size replicas of a dozen varieties of Homo sapiens, from Cro-Magnon and Neanderthal to Peking Man. Don't overlook the annex across the street, which houses more exhibits. The museum's annual Indian Fair, held in June, features American Indians from all of the Southwest demonstrating tribal dances and selling ethnic food, arts, and crafts.

Mingei International Museum of World Folk Art

1439 El Prado, in the House of Charm. ☎ **619/239-0003.** Admission $5 adults, $2 children 6–17 and students with ID, free children 5 and under. AE, MC, V. Free 3rd Tues of each month. Tues–Sun 10am–4pm.

The name of this museum is pronounced *Min*-gay (meaning "art of the people" in Japanese), and it offers changing exhibitions celebrating human creativity manifested in textiles, costumes, jewelry, toys, pottery, paintings, and sculpture—all crafted from natural materials. Countries all over the world are represented. Martha Longenecker, a potter and professor emeritus of art at San Diego State University, founded the museum in 1977, and it is one of only two major museums in the United States devoted to folk crafts on a worldwide scale (the other is in Santa Fe, New Mexico).

The San Diego Automotive Museum

2080 Pan American Plaza, Balboa Park. ☎ **619/231-2886.** Admission $6 adults, $5 seniors and active military, $2 children 6–15, free for children under 6. Free 4th Tues of each month. MC, V. Sept 2–May 31 open daily 10am–4:30pm, June 1–Sept 1 open daily 10am–5:30pm. Last admission $1/2$ hour prior to closing. Bus: 7/7B, 16, or 25.

Classic, antique, and exotic cars and motorcycles are on display here in changing shows. The museum has an extensive automotive-related gift shop and a full automotive research library. On your visit you might see a 1927 Bentley, a 1931 Duesenberg Model J, a 1931 Rolls-Royce Phaeton, the late actor Steve McQueen's 1953 Allard, as well as the ill-fated 1948 Tucker and 1981 DeLorean.

Botanical Building and Lily Pond

El Prado. Free admission. Fri–Wed 10am–4pm. Bus: 7/7B, 16, or 25.

Within a serene park, ivy, ferns, orchids, impatiens, begonias, and other plants— about 1,200 tropical and flowering varieties—are sheltered beneath the domed lath house. The building, part of the 1915 Panama-California Exposition, measures 250 feet long by 75 feet wide by 60 feet high and is one of the world's largest lath structures. The lily pond out front attracts sun worshipers and street entertainers.

Hall of Champions

1649 El Prado, in Casa del Balboa, Balboa Park. ☎ **619/234-2544.** Admission $3 adults, $2 seniors 65 and older and military, $1 children 6–17, free for children 5 and under. Free 2nd Tues of each month. Daily 10am–4:30pm. Bus: 7/7B, 16, or 25.

As one of the country's few multisport museums, Hall of Champions has been popular with sports fans since 1961. The museum highlights more than 40 different professional and amateur sports. More than 25 exhibits surround a centerpiece statue, the Discus Thrower. One particularly interesting exhibit is devoted to athletes with disabilities. The best way to tour the exhibits is to move through them in a counterclockwise direction.

House of Pacific Relations International Cottages

Adjacent to Pan-American Plaza. ☎ **619/234-0739**. Free admission; donations welcome. Sun 12:30–4:30pm and 4th Tues of each month 11:30am–3pm. Bus: 7/7B, 16, or 25.

This cluster of one- and two-room cottages disseminates information about the culture, traditions, and history of 31 countries. Light refreshments are served, and outdoor lawn programs are presented March through October.

Japanese Friendship Garden

Adjacent to the Organ Pavilion. ☎ **619/232-2780**. Admission $2 adults, $1 seniors 65 and older, military, handicapped, and children 7–17, $5 family pass, free for children under 7. Free 3rd Tues of each month. Tues and Fri–Sun 10am–4pm. Bus: 7/7B, 16, or 25.

Of the $11\frac{1}{2}$ acres designated for the garden, only an acre—a beautiful, peaceful one—has been developed. However, the garden's Information Center shows a model of the future garden, named San-Kei-En (Three-Scenery Garden), which will eventually include a shallow lake with a shoreline of Japanese irises; a pastoral scene, such as a meadow abloom with springtime trees; and a rushing mountain waterfall and a stream filled with colorful koi. A self-guided tour is available at the main gate. From the gate, a crooked path (to confound evil spirits, who move only in a straight line) threads its way to the information center in a Zen-style house; here you can view the most ancient kind of garden, the *sekitei,* made only of sand and stone. Refreshments are served on a Japanese-style deck to the left of the entrance. Japanese holidays are celebrated here, and the public is invited.

Marston House Museum

3525 Seventh Ave. (the northwest corner of Balboa Park at Balboa Dr. and Upas St.). ☎ **619/ 298-3142**. Admission $3, $5 in combination with Villa Montezuma, free for children under 13. Fri–Sun 10am–4pm (last tour at 3:45pm). Bus: 1, 3, 16, or 25.

The noted San Diego architect Irving Gill designed this house in 1905 for George Marston, a local businessman and philanthropist. The San Diego Historical Society manages the house, which is a classic example of Craftsman-style architecture, reminiscent of Frank Lloyd Wright's work. Some of the interesting features of the house are wide hallways, brick fireplaces, and redwood paneling. Opened to the public in 1991, it contains few original pieces, but does exhibit Roycroft, Stickley, and Lampert furniture and is slowly being furnished with Craftsman-era pieces or copies as funds become available. Enter at the left side. There's a small bookstore and gift shop.

✪ Model Railroad Museum

Casa de Balboa Building, El Prado, Balboa Park. ☎ **619/696-0199**. E-mail sdmodrailm@aol.com. Admission $3 adults, with discounts for seniors, students, and military with ID, free for children under 15. Free 1st Tues of each month. Tues–Fri 11am–4pm, Sat–Sun 11am–5pm. Bus: 7/7B, 16, or 25.

Four permanent scale-model railroads depict southern California's transportation history and terrain, including San Diego County's "Grand Canyon," the Carriso Gorge. Children will enjoy the hands-on Lionel trains, and train buffs of all ages will appreciate the interactive multimedia exhibits. The gift shop sells rail-related items, including toys, mugs, signs, and kids' overalls and shirts.

Museum of San Diego History

1649 El Prado, in Casa del Balboa, Balboa Park. ☎ **619/232-6203.** Admission $4 adults, $3 seniors and military with ID, $3 for groups of 10 or more, $1.50 for children 5–12, free for children under 5. Free 2nd Tues of each month. Tues–Sun 10am–4:30pm. Bus: 7/7B, 16, or 25.

A good place to start if you are a newcomer to San Diego, the recently remodeled museum offers permanent and changing exhibits on topics related to the history of the San Diego region from pioneer outposts in the 1800's to present day. Many of the museum's photographs depict Balboa Park and the growth of the city. Docent tours are available; call ☎ **619/232-6203,** ext. 117 for information and reservations. Books about San Diego's history are available in the gift shop.

Spreckels Organ Pavilion

South of El Prado. ☎ **619/226-0819.** Free 1-hr. concerts Sun year-round and free Summer Festival concerts July–Aug, 8pm Mon and 6:15pm Tues–Thurs. Seating for 2,400. Bus: 7/7B, 16, or 25.

Given to San Diego citizens in 1914 by brothers John D. and Adolph Spreckels, the ornate, curved pavilion houses a magnificent organ with 4,445 individual pipes, ranging in length from less than a half-inch to more than 32 feet. With only brief interruptions, the organ has been in continuous use in the park, and today visitors can enjoy free hour-long concerts on Sundays at 2pm.

Timken Museum of Art

1500 El Prado, Balboa Park. ☎ **619/239-5548.** Web site: gort.ucsd.edu/sj/timken. Free admission. Tues–Sat 10am–4:30pm, Sun 1:30–4:30pm. Closed Sept. Bus: 7/7B, 16, or 25.

Called the "Jewel of the Park," this museum houses the Putnam Foundation's collection of 19th-century American paintings and works by European old masters, as well as an outstanding display of Russian icons.

4 More Attractions

DOWNTOWN & BEYOND

In downtown San Diego, you can wander in the **Gaslamp Quarter** (see "Walking Tour 2" in chapter 8) or **Horton Plaza,** where you can shop for hours, stroll, snack or dine, enjoy free entertainment, see a movie, and people-watch—all within a unique and colorful architectural framework. The Gaslamp Quarter is San Diego's hottest, trendiest area. It consists of 16 or so blocks of historic buildings which have been restored. The area gets its name from the old-fashioned style street lamps which line the brick sidewalks.

Seaport Village is a shopping/dining complex on the waterfront. It was designed to look like a New England seaport community. The views across the water are terrific.

The **Convention Center** is a dramatic element of the city's skyline.

✪ Cabrillo National Monument

1800 Cabrillo Memorial Dr., Point Loma. ☎ **619/557-5450.** Admission $4 per vehicle, $2 for walk-ins, free for American citizens age 62 and older, who have a National Parks Service Golden Age Passport, and children 16 and younger. Daily 9am–5:15pm. Take I-5 to Rosecrans St. west, which leads to Point Loma, then take Catalina Blvd. to the monument. Bus: 6.

Breathtaking views mingle with the early history of San Diego, which began when Juan Rodríguez Cabrillo arrived in 1542. His statue dominates the tip of Point Loma, which is also a vantage point for watching **migrating gray whales** en route from the Arctic Ocean to Baja California from December through March. The restored lighthouse (1855) allows a glimpse of what life was like here in the past century. The road

Downtown San Diego Attractions

Cabrillo National Monument ❺
Children's Museum ❸
Convention Center ❹
Firehouse Museum ❽

Maritime Museum ❼
Museum of Contemporary Art ❻
William Heath Davis House ❷
Villa Montezuma ❶

into the monument passes Fort Rosecrans National Cemetery, with row after row of white markers. National Park Service rangers lead walks at the monument, and there are tide pools that beg for exploration. Free 30-minute films on Cabrillo, tide pools, and California gray whales are shown on the hour daily from 10am to 4pm. Cabrillo National Monument welcomes almost 1.2 million visitors annually, making it one of the country's most visited national monuments. Only a half-hour ride from downtown, a trip here will be worth your time. Gray Line tours also offer an excursion to the monument (see page 132).

Children's Museum of San Diego

200 W. Island Ave. ☎ **619/233-8792.** Admission $5 for adults and children over 2, $3 for seniors, free for children under 2. Tues–Sat 10am–4:30pm, Sun noon–4:30pm. Trolley: Convention Center stop; the museum is a block away. There's all-day parking across the street for about $3.

This interactive "museum," which encourages participation, is a home away from home for kids. It provides ongoing supervised activities, as well as a monthly special celebration, recognizing important issues such as earth awareness or African-American history. A big draw for kids ages 2 to 10 is the indoor/outdoor art studio. There is also a theater with costumes for budding actors to don, plus an observation walk above the exhibits that kids climb up on and exit via a spiral slide. The museum shop is filled with toys, games, crafts, and books. School groups come in the morning, so you might want to schedule your visit for the afternoon.

Firehouse Museum

1572 Columbia St. (at Cedar). ☎ **619/232-FIRE.** Admission $2 adults, $1 seniors and military in uniform, $1 children 13–17, free for children 12 and under. Wed–Fri 10am–2pm, Sat–Sun 10am–4pm. Bus: 5, 16, or 105.

Appropriately housed in San Diego's oldest firehouse, the museum features shiny fire engines, including hand-drawn and horse-drawn models, a 1903 steam pumper, and memorabilia such as antique alarms, fire hats, and foundry molds for fire hydrants. There's also a small gift shop.

✪ Maritime Museum

1306 N. Harbor Dr. ☎ **619/234-9153.** Admission $5 adults, $4 seniors over 62 and teens 13–17, $2 children 6–12, free for children 5 and under. Daily 9am–8pm. Bus: 2. Trolley: America Plaza.

This unique museum consists of a trio of fine ships: the full-rigged merchant ship *Star of India* (1863), whose impressive masts are an integral part of the San Diego cityscape; the gleaming white San Francisco–Oakland steam-powered ferryboat *Berkeley* (1898), which worked round-the-clock to carry people to safety following the 1906 San Francisco earthquake; and the sleek steam yacht *Medea* (1904), one of the world's few remaining large steam yachts. You can board and explore each vessel, and from April through October you can watch movies on deck (see chapter 10, "San Diego After Dark," for details).

Museum of Contemporary Art, Downtown (MCA)

1001 Kettner Blvd. (at Broadway). ☎ **619/234-1001.** Admission $4 adults; $2 students, military with ID, and seniors; free for children 12 and under. Free 1st Tues and Sun of each month. Tues–Sat 10:30am–5pm, Fri 10:30am–8pm, Sun noon–5pm. Parking $2 with validation at America Plaza Complex. Trolley: America Plaza.

MCA Downtown is the second location of the Museum of Contemporary Art, San Diego (the first is in La Jolla). Two large galleries and two smaller ones present changing exhibitions of nationally and internationally distinguished contemporary artists. Lectures and tours for adults and children are also offered. There's a gift shop/bookstore on the premises.

Villa Montezuma

1925 K St. (at 20th Ave.). ☎ **619/239-2211.** Admission $3 adults, $5 in combination with Marston House (in Balboa Park), free for children 12 and under. Sat–Sun noon–4:30pm. Drive along K St. to the house. Bus: 3, 3A, 4, 5, 16, or 105 to Market and Imperial sts.

Just east of downtown, this stunning mansion was built in 1887 for internationally acclaimed musician and author Jesse Shepard. Lush with Victoriana, it features more stained glass than most churches have; windows depict Mozart, Beethoven, Sappho, Rubens, St. Cecilia (patron saint of musicians), and other notables. The striking ceilings are of pressed canvas coated with linseed oil (called Lincrusta Walton), a forerunner of linoleum, which never looked this good. Shepard lived in the house with his life companion, Lawrence Tonner, for only 2 years and died in obscurity in Los Angeles in 1927. The San Diego Historical Society painstakingly restored the house, which is on the National Register of Historic Places, and furnished it with period pieces. Unfortunately, the neighborhood is not as fashionable as the house, but it's safe to park your car here in the daytime. If you love Victorian houses, don't miss this one for its quirkiness.

William Heath Davis House Museum and Information Center

410 Island Ave. (at Fourth Ave.). ☎ **619/233-4692.** Admission $2. Mon–Fri 10am–2pm, Sat 10am–4pm, Sun noon–4pm. Museum is staffed by volunteers; call to verify hours. Bus: 1, 3, or 3A. Trolley: Gaslamp Quarter/Convention Center W.

Shipped by boat to San Diego in 1850 from Portland, Maine, this is the oldest structure in the Gaslamp Quarter. It is a well-preserved example of a prefabricated "saltbox" family home and has remained structurally unchanged for over 120 years. A museum, on the first and second floors, is open to the public, as is the small park adjacent to the house. The house is also home to the Gaslamp Quarter Historical Foundation, which sponsors walking tours of the quarter every Saturday at 11am for $5 (see "Organized Tours" later in this chapter).

OLD TOWN, HOTEL CIRCLE & BEYOND

The birthplace of San Diego—indeed, of California—Old Town takes you back to the Mexican California, which existed here until the mid-1800s. In chapter 8, "Walking Tour 4" goes through Old Town. In addition, free walking tours leave daily at 2pm from the **Old Town State Historic Park Headquarters,** 4002 Wallace St. (☎ **619/220-5422**), located at the head of the pedestrian walkway that is the continuation of San Diego Avenue. Admission to the center, open daily from 10am to 5pm, is free. Seven of the park's 20 structures are original; the rest are reconstructed. All museums are free, although donations are welcomed at Park Headquarters; La Casa de Estudillo, which depicts the living conditions of a wealthy family in 1872; and Seeley Stables, named after A. L. Seeley, who ran the stagecoach and mail service in these parts from 1867 to 1871. The stables have two floors of wagons, carriages, stagecoaches, and other memorabilia, including washboards, slot machines, and hand-worked saddles, as well as a 17-minute slide show. On weekdays during the school year, Old Town buzzes with fourth graders; it's an enormous classroom.

Heritage Park

2455 Heritage Park Row (corner of Juan and Harney sts.), Old Town. ☎ **619/694-3049.** Free admission. Daily 9:30am–3pm. Bus: 4 or 5/105.

This small 7.8-acre county park is filled with seven original 19th-century houses moved here from other places and given new uses, among them a bed-and-breakfast, a doll shop, and a gift shop. The most recent addition is the small synagogue, placed near the park's entrance in 1989. A glorious coral tree crowns the top of the hill.

Junípero Serra Museum

2727 Presidio Dr., Presidio Park, Old Town. ☎ **619/297-3258.** Admission $3 adults, free for children 12 and under. Tues–Sat 10am–4pm, Sun noon–4pm. Take Interstate 8 to the Taylor St. exit. Turn right on Taylor, then left on Presidio Dr.

Perched on a hill above Old Town, the stately mission-style building overlooks the hillside where California began. Here, in 1769, the first mission and first non-Indian settlement on the west coast of the United States and Canada were founded. Inside, the museum's exhibits introduce visitors to California's origins and to the native American, Spanish, and Mexican people who first called this place home. On display are their belongings, from cannons to cookware; a Spanish furniture collection; and one of the first paintings brought to California, which survived being damaged in an Indian attack. The mission remained San Diego's only settlement until the 1820s, when families began to move down the hill into what is now known as Old Town. Here, you can also watch an ongoing archaeological dig uncovering more of the items

Old Town Attractions

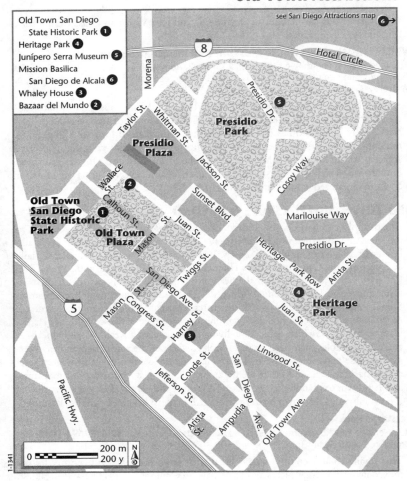

see San Diego Attractions map ➏ →

Old Town San Diego
   State Historic Park ➊
Heritage Park ➍
Junípero Serra Museum ➎
Mission Basilica
   San Diego de Alcala ➏
Whaley House ➌
Bazaar del Mundo ➋

0   200 m
0   200 y

used by early settlers. From the 70-foot tower, visitors can compare the spectacular view with historic photos to see how this land has changed over time.

The museum is located in **Presidio Park,** called the "Plymouth Rock of the Pacific." The large cross in the park was made from floor tile from the Presidio ruins. Sculptor Arthur Putnam made the statues of Father Serra, founder of the missions in California. Climb up to Inspiration Point, as many have done for marriage ceremonies, for a sweeping view of the area.

Mission Basilica San Diego de Alcala

10818 San Diego Mission Rd., Mission Valley. ☎ **619/281-8449.** Admission $2 adults, $1 seniors and students, 50¢ children 12 and under. Free on Sun and for daily services. Daily 9am–5pm; mass daily 7am and 5:30pm. Take I-8 to Mission Gorge Rd. to Twain Ave. Bus: 6, 16, 25, 43, or 81.

Established in 1769, this was the first link in a chain of 21 missions founded by Spanish missionary Junípero Serra. In 1774, the mission was moved to its present site for agricultural reasons and to separate native-American converts from a fortress that included the original building. A few bricks belonging to the original mission can be seen in Presidio Park in Old Town. Mass is held daily in this still-active Catholic parish. Other missions in the San Diego area include Mission San Luis Rey de Francia in Oceanside, Mission San Antonia de Pala near Mount Palomar, and Mission Santa Ysabel near Julian.

Whaley House
2482 San Diego Ave. ☎ **619/298-2482.** Admission $4 adults, $3 seniors over 60, $2 children 5–18, free for children under 5. Daily 10am–5pm. Closed on major holidays.

In 1856, this striking two-story brick house (the first one in these parts) just outside Old Town State Historic Park was built for Thomas Whaley and his family. Whaley was a New Yorker who arrived here via San Francisco, where he had been lured by the gold rush. The house is one of only two authenticated haunted houses in California, and 10,000 schoolchildren come here each year to see for themselves. Apparently, four spirits haunt the house, and other paranormal phenomena have taken place here. Exhibits include a life mask of Abraham Lincoln, one of only six made; the spinet piano used in the movie *Gone With the Wind;* and the concert piano that accompanied Swedish soprano Jenny Lind on her final U.S. tour in 1852. Director June Reading will make you feel at home, in spite of the ghosts.

MISSION BAY, PACIFIC BEACH & BEYOND
This is a great area for walking, jogging, in-line skating, biking, and boating. See the appropriate headings in "Outdoor Pursuits," below.

Giant Dipper Roller Coaster
3146 Mission Blvd. ☎ **619/488-1549.** Ride on the Giant Dipper $3. MC, V. Sun–Thurs 11am–10pm, Fri–Sat 11am–11pm. Take I-5 to the Sea World exit, and follow W. Mission Bay Park to Belmont Park.

A local landmark for 70 years, the Giant Dipper is one of two surviving fixtures from the original Belmont Amusement Park (the other is the Plunge swimming pool). After sitting dormant for 15 years, this vintage wooden roller coaster, with more than 2,600 feet of track and 13 hills, underwent an extensive restoration and reopened in 1991. The minimum-height requirement to ride the roller coaster is 50 inches. You can also ride on the Giant Dipper's neighbor, the Liberty Carousel ($1).

LA JOLLA
My favorite spot is the **La Jolla Cove** and **Ellen Browning Scripps Park** on the cliff above it. Here, swimming, sunning, picnicking, barbecuing, reading, and strolling along the oceanfront walkway are ongoing activities. They are both located on Coast Boulevard. The unique 6,000-acre **San Diego–La Jolla Underwater Park**, established in 1970, stretches from La Jolla Cove to the northern end of Torrey Pines State Reserve. It can be accessed from La Jolla Cove or La Jolla Shores.

Insider's tip: While droves of folks stroll the sidewalks adjacent to the San Diego–La Jolla Underwater Park and La Jolla Cove, only a few know about **Coast Walk** which starts near the **La Jolla Cave & Shell Shop,** 1325 Coast Blvd. (☎ **619/454-6080**), and affords a wonderful view of beach and beyond.

For a scenic drive, follow La Jolla Boulevard to Nautilus Street and turn east to get to **Mount Soledad,** which offers a 360° view of the area. The cross on top, erected in 1954, is 43 feet high and 12 feet wide.

Highlights in town include: **Mary Star of the Sea,** a beautiful Roman Catholic church, which stands at 7727 Girard (at Kline); and the **La Valencia Hotel** at 1132 Prospect St., a fine example of Spanish-colonial structure. The **La Jolla Woman's Club,** located at 7791 Draper Ave., the adjacent **Museum of Contemporary Art,**

San Diego, the **La Jolla Recreation Center,** and **The Bishop's School** are all examples of village buildings designed by architect Irving Gill.

At La Jolla's north end, you'll find the 1,200-acre, 15,000-student **University of California San Diego** (UCSD), established in 1960. The campus features the Stuart Collection of public sculpture and the Birch Aquarium at Scripps Institution of Oceanography (see individual listings, below). Louis Kahn designed the **Salk Institute for Biological Studies,** at 10010 North Torrey Pines Rd.

Museum of Contemporary Art, San Diego

700 Prospect St. ☎ **619/454-3541.** Fax 619/454-6985. Admission $4 adults, $2 students and seniors, 50¢ children 5–12; free 1st Tues and Sun of each month. Take the Ardath Rd. exit off I-5 north or the La Jolla Village Dr. west exit off I-5 south. Take Torrey Pines Rd. to Prospect Place and turn right. Prospect Place becomes Prospect St.

Focusing primarily on work produced since 1950, the museum is known internationally for its permanent collection and thought-provoking exhibitions. The MCA's collection of contemporary art comprises more than 3,000 works of painting, sculpture, drawings, prints, photography, video, and multimedia works. The holdings include every major art movement of the past half-century, with a strong representation by California artists and particularly noteworthy examples of minimalism, light and space work, conceptualism, installation, and site-specific art, as the outside sculptures were designed specifically for this site. The museum is perched on a cliff overlooking the Pacific Ocean, and the views from the galleries are gorgeous. The original building on the site was the residence of the legendary Ellen Browning Scripps, designed by Irving Gill in 1916. It became an art museum in 1941.

Insider's tip: The museum's cafe offers California cuisine. I particularly like their chicken soup.

✪ Birch Aquarium at Scripps

2300 Expedition Way, La Jolla. ☎ **619/534-FISH** (3414). Fax 619/534-7114. Admission $6.50 adults, $5.50 seniors, $4.50 students and teenagers 13–17, $3.50 children 3–12, free for children under 3. Parking $3. AE, MC, V. Daily 9am–5pm. Take I-5 to La Jolla Village Dr. exit, go west 1 mile, and turn left at Expedition Way. Bus: 34.

The Birch Aquarium is operated by Scripps Institution of Oceanography, at the University of California San Diego. This beautiful facility is both an aquarium and a museum. The aquarium is to the right of the entrance, the museum to the left. To make the most of this self-guided experience, be sure to pick up a visitor guide from the information booth just inside the entrance and take time to read the text on each of the exhibits. The aquarium affords close-up views of the Pacific Northwest, the California coast, Mexico's Sea of Cortez, and the tropical seas, which are all presented in 33 marine life tanks. The giant kelp forest is particularly impressive (keep an eye out for a tiger shark or an eel swimming through it). Be sure to notice my favorite sea creatures: the fanciful white anemones and the ethereal moon jellies (which look like parachutes). The rooftop demonstration tide pool not only shows visitors marine coastal life but offers an amazing view of Scripps Pier, La Jolla Shores Beach, the village of La Jolla, and the ocean. Free tide-pool talks are offered on weekends, but this is also when the aquarium is most crowded.

The museum section has numerous interpretive exhibits on the current and historic research done at the Scripps Institution, which was established in 1903 and became part of the university in 1912. Here you'll learn what fog is and why salt melts snow, be astounded at the number of supermarket products that come from the sea (toothpaste, ice cream, and matches, to name a few), feel what an earthquake is like, and experience a 12-minute simulated submarine ride. The bookstore is well stocked with textbooks, science books, educational toys, gifts, and T-shirts.

La Jolla Attractions

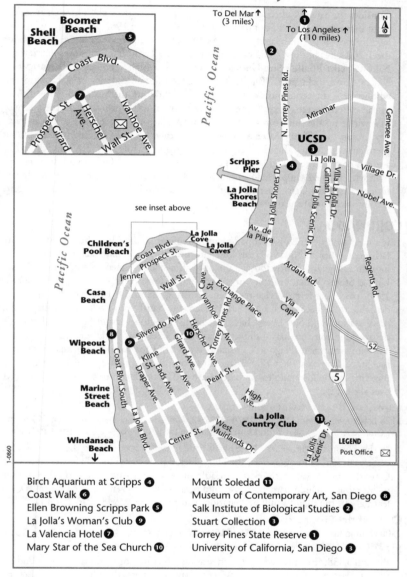

Birch Aquarium at Scripps **4**

Coast Walk **6**

Ellen Browning Scripps Park **5**

La Jolla's Woman's Club **9**

La Valencia Hotel **7**

Mary Star of the Sea Church **10**

Mount Soledad **11**

Museum of Contemporary Art, San Diego **8**

Salk Institute of Biological Studies **2**

Stuart Collection **3**

Torrey Pines State Reserve **1**

University of California, San Diego **3**

A series of **"Seaside Explorations,"** such as the La Jolla Coast Walk, Tidepooling Adventures, and Running with Grunion, are offered. Call ☎ **619/543-6691** for information and prices.

Stuart Collection

University of California, San Diego (UCSD). ☎ **619/534-2117.** Free admission. From La Jolla, take Torrey Pines Rd. to La Jolla Village Dr., turn right, go 2 blocks to Gilman Dr. and turn left into the campus; in about a block the information booth will be visible on the right.

Consider the Stuart Collection a work in progress on a large scale. Through an agreement between the Stuart Foundation and UCSD back in 1982, the still-growing collection consists of site-related sculptures by leading contemporary artists throughout the 1,200 acres of the UCSD campus. Among the 12 diverse sculptures on view are **Niki de Saint-Phalle's Sun God,** a jubilant 14-foot-high fiberglass bird on a 15-foot concrete base, nicknamed **"Big Bird"** and made an unofficial mascot by the students, who make it the centerpiece of their annual celebration, the Sun God Festival. Also in the collection are Alexis Smith's **Snake Path,** a 560-foot-long slate-tile pathway that winds up the hill from the Engineering Mall to the east terrace of the University Library; and **Terry Allen's Trees,** three eucalyptus trees encased in lead, one of them emitting songs and another poems and stories, while the third stands silent in a grove of trees the students call "The Enchanted Forest." Pick up a brochure and map with marked sculpture locations from the information booth at the Northview Drive or Gilman Drive entrance to the campus. Guides, parking permits, and general information are also available.

CORONADO

It's hard to miss one of Coronado's most famous landmarks: The **Coronado Bay Bridge.** Completed in 1969, this four-lane bridge spans 2 miles across the bay, linking San Diego and Coronado; it's the only officially dedicated scenic highway in the United States. When built, it put the commuter ferries out of business, although in 1986, passenger ferry service restarted. Crossing the bridge by car or bus is an undeniable thrill because you can see Mexico, the San Diego skyline, Coronado, the naval station, and San Diego Bay. The bridge's middle section floats, so that if it's destroyed in wartime, naval ships will still have access to the harbor and sea beyond. Traveling from San Diego to Coronado, a toll of $1 for vehicles with solo occupants is charged; however, there's no charge if two or more people are in the car or if you're traveling from Coronado to San Diego. Bus 901 from Downtown will also take you over the bridge.

Coronado Beach Historical Museum

1126 Loma Ave., Coronado. ☎ **619/435-7242.** Free admission. Wed–Sun 10am–4pm. Follow Orange Ave. to Loma Ave. and turn right; it's on the left side beside Chez Loma restaurant.

In the Thomson House (ca. 1898), this little museum goes back to the Coronado of yesteryear, with photographs of the Hotel Del in its infancy; the old ferries; and Tent City, the seaside campground for middle-income folks from 1900 to 1939. Other memorabilia include army uniforms, old postcards, and even recorded music. You'll learn about the island's military aviation history during World Wars I and II.

✪ Hotel del Coronado

1500 Orange Ave., Coronado. ☎ **619/435-6611.** Free admission. Bus: no. 901. Ferry: Broadway Pier, then $1/2$-hr. walk, or take a bus, the Coronado trolley, or rent a bike.

Built in 1888, this turreted Victorian seaside resort in Coronado remains an enduring, endearing national treasure. Whether you stay here, dine here, dance here, or simply wander through on a tour of its grounds and photo gallery, prepare to be enchanted. See "A Hotel with History: Scenes from the Hotel del Coronado" in chapter 5 for more details.

5 Free of Charge & Full of Fun

It's easy to get charged up on a vacation—$10 here, $5 there, and pretty soon your credit-card statement looks like the National Debt. To keep that from happening, I've compiled a list of free San Diego activities. In addition, scan the lists of

"Outdoor Pursuits," "Spectator Sports," and "Special-Interest Sightseeing," below, and the "San Diego Calendar of Events" in chapter 2. Many events listed in these sections, such as the **Annual U.S. Open Sandcastle Competition,** are free of charge. San Diego also has numerous **parades,** such as the Holiday Bowl Parade and the Parade of Lights (both in December). The Centre City Development Corporation's Downtown Information Center offers free trolley and downtown walking tours; see page 132 for more information.

DOWNTOWN & BEYOND

It doesn't cost a penny to stroll around the **Gaslamp Quarter,** which is full or restaurants, shops, and historic buildings, or along the **Embarcadero** (waterfront), and around the shops at **Seaport Village** or **Horton Plaza.** And don't forget: **Walkabout International** offers free guided walking tours as described below.

If you'd rather drive around, ask for the map of the 52-mile **San Diego Scenic Drive** when you're at the International Visitor Information Center.

The downtown branch of the **Museum of Contemporary Art, San Diego,** is free on the 1st Tuesday and Sunday of each month. Another fun activity is the **Sunset Cinema,** discussed in "Only in San Diego" in chapter 10. And you can **fish** free of charge from any municipal pier. The **Children's Park,** situated across the street from the Children's Museum of San Diego, is free, as are all parks in San Diego.

BALBOA PARK

The **San Diego Zoo** is free to all on the 1st Monday of October, Founders Day, and children ages 11 and under get in free every day during October.

All the museums in Balboa Park are open to the public without charge 1 day a month. Here's a list of the free days:

1st Tuesday of each month: Natural History Museum, Reuben H. Fleet Science Center, and Model Railroad Museum.

2nd Tuesday of each month: Museum of Photographic Arts, Hall of Champions, and Museum of San Diego History.

3rd Tuesday of each month: Museum of Art, Museum of Man, Mingei International Museum of World Folk Art, and Japanese Friendship Garden.

4th Tuesday of each month: San Diego Aerospace Museum and San Diego Automotive Museum.

These Balboa Park attractions are always free: The **Botanical Building and Lily Pond, House of Pacific Relations International Cottages,** and **Timken Museum of Art.**

Free 1-hour Sunday concerts and free Summer Festival concerts are given at the **Spreckels Organ Pavilion.**

OLD TOWN, HOTEL CIRCLE & BEYOND

Explore **Heritage Park, Presidio Park,** or **Old Town State Historic Park.** There's free entertainment (mariachis and folk dancers) at the **Bazaar del Mundo,** 2754 Calhoun (☎ 619/296-3161), on Saturday and Sunday. There's also free admission to **Mission Trails Regional Park,** which offers hiking trails and an interpretive center and is located at the east end of Highway 52.

MISSION BAY, PACIFIC BEACH & BEYOND

Walk along the beach or around the bay—it's free, fun, and good for you. (See "Hiking/Walking" in "Outdoor Pursuits" later in this chapter.)

LA JOLLA

Enjoy the ✪ **free outdoor concerts** at Scripps Park on Sundays from 2 to 4pm, mid-June through mid-September (☎ **619/525-3160**).

Anytime is a good time to walk around the **La Jolla Cove, Ellen Browning Scripps Park,** and **Torrey Pines State Reserve** or watch the fur-seal colony at **Seal Rock** or the Children's Pool. If you're a diver, check out the 6,000-acre **San Diego–La Jolla Underwater Park,** which stretches from La Jolla Cove to the northern end of Torrey Pines State Reserve.

If you like arts and crafts, you'll love the **La Jolla Arts Festival,** held the last weekend in September. It's also fun to meander around the campus of the University of California San Diego (UCSD) and view the **Stuart Collection of Outdoor Sculpture.** The La Jolla branch of the **Museum of Contemporary Art, San Diego,** is free on the first Tuesday and Sunday of each month.

For the best vista, follow the "Scenic Drive" signs to **Mount Soledad** and a 360° view of the area.

CORONADO

Drive across the **Coronado Bay Bridge** (free for two or more people in a car) and take a self-guided tour of the **Hotel del Coronado's** grounds and photo gallery. Take a walk on the beach and continue on to the **Coronado Beach Historical Museum.**

FARTHER AFIELD: ARCO TRAINING CENTER

Free tours of the ARCO Training Center in Chula Vista are given year-round. This is the country's first warm weather, year-round, multisport Olympic training complex. It's located on the western shore of Lower Otay Reservoir in Chula Vista and is one of three United States Olympic Committee training centers. The others are in Colorado Springs, Colorado, and Lake Placid, New York. Visitors are shown a short (6-min.) film about the Olympic movement followed by a narrated tour (1.5-mile walk) of the 150-acre campus. The hourly tours are available daily from 9am to 3:30pm. Call ☎ **619/482-6222** for more information.

To get here, take I-805 south to Telegraph Canyon Road, then go east about 7 miles until you reach a sign directing you to turn right, follow this road to the visitor center.

6 Especially for Kids

If you didn't know better, you would think that San Diego was designed by parents planning for a long summer vacation. Activities abound for toddlers to teens. Dozens of public parks, 70 miles of beaches, and myriad museums are just part of what awaits kids of all ages. For up-to-the-minute information about activities for children, pick up a free copy of the monthly *San Diego Family Press;* its calendar of events is geared toward family activities and kids' interests. The **International Visitor Information Center,** at First Avenue and F Street (☎ **619/236-1212**), is always a great resource.

THE TOP ATTRACTIONS

- **Balboa Park** *(see p. 113)* has street entertainers and clowns that always rate high with kids. They can usually be found around El Prado on weekends. The **Natural History Museum** and the **Reuben H. Fleet Space Theater and Science Center,** with its hands-on exhibits and IMAX/OMNIMAX theater, draw kids like magnets.

- The **San Diego Zoo** *(see p. 105)* is appealing to children of all ages, and the double-decker bus tours bring all the animals into easy view of even the smallest, shortest visitors.
- **Sea World** *(see p. 109)*, on Mission Bay, entertains everyone with killer whales, pettable dolphins, and plenty of penguins—the park's penguin exhibit is home to more penguins than all other zoos combined. Try out the new family adventure land, Shamu's Happy Harbor, where everyone is encouraged to explore, crawl, climb, jump, and get wet in more than 20 interactive areas; or take a one-way ride on Mission Bermuda Triangle.
- The **Wild Animal Park** *(see p. 109)* brings geography classes to life when kids find themselves gliding through the wilds of Africa and Asia in a monorail.

OTHER ATTRACTIONS

Children's Museum of San Diego *(see p. 119)*   This museum is a wonderful interactive, imagination-probing experience.

Children's Park *(see p. 127)*   Located across the street from the Children's Museum, the park includes grassy knolls, trees, lighted pathways, and a 200-foot-diameter pond with spray-fountain. Children's Park is a 1996 addition to **Martin Luther King, Jr. Promenade**—a 12-acre park that faces Harbor Drive and includes a walkway with landscaping and benches. Fifteen granite pavers along the walkway focus on Dr. King's philosophy.

Seaport Village *(see p. 127)*   Here your children can enjoy an old-fashioned carousel.

Old Town State Historic Park *(see p. 127)*   This park has a one-room schoolhouse that rates high with kids. They also love the haunted Whaley House, just outside the park.

Birch Aquarium at Scripps *(see p. 128)*   In La Jolla, the aquarium lets kids explore the realms of the deep and learn about life in the sea.

La Jolla Cove *(see p. 128)*   Kids enjoy splashing in tranquil waters that are bathtub smooth.

Belmont Park   Located in Mission Beach, the park lures kids with bumper cars; a carousel; a games arcade; the Plunge, an enormous indoor swimming pool; and the Giant Dipper (see page 123), a restored wooden roller coaster with 2,600 feet of tracks.

White Water Canyon Water Park

2052 Otay Valley Rd., Chula Vista. ☎ **619/426-7275.** Admission $20.99; children under 48 in. tall $14.99; free for children 2 and under. Parking $4 per vehicle. May 24–June 15 10am–6pm weekends only; June 16–Sept 1 daily 10am–6pm.

Located 7 miles south of downtown, this 25-acre water park opened in mid-1997. The theme for this park is a western gold mining town. Features include 16 water slides, a wave pool, a children's pool with minislides, and "Jumping Water Jets." Fort White Water, a four-story interactive play structure, has shallow pools, slides, water cannons, cargo nets, and a floating lily-pad bridge across the pool. Still Water River is a leisurely inner-tube ride along a 1,200 foot river. There are shade structures throughout, food and picnic facilities, a ballpark, and sand volleyball pits.

ENTERTAINMENT

San Diego Junior Theater is located in Balboa Park's Casa del Prado (☎ **619/239-8355**). The theatrical productions here are acted and managed by kids 6 to 18. Sunday afternoon is a great time for kids in Balboa Park, because they can visit the outdoor **Spreckels Organ Pavilion** *(see p. 127)* for a free concert (the mix of music isn't too highbrow for a young audience) and the **House of Pacific Relations** *(see p. 127)* to watch folk dancing on the lawn and experience food from many nations. Or get a taste of Punch and Judy at **Marie Hitchcock Puppet Theatre,** in Balboa Park's Palisades Building (☎ **619/685-5045**). Shows are given Wednesday to Friday at 10am and 11:30am and Saturday and Sunday at 11am, 1, and 2:30pm. These cost $2 for adults and $1.50 for children 3 and over; free for children under 2.

7 Special-Interest Sightseeing

FOR THE ARCHITECTURE ENTHUSIAST   Lovers of period houses will enjoy walking through the Victorian **Villa Montezuma** and the Craftsman-style **Marston House Museum** (described earlier in this chapter). The Gaslamp Quarter walking tour (outlined as "Walking Tour 2" in chapter 8) will lead you past the area's **restored Victorian commercial buildings.**

Downtown high-rises of particular interest include the **Hyatt Regency San Diego,** the **Emerald-Shapery Center,** at 400 W. Broadway, and **One America Plaza** at 600 W. Broadway. This last building is 498 feet high, which is 24 inches under the maximum height allowed by the FAA. Some people say San Diego's new skyline resembles the contents of a toolbox: a straight screwdriver, a Phillips screwdriver, and a cluster of Allen wrenches. Take a look and see what you think.

While you're in the central business district, the 12-by-12-foot scale model of the city at the **Center City Development Corporation Downtown Information Center,** at 225 Broadway (☎ **619/235-2200**), might be of interest.

Students of architecture will also want to see the Louis Kahn–designed **Salk Institute** and the **classic buildings created by Irving Gill** (see "La Jolla" in Section 4 of this chapter). La Jolla's **Wall Street Cafe** and **Brockton Villa** (both described in chapter 6, "Dining") have received architectural awards for excellence.

In contrast, the **Hyatt Regency San Diego** was bestowed a Major Raw Onion (an award given for architectural flops)—the same year the Salk Institute was lambasted for adding an extension that compromised Louis Kahn's design. Not far from the Salk Institute, the Michael Graves–designed **Hyatt Regency La Jolla** has also garnered an Onion.

Two of my favorite buildings are the **Jacob Weinberger Courthouse,** on F Street between State and Union streets, and the ✪ **Treehouse restaurant complex at the San Diego Zoo.** For further information, phone the AIA (☎ **619/232-0109**).

FOR GARDENERS   San Diego is a gardener's paradise, thanks in part to the efforts and inspiration of Kate Sessions. In Balboa Park, visit the **Japanese Friendship Garden,** the **Botanical Building and Lily Pond,** and the **rose and desert gardens** (across the road from Plaza de Balboa). And when you're at the **San Diego Zoo** and **Wild Animal Park,** you'll notice that these are both outstanding botanical gardens. Many visitors who admire the landscaping at the zoo, don't realize that the plantings have been carefully developed over the years. The 100 acres here were once scrub-covered hillsides with few trees. Today, towering eucalyptus and graceful palms, birds-of-paradise, and hibiscus are just a few of the 6,500 botanical species from all over the world that flourish here, providing a beautiful garden setting as well as dinner for some animals. In fact, the plant collection is worth more than the zoo animals.

In North County, garden enthusiasts will want to visit the 30-acre **Quail Botanical Gardens** (see chapter 11 for details). If you'd like to take plants home with you, visit some of the area's nurseries, including the one started in 1910 by Kate Sessions, **Mission Hills Nursery,** 1525 Fort Stockton Dr., San Diego (☎ **619/295-2808**). **Walter**

Andersen's Nursery, 3642 Enterprise St., San Diego (☎ **619/224-8271**), is also a local favorite. See chapter 11 for information on nurseries in North County. Flower growing is big business in this area, and plant enthusiasts could spend a week just visiting the retail and wholesale purveyors of everything from pansies to palm trees. The **San Diego Floral Association,** in the Casa del Prado in Balboa Park (☎ **619/ 232-5762**), may also be able to provide information.

FOR MILITARY BUFFS   The public is welcome at the **Broadway Pier,** near the intersection of Broadway and Harbor Drive, where a Navy ship is in port and open for free tours most Saturdays and Sundays from 1 to 4pm (☎ **619/532-1430,** ext. 9).

You can also attend a marine corps recruit parade at the Marine Corps Recruit Depot (MCRD), off Pacific Coast Highway, most Friday mornings at 10am (☎ **619/524-1765**). **Old Town Trolley Tours** (☎ **619/298-TOUR** [8687]) is the only company allowed on San Diego military bases. On their Friday morning tour to North Island Naval Air Station, passengers get a close-up look at any aircraft carriers that are in port. The tour lasts two to three hours and allows an opportunity to purchase military memorabilia.

FOR WINE LOVERS   Visit **Orfila Vineyards** (☎ **760/738-6500;** Web site: www.orfila.com) near the Wild Animal Park in Escondido. Italian-born wine-maker Leon Santoro is a veteran of Napa Valley (Louis Martini and Stag's Leap). In addition to producing excellent chardonnay and merlot, the winery also makes several Rhone and Italian varietals, including Sangiovese. Tours and tastings are offered daily from 10am to 6pm. The property includes a parklike picnic area and a shop.

If you have time to go farther afield, the wineries along Rancho California Road in Temecula, just across the San Diego County line, are open for tours and tastings. For further details, see chapter 11.

8 Organized Tours

In San Diego, I'd recommend starting with a bus or trolley tour, complemented by a downtown walking tour or a bay excursion.

ORIENTATION TOURS
BAY EXCURSIONS

Bahia Belle
998 W. Mission Bay Dr. ☎ **619/539-7779.** Tickets $5 adults, $3 children under 12. June and Sept Wed–Sat 6:30pm–12:30am; July–Aug Wed–Sun 6:30pm–12:30am; Oct 1–Nov 30 and Jan 1–May 31 Fri–Sat 7:30pm–12:30am. Children accompanied by an adult allowed until 9:30pm; after 9:30pm, 21 or over only (with valid ID).

Cruise Mission Bay aboard this festive stern-wheeler, which picks up passengers at the dock of the Bahia Hotel, 998 W. Mission Bay Dr., on the half hour from 7:30pm to 12:30am, and at the Catamaran Resort Hotels, 3999 Mission Blvd., on the hour from 8pm to midnight.

Hornblower Invader Cruises
1066 N. Harbor Dr. ☎ **619/234-8687.** Tickets $41 for dinner cruise; $30.80 brunch cruise; half price for children.

This company offers 1- and 2-hour narrated tours of San Diego Bay. Nightly dinner cruises with music and dancing are also available from 7 to 9pm, as well as Sunday-brunch cruises from 11am to 1pm. Whale-watching trips are offered in the winter.

Gondola di Venezia

Kona Kai Continental Resort & Marina, 1551 Shelter Island Dr. ☎ **619/221-2999**. Tickets $62 per couple; $17 for each additional passenger.

This is a relaxing and romantic way to view the San Diego skyline and Shelter Island. The watercraft, which can carry up to six passengers, were handcrafted following plans from a Venetian gondola builder. Gondoliers wear authentic attire—striped shirt and hat with ribbon. The 1-hour cruise includes Italian music, hors d'oeuvres, and a bucket of ice with wine and glasses. Boarding is at the Kona Kai Continental Resort & Marina on Shelter Island.

San Diego Harbor Excursion

1050 N. Harbor Dr. (foot of Broadway). ☎ **800/442-7847** or 619/234-4111. Tickets $12 1-hr. excursion; $17 2-hr. excursion; half price for children.

The company offers daily 1- and 2-hour narrated tours of the bay, plus dinner cruises, and in winter, whale-watching excursions. Each narrator has been with the company for at least 5 years. Times and frequency vary seasonally.

BUS TOURS

San Diego Mini Tours (☎ 619/477-8687) offers city sightseeing tours, including a "Grand Tour" that includes San Diego, Tijuana, and a 1-hour harbor cruise. They also offer trips to the San Diego Zoo, Sea World, Disneyland, Universal Studios, Tijuana, Rosarito Beach, and Ensenada. Prices range from $26 to $62 for adults, $14 to $44 for children under 12, and include admissions. Multiple tours can be combined for discounts.

Gray Line Tours (☎ 619/491-0011) offers city sightseeing, including Cabrillo National Monument, Sea World, and La Jolla, along with trips that take you farther afield to the Wild Animal Park, wine country, and Tijuana and Ensenada, Mexico. Prices range from $24 to $56 for adults and $10 to $35 for children.

Centre City Development Corporation's Downtown Information Center (☎ 619/235-2222) offers free trolley tours of the downtown area on the 1st and 3rd Saturdays of the month from 10am to noon. Downtown residential walking tours for five or more people are offered from 1pm to 3pm. The tours require reservations and start at 225 Broadway, Suite 160. Go inside to see models of the Gaslamp Quarter and the downtown area. The office is open Monday through Saturday from 9am to 5pm.

TROLLEY TOURS

In San Diego, it's a good idea to invest at least an hour and a half in a narrated ✪ **Old Town Trolley** tour (☎ 619/298-TOUR [8687]). The 30-mile route has more than a dozen stops, and you can get off at any of them, explore at leisure, and reboard when you please (a bus-cum-trolley passes each stop every half hour). Stops include the Embarcadero, downtown area, Horton Plaza, Gaslamp Quarter, Coronado, San Diego Zoo, Balboa Park, Heritage Park, and Presidio Park. The tour costs $20 for adults, $8 for children 6 to 12, and is free for children under 5, for one complete loop, no matter how many times you hop on or off the trolley. One complete loop takes 90 minutes; once you've finished the circuit, you can't go around again. It's a good idea to start early in the day. Old Town Trolley Tours offers tours to Naval Air Station North Island on Friday morning.

SPECIALTY TOURS
WHALE WATCHING

It's fun to be in San Diego from December through March when the California gray whales migrate to the warmer waters of Baja California to mate. Many local tour operators provide special excursions this time of year to help you catch a glimpse of the mighty animals; two are **Hornblower Invader Cruises** and **San Diego Harbor Excursion** (see "Bay Excursions," above). The **Birch Aquarium at Scripps** (☎ **619/ 534-FISH**) offers expeditions out of Mission Bay, with a naturalist onboard to talk with passengers and answer questions.

WALKING TOURS

Walkabout International, 235 Fifth Ave., #407 (☎ **619/231-7463**), sponsors more than 100 free walking tours every month, led by volunteers in the San Diego area. A lively guide known as Downtown Sam, who retired from the Air Force in 1972, leads downtown tours, which are particularly popular with retired San Diegans eager for exercise and camaraderie. He's easy to spot, in walking shorts and a cap with a button proclaiming "No thanks, I'd rather walk." Sam's Saturday-morning tours draw 20 to 40 people, and they end with a stop for coffee or a meal. Sam also leads a 1¹/₂-hour downtown theme tour at 11am on Tuesday, focusing on bookstores, shopping, pubs, thrift shops, bank lobbies—you name it.

On Saturday from 1 to 3pm, the **Centre City Development Corporation (CCDC),** 225 Broadway, Suite 160 (☎ **619/235-2222**), offers free walking tours that focus on downtown-area development. Reservations are required.

Coronado Touring, 1110 Isabella Ave., Coronado (☎ **619/435-5993** or 619/ 435-5444), provides upbeat, informative 90-minute walking tours of Coronado, including the Hotel del Coronado. Enthusiastic guides Nancy Cobb and Gerry MacCartee have been doing this since 1980, so they know their subject well. Tours leave at 11am on Tuesday, Thursday, and Saturday from the Glorietta Bay Inn. The price is $7.

At the **Cabrillo National Monument** on the tip of Point Loma, rangers often lead free walking tours (see "More Attractions," earlier in this chapter). The **Gaslamp Quarter Association** offers tours of the Gaslamp Quarter on Saturday at 11am for a $5 donation. Tours leave from William Heath Davis House at 410 Island Ave. (☎ **619/233-5227**).

Docents at **Torrey Pines State Reserve** in La Jolla lead guided nature walks on weekends (see "Hiking/Walking" under "Outdoor Pursuits," below).

You can explore **La Jolla** by taking walking and/or shopping tours conducted by **La Jolla Walking Tours** (☎ **619/453-8219**). These leave from the Colonial Inn, 910 Prospect St., on Friday and Saturday mornings at 10am and cost $9.

Volunteers from the **Natural History Museum** (☎ **619/232-3821**, ext. 203) lead nature walks throughout San Diego County.

9 Outdoor Pursuits

BALLOONING

For a balloon's-eye glimpse of the area at sunrise or sunset, followed by champagne and hors d'oeuvres, contact **A Skysurfer Balloon Company** (☎ **619/481-6800**) or—my favorite—✪ **California Dreamin'** (☎ **800/748-5959**). The balloon rides provide sweeping vistas of the southern California coast, rambling estates, and golf courses. You may also be interested in the **Temecula Balloon and Wine Festival** held in late April. Call ☎ **909/676-4713** for information.

BIKING

For information on bike rentals, see "Getting Around" in chapter 4.

Most major thoroughfares offer bike lanes. To receive a really great map of San Diego County's bike lanes and routes, call **Ride Link Bicycle Information**

(☎ **619/231-BIKE** [2453] or ☎ 619/237-POOL [7665]). You might also want to talk to the **City of San Diego Bicycle Coordinator** (☎ **619/533-3110**), the **San Diego Bicycle Coalition** (☎ **619/685-7742**), or the **County of San Diego Bicycle Coordinator** (☎ **619/694-2811**). Just remember to wear a helmet; it's the law.

The Mission Bay and Coronado areas, in particular, are good for leisurely bike rides. The boardwalk in Pacific Beach and Mission Beach can get very crowded, especially on weekends. Coronado also has a 16-mile round-trip bike trail which starts at the Ferry Landing Marketplace and follows a well-marked route around Coronado and to Imperial Beach.

Adventure Bike Tours, 333 W. Harbor Dr., in the San Diego Marriott Marina (☎ **619/234-1500,** ext. 6514) conducts bicycle tours from San Diego to Coronado. These cost about $40 including ferry fare and equipment. They also offer a Bayside Glide for $22 per person and rent bikes for $8 an hour, $18 for half a day, or $25 for a full day. In-line skates are also for hire here.

For a downhill thrill of a lifetime, take the **Palomar Plunge.** From the top of Palomar Mountain to its base, you'll experience, courtesy of gravity, a 5,000-foot vertical drop stretched out over 16 miles. Or try the **Desert Descent,** a 12-mile, 3,700-foot descent down the Montezuma Valley Grade to the desert floor, followed by a tour of the Visitor Center and a delicious lunch. **Gravity Activated Sports** (☎ **800/985-4427** or 760/742-2294; Web site: www.gasports.com) supplies the mountain bike, helmet, gloves, souvenir photo, and T-shirt. They also offer a bike tour through the Temecula wine region.

Adventurous cyclists might also like to participate in the **Rosarito-Ensenada 50-Mile Fun Bicycle Ride,** held every April and September. This event attracts more than 8,000 riders of all ages and abilities. It starts at the Rosarito Beach Hotel and finishes in Ensenada. For information, contact **Bicycling West, Inc.** (☎ **619/583-3001**).

BOATING

Club Nautico, a concession at the San Diego Marriott Marina, 333 W. Harbor Dr. (☎ **619/233-9311**), provides guests and nonguests with an exhilarating way to see the bay by the hour, half day, or full day in 20- to 27-foot offshore power boats. Rentals start at $89 an hour. They allow their boats to be taken into the ocean and also provide diving, waterskiing, and fishing packages.

Seaforth Boat Rental, 1641 Quivira Rd., Mission Bay (☎ and fax **619/ 223-1681**), has a wide variety of boats for bay and ocean, 15- to 90-horsepower powerboats for $45 to $90 an hour, 14- to 30-foot sailboats for $20 to $45 an hour, ski boats and jet skis for $60 an hour; half-day and full-day rates are available. Canoes, pedal boats, and rowboats are available for those who prefer a slower pace. American Express, MasterCard, and Visa are accepted.

Seaforth also owns **Downtown Boat Rental,** at 333 W. Harbor Drive in the Marriott Hotel & Marina (☎ **619/239-2628**). They offer 14- to 36-foot sailboats for $20 to $45 an hour and kayaks for $12 an hour.

Mission Bay Sportcenter, 1010 Santa Clara Place (☎ **619/488-1004**), rents sailboats, catamarans, sailboards, kayaks, jet skis, and motorboats, with prices at $10 an hour, $30 for 4 hours, and $40 for a full day. Instruction is available. Diners Club, MasterCard, and Visa are accepted.

San Diego Yacht & Breakfast Club, 1880 Harbor Island Dr. (☎ **619/ 298-6623**), rents kayaks for $20 an hour, 3-horsepower dinghies for $15 an hour, Windriders for $40 an hour, and Waverunners for $65 an hour. Half- and full-day rentals are also available. The **San Diego Sailing Club,** at the same address and phone number, rents yachts and offers sailing lessons.

Outdoor Pursuits in the San Diego Area

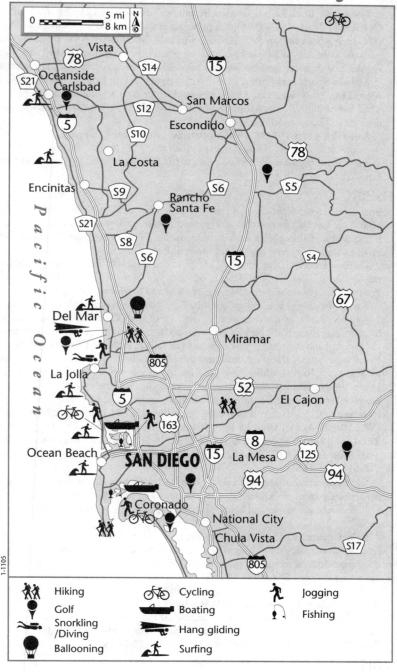

Hiking	Cycling	Jogging
Golf	Boating	Fishing
Snorkling /Diving	Hang gliding	
Ballooning	Surfing	

1-1105

Coronado Boat Rental (owned by the Seaforth folks), 1715 Strand Way, in Coronado (☎ 619/437-1514), has powerboats with 90- and 110-horsepower motors renting from $60 to $90 an hour, with half- and full-day rates; 14- to 30-foot sailboats from $30 to $45 an hour; and jet skis, ski boats, canoes, pedal boats, fishing skiffs, and charter boats. American Express, MasterCard, and Visa are accepted.

La Jolla Sports and Photo, 2199 Avenida de la Playa, in La Jolla Shores (☎ 619/459-1114), rents single and double kayaks. A single costs $30 for half a day, $45 for a full day; a double costs $40 for half a day and $55 for a full day. They also conduct guided kayak tours and rent bicycles.

Sail USA (☎ 619/298-6822), offers custom-tailored skippered cruises on a 34-foot Catalina sloop. A half-day bay cruise costs $295 for six passengers. Full-day and overnight trips are also available, as are trips along the coast to Ensenada and to Catalina.

FISHING

For information on fishing, call the **City Fish Line** at ☎ 619/465-3474. Anglers of any age can fish free of charge without a license off any municipal pier in California. **Public fishing piers** are located on Shelter Island (where there's a statue dedicated to anglers), Ocean Beach, and Imperial Beach.

Fishing charters depart from Harbor and Shelter islands, Point Loma, the Imperial Beach pier, and Quivira Basin in Mission Bay (near the Hyatt Islandia Hotel). Participants in these trips over the age of 16 need a California fishing license.

For **sportfishing,** you can go out on a large boat for about $25 for half a day or $35 to $85 for three-quarters to a full day. To charter a boat for up to six people, the rates run about $550 for half a day and $850 for an entire day; more in summer. Call around and compare prices. Summer and fall are excellent times for excursions. Locally, the waters around Point Loma are filled with bass, bonito, and barracuda; the Coronado Islands, which belong to Mexico but are only about 18 miles from San Diego, are popular for abalone, yellowtail, yellowfin, and big-eyed tuna. Some outfitters will take you farther into Baja California waters. The following outfitters offer short or extended outings with daily departures: **H & M Landing,** 2803 Emerson (☎ 619/222-1144); **Islandia Sportfishing,** 1551 W. Mission Bay Rd. (☎ 619/222-1164); **Lee Palm Sportfishers** (☎ 619/224-3857); **Point Loma Sportfishing,** 1403 Scott St. (☎ 619/223-1627); and **Seaforth Boat Rentals,** 1641 Quivira Rd. (☎ 619/233-1681).

For **freshwater fishing,** San Diego's lakes and rivers provide catches of bass, channel and bullhead catfish, bluegill, trout, crappie, and sunfish. Most lakes have rental facilities for boats, tackle, and bait, and they also provide picnic and (usually) camping areas.

Lake Cuyamaca, 45 minutes from San Diego near Julian, is 5,000 feet above sea level, set in the midst of pines and cedars, and filled with trout year-round. It's open daily from sunrise to sunset; there are motorboat and rowboat rentals and a small charge for fishing (☎ 619/447-8123).

For more information on fishing in California, contact the **California Department of Fish and Game** at ☎ 619/467-4201.

For fishing in Mexican waters, including off the Coronado Islands, angling permits are required. Contact the **Mexican Department of Fisheries,** 2550 Fifth Ave., Suite 101, San Diego, CA 92103-6622 (☎ 619/233-6956).

GOLF

With nearly 80 courses, 50 of them open to the public, golf enthusiasts have innumerable opportunities to play their game in San Diego County. Courses are diverse, some with vistas of the Pacific, others with views of country hillsides or of desert landscapes.

M & M Tee Times (☎ 619/456-8366) can arrange tee times for you at most golf courses, as can **PAR-TEE GOLF** (☎ 800/PAR-TEE-1). **Greenlink** (☎ 619/I-LOVE-GOLF** [456-8346]) is also a valuable source of information about golf courses, schools, and equipment.

And where else but San Diego can you practice your golf swing in the middle of the central business district? **Metro Golf Harborside,** 801 W. Ash St. at Pacific Highway (☎ 619/239-GOLF), is open from 7am to 10pm Monday to Friday, from 8am to 10pm on Saturday, and from 9am to 9pm on Sunday. Here you will find 80 tees, a putting and chipping area, night lighting, a pro shop, and golf instruction. Club rental is available at $1 each; a large bucket of balls costs $6, a small bucket, $3.

Coronado Municipal Golf Course
2000 Visalia Row, Coronado. ☎ 619/435-3121.

This is the first sight that welcomes you as you cross the Coronado Bay Bridge (the course is off to the left). The 18-hole, par-72 course overlooks Glorietta Bay, and there's a coffee shop, pro shop, and driving range. Two-day prior reservations are strongly recommended; call anytime after 7am. Greens fees are $20 for 18 holes.

The Four Seasons Resort Aviara Golf Club
7447 Batiquitos Dr., Carlsbad. ☎ 760/929-0077.

This spot has a reputation as one of the area's most memorable courses. The 18 holes (each with four tees) spread out over 500 acres overlooking the Pacific Ocean and the Batiquitos Lagoon, California's largest lagoon and home to more than 130 species of birds. The 7,007-yard, par-72 course is open to the public, and greens fees ($110 Monday through Thursday; $135 Friday through Sunday; $75 after 3pm) include a golf cart and use of the clubhouse, which has lockers, saunas, and showers. The Argyle restaurant and lounge is on the premises.

Morgan Run
5690 Cancha de Golf, Rancho Santa Fe. ☎ 619/756-3255.

Formerly Whispering Palms, these three 9-hole courses (one par 35; two par 36) are part of a resort, but you don't have to stay there to play. Course architect Jay Morrish redesigned one of the courses in 1995. There's also a driving range. Greens fees are $65 during the week and $80 on weekends, including a cart.

Mount Woodson Country Club
16422 N. Woodson Dr., Ramona. ☎ 760/788-3555.

One of San Diego County's dramatic golf courses, Mount Woodson is a par-70, 6,180-yard course on 150 beautiful acres. The award-winning 18-hole course, which opened in 1991, meanders up and down hills, across bridges, and around granite boulders. Elevated tees provide striking views of Ramona and Mount Palomar, and on a clear day you can see for almost 100 miles. It's easy to combine a game of golf with a weekend getaway to Julian (see chapter 11). Greens fees here for 18 holes are $45 to $48 Monday through Thursday, $50 to $55 Friday, and $65 to $70 on Saturday and Sunday. Lower twilight rates are also available. Mount Woodson is about 40 minutes north of San Diego. To get there, exit I-5 at Poway Road; at the end of Poway Road turn left (north) onto Route 67 and drive 3³/₄ miles to Archie Moore Road; turn left. The golf course entrance is on the left.

Pala Mesa
2001 Old Hwy. 395, Fallbrook. ☎ 760/728-5881.

This hilly course in Fallbrook's avocado country offers stunning views. Greens are excellent, fast, and firm. Women will particularly appreciate this course. It was listed in the magazine *Golf for Women* on their 1997 Top Fairways list as one of the courses that "best meets women golfers' needs" because of its golf clinics that are specifically geared toward women. Pala Mesa is a popular golf resort in a country setting that offers tennis courts, a swimming pool, fine dining, and attractive guest rooms in addition to the highly rated 18-hole par-72 course.

Rancho Bernardo Inn

17550 Bernardo Oaks Dr., Rancho Bernardo. ☎ **800/542-6096** or 619/675-8500.

Home to Ken Blanchard's Golf University of San Diego since 1992, Rancho Bernardo's attributes include a mature 18-hole, 72-par championship course with terrains, water hazards, sand traps, lakes, and waterfalls. Lessons or 1-hour clinics with a pro, 2- to 4-day schools through the Golf University with meals and lodging included, and a standard golf package are available. Greens fees are $65 during the week and $80 Friday through Sunday, including a cart. Twilight rates (after 2pm) are $35 weekdays and $45 weekends.

Singing Hills

3007 Dehesa Rd., El Cajon. ☎ **800/457-5568** or 619/442-3425.

The only resort in Southern California offering 54 holes of golf (two championship courses and a par-54 executive course), Singing Hills has taken advantage of the area's natural terrain, using mountains, natural rock outcroppings, and aged oaks and sycamores to add character to individual holes. In 1997, this course was also chosen by *Golf for Women* magazine for their Top Fairways list as one of the courses that "best meet women golfers' needs." Singing Hills is the home of the 17-year-old School of Golf for Women. The golf courses are part of the Singing Hills Resort, but nonguests are welcome to play here. Greens fees are $30 Monday through Thursday, $35 Friday, and $40 Saturday and Sunday for the two par-72 courses and $12 on the shorter course. Cart rental costs an additional $20. The resort offers a variety of good-value packages.

Temecula Creek Inn

44501 Rainbow Canyon Rd., Temecula. ☎ **800/96-CREEK.**

The resort is 1 hour north of San Diego in a country setting. The 27-hole, 10,014-yard championship golf course is a par-36 per 9 holes and features rolling hills and fairways lined with 100-year-old live oaks. Pheasants and bobcats put in occasional appearances. The stone house on one of the nines is one of Temecula's oldest buildings (see chapter 11). Lessons and golf package available. Greens fees for 18 holes are $48 Monday through Thursday, $55 on Friday, and $70 on Saturday and Sunday, including a cart.

✪ Torrey Pines Golf Course

11480 Torrey Pines Rd., La Jolla. ☎ **619/552-1784** for information, 619/570-1234 to book a tee time, 619/452-3226 for the pro shop.

Two gorgeous 18-hole championship courses are located on the coast between La Jolla and Del Mar, only 15 minutes from downtown San Diego. Home of the Buick Invitational Tournament, these municipal courses are very popular. Both overlook the ocean; the north course is more picturesque, the south course more challenging.

Tee times are taken by computer, starting at 5am, up to 7 days in advance by telephone only. Confirmation numbers are issued, and you must have the number and photo identification with you when you check in with the starter 15 minutes ahead of time. If you're late, your time may be forfeited.

Insider's tip: Single golfers stand a good chance of getting on the course if they just turn up and wait for a threesome. Likewise, the locals also sometimes circumvent the reservation system by spending the night in a camper in the parking lot. The starter lets these diehards on before the reservations made by the computer go into effect at 7:30am.

Golf professionals are available for lessons, and the pro shop rents clubs, if you left yours at home. Greens fees for out-of-towners are $46 during the week and $51 Saturday, Sunday, and holidays for 18 holes (after 4pm April through October and 3pm November through March the fee is only $26); $26 for 9 holes. San Diego city and county residents are charged much less.

HANG GLIDING

If you have a U.S. Hang Gliding Association rating card to prove your proficiency, you can soar above the cliffs and coast at Torrey Pines State Reserve, about 4 miles north of La Jolla. For information about lessons or gear, contact the **Hang Gliding Center** at ☎ 619/450-9008.

HIKING/WALKING

San Diego's mild climate makes it a great place to walk or hike most of the year and the options are very diverse. Walking along the water is particularly popular. The best beaches for walking are La Jolla Shores, Mission Beach, and Coronado, but pretty much any beach is a good choice. You can also walk around **Mission Bay** on a series of connected footpaths. If a four-legged friend is your walking companion, head for **Dog Beach** in Ocean Beach or Fiesta Island in Mission Bay—two of the few areas where dogs can legally go unleashed. **Coast Walk** in La Jolla offers supreme surf-line views (see "La Jolla" under "More Attractions" above).

The **Sierra Club** sponsors regular hikes in the San Diego area, and nonmembers are welcome to participate. There's always a Wednesday mountain hike, usually in the Cuyamaca Mountains, though sometimes in the Lagunas; there are evening and day hikes as well. Most are free. For a recorded message of upcoming hikes, call ☎ 619/299-1744, or call the office between Monday and Friday from noon to 5pm and on Saturday from 10am to 4pm (☎ 619/299-1743).

Torrey Pines State Reserve in La Jolla (☎ 619/755-2063) offers hiking trails with wonderful ocean views and a chance to see the rare torrey pine. Access is via North Torrey Pines Road. The trails are free of charge; parking costs $4 per car, $3 for seniors. Guided nature walks are also available here on the weekends.

The Bayside Trail near **Cabrillo National Monument** also affords great views. Drive to the monument and follow signs to the trail.

✪ **Mission Trails Regional Park,** 8 miles northeast of downtown, offers a glimpse of what San Diego looked like before development. Located between Highway 52 and I-8 and east of I-15, rugged hills, valleys, and open areas provide a quick escape from the urban hustle-bustle. A visitor and interpretive center (☎ 619/668-3275) is open daily from 9am to 5pm. Access is via Mission Gorge Road.

Marian Bear Memorial Park, a.k.a. San Clemente Canyon (☎ 619/581-9952 for park ranger), is a 10-mile round-trip trail that runs directly underneath Highway 52. Most of the trail is flat, hard-packed dirt, but some areas along the trails are rocky. There are benches and places for people to sit and have a quiet picnic. From Highway 52 west, take the Genesee South exit; at the light make a U-turn and an immediate right into the parking lot. From Highway 52 east, exit at Genesee and make a right at the light, then an immediate right into the parking lot.

Lake Miramar Reservoir provides a 5-mile, paved, looped trail that provides a wonderful view of the lake and mountains. Take I-15 north and exit on Mira Mesa

Boulevard, turn right on Scripps Ranch Boulevard, then left on Scripps Lake Drive, and make a left at the LAKE MIRAMAR sign. Parking is free but the lot closes at 6:30pm. There's also a wonderful walkway around **Lake Murray.** Take the Lake Murray Boulevard exit off I-8 and follow the signs.

The **Coronado bike trail** (see "Biking," above) is also a great place to walk. For additional hiking-trail information, see "Julian" in chapter 11.

You should also note that volunteers from the **Natural History Museum** (☎ 619/232-3821, ext. 203) lead nature walks throughout San Diego County.

HORSEBACK RIDING

Hosts Earl and Liz Hammond at ✪ **Holidays on Horseback** (☎ 619/445-3997 or 619/659-6097), located 40 miles east of San Diego in Descanso, offer trail rides from 1¹/₂ to 9 hours in the mountains of the Cuyamaca Rancho State Park, which has 135 miles of wilderness trails. Riders pass through beautiful scenery that includes native chaparral, live oak, and manzanita. The Hammonds have 14 horses; many are smooth-gaited breeds such as the Missouri fox-trotter. A 4-hour ride with a picnic lunch on the trail costs $60. American Express, Diners Club, MasterCard, and Visa are accepted. The Hammonds also offer bed-and-breakfast packages.

JOGGING/RUNNING

One of my favorite places to jog is the sidewalk that follows the east side of **Mission Bay.** Start at the Visitor Information Center and head south past the Hilton to Fiesta Island. A good spot for a short run is **La Jolla Shores Beach,** because there's hard-packed sand to run on even when it isn't low tide. The beach at **Coronado** is also a good place for jogging, as is the shore at **Pacific Beach** and **Mission Beach**— just watch your tide chart to make sure you won't be there at high tide.

Safety note: Avoid secluded areas of Balboa Park even in broad daylight.

SKATING

Gliding around San Diego, especially the Mission Bay area, on in-line skates is the quintessential Southern California experience. In Mission Beach, rent a pair of regular or in-line skates from **Skates Plus,** 3830 Mission Blvd. (☎ 619/488-PLUS), or **Hamel's Action Sports Center,** 704 Ventura Place, off Mission Boulevard at Ocean Front Walk (☎ 619/488-5050); and in Pacific Beach, at **Pacific Beach Sun and Sea,** 4539 Ocean Blvd. (☎ 619/483-6613). In Coronado, go to **Mike's Bikes,** at 1343 Orange Ave. (☎ 619/435-7744), or **Bikes and Beyond,** 1201 First St. and at the Ferry Landing (☎ 619/435-7180). Be sure to ask for protective gear.

If you'd rather ice-skate, try the **Ice Capades Chalet** at University Towne Center, La Jolla Village Drive at Genesee Street (☎ 619/452-9110).

SCUBA DIVING & SNORKELING

San Diego Divers Supply at 4004 Sports Arena Blvd. (☎ 619/224-3439), and at 5701 La Jolla Blvd. (☎ 619/459-2691), will set you up with scuba and snorkeling equipment. The **San Diego–La Jolla Underwater Park,** especially the La Jolla Cove, is the best spot for scuba diving and snorkeling. For more information, see "San Diego Beaches," earlier in this chapter. The **Underwater Pumpkin Carving Contest,** held at Halloween, is a fun local event. For information, call ☎ 619/565-6054.

SPAS

San Diego County hosts some of the best spas in the country, including the Golden Door and Cal-a-Vie. For further details, see "Select Spas" in chapter 11.

SURFING

With its miles of beaches, San Diego is a popular surf destination. Some of the best spots include Windansea, La Jolla Shores, Pacific Beach, Mission Beach, Ocean Beach, and Imperial Beach. In North County, you might consider Carlsbad State Beach and Oceanside.

If you didn't bring your own stick, they are available for rent at stands at many popular beaches. Many local surf shops also rent equipment; these include **La Jolla Surf Systems,** 2132 Avenida de la Playa, La Jolla Shores (☎ **619/456-2777**), and **Emerald Surf & Sport,** 1118 Orange Ave., Coronado (☎ **619/435-6677**).

SWIMMING

San Diego's resort hotels and the Embassy Suites downtown have pools, as does the **YMCA,** located at 500 W. Broadway, between Columbia and India streets (☎ **619/ 232-7451**). The charge for use of the Y's pool and other health facilities, including a sauna, Jacuzzi, free weights, aerobics classes, and a gym with running track, is $10 a day, $7 for ages 18 to 22, free for members of a Y outside San Diego County; it's open Monday through Friday from 5:45am to 9pm and on Saturday from 8am to 5pm (towels are supplied).

In Balboa Park, you can swim in the **Kearns Memorial Swimming Pool,** 2229 Morley Field Dr. (☎ **619/692-4920**). The fee for using this public pool is $2 for adults and $1 for children under 16 and seniors. During the summer, they are open for laps Monday to Friday from 9am to 3:55pm and 6:35 to 7:45pm, Saturday from 9:30am to 4pm, and Sunday 11am to 4pm; recreational swimming hours are Monday through Friday from 1 to 3:55pm and 6:35 to 7:45pm and Saturday and Sunday from 11am to 4pm (winter hours are shorter).

In Mission Bay, you'll find a famous and well-maintained pool called **The Plunge,** 3115 Oceanfront Walk, (☎ **619/488-3110**), part of **Belmont Park** since 1925. Pool capacity is 525 and there are 10 lap lanes and a viewing area inside. It's open to the public Monday through Friday from 6am to 8am, noon to 1pm, and 2:30 to 8pm and Saturday and Sunday from 8am to 4pm. Admission is $2.50 for adults and $2.25 for children.

In La Jolla you can swim at the **Jewish Community Center,** 4126 Executive Drive, ☎ **619/457-3161.** They have an ozone pool (kept clean by an ozone generator), instead of the typical chlorinated pool. It is open to the public Monday through Thursday from 6:30am to 7:30pm, Friday from 6:30am to 6pm, Saturday 11am to 6pm, and Sunday from 10am to 6pm. Admission is $5 for adults and $3 for children under 17.

Swimmers may want to compete in (or watch) one of the rough-water swims held in the area. These include the **Oceanside Rough Water Swim** (☎ **760/941-0946**) and the **La Jolla Rough Water Swim** (☎ **619/456-2100**), both held in the beginning of September around Labor Day.

If you are looking to swim in the Pacific, Mission Bay is a popular spot.

TENNIS

There are 1,200 public and private tennis courts in San Diego. Public courts are located throughout the city, including the **La Jolla Tennis Club,** 7632 Draper, at Prospect (☎ **619/454-4434**), which is free and open daily from dawn until the lights go off at 9pm; and the **Balboa Tennis Club,** 2221 Morley Field Dr., in Balboa Park (☎ **619/295-9278**). Court use is free, but reservations are required; they are open Monday through Friday from 10am to 8pm and Saturday and Sunday from 8am to

6pm. Many resort hotels, including the ones listed below, offer tennis courts that are available to the public.

Hilton Beach & Tennis Resort

1775 E. Mission Bay Dr. ☎ **619/276-4010.**

There are five lighted courts and a practice half-court with a ball machine; tennis packages are available. Only the half-court and ball machine are available to nonguests.

La Costa Resort and Spa

Costa del Mar Rd., Carlsbad. ☎ **619/438-9111.**

The 23 courts here provide play on three different surfaces: two Wimbledon-quality grass courts, four clay courts, and 15 hard courts. Eight courts are lighted for evening play, and six professional practice lanes are available. The courts are available to spa guests and members only; professional coaching and video assessment are available.

Rancho Bernardo Inn

17550 Bernardo Oaks Dr., Rancho Bernardo. ☎ **800/542-6096** or 619/487-1611.

Combine a visit to San Diego with some work on your backhand by enrolling in the Rancho Bernardo Tennis College, which has improved more than 35,000 games since 1971 and is open to nonhotel guests. Programs include a Tennis Holiday package with a 2-night minimum and daily court time but no instruction, a 2-day Stroke and Strategy package for all levels, a 2-day Drill and Play package for experienced players, a comprehensive 5-day "Set" program, and a 2-day doubles clinic. Rancho Bernardo has 12 courts, four lighted for night play.

Sheraton San Diego Hotel & Marina

1380 Harbor Island Dr. ☎ **619/291-2900.**

Right across the street from the airport, the hotel has four lit tennis courts where nonguests are welcome. There's also a pro shop.

10 Spectator Sports

AUTO RACING

The **Score Baja 500,** held in June, is an annual off-road car, motorcycle, and truck loop race that starts and ends in Ensenada. The **Score Baja 1,000** is held in November. For information, call ☎ **818/583-8068.**

BASEBALL

The National League **San Diego Padres** play April through September at Qualcomm Stadium, 9449 Friars Rd., in Mission Valley (☎ **619/283-4494** for schedules and information; 619/29-PADRES for tickets). The Padres Express bus costs $5 round-trip and picks up fans at several locations throughout the city, beginning 2 hours before the game (☎ **619/233-3004** for bus information). The bus operates only for home games on Friday, Saturday, and Sunday. Tickets are readily available.

BOATING

San Diego has probably hosted the America's Cup for the last time, but several other boating events of interest are held here. These include the **America's Schooner Cup,** held every March or April (☎ **619/223-3138**), and the **Annual San Diego Crew Classic,** held on Mission Bay every April (☎ **619/488-0700**). The Crew Classic rowing competition draws teams from throughout the United States and Canada. The **Wooden Boat Festival** is held on Shelter Island every May (☎ 619/574-8020). Approximately 90 boats participate in the festival, which features nautical displays, food, music, and crafts.

FISHING TOURNAMENTS

Enthusiasts will want to attend the **Day at the Docks** event held at the San Diego Sportfishing Landing, Harbor Drive and Scott Street, in Point Loma, every April. For information, call ☎ **619/294-7912.**

FOOTBALL

San Diego's professional football team, the **San Diego Chargers,** played in the 1995 Super Bowl, losing to the San Francisco 49ers. In 1998, San Diego will host the Super Bowl. The Chargers play their home games at **Qualcomm Stadium,** "The Q," 9449 Friars Rd., Mission Valley (☎ **619/280-2121**). The season runs from August through December. The **Chargers Express bus** costs $5 round-trip and picks up passengers at several locations throughout the city, beginning 2 hours before the game (☎ **619/233-3004** for bus information). The bus operates for all home games.

San Diego hosts the collegiate **Holiday Bowl** every December. This event, held at Qualcomm Stadium, pits the Western Athletic Conference Champion against a team from the Big 10. For information, call ☎ **619/283-5808.**

GOLF

San Diego hosts some of the country's most important golf tournaments, including the **Mercedes Championships,** held at La Costa Resort in Carlsbad in early January (☎ **800/918-4653** for tickets and information; 619/438-9111, ext. 4612 for information only). Another popular event is the **Buick Invitational of California,** held every February at Torrey Pines Golf Course in La Jolla (☎ **800/888-BUICK** or ☎ 619/281-4653). The **HGH Pro-Am Golf Classic** is held at Carlton Oaks Country Club every September (☎ **619/448-8500**).

HORSE RACING

Live thoroughbred racing takes place at the **Del Mar Racetrack** from late July through mid-September every year. Post time is 2pm for the nine-race program; there is no racing on Tuesdays. There is a 4pm post time on the first 4 Fridays of the meet. Admission is $6 in the Clubhouse and $3 in the Grandstand. For information, call ☎ **619/755-1141;** the ticket-office number is ☎ **619/792-4242** (Web site: **http://www.dmtc.com**). Bing Crosby and Pat O'Brien founded the track in 1937, and it has been frequented by stars such as Lucille Ball and Desi Arnaz, Dorothy Lamour, Red Skelton, Paulette Goddard, Jimmy Durante, and Ava Gardner. Del Mar's 1993 season marked the opening of a new $80-million grandstand, built in the Spanish mission style of the original structure. The new grandstand features more seats, better race viewing, and a centrally located scenic paddock. The $1-million **Pacific Classic,** featuring the top horses in the country, is held during the 2nd weekend in August (see chapter 11).

HORSE SHOWS

The **Del Mar National Horse Show** takes place at the Del Mar Fairgrounds from late April to mid-May. Olympic-caliber and national championship riders participate. For information, call ☎**619/792-4288** or 619/755-1161.

ICE HOCKEY

The **San Diego Gulls** ice-hockey team of the International Hockey League skate their games at the San Diego Sports Arena. For schedules, tickets, and information, call ☎ 619/688-1800.

JAI ALAI

Experience the excitement of this fast-action game (only legal in two states in the U.S.) at the **Caliente Fronton Palace** (Jai Alai Palace), Calle 7 and Revolución (☎ 619/260-0454 in San Diego, 85-36-87 in Tijuana), in the heart of downtown Tijuana. Admission ranges from $3 to $5. Doors open Thursday through Tuesday at 7pm; play starts at 8pm. It's closed 2 weeks during the Christmas/New Year's period.

MARATHONS/TRIATHLONS

San Diego is a wonderful place to run or watch a marathon because the weather is usually mild. The **San Diego Marathon** takes place in January; it actually starts in Carlsbad, 35 miles north of San Diego, and stretches mostly along the coastline. For more information, contact the **San Diego Track Club** (☎ 619/452-7382) or **In Motion** (☎ 619/792-2900).

Another popular event is the **La Jolla Half Marathon,** held every April. It begins at the Del Mar Fairgrounds and finishes at La Jolla Cove. For information, call ☎ 619/454-1262.

The **America's Finest City Half Marathon** is held in August every year. The race begins at Cabrillo National Monument, winds through downtown, and ends in Balboa Park. For information, call ☎ 619/297-3901.

The **San Diego International Triathlon** held in the middle of June includes a 1,000-meter swim, 30-kilometer bike ride, and 10K run. It starts at Spanish Landing on Harbor Island. For information, call ☎ 619/627-9111 or 619/687-1000.

POLO

The public is invited to watch polo matches on Sundays from June through October at the **Rancho Santa Fe Polo Club,** 14555 El Camino Real, Rancho Santa Fe (☎ 619/481-9217). Admission is $5.

RODEOS

In the outlying areas of the county, you can watch bull riding, bronco busting, and calf roping several times a year. In April, there's **Lakeside Western Days,** which features seven major rodeo events as well as food and entertainment. For information, call ☎ 619/561-1031 or 619/561-4331. The **Ramona Rodeo,** held in May, is one of the country's top 50 rodeos. For information, call ☎ 619/789-1311. The **KSON Country Fest Rodeo,** held in Lakeside every June, features bands, music, and a full-scale rodeo. For information, call ☎ 619/561-6070.

SANDCASTLE COMPETITIONS

Sandcastle enthusiasts will enjoy the 2-day **Annual U.S. Open Sandcastle Competition** at the pier in Imperial Beach in July or August. There is a parade and children's castle contest on Saturday at 2pm, and the main event is on Sunday. For information, call ☎ 619/424-6663. A similar event is held in October: the ✪ **Ocean Beach Sandcastle Event and Family Fun Carnival.** For information, call ☎ 619/222-2683.

SOCCER

The **San Diego Sockers,** 10-time champions of the Major Indoor Soccer League, have joined the new Continental Indoor Soccer League. They play from June through October at the **San Diego Sports Arena,** 3500 Sports Arena Blvd. (☎ **619/ 224-GOAL**). Admission costs from $5 to $12.50.

SOFTBALL

The highlight of many San Diegans' summer is the softball event known as the **World Championship Over-the-Line Tournament,** held on Fiesta Island in Mission Bay on the 2nd and 3rd weekends of July. For more information see the "San Diego Calendar of Events" in chapter 2.

TENNIS

San Diego hosts some major tennis tournaments, including the **Toshiba Tennis Classic,** held at the La Costa Resort and Spa in Carlsbad. The tournament is usually held between late July and early August. For tickets, call ☎ **619/438-LOVE;** for information, ☎ **619/436-3551.**

8 City Strolls

San Diego lends itself to strolling, and the following five walking tours will give you a sense of the city as well as a look at some of its most appealing sights and structures. There is no better way to get to know a place than by walking. Wandering a city's streets and parks gives you insights that are hard to come by any other way—and the exercise can't be beat, especially under the warm (but usually not unbearably hot) Southern California sun.

WALKING TOUR 1
Downtown

Start: First Avenue and F Street.
Finish: Horton Plaza, at Broadway and Fourth Avenue.
Time: Allow approximately 2 hours, not including shopping or dining.
Best Times: Mornings or afternoons during the week.
Worst Times: Lunch hour on weekdays, when the streets are filled with office workers on break, and weekends, when office buildings and some stores are closed.

Downtown San Diego is an exhilarating place, with an ever-changing skyline, interesting architecture, and generous use of public sculpture. Since the mid-1980s, the city core has experienced a resurgence and growth; this positive energy is readily apparent.

Start at the:

1. **International Visitor Information Center,** on First Avenue at F Street. You won't find "Information Anderson" here (Adolph H. Anderson manned the information booth at the original Horton Plaza from 1915 to 1948 and answered an estimated 22 million questions on all aspects of San Diego), but you will find a friendly staff who can answer all your questions. You can also stock up on maps and brochures before starting out on your walk. From here, follow F Street to Union Street. In front of you, to the left, on F Street is the:

2. **Jacob Weinberger Courthouse.** This historic building was the city's first post office and now serves as the bankruptcy court.

   Across F Street is a single tall brown building. This is the:

3. **Metropolitan Corrections Center,** which has played host to Timothy Leary and Patty Hearst, among others. A holding

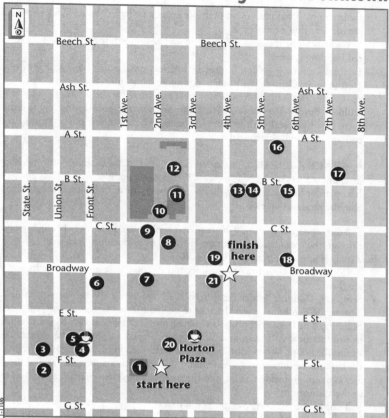

1. International Visitor Information Center
2. Jacob Weinberger Courthouse
3. Metropolitan Corrections Center
4. Federal Building
5. Ex-caliber
6. *Light, Water, and Rock*
7. Spreckels Building
8. Westgate Hotel
9. Trolley stop
10. City Administration Building
11. Civic Center
12. *The Bow Waves*
13. Wells Fargo Bank Plaza
14. *The Fountain of Two Oceans*
15. View of El Cortez Center
16. World Trade Center San Diego
17. Copley Symphony Hall
18. First Interstate Bank
19. U.S. Grant Hotel
20. Horton Plaza
21. Horton Plaza Park

facility only, it has phones on each floor and a volleyball court for detainees. The guards here don't carry guns.

Backtrack one block to Front Street and walk north for a half block. The large red building is the:

4. **Federal Building,** which houses FBI offices on the top floor and INS on the ground floor. Outside is a black pyramidlike sculpture called:

5. *Ex-caliber,* a 32-by-40-by-60-foot structure built by the internationally known sculptor Beverly Pepper in 1976. From one vantage point, some say it reminds them of a sleek seal with its nose in the air. The fence was put around it to discourage daredevil skateboarders.

☕ **TAKE A BREAK**   The **cafeteria** on the Federal Building's second floor—little known to visitors or many San Diegans—is popular with judges and juries. It's open for breakfast and lunch. Enter through the door beside the sculpture and take the escalator up to it.

After some coffee, you'll be ready to walk a few blocks up Front Street and through the small landscaped plaza with the kinetic sculpture called:

6. *Light, Water, and Rock,* by Charles Ross.

Continue on Broadway toward Second Avenue, where on your right you will see the:

7. **Spreckels Building,** which dates from 1912 and houses the neo-baroque Spreckels Theater. When built, it was thought to be California's largest reinforced concrete building. The large exits on either side of the stage made it easy to use live horses in productions. Al Jolson and Will Rogers played here when the theater was a vaudeville house. When John Barrymore performed here, he supposedly retired to the bar around the corner (now Dobson's) for a quick one between acts. If the theater is open, go inside and admire the marble lobby; the guard may let you look in the auditorium.

Turn left on Second Avenue. You'll pass the:

8. **Westgate Hotel** on your right, a member of Leading Hotels of the World. If you venture into the lobby, you'll feel you've suddenly stepped into a hall at the palace at Versailles. Afternoon tea is served here Monday through Saturday.

Continue on Second Avenue to C Street; this intersection is a:

9. **trolley stop.** In 1981 when the bright-red San Diego Trolley was unveiled, many San Diegans felt this "modern" mode of transportation was an answer to the mounting challenges of parking, pollution, and traffic. Most didn't realize that San Diego had an electric streetcar system from 1892 to 1949 that was retired due to the popularity of the automobile. In fact, the trolley follows many of the old streetcar routes.

Cross C Street and go through the glass doors of the:

10. **City Administration Building** at 202 C St. City offices mainly fill this tall crenellated building; the San Diego Opera administrative offices are also housed here.

Proceed through the concourse; on your right will be the curving facade of the:

11. **Civic Center.** Straight ahead (follow the splashing sounds) is a public sculpture called:

12. *The Bow Waves,* by Malcolm Leland, resembling the prow of a ship cutting its way through the sea.

From here, go east to B Street and walk along the street's right side. At B Street between Fourth and Fifth avenues, on your right, is the:

13. **Wells Fargo Bank Plaza** with an entrance at Fifth Avenue and B Street. Inside the lobby stands a bright-red 1868 Concord stagecoach, an engineering marvel of its day that Mark Twain praised as "a cradle on wheels." Six horses pulled the Concord coaches that carried nine passengers and eagerly awaited mail. In 1852, Henry Wells and William Fargo founded the Wells Fargo Company in San Francisco. Wells, an advocate for women's education, also founded Wells College for women in Aurora, New York, in 1868. Fargo, who had been a mail carrier on horseback at the age of 13, was mayor of Buffalo, New York, during the Civil War, and the city of Fargo, North Dakota, was named for him.

   In front of the building, you'll find:

14. *The Fountain of Two Oceans,* by Sergio Benvenuti. The male and female figures atop the fountain appear to be discussing the events of the day.

   Proceed to:

15. **The corner of Sixth Avenue and B Street;** from here if you turn and look northeast to the corner of Seventh Avenue and Ash Street, you can see the **El Cortez Center,** once a fine downtown hotel. When the El Cortez Hotel opened in 1956, it was featured in *Time, Life,* and *Business Week,* because it had the world's first outside glass hydraulic elevator. As many as 16 passengers could ride up to the 15th floor and get a panoramic view of the city. In 1978, Rev. Morris Cerullo bought the hotel, and it was used as an international ministry school until 1981. After that, it became a white elephant, but it has recently been sold, and the new owners plan to restore the building to its 1927 splendor and convert it to apartments or resurrect it as an elegant hotel.

   Cross Sixth Avenue and look to the north; the white building with blue trim and awnings is the:

16. **World Trade Center San Diego,** donated to the city by Harcourt Brace and Company in 1993. For many years, the 13-story building served as headquarters for the publishing company Harcourt Brace and Jovanovich; now it houses city offices and trade-related businesses.

   Continue down B Street. At 700 B St. is:

17. **Copley Symphony Hall.** Once known as the Fox Theatre, this lavish rococo-style theater opened November 8, 1929, and was the third-largest theater in the West. Originally designed for vaudeville and movies, the theater still has its original Robert Morton organ, which has been restored. Its 2,478 pipes make it the largest pipe organ in a California theater. In 1985, the theater was restored and reopened as Symphony Hall, and is now topped by the soaring Symphony Towers. Peek inside at the 80-foot-long mural by Denver artist James Jackson. The work, which captures the mood and movements of an orchestra at work, is oil on canvas that has been adhered to the wall. The building is still called Copley Symphony Hall in spite of the fact that the San Diego Symphony declared bankruptcy in 1996 and disbanded in 1997.

   From here, walk down Seventh Avenue to C Street and turn right; proceed to Sixth Avenue and turn left. The building with the pagoda-shape tower (its familiar outline is lit at night) is the:

18. **First Interstate Building** (the former home of **San Diego Trust and Savings Bank**), built in 1928 and once San Diego's tallest building. A tall Romanesque archway decorated with three bands of carved sandstone surrounds a large revolving door (downtown's only one) between two hinged doors. The roof was home to the first aviation beacon and a shooting gallery, which were installed during the original construction. The lights, in a cupola 240 feet above the sidewalk, were visible for a radius of more than 25 miles. Bank employees used the shooting gallery for

In the arts of landscaping and architecture, the spirit of a city can be perpetuated for the ages.

—George Marston, philanthropist, 1929

recreation and to discourage bank robbers. The bank supplied the ammunition for rifles and revolvers. The FBI also made use of this 75-foot-deep, soundproof range. It was converted to offices in the 1950s when the FBI relocated.

You are standing in the heart of the city's business district. Continue walking west along Broadway for two blocks to Fourth Avenue. On the corner of Fourth and Broadway is the:

19. **U.S. Grant Hotel,** built by Ulysses S. Grant, Jr., as a memorial to his father. Grant Jr. had come to San Diego in 1893 for the benefit of his wife's health. The $1.95-million hotel opened in 1910 after many delays. The hotel featured a marble staircase, 426 rooms, a roof garden, two indoor pools, and Turkish baths. Take a look at the lobby before crossing Broadway to explore:

20. **Horton Plaza,** a colorful conglomeration of shops, eateries, and architecture—and a tourist attraction in its own right. Ernest W. Hahn, selected to plan and implement the redevelopment and revitalization of downtown San Diego, built the plaza in 1985. This core project, which covers 11.5 acres and 6.5 city blocks in the very heart of downtown, represents the successful integration of public and private funding.

The ground floor at Horton Plaza is home to the 1906 Jessop Street Clock. This timepiece has 20 dials, 12 of which tell the time in places throughout the world. Designed by Joseph Jessop, Sr., and built primarily by Claude D. Ledger, the clock stood outside Jessop's Jewelry Store on Fifth Avenue from 1927 until they moved to Horton Plaza in 1985. In 1935, when Mr. Ledger died, the clock stopped; it was restarted, but it stopped again 3 days later—the day of his funeral.

In front of Horton Plaza is:

21. **Horton Plaza Park.** Its centerpiece is a fountain designed by well-known local architect Irving Gill and modeled after the choragic monument of Lysicrates in Athens. Dedicated October 15, 1910, it was the first successful attempt to combine colored lights with flowing water. On the fountain's base are bronze medallions of Juan Rodríguez Cabrillo, Father Junípero Serra, and Alonzo Horton, three men who were important to San Diego's development.

WINDING DOWN The **Grant Grill,** in the U.S. Grant Hotel (☎ **619/232-3121**), one of San Diego's finest restaurants, is steeped in tradition, boasts a talented French chef, and is open for lunch and dinner and afternoon tea Tuesday through Sunday. Or, try **Horton Plaza** where you can choose from many kinds of cuisine, from California to Chinese along with good old American fast food.

WALKING TOUR 2
Gaslamp Quarter

Start: Fourth Avenue and E Street, at Horton Plaza.
Finish: Fourth Avenue and F Street.
Time: Allow approximately 1½ hours, not including shopping and dining.
Best Times: During the day.

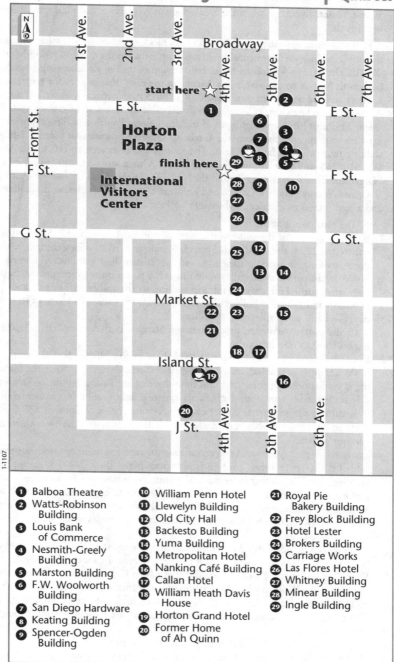

1. Balboa Theatre
2. Watts-Robinson Building
3. Louis Bank of Commerce
4. Nesmith-Greely Building
5. Marston Building
6. F.W. Woolworth Building
7. San Diego Hardware
8. Keating Building
9. Spencer-Ogden Building
10. William Penn Hotel
11. Llewelyn Building
12. Old City Hall
13. Backesto Building
14. Yuma Building
15. Metropolitan Hotel
16. Nanking Café Building
17. Callan Hotel
18. William Heath Davis House
19. Horton Grand Hotel
20. Former Home of Ah Quinn
21. Royal Pie Bakery Building
22. Frey Block Building
23. Hotel Lester
24. Brokers Building
25. Carriage Works
26. Las Flores Hotel
27. Whitney Building
28. Minear Building
29. Ingle Building

Worst Times: Evenings, when the area's popular restaurants and nightspots attract big crowds.

A National Historic District covering 16½ city blocks, the Gaslamp Quarter contains many Victorian-style commercial buildings built between the Civil War and World War II. The quarter—set off by the electric version of the old gas lamps—is bounded by Fourth Avenue to the west, Sixth Avenue to the east, Broadway to the north, and L Street and the waterfront to the south. The blocks are noticeably short; developer Alonzo Horton knew corner lots were more desirable to buyers, so he created more of them. This tour hits some highlights of buildings along Fourth and Fifth avenues. If it whets your appetite for more, the **Gaslamp Quarter Foundation** offers a 2-hour walking tour on Saturdays at 11am. The foundation is located at 410 Island Ave. (☎ **619/233-4692,** or hot line 619/233-4691). Other tours are also available (see "Organized Tours" in chapter 7), and the book *San Diego's Historic Gaslamp Quarter: Then and Now* by Susan H. Carrico and Kathleen Flanagan, with photos, illustrations, and a map, makes an excellent, lightweight walking companion.

The tour begins at the:

1. Balboa Theatre, at the southwest corner of Fourth Avenue and E Street. Constructed in 1924, the building is Spanish Renaissance style, with a distinctive tile dome, striking tile work in the entry, and two 20-foot-high ornamental waterfalls inside. In the past the waterfalls would run at full power during intermission; however, when turned off, they would drip and irritate the audience. The ship mosaic at Fourth and E depicts Balboa discovering the Pacific Ocean in 1513. In its heyday, plays and vaudeville took top billing.

Cross Fourth Avenue and proceed along E Street to Fifth Avenue. The tall, striking building to your left is the:

2. Watts-Robinson Building, built in 1913. One of San Diego's first skyscrapers, it was a favorite of jewelers, once housing 70 of them. Currently a hotel, the building is gradually being converted into time-share units. Take a minute to look inside at the marble wainscoting, tile floors, ornate ceiling, and brass ornamentation.

Return to the southwest corner of Fifth Avenue. To your right, at 837 Fifth Ave., is the unmistakable "grand old lady of the Gaslamp," the twin-towered baroque revival:

3. Louis Bank of Commerce. (You can admire the next few buildings from the west side of the street and then continue south from here.) Built in 1888, this proud building, San Diego's first to be made of granite, once housed a 24-hour ice-cream parlor for which streetcars made unscheduled stops; an oyster bar frequented by Wyatt Earp; and upstairs, a number of rooms inhabited by ladies of the night. After a fire in 1903, the original towers of the building, with eagles perched atop them, were removed.

Next door, at 831 Fifth Ave., is the Romanesque revival:

4. Nesmith-Greely Building, also built in 1888, with its 12-foot-wide entry. Clara Shortridge Foltz, the first woman admitted to the California State Bar and the founder of the Woman's Bar Association of California, once had an office in this building, as did Daniel Cleveland, a lawyer who founded the city's public library. The face of this building, with the exception of the fire escapes, retains its original appearance.

On the corner, at 809 Fifth Ave., stands the two-story:

5. Marston Building. This Italianate Victorian style building dates from 1881 and housed humanitarian George W. Marston's department store for 15 years. In 1885, San Diego Federal Saving's first office was located here, and the Prohibition

Temperance Union held its meetings here in the late 1880s. After a fire in 1903, the building was remodeled extensively.

On the west side of Fifth Avenue, at no. 840, near E Street, you'll find the:

6. **F. W. Woolworth Building,** built in 1910. It has housed:

7. **San Diego Hardware** since 1922; the original tin ceiling, wooden floors, and storefront windows remain, and the store deserves a quick browse. The redbrick Romanesque revival:

8. **Keating Building,** on the northwest corner of Fifth Avenue and F Street, is a San Diego landmark dating from 1890. Mrs. Keating built it as a tribute to her late husband George, whose name can still be seen in the top cornice. Originally heralded as one of the city's most prestigious office buildings, it featured conveniences such as steam heat and a wire-cage elevator. Note the architecturally distinctive rounded corner and windows.

☕ **TAKE A BREAK**   Housed in the Keating Building, **Croce's** (☎ 619/233-4355) cluster of dining and entertainment possibilities serves up generous portions of good food and drink, live jazz, national acts, and inviting ambiance. Owner Ingrid Croce has created a memorial to the life and music of her late husband, musician Jim Croce, with photos, guitars, and other memorabilia. Across the street is the perennially popular **Fio's** (☎ 619/234-3467) Italian restaurant.

Continuing south on Fifth Avenue, cross F Street and stand in front of the:

9. **Spencer-Ogden Building,** on the southwest corner at 429 F St. Built in 1874, it was purchased by business partners Spencer and Ogden in 1881 and has been owned by the same families ever since. In *San Diego's Historic Gaslamp Quarter: Then and Now,* it is noted that a number of druggists leased space in the building over the years, including the notorious one "who tried to make firecrackers on the second floor [and] ended up blowing away part of the building." Other tenants included Realtors, an import business, a home-furnishing business, and dentists, one of whom called himself "Painless Parker."

Directly across the street stands the:

10. **William Penn Hotel,** built in 1913. In the building's former, more elegant life as the Oxford Hotel, it touted itself as "no rooming house but an up-to-the-minute, first-class, downtown hotel"; a double room with private bath and toilet cost $1.50. It reopened in 1992 as a mostly all-suites hotel at substantially higher prices.

On the west side of the street, at 722–728 Fifth Ave., you'll find the:

11. **Llewelyn Building,** built in 1887 by William Llewelyn; the family shoe store was located here until 1906. Over the years, it has been home to hotels of various names with unsavory reputations. Of architectural note are its arched windows, molding, and cornices.

On the southwest corner of Fifth Avenue and G Street is the:

12. **Old City Hall,** dating from 1874, when it actually was a bank. This Florentine Italianate building features 16-foot ceilings, 12-foot windows framed with brick arches, antique columns, and a wrought-iron cage elevator. Notice that the windows on each floor are different (the top two stories were added in 1887, when it became the city's public library). The entire city government filled this building in 1900, with the police department on the first floor and the council chambers on the fourth.

Continue down Fifth Avenue toward Market, and you'll notice the three-story:

13. **Backesto Building** (1873), which fills most of the block. Originally a one-story structure on the corner, the classical revival/Victorian-style building expanded to its present size and height over its first 15 years.

   Across the street in the middle of the block, at 631–633 Fifth Ave., is the:

14. **Yuma Building,** built in 1882 and later expanded upward two floors to feature inviting bay windows. It was one of the first brick buildings downtown. Across Market Street, on the east side of the street, is the former:

15. **Metropolitan Hotel,** with an arresting trompe l'oeil by artists Nonni McKinnoon and Kitty Anderson. The building had actual bay windows when it was built in 1886.

   The center of the city used to be at Fifth Avenue and Market Street, but as San Diego expanded and gradually moved north, the hub became Fifth and Broadway. When Horton Plaza was completed in 1985, the center moved a block west to Broadway and Fourth Avenue. Back in its heyday, however, when Fifth Avenue was the main drag, it was the scene of many a parade, and Buffalo Bill Cody and John Philip Sousa numbered among those who marched up it.

   Proceed to Island Avenue. On the southeast corner, the unassuming:

16. **Nanking Café Building** illustrates the Chinese influence in the area. At the turn of the century, Chinatown was located nearby. The building currently houses Royal Thai Cuisine Restaurant.

   Turn right on Island. The mural-covered building on the corner is the:

17. **Callan Hotel** (1904). The artwork, by Heidi Hardin, depicts a turn-of-the-century park scene with faces of contemporary San Diego citizens who contributed to the Gaslamp Quarter's rebirth.

   The saltbox house next to the hotel is the:

18. **William Heath Davis House.** This 140-year-old New England prefabricated lumber home was shipped to San Diego around Cape Horn in 1850 and is the oldest surviving structure from Alonzo Horton's "New Town." Horton lived here in 1867. The first floor and the small park next to it are open to the public; the Gaslamp Quarter Association and Gaslamp Quarter Historical Foundation have their headquarters on the second floor. Saturday morning walking tours of the Gaslamp Quarter leave from here.

   At the southwest corner of Island and Fourth avenues stands a bay-window–clad building sure to steal your heart, the:

19. **Horton Grand Hotel.** It actually is two 1886 hotels that were moved here—very gently—from other sites, then renovated and connected by an atrium; the original Horton Grand is to your left, the Brooklyn Hotel to your right. The life-size papier-mâché horse (Sunshine), in the lobby near the reception area, used to stand in front of the Brooklyn Hotel when it was a saddlery shop. The reception desk is a recycled pew from a choir loft, and old post-office boxes now hold guests' keys. By the concierge desk, to your right, is an old photo of the original Horton Grand Hotel, much less elegant in olden days. In its small museum hangs a portrait of Ida Bailey, a local madam whose establishment, the Canary Cottage, once stood on this spot. Artist Pamela Russ had been asked to retouch the somewhat austere face of her subject, but Russ's husband murdered her before she could get around to it.

   Around the corner from the Horton Grand, at 429–431 Third Ave., stands the:

20. **former home of Ah Quinn,** the first Chinese resident of San Diego, who arrived in 1879 at the age of 27 and became known as the "Mayor of Chinatown," an area bounded by Island, J, Third, and Fourth. Ah Quinn helped hundreds of Chinese

immigrants find work on the railroad and owned a successful general merchandise store on Fifth Avenue. He was a respected father (of 12 children), leader, and spokesperson for the city's Chinese population. When he died in 1914—he was hit by a motorcycle—his amassed wealth included farmland, a mine, and other real estate. The modest house is not open to the public.

☕ **TAKE A BREAK**   The **Palace Bar** (☎ 619/544-1886) in the Horton Grand Hotel is the perfect place to find yourself at teatime or in the evening, when live music, piano or jazz, adds to the already inviting atmosphere. The bar is part of the same choir-loft pew that has been turned into the reception desk.

When you leave the Horton Grand, head north on Fourth Avenue; in the middle of the block on the west side you will come to the:

21. **Royal Pie Bakery Building,** erected in 1911. This particular bakery, preceded by others, has been here since 1920; the second floor used to house the Anchor Hotel, run by "Madam Cora."
     At the southwest corner of Fourth Avenue and Market Street, at the:
22. **Frey Block building** (1911), a plaque reads "Home of the Crossroads, the oldest live jazz club in San Diego."
     Across the street on the southeast corner, at 401–417 Market St., is the:
23. **Hotel Lester,** which dates from 1906. It used to house a saloon, pool hall, and a hotel of ill repute when this was a red-light district.
     On the northeast corner of Fourth Avenue and Market Street, at 402 Market St., stands the:
24. **Brokers Building,** constructed in 1889; it has 16-foot-high wood-beam ceilings and cast-iron columns.
     At the north end of this block, the:
25. **Carriage Works,** established in 1890, now houses the Cheese Shop; instead of wagons and carriages, you get sandwiches and pastries. Cross G Street and walk to the middle of the block.
26. **The Las Flores Hotel,** the gray building with blue-and-red trim at 725–733 Fourth Ave., was built in 1912 and is the only Gaslamp Quarter structure completely designed by architect Irving Gill, whose work can be seen throughout San Diego and in La Jolla.
     Next door, at 739–745 Fourth Ave., is the:
27. **Whitney Building,** dating from 1906, with striking arched windows on the second floor. While you're studying details, take a look at the trim on the top of the:
28. **Minear Building** (1910), at the end of the block, on the southeast corner of Fourth Avenue and F Street.
     Across the street is the:
29. **Ingle Building,** dating from 1907. The mural on the F Street side of the building depicts a group of men toasting inside the original Golden Lion Tavern, which served 'em up from 1907 to 1932. Original stained-glass windows front Fourth Avenue. Inside, the restaurant's stained-glass ceiling was taken from the Elks Club in Stockton, California, and much of the floor is original.

☕ **WINDING DOWN**   Walk to **Cafe Lulu,** 419 F St. (☎ 619/238-0114), near Fourth Avenue, for casual coffeehouse atmosphere and fare, or walk to **Fio's,** in the Marston Building (☎ 619/234-3467), for a drink, some pizza, or an Italian meal. They serve meals at the bar, if you're lucky enough to snag a seat.

WALKING TOUR 3
Embarcadero

Start: The Maritime Museum, at Harbor Drive and Ash Street.
Finish: The Convention Center, at Harbor Drive and Fifth Avenue.
Time: Allow 1¹/₂ hours, not including museum and shopping stops.
Best Times: Weekday mornings.
Worst Times: Weekends, especially in the afternoon, when the Maritime Museum and Seaport Village are crowded; also when cruise ships are in port (days vary).

San Diego's colorful **Embarcadero,** or waterfront, cradles a bevy of seagoing vessels—frigates, ferries, paddle-wheelers, yachts, cruise ships, and even a multimasted merchant vessel. You'll also find the equally colorful **Seaport Village,** a vital aspect of the city's life.

Start at the:

1. **Maritime Museum** on Harbor Drive at Ash Street. Making up part of the floating museum is the magnificent *Star of India,* the world's oldest merchant ship still afloat, built in 1863 as the *Euterpe.* The ship, whose billowing sails are a familiar sight along Harbor Drive, once carried cargo to India and immigrants to New Zealand, and it braved the arctic ice in Alaska to work in the salmon industry. Another member of the Maritime Museum is the ferry *Berkeley,* built in 1898 to operate between San Francisco and Oakland. In service through 1958, it carried survivors to safety 24 hours a day for 4 days after the 1906 San Francisco earthquake. The *Medea,* the third and smallest member of the floating museum, is a private steam yacht. (One ticket gets you onto all three boats.)

   From this vantage point you get a fine view of the:

2. **County Administration Center,** built in 1936 with funds from the Works Progress Administration and dedicated in 1938 by President Franklin D. Roosevelt. The 23-foot-high granite sculpture in front, completed by Donal Hord in 1939 and called *Guardian of Water,* represents a pioneer woman shouldering a water jug. The building is even more impressive from the other side because of the carefully tended gardens; it's well worth the effort and extra few minutes to walk around to Pacific Highway for a look. On weekdays the building is open from 8am to 5pm; there are rest rooms and a cafeteria inside.

   ☕ **TAKE A BREAK**   The **cafeteria** on the fourth floor of the County Administration Center has lovely harbor views; it's open weekdays until 3:35pm. If you can't pass up the chance to have some seafood, return to the waterfront to **Anthony's Fishette** (☎ **619/232-5105**), the simplest entity in the Anthony's group of seafood houses, which provides short orders alfresco.

   Next door is **Anthony's Star of the Sea Room** (☎ **619/232-7408**), one of the city's finest seafood restaurants, where reservations and jackets for men are a must; it's open for dinner only.

   Continue south along the Embarcadero. The large carnival-colored building on your right is the:

3. **San Diego Cruise Ship Terminal** on the B Street Pier, with a large nautical clock at the entrance. Totally renovated in 1985, the terminal's interior is light and airy, with flags for decor. Inside, you'll also find a snack bar and gift shop.

4. **Harbor Cruises** depart from this location from sunup to sundown on their tours of San Diego's harbor; ticket booths are right on the water.

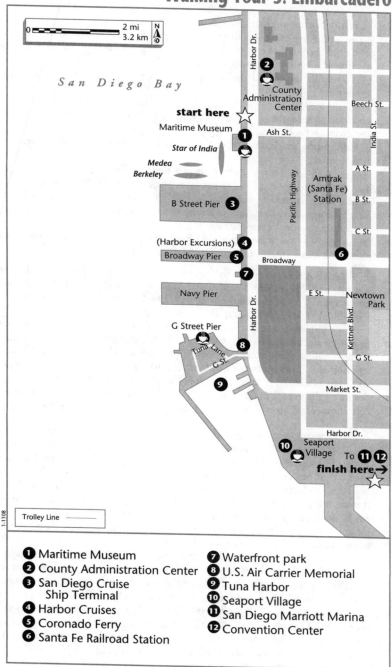

San Diego Bay

2 mi
3.2 km
N

Harbor Dr.

County Administration Center

2

Beech St.

India St.

start here
Maritime Museum

Ash St.

1

Star of India

Medea
Berkeley

A St.

Amtrak (Santa Fe) Station

Pacific Highway

B Street Pier

3

B St.

C St.

(Harbor Excursions)

4

Broadway Pier

5

6

7

Broadway

Navy Pier

E St.

Newtown Park

Kettner Blvd.

G Street Pier

Tuna Lane

G St.

8

Harbor Dr.

9

G St.

Market St.

Harbor Dr.

Seaport Village

10

To 11 12

finish here →

Trolley Line

1 Maritime Museum
2 County Administration Center
3 San Diego Cruise Ship Terminal
4 Harbor Cruises
5 Coronado Ferry
6 Santa Fe Railroad Station
7 Waterfront park
8 U.S. Air Carrier Memorial
9 Tuna Harbor
10 Seaport Village
11 San Diego Marriott Marina
12 Convention Center

1-1108

A little farther south, near the Broadway Pier, the:

5. **Coronado Ferry** makes frequent trips between San Diego and Coronado. See "By Ferry" in Section 2 of chapter 4 for more information. Buy the inexpensive tickets from the Harbor Excursion booth.

To your left as you look up Broadway, you'll see the two gold mission-style towers of the:

6. **Santa Fe Railroad Station,** built in 1915. It's only 1 1/2 blocks away, so stroll up and look inside at the vaulted ceiling, wooden benches, and walls covered in striking green and gold tiles.

Continuing south on Harbor Drive, you'll stroll through a small tree- and bench-lined:

7. **waterfront park.** Then at Pier 11, there is the:

8. **U.S. Air Carrier Memorial,** a compact black-granite obelisk that honors the nation's carriers and crews. Erected in 1993, it stands on the site of the old Navy fleet landing, where thousands of servicemen have boarded ships over the years.

Continue along the walkway to:

9. **Tuna Harbor,** where the commercial fishing boats congregate. San Diego's tuna fleet, with about 100 boats, is one of the world's largest.

☕ **TAKE A BREAK**   The red building off to your right houses the **Fish Market** (☎ **619/232-FISH**), a market and casual restaurant, and its elegant upstairs counterpart, **Top of the Market** (☎ **619/234-4TOP**). You can be assured that a meal here is fresh off the boat. Both serve lunch and dinner, and the Fish Market has a children's menu, as well as an oyster and sushi bar. It's acceptable to drop in just for a drink and to savor the view, which is mighty. Prices here are moderate to expensive, but if you prefer something quick and cheap, save yourself a walk and stop in at casual **Anthony's Fishette** (☎ **619/232-5105**) (a cousin to the one you passed earlier), just outside Seaport Village. For desserts or coffee, go inside Seaport Village to **Upstart Crow** (☎ **619/232-4855**), actually a bookstore/coffeehouse, and sip cappuccino in the company of your favorite authors.

Keep walking south, where you can meander along the winding pathways of:

10. **Seaport Village** with its myriad shops and restaurants. The Broadway Flying Horses Carousel is pure nostalgia. Charles Looff, of Coney Island, carved the animals out of poplar in 1890. The merry-go-round was originally installed at Coney Island and later moved to Salisbury, Massachusetts. Seaport Village purchased it in the 1970s and spent more than 2 years restoring it to its original splendor—the horses even have real horsehair tails. If you decide to take a twirl, pick your mount from the 40 horses, three goats, and three St. Bernard dogs. This carousel comes complete with the ever-elusive brass ring.

As you stroll farther, you will no doubt notice the official symbol of Seaport Village. This 45-foot-high detailed replica of the famous turn-of-the-century Mukilteo Lighthouse of Everett, Washington, towers above the other buildings.

From Seaport Village, continue your waterfront walk south to the:

11. **San Diego Marriott Marina,** adjacent to Embarcadero Marina Park, which is well used by San Diegans for strolling and jogging. A concession at the marina office rents boats by the hour at reasonable rates and arranges diving, waterskiing, and fishing outings. The impressive hotel resembles an ocean liner at berth.

The boardwalk continues to the:

12. **Convention Center,** another striking piece of architecture on the city's waterfront. Completed in late 1989, it also has a seafaring theme, and its presence on the waterfront has contributed to the revitalization of downtown San Diego.

☕ **WINDING DOWN**   The waterfront bar at the Marriott, called the **Yacht Club** (☎ 619/234-1500), looks out onto the marina and the bay beyond and is a choice spot for watching the sunset (you're in luck if the end of your walking tour coincides with it). You can get drinks, appetizers, and short orders here, and if you linger into the evening, there's likely to be live music and dancing. Across from the Convention Center, at the water's edge, the **Chart House** (☎ 619/435-0155), housed in the historic San Diego Rowing Club built in 1899, is a more upscale candidate for a drink or a bite to eat.

WALKING TOUR 4
Old Town

Start: Old Town State Historic Park Headquarters.
Finish: Heritage Park.
Time: Allow approximately 2 hours, not including shopping or dining.
Best Times: Weekends (except the first one in May) and any day before 2pm or after 3pm (so you can take the free park tour from 2 to 3pm if you wish).
Worst Times: Weekdays, when numerous school groups are touring (although it's fun to watch on-site education in action), and Cinco de Mayo weekend, the 1st weekend in May, when Old Town is a madhouse in celebration of Mexico's defeat of the French on May 5, 1862, in the Battle of Puebla.

Old Town is the Williamsburg of the West. When you visit, you go back to a time of one-room schoolhouses and village greens, when many of the people who lived, worked, and played here spoke Spanish. Even today, life moves more slowly in this part of the city, where the buildings are either old or built to look that way. The stillness is palpable, especially at night when you stroll the streets and look up at the stars. You don't have to look hard or very far to see yesterday. Begin at the Park Headquarters, at the eastern end of the park—not so much a park in the sense of having grass and trees, but a historic district that preserves the essence of the small Mexican and fledgling American communities that existed here from 1821 to 1872. The center of Old Town is a six-block area with no vehicular traffic.

The headquarters are in the:

1. Robinson-Rose House, built in 1853 as a family home; it has also served as a newspaper and railroad office. Here you will see a large model of Old Town the way it looked in 1872, the year a large fire broke out (or was set), destroying much of the town and initiating the exodus of the local citizenry to New Town, now downtown San Diego. Old Town State Historic Park contains seven original buildings, including the Robinson-Rose House, and a growing amount of reconstruction of buildings that once existed here.

From here, turn left and stroll into the colorful world of Mexican California called:

2. Bazaar del Mundo, 2754 Calhoun, where international shops and restaurants spill into a flower-filled courtyard. Designer Diane Powers created the unique setting from the dilapidated Casa de Pico motel, constructed here in 1936. On Saturday and Sunday afternoons, Mexican dancers perform for free at the bazaar. While you're here, be sure to visit the **Guatemala Shop,** the **Design Center,** and **Libros Bookstore.**

☕ **TAKE A BREAK**   You can't leave San Diego without sampling the Mexican food in Bazaar del Mundo. Try **Rancho El Nopal** (☎ 619/295-0584), **Casa** de Pico (☎ 619/296-3267), or, a block away, **Casa de Bandini** (☎ 619/297-8211). You can also enjoy Italian food at **Lino's** (☎ 619/299-7124) All offer indoor and outdoor dining and lively ambiance. Historic Casa de Bandini, completed in 1829, was the home of Peruvian-born Juan Bandini, who became a Mexican citizen; in 1869, the building, with a second story added, became the Cosmopolitan Hotel. Within the park, restaurants are open from 10am to 9pm and stores from 10am to 8pm (9pm in Bazaar del Mundo).

From Bazaar del Mundo, stroll into the grassy plaza, where you'll see a:

3. **Large Rock Monument,** which commemorates the first U.S. flag flown in southern California (on July 29, 1846). In the plaza's center stands a flagpole that resembles a ship's mast. There's a reason: the original flag hung from the mast of an abandoned ship.

Straight ahead, at the plaza's western edge, is the:

4. **La Casa de Estudillo.** An original adobe building dating from 1827, it has covered walkways and an open central patio. The patio covering of the U-shaped house is made of corraza cane, the seeds for which were brought by Father Serra in 1769. The walls are 3 to 5 feet thick, holding up the heavy beams and tiles, and they work as terrific insulators against summer heat. In those days, the thicker the walls the wealthier the family. The furnishings in the "upper-class" house are representative of the 19th century (don't overlook the beautiful four-poster beds); the original furniture came from the East Coast and from as far away as Asia. The Estudillo family, which then numbered 12, lived in the house until 1887; today family members still live in San Diego.

After you exit La Casa de Estudillo, turn left. In front of you is the reconstruction of the three-story:

5. **Colorado House,** built in 1851 and destroyed by fire in 1872, as were most buildings on this side of the park. Today it's the home of the **Wells Fargo Historical Museum,** but the original housed San Diego's first two-story hotel. The museum features an original Wells Fargo stagecoach, numerous displays of the overland-express business, and a video show. Next door to the Wells Fargo museum, and kitty-corner to La Casa de Estudillo, is the small redbrick **San Diego Court House** and **City Hall.** (A reconstruction of the three-story Franklin House is planned to the right of the Colorado House.)

From here, continue along the pedestrian walkway one short block, turn right, and walk another short block to the one-room:

6. **Mason Street School** (a reddish-brown building to your right), an original building dating from 1865. It was commissioned by Joshua Bean, uncle to the notorious "hanging judge" Roy Bean; Joshua Bean was also San Diego's first mayor and the state of California's first governor. If you look inside you'll notice that the boards that make up the walls don't match; they were leftovers from the construction of San Diego homes. Mary Chase Walker, the first teacher, ventured here from the East when she was 38 years old. She enjoyed the larger salary but hated the fleas, mosquitoes, and truancy; after a year, she resigned to marry the president of the school board.

When you leave the schoolhouse, retrace your steps to the walkway (which is the extension of San Diego Avenue) and turn right. On your left, you will see two buildings with brown-shingle roofs. The first, the:

7. **Pedroreña House** (no. 2616), is an original Old Town house built in 1869, with stained glass over the doorway. The owner, Miguel Pedroreña, also owned the house next door, which would become the:

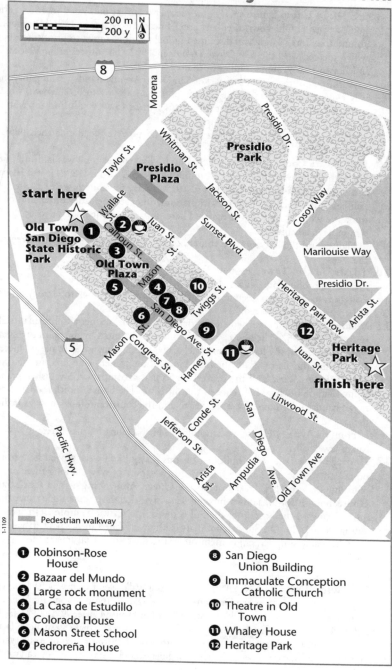

start here

Old Town
San Diego
State Historic
Park

Presidio
Plaza

Presidio
Park

Old Town
Plaza

Heritage
Park

finish here

Pedestrian walkway

❶ Robinson-Rose
   House
❷ Bazaar del Mundo
❸ Large rock monument
❹ La Casa de Estudillo
❺ Colorado House
❻ Mason Street School
❼ Pedroreña House

❽ San Diego
   Union Building
❾ Immaculate Conception
   Catholic Church
❿ Theatre in Old
   Town
⓫ Whaley House
⓬ Heritage Park

8. **San Diego Union Building.** The newspaper was first published in 1868. This house arrived in Old Town after being prefabricated in Maine in 1851 and shipped around the Horn. Inside you'll see the original handpress used to print the paper, which merged with the *San Diego Tribune* in 1992. The offices are now located in Mission Valley, about 3 miles from here.

At the end of the pedestrian part of San Diego Avenue stands a railing; beyond it is Twiggs Street, dividing the historic park from the rest of Old Town, which is more commercial in comparison. In this part of town you'll find interesting shops and galleries and outstanding restaurants.

At the corner of Twiggs Street and San Diego Avenue stands the Spanish mission–style:

9. **Immaculate Conception Catholic Church.** The cornerstone was laid in 1868, but with the movement of the community to New Town in 1872, it lost its parishioners and was not dedicated until 1919. Today the church serves about 300 families in the Old Town area. (Visitors sometimes see the little church and on a romantic whim decide to get married here, but arrangements have to be made 9 months in advance.)

Halfway up the hill from the church, on the opposite side of Twiggs Street, is the:

10. **Theatre in Old Town,** at 4040 Twiggs St., where there's usually a comedy or musical in production. This is also an Old Town Trolley stop.

Return to San Diego Avenue and continue along it one block to Harney Street. On your left is the restored:

11. **Whaley House,** the first two-story brick structure in southern California, built from 1855 to 1857. The house, which is said to be haunted by the ghost of a man who was executed (by hanging) out back, is beautifully furnished in period pieces and features the life mask of Abraham Lincoln, the spinet piano used in the film *Gone With the Wind,* and the concert piano that accompanied Swedish soprano Jenny Lind on her final U.S. concert tour in 1852. The house's north room served as the county courthouse for a few years, and the courtroom looks now as it did then.

From the Whaley House, walk uphill 1½ blocks along Harney Street to a Victorian jewel called:

12. **Heritage Park.** The seven buildings on this grassy knoll were moved here from other parts of the city and are now used in a variety of ways; among them are a winsome bed-and-breakfast inn (in the Queen Anne shingle-style **Christian House,** built in 1889), a down-memory-lane–style doll shop, an antique store, and offices. Toward the bottom of the hill is the classic revival **Temple Beth Israel,** dating from 1889. On Sunday, local art is often exhibited in the park. If you've brought picnic supplies, enjoy them under the sheltering coral tree at the top of the hill.

🕮 **WINDING DOWN** At the end of your walk, wend your way back down Harney Street, turn left at San Diego Avenue, and take a left just beyond the Whaley House. The brick walkway will lead you to **Garden House Coffee & Tea** (☎ 619/220-0723), a small coffee shop in a turn-of-the-century house that's so small, in fact, that you have to take your fresh brew and sip it on the front porch or in the yard under the gnarled old pepper trees. This is a quiet, secluded spot where you can catch your breath and enjoy the scenery.

WALKING TOUR 5
Balboa Park

Start: Cabrillo Bridge, entry at Laurel Street and Sixth Avenue.

Finish: San Diego Zoo.

Time: Allow 2 hours, not including museum or zoo stops. If you get tired at any point, hop on the free park tram, which will get you around effortlessly.

Best Times: Anytime, but if you want to get good photographs, come in the afternoon. Most museums are open until 4:30pm. The zoo closes at 5pm in the summer, 4pm other times of the year.

Worst Times: Some say weekends, when more people (especially families) visit the park, but I love it then—particularly on Sunday afternoons, when at 2pm there is a free organ concert at the outdoor Spreckels Organ Pavilion.

Balboa Park is the second-oldest city park in the United States, after New York's Central Park. Its striking architecture, much of which was the product of the Panama-California Exposition in 1915–16 and the California Pacific International Exposition in 1935–36, now houses outstanding museums and contributes to the park's uniqueness and beauty. The park, previously called "City Park," was renamed in 1910 when Mrs. Harriet Phillips won a name contest; she submitted "Balboa Park" in honor of the Spanish explorer who, in 1513, was the first European to see the Pacific Ocean.

Take bus no. 1 or 3 via Fifth Avenue or bus no. 25 via Sixth Avenue to Laurel Street, which leads into Balboa Park via its most dramatic entrance, the:

1. **Cabrillo Bridge,** with its striking views of downtown San Diego and scenic sycamore-lined Highway 163. Built in 1915 for the Panama-California Exposition and patterned after a bridge in Ronda, Spain, this cantilever-style bridge, with seven pseudo-arches, makes a dramatic entrance to Balboa Park. As you cross the bridge, to your left you'll see the yellow cars of the zoo's Skyfari and, directly ahead, the distinctive California Tower of the Museum of Man. The delightful sounds of the 100-bell Symphonic Carillon can be heard every quarter hour. Sitting atop this San Diego landmark is a weather vane shaped similarly to the ship that Cabrillo sailed to California in 1542. The city skyline lies to your right.

   Once you've crossed the bridge, go through the:

2. **Arch** (the two figures represent the Atlantic and Pacific oceans) and into the park itself, a treasure of nature and culture. For now, just view the museums from the outside (read more about them in chapter 7). You have entered the park's major thoroughfare, called El Prado, and to your left is the:

3. **Museum of Man,** an anthropological museum focusing on the peoples of North and South America. Architect Bertram Goodhue designed this building, originally known as the California Building, in 1915. Goodhue, considered the world's foremost authority on Spanish-colonial architecture, was the master architect for the 1915–16 exposition.

   Just beyond it and up the steps to the left is the nationally acclaimed:

4. **Old Globe Theatre,** part of the Simon Edison Centre for the Performing Arts. The Globe, as the locals refer to it, was built for the 1935 exposition. This replica of Shakespeare's Old Globe Theatre was meant to be demolished after the exposition but was not, and it has survived to be California's oldest professional theater. In 1978, an arsonist destroyed the theater, which was subsequently rebuilt into what it is today. If you have the opportunity to go inside, you can see the bronze bust of Shakespeare that miraculously survived the fire with minor damage.

This is the most beautiful highway I've ever seen.
—John F. Kennedy (speaking about Highway 163,
which winds through Balboa Park), 1963

Beside the theater is the:

5. **Sculpture Garden** of the Museum of Art.

Across the street, to your right as you stroll along the Prado, is the:

6. **Alcazar Garden,** designed in 1935 by Richard Requa, who patterned it after the gardens surrounding the Alcazar Castle in Seville, Spain. The garden, is formally laid out and trimmed with low clipped hedges; in the center walkway are two star-shaped yellow-and-blue tile fountains.

Exit to your left at the opposite end of the garden, and you'll be back on El Prado. Proceed to the corner; on your right is the site of the:

7. **House of Charm,** the site of the San Diego Art Institute Gallery, a nonprofit gallery that primarily exhibits works of local artists, and the **Mingei International Museum of World Folk Art,** which offers changing exhibitions celebrating human creativity manifested in textiles, costumes, jewelry, toys, pottery, paintings, and sculpture.

To your left is the imposing:

8. **Museum of Art,** a must for anyone who fancies fine art. The latticework building you see beyond it is the:

9. **Botanical Building,** where colorful flowers and plants are shaded within.

Directly in front of you are the newly renovated House of Hospitality and the park's:

10. **Visitor Center,** where you can pick up maps and a discount ticket to some of the museums.

Turn right toward the statue of the mounted:

11. **El Cid Campeador,** created by Anna Hyatt Huntington and dedicated in 1930. This sculpture of the 11th-century Spanish hero was made from a mold of the original statue in the court of the Museum of Hispanic Society in New York. A third one is in Seville, Spain.

Walk down to the ornate:

12. **Spreckels Organ Pavilion,** donated to San Diego by brothers John D. and Adolph B. Spreckels. Famed contralto Madame Ernestine Schumann-Heink sang at the December 31, 1914, dedication; a brass plaque honors her charity and patriotism. Free, lively recitals featuring the largest outdoor organ in the world (its vast structure contains 4,428 pipes) are given Sunday at 2pm.

Exit to your right, cross the two-lane road, and follow the sidewalk down the hill. The pathway leading into the ravine to your right will take you to the:

13. **Palm Arboretum,** which requires some climbing. More secluded, it may not always be as safe as the main roads, but you can get a good sense of its beauty by venturing only a short distance along it. As you walk down the hill, you'll see the **Hall of Nations** on your left, and beside it, the:

14. **United Nations Building,** which houses the United Nations International Gift Shop, a favorite for its diverse merchandise, much of it handmade by peoples from around the world. You'll recognize the shop by the U.S. and U.N. flags out front. Check the bulletin board, or ask inside, for the park's calendar of events. If you need to rest, there's a pleasant spot with a few benches opposite the gift shop.

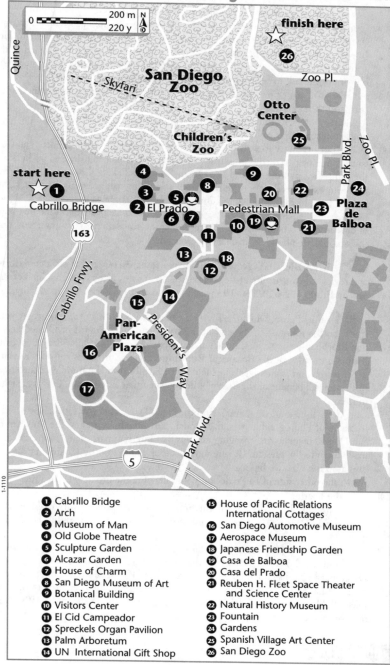

0   200 m
    220 y   N

Quince

San Diego Zoo

Skyfari

Otto Center

Children's Zoo

finish here
26

Zoo Pl.

25

start here
1

Cabrillo Bridge

4

3

5

2   El Prado

6   7

8

9

20

22

23

24

Plaza de Balboa

21

Pedestrian Mall

10   19

11

13

18

12

15   14

Pan-American Plaza

President's Way

16

17

Cabrillo Frwy.

163

Park Blvd.

Zoo Pl.

Park Blvd.

5

1-1110

① Cabrillo Bridge
② Arch
③ Museum of Man
④ Old Globe Theatre
⑤ Sculpture Garden
⑥ Alcazar Garden
⑦ House of Charm
⑧ San Diego Museum of Art
⑨ Botanical Building
⑩ Visitors Center
⑪ El Cid Campeador
⑫ Spreckels Organ Pavilion
⑬ Palm Arboretum
⑭ UN International Gift Shop

⑮ House of Pacific Relations
    International Cottages
⑯ San Diego Automotive Museum
⑰ Aerospace Museum
⑱ Japanese Friendship Garden
⑲ Casa de Balboa
⑳ Casa del Prado
㉑ Reuben H. Fleet Space Theater
    and Science Center
㉒ Natural History Museum
㉓ Fountain
㉔ Gardens
㉕ Spanish Village Art Center
㉖ San Diego Zoo

You will notice a cluster of small houses with red tile roofs. They are the:

15. House of Pacific Relations International Cottages, which promote ethnic and cultural awareness and are open to the public on Sunday afternoons year-round. In March through October, lawn programs are presented with folk dancing. Take a quick peek into some of the cottages, then continue following the road to the bottom of the hill to see more of the park's museums, most notably the:

16. San Diego Automotive Museum to your right, filled with exquisite and exotic cars, and the cylindrical:

17. Aerospace Museum straight ahead. The museums in this part of the park are housed in structures built for the 1935 exposition.

It is not necessary to walk all the way to the bottom of the hill, unless you plan to tour one or two of the museums now. Instead, cross the road and go back up the hill past a parking lot and the Organ Pavilion. Take a short cut through the pavilion, exit directly opposite the stage, and follow the sidewalk to your right, leading back to El Prado. Almost immediately, you come to the:

18. Japanese Friendship Garden of San Diego, an 11¹/₂-acre canyon in the first stage of development. Its information center is inside a teahouse with shoji screens, and the small garden beside it inspires meditation.

☕ **TAKE A BREAK** Now is your chance to have a bite to eat, sip a cool drink, and review the tourist literature you picked up at the Visitor Center. The **Terrace on the Prado** (☎ 619/236-1935) in the House of Hospitality is open daily.

Back on El Prado, which is strictly a pedestrian mall from this point, set your sights on the fountain at the end of the street and head toward it. On weekends you'll probably pass street musicians, artists, and clowns. One of their favorite haunts is in front of the **Botanical Building;** it takes only a few minutes to wander through and is a delightful little detour. Stroll down the middle of the street to get the full benefit of the lovely buildings on either side of you. On your right, in the:

19. Casa de Balboa Building, you'll find the Hall of Champions Sports Museum, the Museum of Photographic Arts, the Model Railroad Museum, and the Museum of San Diego History, with engaging exhibits that interpret past events in the city and relate them to the present. Be sure to take a look at the realistic-looking female figures atop the Casa de Balboa.

On the other side of El Prado, on your left, note the ornate work on the:

20. Casa del Prado.

At the end of El Prado are two museums particularly popular with children, the:

21. Reuben H. Fleet Space Theater and Science Center to your right. To the left is the:

22. Natural History Museum, where kids are likely to be climbing atop the whale statue outside. Look for the sundial that is inscribed "Presented by Joseph Jessop; December 1908; I stand amid ye sommere flowers To tell ye passage of ye houres." This sundial, which is accurate to the second, was originally presented to the San Diego Public Library and relocated in front of the museum in the mid-1950s when the library moved.

Impressions

Wouldn't it be splendid if San Diego had a zoo!
—Dr. Harry Wegeforth, San Diego Zoo founder, 1916

In the center of the Plaza de Balboa is a high-spouting:

23. fountain. This seemingly ordinary fountain, built in 1972, holds 25,000 gallons of water and spouts 50 to 60 feet into the air. The unique feature is actually on top of the Natural History Museum, where a wind-regulator is located. As the wind increases, the fountain's water pressure is lowered so that the water doesn't spray out over the edges. The fountain fascinates children, who giggle when it sprays them and marvel at the rainbows it creates.

From here, cross the road to visit the near-secret:

24. Gardens tucked away on the other side of the highway: to your left, a garden for cacti and other plants at home in an arid landscape; to your right, formal rose gardens. After you've enjoyed the flowers and plants, return to El Prado.

☕ **TAKE A BREAK**   Tucked in the Casa de Balboa building, there's a tiny **snack bar** with seating. A block from El Prado on Village Place (the street is on your left as you stand on El Prado and face the fountain) is another snack bar with picnic tables. You can get almost anything: sodas, iced tea, lemonade, milkshakes, pizza, burritos, sandwiches, nachos, chili, and hot dogs. In this lovely spot, towering eucalyptus trees flank the Casa del Prado Theatre. The voluptuous Moreton Bay Fig tree, which is fenced off across the street, was planted in 1915 for the exposition; now it's more than 62 feet tall, with a canopy 100 feet in diameter.

Across Village Place from the snack bar is the sleepy:

25. Spanish Village Art Center, where artists are at work daily from 11am to 4pm, creating jewelry, paintings, and sculptures in tile-roof studios around a courtyard. (There are rest rooms here.)

Exit at the back of the Spanish Village Art Center and take the paved, palm-lined sidewalk to the left. Then turn right onto the palm-lined path that will take you to the world-famous:

26. San Diego Zoo (or retrace your steps and visit some of those tempting museums you've just passed, and save the zoo for another day). From here, you can also walk out to Park Boulevard through the zoo parking lot to the bus stop, on your right, where the no. 7 bus will take you back to downtown San Diego. You'll pass, on the right, the **San Diego Miniature Railroad.** The Miniature Train Company of Rensaeler, Indiana, made this 1:5-scale, 16-inch-gauge train that has been a fixture here since 1948. The railroad is open every day that public schools are closed and the half-mile ride through "San Diego's back country" takes about 4 minutes (☎ **619/239-4748**). Just before you reach Park Boulevard you will see the **Balboa Park Carousel** (☎ **619/460-9000**). The historic carousel was made in North Tonawanda, New York, in 1910 and was temporarily located in Luna Park (Los Angeles) and Tent City (Coronado). The carousel and its menagerie of original European hand-carved animals (except for two pairs of miniature horses) permanently settled in Balboa Park in 1922. The bus stop is a brown-shingled kiosk.

9 Shopping

Whether you're looking for a souvenir, a gift, or a quick replacement for an item inadvertently left at home, you'll find no shortage of stores in San Diego. This is, after all, Southern California, where looking good is a high priority and shopping is a way of life.

1 The Shopping Scene

The best buys in San Diego are often unusual or one-of-a-kind gift items. Many galleries sell wearable art, and you can still find art by up-and-coming local artists priced within your budget. The city has outstanding galleries, and while some work has high prices, it's not unusual to find something you fancy for $25 or $50. And don't forget that Mexico is only half an hour away; *tiendas* in Tijuana, Rosarito Beach, and Ensenada are stocked with colorful crafts.

Shops here tend to stay open late. Expect to find the welcome mat out until 9pm on weeknights and 6pm on Saturdays and Sundays, particularly in shopping clusters (much more creative than malls) such as Horton Plaza, Seaport Village, and Bazaar del Mundo. Exploring them is fun because the stores are part of an environment that is architecturally interesting and incorporates shopping, strolling, snacking, dining, and lolling.

Department store names you'll recognize after only a brief stay in San Diego are Nordstrom, Robinsons-May, and Macy's, located at Horton Plaza and elsewhere. In Old Town, shops are strung along San Diego Avenue and within Old Town State Historic Park. In Coronado, Orange Avenue is a magnet for shoppers, and in La Jolla, the most elegant stores and galleries line Prospect Street and Girard Avenue.

Sales tax in San Diego is 7.75%.

SHOPPING COMPLEXES

Bazaar del Mundo
2754 Calhoun St., Old Town State Historic Park. ☎ **619/296-3161.** Bus: 4 or 5/105.

Take a stroll down Mexico way and points south through the arched passageways of this colorful corner of Old Town. Always festive, its central courtyard vibrates with folkloric music, mariachis, and a splashing fountain. Shops feature one-of-a-kind folk art, home furnishings, clothing, and textiles from Mexico and South America. You'll also find a top-notch bookstore called **Libros,** with a large kids' selection. Don't miss the **Design Center** and the **Guatemala Store.** You won't find any bargains here, but there isn't a more colorful place to browse in San Diego. Open daily from 10am to 9pm.

The Ferry Landing Marketplace

1201 First St. (at B Ave.), Coronado. ☎ **619/435-8895.** Fax 619/522-6150. Take I-5 to Coronado Bay Bridge, to B Ave., and turn right. Bus: 901. Ferry: From Broadway Pier.

The entrance is impressive—turreted red rooftops with jaunty blue flags that draw closer as the ferry to Coronado pulls into the slip. As you stroll up the pier, you'll find yourself in the midst of shops filled with gifts, imported and designer fashions, jewelry, and crafts. You can get a quick bite to eat or have a leisurely dinner with a view, wander along landscaped walkways, or laze on a friendly beach or grassy bank. Open daily from 10am to 9pm.

Horton Plaza

324 Horton Plaza. ☎ **619/238-1596.** Web site: hortonplaza.com. Bus: 2, 7, 9, 29, 34, or 35. Trolley: City Center.

The Disneyland of shopping malls, it is right in the heart of San Diego; in fact, it *is* the heart of the revitalized city center, bounded by Broadway, First and Fourth avenues, and G Street. Covering 7$^{1}/_{2}$ city blocks, this multilevel shopping center has 140 specialty shops, including art galleries, clothing and shoe stores, several fun shops for kids, bookstores, a 14-screen cinema, three major department stores, and a variety of restaurants and short-order eateries. It's almost as much a San Diego attraction as Sea World or the San Diego Zoo, partly for its unusual eclectic designs and colors. The plaza is purposefully designed for meandering, so expect to take some wrong turns and make some delightful discoveries (or stay close to the escalator, which you can pick up at the front of the plaza beside **Long's Pharmacy,** or take the elevator beside Nordstrom).

Among the favorite shops here are the **Nature Company,** for items that are natural or reflect nature such as insect-collecting kits; **Horton Toy & Doll,** for inexpensive toys for kids and great gag gifts for adults; and **Eddie Bauer** for travel supplies and outdoor gear. Various performers entertain customers throughout the year. Parking is free the first 3 hours with validation (4 hours at the movie theater and the Lyceum Theatre), $1 per half hour thereafter; parking levels are confusing, and temporarily losing your car is part of the Horton Plaza experience. Open Monday through Friday from 10am to 9pm, Saturday from 10am to 6pm, and Sunday from 11am to 6pm (extended summer and holiday hours).

The Paladion

777 Front St. (opposite Horton Plaza between First and G sts.). ☎ **619/232-1627.** Bus: 2, 7, 9, 29, 34, or 35. Trolley: Civic Center.

The posh Paladion brought world-class shopping to downtown San Diego when it opened early in 1992, with tony tenants like **Cartier, Tiffany & Co., H. Stern, House of Windsor,** and **Hemingway's Fine Cigars.** Sadly, the timing couldn't have been worse from the developer's point of view. The combined devaluation of the Mexican peso and economic downturn of San Diego caused many of the original businesses in this center to close for lack of customers. As we go to press, the fate of the Paladion is uncertain; discussions include the addition of theaters and midpriced shops. Bellisima Day Spa is on the top floor. The center offers free valet parking and concierge service.

Seaport Village

849 W. Harbor Dr. (at Kettner Blvd.). ☎ **619/235-4014,** or 619/235-4013 for events information. Bus: 7. Trolley: Seaport Village.

San Diego Shopping

See La Jolla
Shopping Map

Fashion Valley Shopping Center ❾
John's Fifth Avenue Luggage ❻
Kobey's ❹
Kippy's ❷
Map Centre ❽
Mission Valley Center ❿
Obelisk Book Store ❼
Pilar's ⓫
Point Loma Camera ❸
S.D. Factory Outlet ❶
Tower Records ❺
Traveler's Depot ⓬

Miramar Naval
Air Staion

Miramar Rd.

Qualcomm
Stadium

SDSU ■

Mission Gorge Rd.

8

15

274

805

163

Friars Rd.

Mission Village Dr.

Aero Dr.

Linda Vista Rd.

Genesee Ave.

Claremont Mesa Blvd.

Balboa Ave.

Clairmont Dr.

Morena Blvd

274

Eastgate Mall

805

University
Towne
Center

Genesee Ave.

La Jolla Village Dr.

Nobel Dr.

La Jolla
Village Square

5

UCSD

Gilman Dr.

Ardath Rd

La Jolla Village Dr.

52

5

Soledad Mountain Rd.

Soledad Rd.

Lamont St. ⓬

Mission Bay
Park

Mission Bay

MISSION BAY

Ingraham St.

Pacific Beach Dr.

Grand Ave.

Garnet Ave.

Diamond St.

Dawsed St.

Mission Blvd.

PACIFIC
BEACH ⓫

La Jolla Mesa

La Jolla
Scenic Dr.

Torrey Pines Rd.

La Jolla Shores

La Jolla Mesa

Prospect
St.

High Ave.

Nautilus

Rushville St.

LA JOLLA

Pearl St.

Girard

Coast Blvd

La Jolla Cove

Pacific
Ocean

La Jolla Blvd.

1-1342

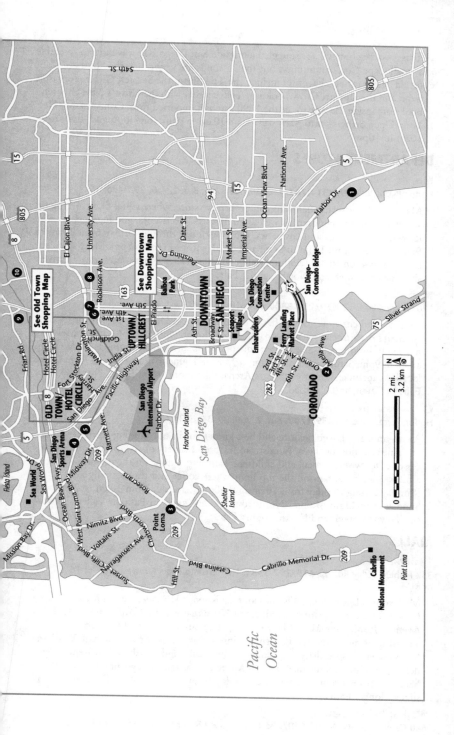

See Old Town Shopping Map

See Downtown Shopping Map

UPTOWN/HILLCREST

DOWNTOWN SAN DIEGO

Balboa Park

San Diego Convention Center

Seaport Village

Embarcadero

Ferry Landing Market Place

San Diego–Coronado Bridge

CORONADO

Silver Strand

San Diego Bay

San Diego International Airport

Harbor Island

Shelter Island

HOTEL CIRCLE

OLD TOWN

San Diego Sports Arena

Sea World

Fiesta Island

Mission Bay Dr.

Point Loma

Cabrillo National Monument

Point Loma

Pacific Ocean

N

0   2 mi.
      3.2 km

171

This 14-acre ersatz village snuggled alongside San Diego Bay was built to resemble a small Cape Cod community, but the 75 shops are very much the Southern California cutesy variety. Favorites include the **Tile Shop;** the **Seasick Giraffe** for resort wear; and the **Upstart Crow** bookshop/coffeehouse, with the **Crow's Nest** children's bookstore inside. Be sure to see the 1890 carousel imported from Coney Island, New York. Open September to May, daily from 10am to 9pm; June to August, daily from 10am to 10pm.

DEPARTMENT STORES

Macy's
Horton Plaza. ☎ **619/231-4747.** Fax 619/645-3295. Bus: 2, 7, 9, 29, 34, or 35.

Many San Diegans frequent this comprehensive store, where you'll find clothing for women, men, and children, as well as housewares, electronics, and luggage. It's well known for handbags and cosmetics. Open Monday through Friday from 10am to 9pm, Saturday from 10am to 8pm, and Sunday from 11am to 7pm. Macy's also has stores in Fashion Valley (clothing only), Mission Valley (housewares only), University Towne Center, and North County Fair.

Mervyn's
120 Horton Plaza. ☎ **619/231-8800.** Fax 619/231-8800, ext. 208.

This department store, not as flashy as others in San Diego, is known for its large children's department, with reasonably priced clothing for the entire family. Mervyn's has many locations in San Diego; this one is open Monday through Friday from 10am to 9pm, Saturday from 9:30am to 9pm, and Sunday from 10am to 7pm. Other locations include: Rosecrans/Sports Arena, Clairmont, Mira Mesa, North County Fair, El Cajon, and Carlsbad.

✪ Nordstrom
Horton Plaza. ☎ **619/239-1700.** Bus: 2, 7, 9, 29, 34, or 35.

An all-time San Diego favorite and best known for its outstanding customer service and fine selection of shoes, Nordstrom features a variety of stylish fashions and accessories for women, men, and children. Tailoring is done on the premises. There's a full-service restaurant on the top floor where coffee and tea cost only 25¢. Open Monday through Friday from 10am to 9:30pm, Saturday from 10am to 7pm, and Sunday from 11am to 6pm. Nordstrom also has stores in Fashion Valley, University Towne Center, and North County Fair.

MALLS

Fashion Valley
352 Fashion Valley Rd. ☎ **619/297-3381.** Hwy. 163 to Friars Rd. west. Bus: 6, 16, 25, 43, or 81.

My favorite place to shop, this outdoor mall is about 1 $1/2$ miles west of Mission Valley Center. Department stores here include **Neiman-Marcus, Nordstrom, Saks Fifth Avenue, Robinsons-May, Macy's,** and **J. C. Penney,** plus 140 specialty shops and a quadriplex movie theater. Particularly interesting specialty shops include **Williams Sonoma** which specializes in cooking paraphernalia, and **Smith & Hawken,** for gardening provisions. This mall is open Monday through Friday from 10am to 9pm, Saturday from 10am to 6pm, and Sunday from 11am to 6pm. (Nordstrom has slightly longer hours.)

Mission Valley Center
1640 Camino del Rio N. ☎ **619/296-6375.** Take I-8 to Mission Center Rd. Bus: 6, 16, 25, 43, or 81.

About 5 miles from downtown San Diego and just over 2 miles east of Old Town on I-8, you'll find San Diego's largest outdoor shopping center. Among the stores here are **Macy's, Montgomery Ward,** and **Robinsons-May,** a 20-plex cinema, plus more than 150 specialty shops and eateries. The store **Michaels** is great for arts and crafts materials. Mission Valley Center is open Monday through Friday from 10am to 9pm, Saturday from 10am to 6pm, and Sunday from 11am to 6pm.

University Towne Center (UTC)

4545 La Jolla Village Dr. ☎ **619/546-8858.** Fax 619/552-9065. Take I-5 to La Jolla Village Dr. and go east to UTC, or from I-805 take La Jolla Village Dr. and go west. Bus: 50 express, 34, or 34A.

This outdoor shopping complex has a landscaped plaza and 160 stores, including some big ones like **Nordstrom, Sears,** and **Macy's.** It is also home to a year-round ice-skating rink, the popular **Hops Bistro and Brewery,** and a six-plex cinema. Open Monday through Friday from 10am to 9pm, Saturday from 10am to 7pm, and Sunday from 11am to 6pm.

DISCOUNT SHOPPING

Kobey's Swap Meet

Sports Arena Parking Lot (west end), 3500 Sports Arena Blvd. ☎ **619/226-0650** (24-hr. information). Admission Thurs–Fri 50¢, Sat–Sun $1; children under 12 free. Take I-8 to Sports Arena Blvd. turnoff or I-5 to Rosecrans St., turn right on Sports Arena Blvd.

Since 1980, this gigantic open-air market has been a bargain-hunter's dream come true. Approximately 3,000 vendors fill row after row with new and used clothing, jewelry, electronics, hardware, appliances, furniture, collectibles, crafts, antiques, auto accessories, toys, and books. There's produce, too, along with food stalls and rest rooms. Open Thursday through Sunday from 7am to 3pm.

San Diego Factory Outlet Center

4498 Camino de la Plaza, San Ysidro. ☎ **619/690-2999.** Trolley: Take the southbound trolley to the San Ysidro (last) stop, walk back (north) 1 block, and turn left on Camino de la Plaza; it's a ¹/₂-mile walk or a very short taxi ride. Take I-5 or I-805 south to Camino de la Plaza exit (last U.S. exit before Mexico); turn right and continue 1 block—center is on right.

This strip of 35 factory outlets saves you money because you buy directly from the manufacturers. Some familiar names represented include Mikasa, Levi's, Calvin Klein, Guess?, Maidenform, Van Heusen, Bass, Nike, Carter's, Osh Kosh B'Gosh, Ray-Ban, and Jockey. Open Monday through Friday from 10am to 8pm, Saturday from 10am to 7pm, and Sunday from 10am to 6pm.

2 Shopping A to Z

ANTIQUES

The Cracker Factory Antiques Shopping Center

448 W. Market St. (at Columbia St.). ☎ **619/233-1669.** Bus: 7. Trolley: Seaport Village. It's across the street from the Hyatt Regency San Diego.

Prepare to spend some time here exploring three floors of individually owned and operated shops filled with antiques and collectibles. It's a block north of Seaport Village. Open daily from 11am to 5pm.

Unicorn Antique Mall

704 J St. (at Seventh Ave.). ☎ **619/232-1696.**

Antiques and collectibles fill three floors of this 30,000-square-foot building, presenting a wide selection of American oak and European furniture. Free off-street parking is available. Open Monday through Saturday from 10am to 5:30pm and Sunday from noon to 5:30pm.

ART

The San Diego area hosts numerous fairs where arts and crafts can be purchased, such as the **La Jolla Arts Festival**, which is held every September (☎ **619/454-5718**).

The Artist's Gallery
7420 Girard Ave., La Jolla (☎ **619/459-5844**).

This gallery features 20 regional artists in a variety of media including paintings, sculpture, and three-dimensional paper wall sculptures.

Brushworks
425 Market St., Downtown. ☎ **619/238-4381.**

Brushworks presents changing exhibits of contemporary work.

Galeria Dos Damas
415 Market St., Downtown. ☎ **619/231-3030.** Fax 619/233-9201.

This gallery specializes in art from Mexico and California.

Hager Fine Art
Ferry Landing Marketplace in Coronado. ☎ **619/435-9474.**

The focus here is on original contemporary work, particularly abstract impressionism.

International Gallery
643 G St. ☎ **619/235-8255.**

Here, you'll find authentic African and Melanesian primitive art, including ritual masks and sculpture, as well as contemporary American crafts in ceramics, glass, jewelry, and wood.

Pratt Gallery
2400 Kettner Blvd. (located between Downtown and Hillcrest/Uptown). ☎ **619/236-0211.**

Pratt displays original paintings, including landscapes and cityscapes by southern California artists.

SOMA and Quint
7661 Girard Ave., La Jolla. SOMA ☎ **619/551-5821;** Quint ☎ **619/454-3409.**

These galleries both occupy the space once held by I. Magnin and specialize in contemporary art.

David Zapf Gallery
2400 Kettner Blvd. (just south of Laurel). ☎ **619/232-5004.**

David Zapf specializes in the works of San Diego–area artists. Contact the David Zapf Gallery for a copy of the *Arts Down Town,* a guide to San Diego's downtown art scene.

BOOKS

John Cole's Book Shop
780 Prospect St., La Jolla. ☎ **619/454-4766.** Fax 619/454-8377.

Cole's, a favorite of many locals, is housed in a turn-of-the-century wisteria-covered cottage, the former guest house of philanthropist Ellen Browning Scripps. John and Barbara Cole founded the shop in 1946 and moved it into the cottage 20 years later. Barbara and her children continue to run it today. Visitors will find cookbooks in the old kitchen, paperbacks in a former classroom, and CDs and harmonicas in Zach's music corner. The children's-book section bulges forth with a diverse selection, and there are plenty of books about La Jolla and San Diego. Sitting and

Downtown San Diego Shopping

Brushworks **5**
Cracker Factory Antiques
 Shopping Center **4**
David Zapf **15**
Galeria Dos Damas **6**
International Gallery **8**
Le Travel **10**
Many Hands **3**
Nelson Photo **13**

One Hour Photo Shop **12**
Pannikin Coffee **9**
Pratt Gallery **14**
Taboo Studio **7**
Unicorn Antique Mall **2**
United Nations
 International
 Gift Shop **16**
Upstart Crow **1**

Horton Plaza: 11
Eddie Bauer
Horton Marketplace
Jessop's
Macy's
Mervyn's
Nature Company
Nordstrom
Paladion
Village Hat Shop

1-1343

reading in the patio garden is acceptable, even encouraged. Open Monday through Saturday from 9:30am to 5:30pm.

Obelisk Bookstore

1029 University Ave., Hillcrest. ☎ **619/297-4171.** Fax 619/297-5803.

This bookstore, which caters to gay men and lesbians, is where Greg Louganis signed copies of his book *Breaking the Surface.* Open Monday through Saturday from 10am to 11pm and Sunday noon to 8pm.

Traveler's Depot

1655 Garnet Ave., Pacific Beach. ☎ **619/483-1421.** Fax 619/483-2743.

This bookstore offers an extensive selection of travel books and maps, plus a great array of travel gear and accessories, with discounted prices for backpacks and luggage. The well-traveled owners, Ward and Lisl Hampton, are happy to give advice about favorite restaurants in a given city while pointing you to the right shelf for the appropriate book or map. Open Monday to Friday from 10am to 6pm (until 8pm in summer), Saturday from 10am to 5pm, and Sunday noon to 5pm.

Upstart Crow
835 Harbor Dr., Seaport Village. ☎ **619/232-4855.** Fax 619/232-4856. Bus: 7. Trolley: Seaport Village.

This wonderful place combines a well-stocked bookstore and a coffeehouse with tables and chairs nestled amid the volumes. It smells heavenly—of new books and fresh-brewed coffee—and refills are only 25¢. Open Sunday through Thursday from 9am to 10pm and Friday and Saturday from 9am to 11pm (until 11pm every night in summer).

Warwick's Books
7812 Girard Ave., La Jolla. ☎ **619/454-0347.**

This popular family-run bookstore is a browser's delight, with more than 40,000 titles to choose from, including a large travel section, not to mention gifts, cards, and stationery. The well-read Warwick family has been in the book and stationery business for almost 100 years, and the current owners are the third generation involved with the store. Open Monday through Saturday from 9am to 5:30pm and Sunday from 11am to 4pm.

COFFEE & TEA

Pannikin Coffee & Tea
675 G St. ☎ **619/239-7891.** Bus: 3, 5/105, or 16.

Coffees, teas, herbs, and spices are the order of the day here, and you can buy a pound or one-half pound, from aged java to Sumatra Mandheling. Decaffeinated beans and a large assortment of teas, from Lapsang Souchong to English Breakfast, are also available, plus all sorts of kitchen paraphernalia. Open Monday through Friday from 9am to 5:30pm and Saturday and Sunday from 10am to 5pm. Pannikin has many locations throughout San Diego including 523 University Ave., Hillcrest/Uptown; 7467 Girard Ave., La Jolla; and 2670 Via de la Valle, Del Mar.

CRAFTS

Lowrey's Hot Glass
3985 Harney St., Old Town. ☎ **619/297-3473.**

This is the only place in San Diego where you can watch glass artisans create colorful handblown works of art. The gallery has many one-of-a-kind mementos. Open daily from 10am to 5pm.

Many Hands
302 Island Ave., Suite 101. ☎ **619/557-8303.** Bus: 1, 4, 16, or 5/105. Trolley: Gaslamp Quarter.

This cooperative gallery, in existence since 1972, has 35 members who engage in a variety of crafts, including toys, jewelry, posters, pottery, baskets, and wearable art. Open Sunday through Thursday and Saturday from 11am to 6pm, Friday from 11am to 9pm.

DOLLS

Ye Olde Doll Shoppe
2454 Heritage Park Row, Old Town. ☎ **619/291-1979.** Bus: 4 or 5/105.

Doll lovers small and large will find treasures in this five-room Victorian house—mostly American-made black, white, Asian, and Latin porcelain dolls along with some wax ones, priced from $25 to $3,600. There are also black figurines and nativity sets, as well as international miniatures and collectibles. Owner Arlys Rapp also sells cases

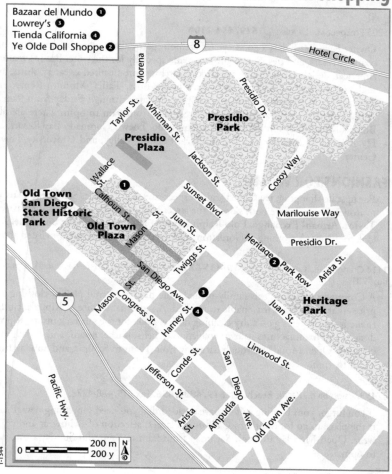

for dolls, dollhouse kits (from $20 to $400), trains, and music boxes. Open daily from 10:30am to 5:30pm.

FASHIONS FOR CHILDREN

See also the listing below for **Pacific Eyes & T's,** and remember that each of the department stores listed in this chapter sells clothes for kids.

City Kids

7886 Girard Ave., La Jolla. ☎ **619/459-4877.** Fax 619/459-5562.

This is the place to go for really cute garb for newborns to preteens at reasonable prices. Open Monday through Saturday from 9:30am to 5:30pm and Sunday from 10am to 4pm. City Kids also has a store in Del Mar.

FASHIONS FOR MEN

Nordstrom department store (see "Department Stores," earlier in this chapter) has a large menswear section.

Brady's Men's Shop

1205 Prospect St., La Jolla. ☎ **619/454-1100.**

Owner Rick Brady has a good eye for fashion, particularly when it comes to sports coats, sweaters, and ties. Some suits are made specially for the store. Brady's features American designers, including the striking, architecture-inspired sweaters, shirts, and socks of Jhane Barnes. They also carry Hugo Boss, Tallia, Mondo, Remy, and Zanella. Open Monday from 9am to 7pm, Tuesday through Friday from 9am to 9pm, Saturday from 9am to 7pm, and Sunday from 9am to 6pm. There are also Brady's Men's Shops in the Hotel del Coronado, Loew's Coronado Bay Resort, the Hyatt Regency San Diego, Horton Plaza, Fashion Valley, and University Towne Center.

FASHIONS FOR WOMEN

For upscale shopping, try Girard and Prospect streets in La Jolla, San Diego's answer to Rodeo Drive, where both sides of the street are lined with boutiques such as **Ann Taylor, Armani Exchange, Polo Ralph Lauren, Talbots,** and **Sigi's Boutique.** Also look for women's clothing at Nordstrom and the other department stores listed above.

Kippy's

1114 Orange Ave., Coronado. ☎ **619/435-6218.** Fax 619/435-6358. E-mail bob@kippys.com. Bus: 901.

A Coronado tradition, this family-owned store has stylish and playful clothing and prices that range from reasonable to rarefied. An unusual feature of Kippy's: clothes rotate from the ceiling on a dry-cleaning device. Look for the sale rack inside. Kippy's designs and manufactures its own collection of belts, leather goods, and embellished clothing. Open Monday through Saturday from 10am to 5:30pm and Sunday from 11am to 4pm.

Pilar's

3745 Mission Blvd., Pacific Beach. ☎ **619/488-3056.** Fax 619/488-4273.

If you forgot your bathing suit or have decided that you need something new, Pilar's is the place to go for Southern California's largest selection of swimwear and cruise wear. Open Monday through Saturday from 9am to 7pm and Sunday from 9am to 6pm.

GIFTS & SOUVENIRS

Pacific Eyes & T's

1241 Prospect St., La Jolla. ☎ **619/454-7532.**

There's no shortage of places to buy T-shirts and sunglasses in San Diego, but these people have a large selection at reasonable prices. There are sizes ranging from toddlers up to extra-large dads and moms. Locations include Pacific Beach, Mission Valley, Old Town, Horton Plaza, and La Jolla Village Square.

United Nations International Gift Shop

Balboa Park. ☎ **619/233-5044.** Fax 619/233-5838. Bus: 16 or 25.

You'll find inexpensive, imaginative offerings from around the world: origami from Japan, hand-carved boxes from Poland, necklaces from India, Russian nesting dolls, Christmas decorations (year-round) from all over the world, vests, jackets, and T-shirts from across the globe. UNICEF cards are a given. Look for the U.S. and U.N. flags out front. Open daily from 10am to 5pm during summer, 10am to 4pm during winter.

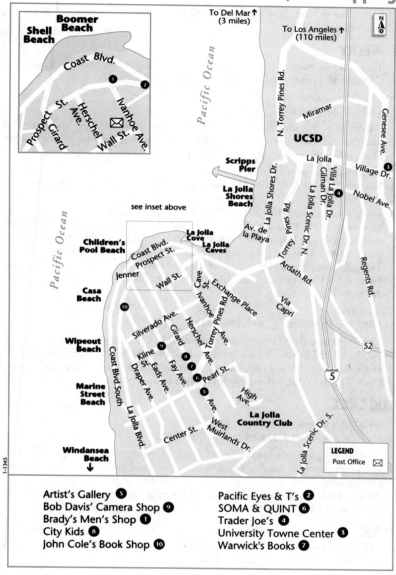

Artist's Gallery **5**
Bob Davis' Camera Shop **9**
Brady's Men's Shop **1**
City Kids **8**
John Cole's Book Shop **10**

Pacific Eyes & T's **2**
SOMA & QUINT **6**
Trader Joe's **4**
University Towne Center **3**
Warwick's Books **7**

HATS

Village Hat Shop

530 Horton Plaza. ☎ **619/232-4997.** Bus: 2, 7, 9, 29, 34, or 35. Trolley: Civic Center.

Entering the portal is like going into a costume shop. Trying on is quite acceptable, and from hat to hat you can become a pilot, a cowpoke, the Mad Hatter, or Davy Crockett. Prices range from $5 to $200, and there's something for men, women, and kids of all tastes. Open Monday through Thursday from 10am to 9pm, Saturday from 10am to 10pm, and Sunday from 11am to 7pm. There's a second shop at Seaport Village.

JEWELRY

There's no shortage of jewelry stores in La Jolla. You'll also find several, including **Cartier and Tiffany,** at The Paladion located downtown.

International Gallery
643 G St. ☎ 619/235-8255.

Besides its outstanding folk and primitive art and quality ceramics and textiles, the International Gallery sells contemporary and costume jewelry by American artists. Much of it is silver, but there are some gold pieces as well.

J. Jessop & Sons Jewelers
149 Horton Plaza. ☎ **619/239-9311.** Fax 619/239-9367. Bus: 2, 7, 9, 29, 34, or 35. Trolley: Civic Center.

Jessop's is well entrenched in San Diego, having sold jewelry and watches to the folks here since 1893. Most everything that glitters here is gold, ornamented with diamonds, rubies, and sapphires if you prefer. You can also find the finest watches and pearls, as well as Mont Blanc pens, Lalique crystal, and Lladro porcelain figurines. The giant clock that stands in front of the store has 21 dials. Open Monday through Friday from 10am to 9pm, Saturday from 10am to 6pm (8pm in summer), and Sunday from 11am to 6pm.

Taboo Studio
542 Fifth Ave. (at Market). ☎ **619/696-0055.**

This impressive shop exhibits and sells the work of jewelry designers from throughout the United States. The jewelry is made of silver, gold, and inlaid stones, in one-of-a-kind pieces, limited editions, or custom work. The gallery represents 65 artists. Open Tuesday through Saturday from 11am to 6pm.

LUGGAGE

John's Fifth Avenue Luggage
3833 Fourth Ave. ☎ **619/298-0993** or 619/298-0995.

This San Diego institution carries just about everything you can imagine in the way of luggage, travel accessories, business cases, pens, and giftware. On the premises is a luggage-repair center, which is an authorized airline repair facility. Open Monday through Friday from 9am to 5:30pm and Saturday from 9am to 4pm. There is also a store in Fashion Valley.

MAPS

Before you buy maps, remember that some of the best are free of charge to AAA members at offices throughout the United States.

The Map Centre
2611 University Ave. ☎ **619/291-3830.** Fax 619/291-3840. E-mail gayla@mapcentre.com.

This shop three blocks east of Texas Street may be tiny, but it's got the whole world covered—in maps, that is. If you plan to spend some serious time in San Diego or move here, buy the *Thomas Guide;* it's $16.95, but indispensable. The Map Centre is easily recognizable by its bright yellow awning. Open Tuesday through Friday from 10am to 5:30pm and Saturday from 10am to 5pm.

MARKETS

Farmers' markets throughout San Diego County sell fresh local fruits, vegetables, and flowers, as well as specialty items such as raw apple cider (in the fall), macadamia nuts, and rhubarb pies. These open-air events, which are very popular with locals, are the best place to see and sample San Diego County produce. Friendly farmers happily provide information, advice, and sometimes even free samples.

Here's a daily schedule:

Tuesday: Coronado, corner of First and B streets (Ferry Landing Marketplace), from 2:30 to 6pm; and **Escondido,** Grand Avenue at Broadway, from 3 to 7pm.

Wednesday: Escondido, North County Market, 3660 Sunset Dr. (across from North County Fair), from 9am to noon; **Ocean Beach,** 4900 block of Newport Avenue (west of Sunset Cliffs Boulevard), from 4 to 8pm; and **Carlsbad,** on Roosevelt between Grand Avenue and Carlsbad Village Drive, from 2 to 5pm (☎ 760/720-9161).

Thursday: Oceanside, Downtown, corner of Pier View and Pacific Coast Highway, from 9am to 12:30pm; **Mission Valley Center,** in the parking lot behind Bennigans, from 2:30 to 6pm; **Chula Vista,** Third Avenue and E Street, from 3 to 6pm; and **Vista,** April through December, on East Vista Way between Citrus and Santa Fe, from 4 to 7pm;.

Friday: Fallbrook, Village Square at Main and Alvarado, from 9am to 1pm; **Rancho Bernardo,** Bernardo Winery, 13330 Paseo del Verano Norte, from 9am to noon; **Encinitas,** Moonlight Beach parking lot (upper), from 9am to 1pm; and **La Mesa,** 8500 Allison St. (east of Spring Street), from 3 to 6pm.

Saturday: Pacific Beach, Promenade Mall, Mission Boulevard between Reed and Pacific Beach Drive, from 8am to noon; **Vista,** corner of Eucalyptus and Escondido Avenue, (in City Hall parking lot), from 8 to 11am; **Poway** (Old Poway Park), Midland between Temple and Aubrey, from 8 to 11am; and **Del Mar** (City Hall Parking Lot), corner of El Camino Del Mar and 10th Street, from 1 to 4pm.

Sunday: Uptown San Diego, in the DMV parking lot on Normal Street, from 9am to noon ; **Solana Beach,** Solana Beach Plaza, 124 N. Cedros, from 2 to 5pm (☎ 760/720-9161).

MUSIC

Tower Records
3601 Sports Arena Blvd. (across from the Sports Arena). ☎ **619/224-3333.**

Whatever your taste in music, you are sure to find it here. Tower Records has the area's most complete music selection and a knowledgeable staff. Open daily from 9am to midnight.

PHOTOGRAPHY

Bob Davis' Camera Shop
7720 Fay St., La Jolla. ☎ **619/459-7355.**

If your camera starts acting strange while you're in La Jolla, this is the best place to go for advice. It's also a good choice for picking up extra film or batteries. Open Monday through Saturday from 9am to 5:30pm.

Nelson Photo Supply
1909 India St. (at Fir St.). ☎ **619/234-6621.** Fax 619/232-6153. Bus: 5/105. Trolley: America Plaza.

All you need in the way of camera accessories, film, and 1-hour processing is here. Open Monday through Friday from 8:30am to 5:30pm and Saturday from 8:30am to 5pm.

One-Hour Photo Stop
428 C St. ☎ **619/232-8291.** Fax 619/230-0737. Bus: 2, 7, 9, 29, 34, or 35. Trolley: Civic Center or Fifth Ave.

Conveniently located in the heart of downtown, between Fourth and Fifth avenues, the store can process your film in an hour. Just drop it off, have lunch or do a little shopping, then pick it up. They also sell film and batteries. Open Monday through Friday from 8am to 5:30pm.

Point Loma Camera Store
1310 Rosecrans St. ☎ **619/224-2719.**

This is a good source for photography supplies and film processing. They also have an excellent selection of frames and similar accessories. Open Monday through Saturday from 9am to 5:30pm; Sunday lab hours are from 11am to 6pm.

SPECIALTY FOODS

Horton Marketplace
1 Horton Plaza (bottom level). ☎ **619/696-7766.** Bus: 2, 7, 9, 29, 34, or 35. Trolley: Civic Center.

The specialty food section in this large deli/market carries an abundant supply of foodstuffs, produce, and wines. The staff can prepare food baskets with fruit (and/or dried fruit), crackers, cheese, pâtés, caviar, wine, and much more. Open Monday through Friday from 8am to 8pm, Saturday from 8am to 8pm, and Sunday from 10am to 7pm (in winter the market opens at 9am Monday through Saturday; Sunday hours remain the same).

Trader Joe's
8657 Villa La Jolla Dr. (in La Jolla Village Center), La Jolla. ☎ **619/546-8629.**

A local institution, Trader Joe's sells specialty food items, as well as basic grocery supplies. Most items are packaged under their house label and sold for less than they would be as a name brand. Look for great deals on wine, a wide selection of imported beers, and wonderful treats from the bakery (try the cheese scones). This is the place to get the ingredients for your picnic at the beach. Open daily from 9am to 9pm. Trader Joe's can also be found in Hillcrest/Uptown, Pacific Beach, La Mesa, and Rancho Bernardo.

THRIFT SHOPS

For upscale secondhand selections, head for La Jolla and these three stores, where you're sure to find designer items: **Designer Consigner,** 834 Kline St. (☎ **619/459-1737**); **Encore of La Jolla,** 7850 Herschel St. (☎ **619/454-7540**); and **Second Act West,** 7449 Girard Ave. (☎ **619/454-6096**). These are within walking distance of one another. Or try:

Goodwill
402 Fifth Ave. (Between Broadway and Market). ☎ **619/696-6709.**

Filling the whole block, this store sells clothing and housewares, along with vintage clothing in its boutique. It's open Monday through Friday from 10am to 7pm, Saturday from 10am to 6pm, and Sunday from 10am to 5pm.

Now that you know your way around, let's move on to something simple.

1 8 0 0
C A L L
A T T ®

For card and collect calls.

1 800 CALL ATT is the only number you need to know when you're away from home. Dial it from any phone, anywhere* and your calls will always go through to AT&T.

*Available in U.S. and Canada. © 1997 AT&T

AT&T

Homegrown San Diego

Few visitors realize that San Diego County produces a billion (no, that isn't a typo) dollars worth of fruit, vegetables, flowers, and nuts every year.

Avocados, known locally as "green gold," are the most profitable crop and have been grown here for more than 100 years. A common variety is called *fuerte* (Spanish for strong and vigorous), because only this type survived the freeze of 1913 that killed every other tree that had been imported from Mexico. The bright-green trees grow from 20 to 60 feet tall; an average-sized tree bears up to 300 avocados.

Avocado Trivia
1. What has been a long-standing nickname for the avocado?
2. In which U.S. city are the most avocados eaten?
3. What is the best way to ripen an avocado?

Oranges, lemons, and grapefruit also have been grown here since the turn of the century. Oddly enough, the Atchison, Topeka and Santa Fe Railway popularized citrus production here. In 1906, the railway bought a large tract of land, now known as the community of Rancho Santa Fe, where they planted and grew eucalyptus trees. They planned to make railroad ties from the wood, but when it proved unsuitable, they found themselves holding the bag, or the acreage in this case. In order to sell their turf, they promoted the area as ideal for large-scale, commercial citrus groves, which it was.

Flowers are San Diego's third most important crop (after avocados and citrus). Ranunculus bulbs from here are sent all over the world, as are the famous Ecke poinsettias. And proteas like the local Mediterranean climate, even though they're native to South Africa. Macadamias, which are native to Australia, also flourish here; rumor has it that macadamia growing became popular after World War II because some retired admirals wanted business reasons to travel down under.

Answers to Avocado Trivia: 1. alligator pear; 2. Los Angeles; 3. place it in an ordinary paper bag and store at room temperature; including an apple in the bag will accelerate the process.

TOYS

You'll also find toys at the places listed under "Shopping Complexes" and "Crafts" earlier in this chapter.

Tienda California
2505 San Diego Ave., Old Town. ☎ **619/291-4699.** Bus: 4 or 5/105.

Most items sold here are diminutive: figurines, magnets, and striking Hagen-Renaker miniatures, made in California. The tiny animals will steal your heart: cats, dogs, horses, owls, wild animals, pandas, fish, unicorns, and carousel ponies. Most prices are diminutive, too, from $1.50 to $6.50, although the collectible pewter dragons and magicians are more expensive. Open daily from 9am to 9pm.

TRAVEL ACCESSORIES

Try **Eddie Bauer** in Horton Plaza (☎ 619/233-0814) or **Traveler's Depot** (listed under "Books") for travel gear.

Le Travel Store

745 Fourth Ave. (Between F and G sts.). ☎ **619/544-0005.** Fax 619/544-0312. Web site: www.letravelstore.com. Bus: 2, 7, 9, 29, 34, or 35. Trolley: Civic Center.

In business since 1976, Le Travel Store has a nice selection of soft-sided luggage, travel books, language tapes, maps, and lots of travel accessories. A cafe on the premises serves beverages and snacks. The long hours and central location make this spot extra handy. Open Monday through Thursday from 10am to 10pm, Friday and Saturday from 10am to 11pm, and Sunday from 11am to 7pm.

San Diego After Dark

San Diego's rich and varied cultural scene includes more than a dozen theaters mounting classical and contemporary plays throughout the year; performances by the San Diego Opera; rock and pop concerts; and numerous movie houses and multiscreen complexes, including several that feature foreign and avant-garde films. Not all of the city streets pulsate with nightlife, but there are ever-growing areas of late-night activity.

Half-price tickets to theater, music, and dance events are available at the **Times Arts Tix** booth, in Horton Plaza Park, at Broadway and Third Avenue. Park in the Horton Plaza parking garage and have your parking validated, or pause at the curb nearby. The kiosk is open Tuesday through Thursday from 11am to 6pm and Friday and Saturday from 10am to 6pm. Half-price tickets are only available the day of the show except for Sunday performances when half-price tickets are sold on Saturday. Only cash payments are accepted. For a daily listing of half-price offerings, call ☎ **619/497-5000.** Full-price advance tickets are also sold; the kiosk doubles as a Ticketmaster outlet, selling tickets to concerts throughout California.

For a rundown of the latest performances, gallery openings, and other events in the city, check the listings in "Night and Day," the Thursday entertainment section of the *San Diego Union-Tribune,* or the *Reader,* San Diego's free alternative newspaper, published weekly on Thursday. For what's happening at the gay clubs, get the weekly *San Diego Gay and Lesbian Times. What's Playing?,* the San Diego performing arts guide, produced every 2 months by the **San Diego Performing Arts League,** is also very helpful. You can pick one up at the Times Art Tix booth or write to 701 B St., Suite 225, San Diego, CA 92101-8101 (☎ **619/238-0700**). The San Diego Performing Arts League can also be reached through their Web site at **www.sandiego-online.com/sdpal.**

1 The Performing Arts

As San Diego has many talented theater companies, I will focus on the ones that are best known. Don't hesitate, however, to try a lesser-known venue if the show appeals to you. Also, keep in mind that the **California Center for Performing Arts** in Escondido has its own schedule of productions (see chapter 11 for details), as does the **East**

County Performing Arts Center, 210 E. Main St., El Cajon (☎ **800/696-1929** or 619/588-0206).

The **San Diego Repertory Theatre** offers ethnically diverse productions, plus one bilingual (English/Spanish) production each year, at the Lyceum Theatre, 2 Broadway Circle, in Horton Plaza (☎ **619/235-8025** or 619/231-3586). In summer, the theaters—the 550-seat Lyceum Stage and the 250-seat Lyceum Space—host dance and musical programs, as well as other events. Situated at the entrance to Horton Plaza, the two-level subterranean theaters are tucked behind a tile obelisk.

Founded in 1948, the **San Diego Junior Theatre,** at Balboa Park's Casa del Prado Theatre (☎ **619/239-8355;** fax 619/239-5048), is one of the country's oldest continuously producing children's theaters, providing training and performance opportunities for children and young adults. Students act and technically crew six main-stage shows each year.

In Coronado, **Lamb's Players Theatre,** at 1142 Orange Ave. (☎ **619/437-0600;** fax 619/437-6053), is a professional repertory company whose season runs from February through December. Shows take place in their 340-seat theater in Coronado's historic Spreckels building, where no seat is more than seven rows from the stage.

MAJOR THEATER COMPANIES

La Jolla Playhouse

2910 La Jolla Village Dr. (at Torrey Pines Rd. on the edge of the UCSD campus). ☎ **619/ 550-1010.** Fax 619/550-1025. E-mail ljplayhouse@ucsd.edu. Tickets $19 to $37. Bus: 30, 34, or 34A.

Winner of the 1993 Tony Award for outstanding American regional theater, the playhouse stages six productions each year in its 500-seat Mandell Weiss Theater and 400-seat Mandell Weiss Forum on the campus of the University of California, San Diego. Performances are held May through November. Playhouse audiences cheered *The Who's Tommy* and Matthew Broderick in *How to Succeed in Business without Really Trying* before they went on to Broadway fame and fortune. The highlight of the 1997 season was the first West Coast production of the Tony Award–winning *Rent.*

The original La Jolla Playhouse was founded by Gregory Peck, Dorothy McGuire, and Mel Ferrer in 1947 and closed in 1964; this stellar reincarnation emerged on the theatrical scene in 1983. The box office is open Monday from 11am to 6pm and Tuesday through Sunday from 10am to 8pm. Each show designates one Saturday matinee as a "pay what you can" performance. Reduced-price "Public Rush" tickets are available 10 minutes before curtain, subject to availability.

Old Globe Theatre

Balboa Park. ☎ **619/239-2255,** or 619/23-GLOBE for 24-hr. hot line. Fax 619/231-5879. Tickets $32–$39 (previews $22, matinees $30); seniors and students $26 matinees, $29.50 weeknights. Bus: 7 or 25.

Near the entrance to Balboa Park and just behind the Museum of Man, this Tony Award–winning theater, fashioned after Shakespeare's, has produced world premieres of such Broadway hits as *Into the Woods,* plus the revival of *Damn Yankees,* and has billed such notable performers as Marsha Mason, Cliff Robertson, Jon Voight, and Christopher Walken. The 581-seat Old Globe is part of the Simon Edison Centre for the Performing Arts, which also includes the 245-seat Cassius Carter Centre Stage and the 620-seat open-air Lowell Davies Festival Theatre, and mounts a dozen plays a year on the three stages between January and October. Tours are offered Saturday and Sunday at 11am and cost $3 ($1 students, seniors, and military). The box office is open Tuesday through Sunday from noon to 8:30pm.

OPERA

San Diego Opera

Civic Theatre, 202 C St. ☎ **619/236-6510** (box office) or 619/232-7636 (for more information). Fax 619/231-6915. E-mail sdostaff@sdopera.com. Web site: www.sdopera.com. Tickets $23 to $95; ask about standing room or discounts for students and seniors. Bus: 2, 7, 9, 29, 34, or 35. Trolley: Civic Center.

Founded in 1964, the opera showcases internationally renowned performers in operas and occasional special recitals. The season runs January through May. The 1998 season includes *The Barber of Seville* by Gioacchino Rossini, January 24 to February 4; *Salome* by Richard Strauss, February 14 to 22; *Madama Butterfly* by Giacomo Puccini, March 7 to 18; *Romeo and Juliet* by Charles Gounod, April 18 to 26; *The Marriage of Figaro* by Wolfgang Amadeus Mozart, May 9 to 20; and MET Orchestra, conductor James Levine with violinist Maxim Vengerov, Saturday, May 16.

The box office is not in the Civic Theatre but on the outside of the adjacent Golden Hall. It's open Monday through Friday from 10am to 5:30pm; hours vary on weekends on the day of performance. Performances are Tuesday, Wednesday, and Saturday at 7pm, Friday at 8pm, and Sunday at 2pm.

DANCE

San Diego–based dance companies include the **California Ballet,** a traditional ballet company, plus other minor companies. San Diego's **International Dance Festival,** held annually in January, spotlights the city's ethnic dance groups and emerging artists; most performances are at the Lyceum Theatre, but there are free dance performances in public areas. Dance companies generally perform in San Diego from September through June. For specific information about time and place of performances or for a monthly calendar of events, call the **San Diego Area Dance Alliance Calendar** (☎ 619/239-9255).

2 The Club & Music Scene

San Diego has a good supply of popular discos, bars, and clubs. (The legal drinking age is 21.) Currently, the hottest ones are located in the Gaslamp Quarter. They include **Club 66,** at 901 Fifth Ave. (☎ **619/234-4166**), which has a Route 66 motif and caters to an over-28 crowd; **E Street Alley,** on the north side of E Street between Fourth and Fifth avenues (☎ **619/231-9200**), which is a dressier club; **Blue Tattoo,** 835 Fifth Ave. (☎ **619/238-7191**); **Olé Madrid,** 755 Fifth Ave. (☎ **619/ 557-0146;** fax 619/557-0481), the destination of choice for Europhiles; **Dick's Last Resort,** 345 Fourth Ave., with entrances on both Fourth and Fifth avenues (☎ **619/ 231-9100**), popular with the college crowd; and **Buffalo Joe's American Restaurant and Bar,** 600 Fifth Ave. (☎ **619/236-1616**), where you'll find rhythm and blues, jazz, and top-40 dance music. The first four of these are underground discos, and their popularity rises and falls like the tide in the Pacific. I suggest you walk around the Gaslamp Quarter and check them out for yourself. Cover charges vary from nil to $10, depending on the group that is performing, the night of the week, and if it happens to be the "in spot" at the moment.

Fans of alternative music might enjoy the **Casbah,** 2501 Kettner Blvd. (☎ **619/ 232-4355**), where breakthrough bands are the norm.

If you're under 21, **SOMA Live,** 5305 Metro St., Mission Bay (☎ **619/ 239-SOMA** [7662]), is the place for you. This concert venue in a warehouselike building has hosted Courtney Love, Social Distortion, and Faith No More.

COMEDY CLUBS

Comedy Store

916 Pearl St., La Jolla. ☎ **619/454-9176.** Cover Tues–Wed $6, Thurs and Sun $8, Fri–Sat $10. 2-drink minimum all shows.

If you can prove you're 21, you're in for a lot of laughs. Amateur night is Monday, and Sunday and is for nonsmokers. Sunday and Thursday shows start at 8:30pm, Tuesday and Wednesday 8pm, and Friday and Saturday 8 and 10:30pm.

DISCOS

Cannibal Bar

3999 Mission Blvd. (in the Catamaran Hotel). ☎ **619/539-8650.** Cover Fri–Sun $3–$15. Bus: 34 or 34A.

Videos and live bands take center stage in this large, lively, and ever-popular nightspot. Live entertainment Wednesday through Sunday features the best local entertainment and national recording artists. A draft beer costs $1.50. Open Wednesday through Sunday from 7pm to 2am.

The Yacht Club

333 W. Harbor Dr. (in the San Diego Marriott Marina). ☎ **619/234-1500.** No cover. Bus: 2. Trolley: Convention Center.

The nautical theme and waterfront location, with a curving window wall looking onto the marina, make this a comfortable spot to park oneself. There's live dance music nightly, with appetizers and light fare available until 11pm, along with a dinner menu served from 5 to 11pm. It's open daily from 11am to 1am; the band plays 5 nights a week, a DJ, 2 nights at 9pm. Prices range from $3 to $4.50; there's no drink minimum.

JAZZ & BLUES

Croce's

802 Fifth Ave. (at F St.). ☎ **619/233-4355.** No cover to either Croce's Jazz Bar or Croce's Top Hat with the purchase of dinner at Croce's Restaurant or Ingrid's Cantina. Cover for regional bands $3–$7, for national acts $10–$18. Minimum at both bars $5. Bus: 1, 3, or 25. Trolley: Gaslamp Quarter.

Groups and individuals perform traditional jazz every night in Croce's Jazz Bar and rhythm and blues at Croce's Top Hat, both named after the late musician Jim Croce and owned by his widow, Ingrid. Jim Croce's son, A. J., an accomplished musician in his own right, sometimes performs. Jazz from the Jazz Bar drifts easily into the adjoining restaurant; it opens nightly at 5pm and music starts at 8:30pm. Next door, in Croce's Top Hat, balcony seating overlooks the stage, where rhythm 'n' blues is at its liveliest; it's open daily from 11am to 2am, with music starting at 9pm. Prices at either bar range from $2.25 to $6.

BIG BAND

Hotel del Coronado

1500 Orange Ave., Coronado. ☎ **619/435-6611.** Cover $10 without dinner; with dinner (see below). Take the Coronado Bridge to Third St., then left onto Orange Ave. Bus: 901. Ferry: From Broadway Pier, then take taxi.

The West Coast's most glorious Victorian hotel kicks up its heels on Sunday nights, when it's swing time in the Crown Room. Besides the music and dancing, the architecturally memorable room makes the trip here worthwhile. The price is $26.95 with buffet dinner. Open Sunday from 6 to 9:30pm.

CRUISES WITH ENTERTAINMENT

Hornblower/Invader Cruises

1066 N. Harbor Dr. (at Broadway Pier). ☎ **619/234-8687.** Tickets Sun–Fri $35, Sat $40 adults and children; alcoholic beverages are extra. Bus: 2. Trolley: Embarcadero.

Aboard the 151-foot antique-style yacht *Lord Hornblower,* you'll be entertained—and encouraged to dance—by a DJ/host playing a variety of CDs, cassettes, and records. The three-course meal includes a Caesar salad, chicken and beef main course, and double-fudge chocolate cake. Boarding is at 6:30pm, and the cruise runs from 7 to 9:30pm.

San Diego Harbor Excursion

1050 N. Harbor Dr. (at Broadway Pier). ☎ **619/234-4111.** Fax 619/522-6150. Tickets $45 adults, $30 for kids ages 3 to 12. Bus: 2. Trolley: Embarcadero.

The company offers a dinner on board the 150-foot, 3-deck *Spirit of San Diego,* with not one but two main courses, dessert, and cocktails. A DJ plays tunes during the $2^{1}/_{2}$-hour cruise, and you can dance all you like. Sometimes they add a country-western band or even a karaoke sing-along. Boarding is at 7pm, the cruise from 7:30 to 10pm.

CONCERTS

San Diego has become a popular performance destination for many major record-ing artists. In fact, there is a concert just about every week. The *Reader* is the best source of concert information. Tickets typically go on sale at least 6 weeks before the event, and, depending on the popularity of a particular artist or group, last-minute seats are often available through the box office or Ticketmaster (☎ **619/220-8497**). Of course, you can always go through a ticket agency like **Advance Tickets** (☎ **619/ 581-1080**) and pay a higher price for prime tickets at the last minute.

Main concert venues include the **San Diego Sports Arena,** a 15,000- to 18,000-seat indoor venue, where the acoustics are not the best but a majority of concerts are held here because of the seating capacity and availability of paid parking; the **Qualcomm Stadium,** a 50,000-seat outdoor stadium, which has acceptable acous-tics and is only used for major concerts like The Who and the Rolling Stones; **SDSU Open Air Amphitheater,** a 4,000-seat outdoor amphitheater with great acoustics—if you are not able to get a ticket, you can stand outside and hear the entire show; **Embarcadero Marina Park,** a 4,400-seat outdoor setting on San Diego Bay with great acoustics; and—from May through October—a series of contemporary concerts takes place outdoors at **Humphrey's,** 2241 Shelter Island Dr., (☎ **619/523-1010**), a 900-seat outdoor venue on the water that has good acoustics, but seats are close together and parking can be a challenge unless you arrive early. For their concert schedule, call the above number, or check their Web site: **user.aol.com/humconcert.**

3 The Bar & Coffeehouse Scene

POPULAR BARS

In downtown San Diego, the knowing crowd gravitates to bars such as **Dobson's,** 956 Broadway Circle, between Broadway and Horton Place (☎ **619/231-6711**), and **La Gran Tapa,** 611 B St., between Sixth and Seventh (☎ **619/234-8272**). For a quieter scene, try the **Palace Bar** in the Horton Grand hotel, 311 Island Ave., at Fourth Avenue (☎ **619/544-1886**). Pub goers head to **The Princess Pub & Grille,** 1675 India St., at Date Street (☎ **619/702-3021**). In Mission Bay, the **Cannibal Bar** in the Catamaran Resort Hotel at 3999 Mission Blvd. (☎ **619/488-1081**)

Pitcher This: San Diego's Microbreweries

A microbrewery revolution? Well, not exactly, but San Diego suds have come a long way in the last few years. It started in 1989 when Karl Strauss, a Bavarian brew master with 44 years of experience working for Pabst in Milwaukee, came to town. He opened Old Columbia Brewery, the first brewery here in more than 50 years. He named his brews after local attractions—Gaslamp Gold Ale, Red Trolley Ale, Black's Beach Extra Dark, Star of India Pale Ale—but he brought the recipes from the Old World, and they adhere to the Bavarian Purity Laws of 1516.

Karl's crew continues to make 23 beers a year, on a rotational basis, with eight available at any one time. Want to try them all and still be able to walk? You can order a Taster Series, 4 ounces of 8 brews for only $5.95. Free brewery tours are conducted Saturday and Sunday at 1 and 2pm. An in-depth tour, which includes a comparative tasting of Karl Strauss beers with America's best-selling beers, is available both days at 3pm. The cost of $20 per person also includes a T-shirt, appetizers, Karl's Taster Series of beers, plus a pilsner of your favorite. **Karl Strauss Brewery & Grill, Downtown** (formerly Old Columbia), at 1157 Columbia St. (☎ **619/ 234-BREW** [2739]; fax 619/234-2773), serves American fare along with their beer (see listing in chapter 6). Happy hours run from 4 to 6pm Monday through Friday, and 10pm to 1am Thursday through Saturday. Other Karl Strauss locations include **Karl Strauss Brewery & Grill, La Jolla,** at 1044 Wall St. (☎ **619/ 551-BREW**), and **Karl Strauss Brewery Gardens,** 9675 Scranton Rd., in Sorrento Mesa (☎ **619/587-BREW**)

In contrast to the polished atmosphere of the Karl Strauss breweries, the **La Jolla Brewing Company,** at 7536 Fay Ave. (☎ **619/456-BREW**), feels like a neighborhood pub. The wood floor is appropriately worn, and pool and darts are played in the back room. The brew master here is John Atwater, graduate of La Jolla High, class of 1976. During his years at UC Santa Barbara (where he earned a Ph.D. in biochemistry), John home-brewed in 5-gallon bottles. During his postdoctoral fellowship at the Salk Institute, he opened this microbrewery. He makes his handcrafted beers from his own recipes and names them after local spots: Windansea Wheat (an American-style wheat beer), Sea Lane Amber (similar to a California steam beer), Red Roost Ale (a red ale), and Pump House Porter (a dark, slightly sweet ale balanced with a bitter finish). John offers TVs for sports fans and serves meals such as Baja fish tacos, brew-house pasta, and a "cheeseburger in paradise." Oyster shooters are a local favorite. Happy hour is from 4 to 7pm Monday through Friday. If you're trying to decide between the two La Jolla brew pubs. La Jolla Brewing Company has better beer, Karl Shrauss Brewery & Grill has better food.

The San Diego area, once strictly a white-wine or Perrier kind of place, now has many brew pubs. Others you may want to try include **Pizza Port,** 135 N. Hwy. 101, Solana Beach (☎ **619/481-7332**); **Hops Bistro and Brewery,** 4353 La Jolla Village Dr., in University Towne Center (☎ **619/587-6677**; fax 619/587-6739); and **San Diego Brewing Co.,** 10450 Friars Rd., at Mission Gorge (☎ **619/ 284-BREW**).

is a popular spot. In La Jolla, favorites are the **Whaling Bar** in La Valencia hotel, 1132 Prospect St. (☎ **619/454-0771**), and nearby **George's Cafe,** 1250 Prospect St. (☎ **619/454-4244**). The legal drinking age is 21.

Top O' The Cove
1216 Prospect St., La Jolla. ☎ **619/454-7779.**

In this intimate setting, the pianist plays favorites, but leans heavily toward Gershwin. Nab the corner table next to the piano. On nice evenings, the music is piped to the patio, another idyllic spot to sit and sip. Drinks run from $4 to $65 (that's for Louis XIII cognac; buy the last two drinks and you get to keep the Baccarat bottle). Open Wednesday through Sunday from 8pm to late (usually 1am).

SPORTS BARS

If you are in town for the Superbowl and can't get a ticket, or want to mingle with San Diego sports fans, head to **Seau's** at 1640 Camino del Rio North, in Mission Valley Center (☎ **619/291-7328**), which is named for Jr. Seau, one of the key players for the San Diego Chargers. Alternatively, you could try **Trophy's** (☎ **619/450-1400**) in La Jolla at 4282 Esplanade Ct. (in the Costa Verde Center on Genesee Avenue) and in Mission Valley at 7510 Hazard Center Dr. (in Hazard center off Friars Road).

GAY & LESBIAN BARS & CLUBS

Club Bombay
3175 India St. (at Spruce St.). ☎ **619/296-6789.** Cover $2 after 9pm Fri. Bus: 5/105.

This casual place for women has a patio bar in back, where barbecues with a keg of beer are hosted on Sunday beginning at 4pm. There's occasional live entertainment on Friday and Saturday nights and karaoke on Wednesday nights. Prices range from $2 to $4.25. Open Monday through Thursday from 4pm to 2am, Friday and Saturday from 2pm to 2am, and Sunday from 1pm to 2am.

Club Montage
2028 Hancock St. ☎ **619/294-9590.** Fax 619/294-9592. E-mail montage@cts.com. Web site: www.clubmontage.com. Cover $3.

This state-of-the-art modern dance club with three floors of fun features a newly remodeled laser-and-light show, a video bar with 12 screens, and a rooftop patio. It primarily attracts gay men, but lesbians and straight couples are welcome. Pool tables and arcade games round out the largest dance club in San Diego. Dance all night with the latest and hottest sound from San Diego's best DJs, as well as many live performances. Open Wednesday from 9pm to 2am and Friday and Saturday from 9pm to 4am. Friday night's "Studio 64" is particularly popular.

The Flame
3780 Park Blvd. ☎ **619/295-4163.** Cover Sun–Fri $2, Sat $3. Bus: 7 or 7B.

For women, The Flame has a large dance floor and two bars, including a lounge bar open Friday and Saturday. Friday night is martini bar night, and on Tuesday, when it's "Boys Night Out," don't be surprised to find the clientele to be 95% men. The bar often hosts special events. Prices range from $2.75 to $5.25 (often with specials at $1.25). Open Saturday through Thursday from 5pm to 2am and Friday from 4pm to 2am.

Rich's
1051 University Ave. (between 10th and 11th aves). ☎ **619/295-2195,** or 619/497-4588 for upcoming events. Fax 619/295-5518. Thurs–Sat $3–$5; no cover Sun before 9pm, $3 afterward.

This popular club/dance space primarily welcomes gay men 21 and older. Sunday is popular for Tea and Me, when there is no cover between 7 and 9pm, and on Thursday for Club Hedonism, with techno tunes and more. On Friday and Saturday nights, go-go dancers and high-energy music set the tone for the night. Always check the events hot line, since the schedules can change. Open Thursday through Saturday from 9pm to 2am and Sunday from 7pm to 2am.

COFFEEHOUSES

There's no shortage of java joints in the San Diego area. The ones listed below and in "Java Joints in La Jolla" in chapter 6 are just a sampling of the numerous coffee and tea emporiums around town.

Pannikin Hillcrest (formerly Quel Fromage)

523 University Ave., Hillcrest. ☎ **619/295-1600.** Bus: 16 or 25.

This laid-back place looks as if people have been drinking lattes and espresso here for decades. The desserts are rich, and the art on the wall is the work of local artists. Prices range from $1.25 to $5. Open Sunday to Thursday from 7:30am to 11pm and Friday and Saturday from 7:30am to midnight.

Upstart Crow

Seaport Village (central plaza). ☎ **619/232-4855.** Fax 619/232-4856. Bus: 7. Trolley: Seaport Village.

Where else but in a coffeehouse/bookstore can you mix cappuccino and Colette, where tables and chairs fill cozy spaces surrounded by books? The selection of books, coffees, and desserts is scrumptious. And coffee refills are only 25¢. Menu prices range from $1 to $5. Open Sunday through Thursday from 9am to 10pm (until 11pm in summer) and Friday and Saturday from 9am to 11pm.

4 More Entertainment

MOVIES

Many multiscreen complexes around the city show first-release films. Avant-garde and foreign films are screened at **The Guild,** 3827 Fifth Ave., Hillcrest (☎ **619/295-2000**); **Hillcrest Cinema,** 3965 Fifth Ave., Hillcrest, with 3 hours' free parking (☎ **619/299-2100**); the **Ken Cinema,** 4061 Adams Ave., Kensington near Hillcrest (☎ **619/283-5909**); and **The Cove,** 7730 Girard Ave., La Jolla (☎ **619/459-5404**). The irrepressible *Rocky Horror Picture Show* is resurrected every Friday and Saturday at midnight at the Ken. The **OMNIMAX** theater at the Reuben H. Fleet Space Theater in Balboa Park at 1875 El Prado features movies and three-dimensional laser shows projected onto the 76-foot tilted dome screen (☎ **619/238-1233**).

LITERARY READINGS

The best way to find out if and when authors will be reading from their works is to check the daily *San Diego Union-Tribune* or the *Reader* and the *San Diego Gay and Lesbian Times,* which are published weekly. In Del Mar, authors sometimes read at **Esmeralda Books & Coffee,** in the Del Mar Plaza at 1555 Camino Del Mar (☎ **619/755-2707**); in Hillcrest, at the **Blue Door Bookstore,** 3823 Fifth Ave. (☎ **619/298-8610**); and in La Jolla at **Warwick's Books,** 7812 Girard Ave. (☎ **619/454-0347**), and **D. G. Wills** bookstore, 7463 Girard Ave. (☎ **619/456-1800**).

CASINOS

Native American tribes operate three **casinos** located in east county: **Barona Casino,** 1000 Barona Rd., Lakeside (☎ **619/443-2300**); **Sycuan Gaming Center,** 5469 Dehesa Rd., El Cajon (☎ **888/7-BARONA** or 619/445-6016; fax 619/443-2856);

and **Viejas Casino and Turf Club,** 5000 Willows Rd., Alpine (☎ **619/445-5400**). All three offer full casino gambling à la Las Vegas, off-track betting, and bingo.

To bet on the ponies, go to the **Del Mar Thoroughbred Club** during the local racing season (July through September). At any time of the year, bets can be placed on races being run far and wide at **Del Mar Satellite Wagering,** at the Del Mar Fairgrounds (☎ **619/755-1167**). To place a wager on **greyhound racing** or **jai alai,** you have to cross the international border to Tijuana. It's only a 40-minute ride by car or trolley from San Diego; from the border you'll need a cab to get to the racetrack or jai alai palace (see "Tijuana: Going South of the Border," in chapter 11). Bookmaker offices, where you can place a bet on just about any sport, are located throughout Tijuana.

POOL

If your image of a pool hall includes smoke and marginal characters, **Gaslamp Billiard Palace,** 379 Fourth Ave., at J Street (☎ **619/230-1968;** fax 619/230-1976), will be a pleasant surprise, with 34 pool tables, 2 full bars, TVs, and darts. Table rental is $6 an hour during the week and $9 an hour on weekends. Open daily from 11am to 2am.

5 Only in San Diego

San Diego's top three attractions—the San Diego Zoo, Wild Animal Park, and Sea World—all extend their hours into the evenings during summer. Sea World caps its **Summer Nights** off every night at 9pm with a free fireworks display. To catch the fireworks, you can either watch from Sea World or anywhere around Mission Bay.

Free summer concerts are offered on Sunday at 2pm year-round at the Spreckels Organ Pavilion in Balboa Park. In the summer, concerts are also held on Monday nights from 8 to 9:30pm as part of **Twilight in the Park** (☎ **619/235-1105**). **Starlight Theater** presents Broadway musicals in the Starlight Bowl in Balboa Park in July and August (☎ **619/544-STAR** [7827]). This venue is in the flight path to Lindbergh Field, and when planes pass overhead, singers stop midnote and wait for the roar to stop. The **Festival Stage** (☎ **619/239-2255**) in Balboa Park and the **Mount Helix Amphitheater** in La Mesa are popular outdoor theater venues during the summer, as is the **Moonlight Ampitheater** in Vista (☎ **760/639-6199**).

Another Balboa Park event, **Christmas on the Prado,** has been a San Diego tradition since 1977. The weekend of evening events is held the first Friday and Saturday in December. The park's museums and walkways are decked out in holiday finery; the museums are free and open late from 5 to 9pm; and there is entertainment galore, from bell choruses to Renaissance and baroque music to barbershop quartets. Crafts (including unusual Christmas ornaments), ethnic nibbles, hot cider, and sweets are for sale. A Christmas tree and nativity scene are displayed at the Spreckels Organ Pavilion.

Only-in-San-Diego movie venues include **Movies Before the Mast** aboard the *Star of India.* Here, movies of the nautical genre (such as *Black Beard the Pirate, Captain Blood,* and *Hook*) are shown on a special "screensail" April through October (☎ **619/234-9153**); at the **Sunset Cinema Film Festival** in August you can view a mix of classic and current films free of charge from a blanket or chair on the beach. Films are projected on screens mounted on floating barges from San Diego to Imperial Beach (☎ **619/454-7373**). **Dive-In Movies** are shown at the Plunge (☎ **619/488-3110**), an indoor swimming pool in Mission Beach. Viewers float on rafts in 91° water and watch water-related movies projected onto the wall. *Jaws* is a perennial favorite.

11

Side Trips from San Diego

f you have time for a day trip away from San Diego, popular destinations include the beaches and inland towns of "North County" (what locals call the northern part of San Diego County), as well as our south-of-the-border neighbor, Tijuana. You could also go relax at a spa or resort (see p. 203). All are no more than an hour away.

If you have time for a longer trip outside of San Diego, you can choose to explore some very distinct areas, all of them within an hour or two of the city. They include the wine country of Temecula, due north of San Diego; Disneyland, a little farther to the north; the gold-mining town of Julian, now known for its apple pies, to the northeast of San Diego; the vast Anza-Borrego Desert, east of Julian; or to the south of San Diego, just across the border, Baja California and a taste of Mexico. Whichever direction you choose, you're in for a treat.

The following excursions are arranged geographically going north from San Diego, up to Disneyland, and then heading southeast toward Julian and back down south to Mexico.

1 North County Beach Towns: Spots to Surf & Sun

Picturesque beach towns, each poised over their own stretch of sand, dot the coast of San Diego County from Del Mar to Oceanside. These make great day-trip destinations for sun worshipers and surfers. Getting there is easy: Del Mar is only 18 miles north of downtown San Diego; Carlsbad about 33; and Oceanside approximately 36. If you're driving, follow I-5 north: You'll find freeway exits for Del Mar, Solana Beach, Cardiff by the Sea, Encinitas, Leucadia, Carlsbad, and Oceanside. The farthest point, Oceanside, will take you about 45 minutes. The other choice by car is to wander up the coast road—known variously along the way as Camino del Mar, Pacific Coast Highway, Old Highway 101, and County Highway S21. The Coaster provides service to Carlsbad, Encinitas Solana Beach and Oceanside, and Amtrak stops in Solana Beach, just a few minutes north of Del Mar, and Oceanside. Check with **Amtrak** (☎ **800/USA-RAIL**) or call ☎ **619/685-4900** for transit information. **United Airlines** and **American Airlines** fly into Palomar

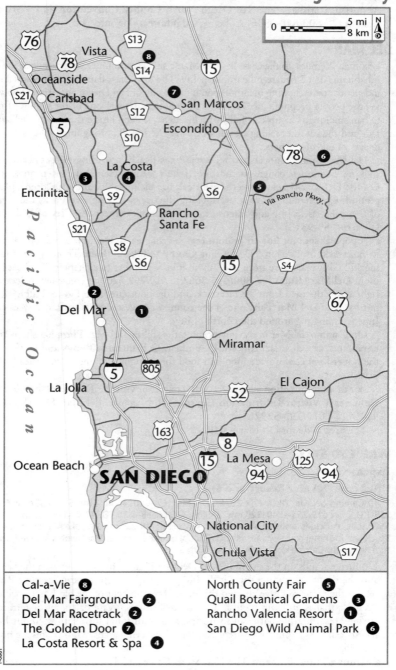

Northern San Diego County

0 | 5 mi
0 | 8 km
N

76
78 Vista **S13**
S14 **8**
Oceanside
S21 Carlsbad
5
7 San Marcos
15
S12
Escondido
S10
La Costa **78** **6**
3 **4**
Encinitas **S9** **S6**
5 Via Rancho Pkwy.
S21
Rancho
Santa Fe
S8
S6 **15** **S4**
2
Del Mar **1** **67**
Miramar
5 **805**
La Jolla
52 El Cajon
163
8
Ocean Beach **15** La Mesa **125**
SAN DIEGO **94** **94**

National City

Chula Vista **S17**

Pacific Ocean

Cal-a-Vie **8**   North County Fair **5**
Del Mar Fairgrounds **2**   Quail Botanical Gardens **3**
Del Mar Racetrack **2**   Rancho Valencia Resort **1**
The Golden Door **7**   San Diego Wild Animal Park **6**
La Costa Resort & Spa **4**

1-0861

Airport in Carlsbad. The **San Diego North County Convention and Visitors Bureau** (☎ **800/848-3336**) is also a good information source.

DEL MAR

Less than 20 miles up the coast lies Del Mar, a small community with just over 5,000 inhabitants in a 2-square-mile municipality. The town has adamantly maintained its independence, eschewing incorporation into the city of San Diego. Sometimes known as "the people's republic of Del Mar," this community was one of the nation's first to ban smoking. The upscale folks who live here grin and bear it during the Del Mar Fair and the summer racing season when the Del Mar Thoroughbred Club attracts droves of out-of-towners.

Del Mar Beach connects with Torrey Pines Beach, providing miles of sand for walking. Swimmers congregate north of **Jake's** seaside restaurant; surfers go south. On the Del Mar Beach, **Powerhouse Park** has picnic tables and a children's playground. On the cliff above it overlooking the ocean is **Seagrove Park,** the scene of free concerts in July and August; for information, contact the **City of Del Mar** (☎ **619/755-9313**).

A popular spot for **hot-air ballooning** (see chapter 7), Del Mar is best known for its **racetrack,** founded in 1937 by Bing Crosby and Pat O'Brien. Thoroughbred racing still takes place here from late July to mid-September (see chapter 7). The 243-room **Del Mar Hilton** (☎ **800/445-8667** or 619/792-5200) is conveniently located right across the road from the racetrack, and the boutique-filled Flower Hill Mall is nearby. The **Del Mar Fair,** one of the country's largest, occurs the last 2 weeks of June, culminating around the Fourth of July.

On Camino del Mar in the town center, the stylish **Del Mar Plaza** has shops and restaurants, as well as jazz concerts in summer. ۞ **Esmeralda Books and Coffee** on the upper level can provide food and food for thought. Parking is underneath the plaza.

For more information about Del Mar, contact or visit the **Del Mar Chamber of Commerce Visitor Information Center,** 1104 Camino del Mar, Del Mar, CA 92014 (☎ **619/793-5292**).

The **area code** for Del Mar is **619.**

WHERE TO STAY

Expensive

L'Auberge Del Mar Resort and Spa

1540 Camino del Mar (P.O. Box 2078), Del Mar, CA 92014. ☎ **800/553-1336** or 619/259-1515. Fax 619/755-4940. 120 rms, 8 suites. A/C MINIBAR TV TEL. $189–$249 double; from $500 suite. Packages available. AE, DC, MC, V. Valet or self-parking $8. Take Amtrak to Solana Beach and the hotel courtesy van will pick you up, or take I-5 to Del Mar Heights Rd. west, then turn right onto Camino del Mar Rd.; it's at 15th St.

L'Auberge stands on the site of the old Del Mar Hotel—midway between the beach and the shops and dining spots in Del Mar Plaza. The resort, near Seagrove Park, retains the same exclusive air, and the lobby is reminiscent of the old hotel's, with a fireplace that is an exact replica. The rooms feature private balconies or terraces, sitting areas, marble baths and vanities, and traditional furnishings; about half have ocean views; some offer fireplaces; some have ceiling fans. Most rooms are non-smoking.

Dining/Entertainment: The 15th Street Grille and Terrace serves three meals a day. There are 3 hours of free music and dancing in the lobby on Friday and Saturday nights, and you can pop into Durante's Pub most anytime.

Services: Room service (6:30am to 10pm), laundry/dry cleaning, complimentary newspaper, in-room coffee service, VIK (Very Important Kids) program during summer months and holidays.

Facilities: Two tennis courts, pool, lap pool, Jacuzzi, full European-style spa (massage, hydrotherapy treatments, herbal wraps, steam room, sauna, spa cuisine, yoga on nearby beach), health club, nearby golf.

Wave Crest

1400 Ocean Ave., Del Mar, CA 92014. ☎ **619/755-0100.** No fax. 31 bungalow/condos. TV TEL. Late July–Sept 15, $175–$200 studio, $210–$240 one-bedroom, $300 two-bedroom. Lower off-seasons rates; weekly rates available year-round. MC, V. From I-5, exit Del Mar Heights Rd. west, turn right onto Camino del Mar and drive to 15th St.; turn left and drive to Ocean Ave., and turn left.

On a bluff overlooking the Pacific, these gray-shingled bungalow/condominiums containing studios and suites are beautifully maintained and wonderfully private. For a honeymoon or romantic getaway, this is tops. All the units surround a landscaped courtyard and have a queen-size bed and sofa beds, artwork by local artists, VCR, stereo, full bath, and fully equipped kitchen with dishwasher. The studios can sleep one or two people; the one-bedroom sleeps up to four. It's only a 5-minute walk to the beach from here, and shopping and dining spots are only a few blocks away. There is an extra fee for maid service.

Facilities: Common lounge with a fireplace, TV, and newspapers; pool and bubbling Jacuzzi overlooking the ocean; irons, ironing boards, and movies are available to guests; laundry facilities.

Moderate

Del Mar Motel on the Beach

1702 Coast Blvd. (at 17th St.), Del Mar, CA 92014. ☎ **800/223-8449** for reservations, or 619/755-1534. 45 rms, all with bath (some with shower only). TV TEL. $95–$120 double. Lower off-season rates; sometimes higher weekends and holidays. Extra person $5. AE, CB, DC, DISC, MC, V. Take I-5 to Via de la Valle exit; go west, then south on Hwy. 101 (Pacific Coast Hwy.), veer west onto Coast Blvd.

The only property in Del Mar right on the beach, this little white-stucco motel with blue trim is clean and simply furnished and has been here since 1946. Upstairs rooms have one king-size bed, while those downstairs come with two double beds. All rooms have a refrigerator, coffeemaker, and fan. Half are nonsmoking rooms, and only those rooms with ocean views have bathtubs (the rest have showers only). This is a good choice for beach lovers, because you can walk from here along the beach for miles, and the popular seaside restaurants Poseidon and Jake's are right next door. The motel has a barbecue and picnic table for guests' use.

WHERE TO DINE

Head to the upper level of the centrally located **Del Mar Plaza,** at Camino del Mar and 15th Street, and consider **Il Fornaio Cucina Italiana** (☎ **619/755-8876**) for excellent Italian cuisine; **Epazote** (☎ **619/259-9966**) for Mexican, Tex-Mex, and Southwestern fare; or **Pacifica Del Mar** (☎ **619/792-0476**) for outstanding seafood. Kids like to eat at **Johnny Rockets** (☎ **619/755-1954**) an old-fashioned diner on the lower level. Down on the beach, ✪ **Jake's Del Mar,** 1660 Coast Blvd. (☎ **619/ 755-2002**), and **Poseidon Restaurant on the Beach,** 1670 Coast Blvd. (☎ **619/ 755-9345**), are both good for California cuisine and sunset views. If you want to eat at either of these popular spots, reserve early. The racetrack crowd congregates at **Bully's Restaurant,** 1404 Camino del Mar (☎ **619/755-1660**) for Bully Burgers, prime rib, and crab legs.

CARLSBAD

Fifteen miles north of Del Mar and 33 miles from downtown San Diego (a 45-min. drive), the pretty beach community of Carlsbad provides many reasons to linger on the California coast: good swimming and surfing beaches; a mile-long, two-tiered beach walk that is accessible for travelers with disabilities; three lagoons perfect for walks or bird watching; small-town atmosphere (the population is 63,000, but it actually feels smaller than Del Mar); landscaped streets; memorable restaurants; an abundance of antique and gift shops; no high-rise buildings (and no plans for any); and a warm welcome to travelers in the town's recycled train depot (1887) that is now home to the **Visitors Information Center** (☎ **760/434-6093**). United Airlines and American Airlines fly into **Palomar Airport,** which serves Carlsbad and nearby communities.

The **area code** for Carlsbad is **760.**

Carlsbad was named for Karlsbad, Bohemia, because of the similar mineral (some say curative) waters they both produced, but the town's once famous artesian well has long been plugged up.

In Carlsbad, a good place to picnic is in small **Florence Magee Park.** While there, peek into **St. Michael's by the Sea Episcopal Church** (1894) across the street; the original organ is to the right. In the spring, fall, and winter, flower fans will want to visit the 200 acres of cultivated **flower fields** at 5802 Paseo del Norte, across from Pea Soup Andersens Windmill restaurant (☎ **760/431-0352**), which transform the hills south of town into a startling floral rainbow from mid-March to late April when the ranunculas are in bloom. From late November through December, 50,000 poinsettia blooms are the big attraction here. Or see 3,000 varieties of flowers, plants, and trees from around the world and the largest bamboo collection in the United States at the serene, 30-acre **Quail Botanical Gardens,** 230 Quail Gardens Dr., Encinitas (☎ **760/436-3036**), which is open daily from 8am to 5pm; admission is $3 for adults and $1.50 for children 5 to 12; free the 1st Tuesday of each month. **Weidners' Gardens,** 695 Normandy Rd., Leucadia (☎ **760/436-2194**), is a wonderful commercial nursery for browsing. If you're interested in gardening, pick up a copy of the *North County Nursery Hoppers Guide* at Weidners' or the Flower Fields. It will give you information on and direction to other nurseries in the area.

In March, the town hosts the **Carlsbad 5000,** one of the top 5-kilometer races in the United States; the men's and women's world records were attained here. **Legoland Carlsbad,** a 35-acre theme park made of the world-famous Lego blocks, is scheduled to open in the spring of 1999. This will be the first Legoland in the United States and will feature eight theme areas, including North-American landmarks built with Lego bricks, hands-on building areas, and rides. For information, contact Legoland Carlsbad (☎ **760/438-5346;** fax 760/438-9499). Admission is expected to be between $20 and $25 for adults.

WHERE TO STAY

As we go to press, the **Four Seaons Resort Aviara** has just opened in Carlsbad (☎ **800/332-3442** in the U.S., 760/603-6800, or 800/268-6282 in Canada. Fax 760/603-6801. Web site: **www.fshr.com.**). The 331-room luxury resort features five dining options, an 18-hole golf course, a Fitness and Spa Center, and six tennis courts.

Expensive

La Costa Resort and Spa

Costa del Mar Rd., Carlsbad, CA 92009. ☎ **800/854-5000** or 760/438-9111. Fax 760/931-7585. 478 rms and suites. A/C TV TEL. $245–$440 double; $500–$2,200 suite. Golf, spa, and tennis packages available. AE, CB, DC, DISC, MC, V. Valet parking $10 overnight; free self-parking.

La Costa resort boasts two championship 18-hole golf courses (home of the annual Mercedes Championships); a 21-court racquet club comprised of 2 grass, 4 clay, and 15 composite courts (home of the WTA Toshiba Tennis Classic); resident tennis pro Pancho Segura (who has coached Jimmy Connors and Andre Agassi); an extensive spa with a multitude of treatments available; and five restaurants. These amenities are spread over 450 landscaped acres. Attractive accommodations offer all the bells and whistles you'd expect at this price level. The big advantage here is that travel partners can do their own things during the day (golf, tennis, or the spa) and still rendezvous for dinner. While this large resort boasts many facilities, it isn't looking as fresh as it once did.

Moderate

Beach Terrace Inn

2775 Ocean St., Carlsbad, CA 92003. ☎ **800/433-5415** outside Calif., or 760/729-5951; 800/622-3224 in Calif. Fax 760/729-1078. 41 rms, 5 suites. A/C TV TEL. Summer $110–$220 double; from $140 suite. Winter $100–$180 double; from $120 suite. Extra person $10. Rates include continental breakfast. AE, CB, DC, DISC, ER, MC, V. Free parking.

Carlsbad's only beachside hostelry (others are across the road or a little farther away), this downtown Best Western property has a helpful staff, and rooms and an outdoor pool with ocean views. Rooms, although not elegant, are extra large, and some have balconies, fireplaces, and kitchenettes; suites have separate living rooms and bedrooms. VCRs and films are available at the front desk. It's good for families. You can walk everywhere from here, and there is street parking.

Pelican Cove Inn

320 Walnut Ave., Carlsbad, CA 92008. ☎ **800/PEL-COVE** or 760/434-5995. E-mail PelicanCoveInn@sandcastleweb.com. Web site: http://www.pelican-cove.com/pelican. 8 rms. $85–$175 double. Rates include full breakfast. Extra person $15. AE, MC, V. From downtown Carlsbad, follow Carlsbad Blvd. south to Walnut Ave.; turn left and drive 2^1/2 blocks.

This Cape Cod–style hideaway near the beach combines romance with luxury—down to the bed covers, which resemble clouds more than comforters. All rooms have fireplaces, private entrances, and baths; some have spa tubs. You can lounge or have breakfast in the garden with a gazebo and a sundeck. Hosts Kris and Nancy Nayudu can provide you with beach towels and chairs or prepare a wonderful picnic basket (with 24-hours notice). Courtesy transportation from Oceanside train station is available.

Tamarack Beach Resort

3200 Carlsbad Blvd., Carlsbad, CA 92008. ☎ **800/334-2199** or 760/729-3500. Fax 760/434-5942. E-mail tamarack@pacbell.net. 23 rms, 54 vacation rentals. A/C TV TEL. $110–$150 double; $160–$260 vacation rental. Children under 12 stay free in parents' room. AE (accepted for rooms, not suites), MC, V. Free underground parking.

This resort property's rooms, in the village and across the street from the beach, are restfully decorated in tropical colors and wicker furniture, with small refrigerators, coffee-making facilities, and VCRs (movies are complimentary). The fully equipped vacation rentals (including washer and dryer) are available on a daily or weekly basis. The pretty Tamarack also has a pleasant lobby, a heated pool in a sunny courtyard setting, two Jacuzzis, exercise facilities, valet services, barbecue grills, and a good restaurant, Dini's by the Sea, that is popular with locals.

WHERE TO DINE

Branci's Caldo Pomodoro, 2907 State St. (☎ 760/720-9998), serves good Italian food in an informal atmosphere; **Neiman's,** 300 Carlsbad Village Dr. (☎ **760/729-4131**), serves California cuisine in historic surroundings; and **Tip Top Meats,**

6118 Paseo del Norte (☎ **760/438-2620**), is known far and wide as one of the best bargains in the county.

OCEANSIDE

The most northerly town in San Diego County (actually, it's a city of 150,000) and 36 miles from San Diego, Oceanside claims almost 4 miles of beaches and one of the West Coast's longest over-the-water wooden piers, where a tram does nothing but transport people from the street to the end of the 1,954-foot-long pier and back for 25¢ one way. The restaurant at the end of the pier called **Ruby's Diner** is a great place for a quick and inexpensive lunch over the ocean. The wide, sandy beach, pier, and well-tended recreational area with playground equipment and an outdoor amphitheater are within easy walking distance of the train station.

Oceanside's world-famous surfing spots attract numerous competitions, including the **Longboard Surf Contest** and **World Bodysurfing Championships,** both in August.

Four blocks west of the pier is the Moorish-style **Oceanside Civic Center,** at 300 N. Coast Hwy. (☎ **760/966-4420**), designed by architect Charles Moore as a postmodern homage to renowned California architect Irving Gill.

The **California Surf Museum,** 223 N. Coast Hwy. (☎ **760/721-6876**), is open Monday, Thursday, and Friday from noon to 4pm and Saturday and Sunday from 10am to 4pm. One of the highlights of the museum is a display showing the evolution of surfboards from the early days of surfing to the boards that exist today.

A launch ramp, visitor boat slips, charter fishing, and a Cape Cod–style village of shops are found at **Oceanside Harbor,** about 1 mile north of the pier. Several excellent restaurants, including **Chart House,** offer harborside dining. The **Marina Inn,** at 2008 Harbor Dr. N., Oceanside, CA 92054 (☎ **800/252-2033** or 760/722-1561; fax 760/439-9758), has comfortable rooms and suites that offer harbor and ocean views. The **Harbor Days Festival** in mid-September typically attracts 100,000 visitors to enjoy a crafts fair, entertainment, and food booths.

The area's biggest attraction is **Mission San Luis Rey** (☎ **760/757-3651**), which is a few miles inland. Founded in 1798, it is the largest of California's 21 missions. There is a small charge to tour the mission, its impressive church, exhibits, grounds, and cemetery. You might recognize it as the backdrop for one of the *Zorro* movies.

For an information packet about Oceanside and its attractions, send a check for $3 to the **Oceanside Chamber of Commerce,** 928 North Coast Hwy., Oceanside, CA 92054 (☎ **760/721-1101;** fax 760/722-8336).

The **area code** for Oceanside is **760.**

2 North County Inland: From Rancho Santa Fe to Palomar Mountain

The coastal and inland sections of North County are as different as night and day. Beaches and laid-back villages where work seems to be the curse of the surfing class characterize the coast, while inland you'll find beautiful barren hills, citrus groves, and conservative communities where agriculture plays an important role.

Rancho Santa Fe is located about 27 miles north of downtown San Diego, and from there the Del Dios Highway (S6) leads to Escondido, almost 32 miles from the city. San Marcos, Vista, and Fallbrook are even farther north. Nearly 70 miles away is Palomar Mountain in the Cleveland National Forest, which spills over the border into Riverside County. The **San Diego North County Convention and Visitors Bureau** (☎ **800/848-3336**) can answer all your questions.

RANCHO SANTA FE

Certainly one of the county's loveliest communities, exclusive Rancho Santa Fe was once the property of the Santa Fe Railroad, and the eucalyptus trees they grew there create a stately atmosphere. To get to Rancho Santa Fe from San Diego, take Interstate 5 north to Via de la Valle east. The Del Dios Highway, which starts here, is the scenic route to Escondido and the Wild Animal Park. This road affords views of Lake Hodges, as well as glimpses of expansive estates, some of the most expensive in the country.

The **area code** for Rancho Santa Fe is **619.**

WHERE TO STAY

✪ Rancho Valencia Resort

5921 Valencia Circle (Box 9126), Rancho Santa Fe, CA 92067. ☎ **800/548-3664** or 619/756-1123. Fax 619/756-0165. E-mail rvr@aol.com. 43 suites in 21 casitas. MINIBAR TV TEL. $360–$535 suite. Spa, tennis, golf, and romance packages available. AE, DC, DISC, MC, V. Free parking. Take I-5 to Via de la Valle and travel east to El Camino Real (Mary's Tack Shop is on the corner); go south to San Dieguito Rd. and turn east; follow the signs for Rancho Valencia.

If you are in need of pampering and relaxation or a romantic getaway, read on. A member of Relais et Châteaux and Preferred Hotels, this sun-baked Spanish- and Mediterranean-style resort sits on 40 acres overlooking the San Dieguito Valley and the rolling hills of Rancho Santa Fe. Small and intimate, the resort is far removed from the fast pace of the real world, even though it's only a short way from I-5 and only 6 miles inland from Del Mar. Imagine having your own casita with cathedral ceilings, terra-cotta tiles, Berber carpets, wood-burning fireplace, ceiling fans, oversize tiled bath, walk-in closet, patio, and private terrace. To boot, spa treatments and massages can be given in the casita itself. Fresh-squeezed juice and a newspaper are left outside your door in the morning, and coffee-making equipment is available. Those who actually do venture outside their casita will discover grounds filled with 2,000 citrus trees, bougainvillea, and air sweetened by flowers and birdsong.

There is a lap pool, a large secluded pool, three Jacuzzis, and a fitness room. Those more athletically inclined can take advantage of the 18 tennis courts and tennis clinics with a four-to-one student/teacher ratio. You might check out the championship croquet lawn or play a round of golf at the private courses adjacent to the resort. Bikes for adults and kids are available at no extra charge, and there are plenty of hiking trails to enjoy. The Clintons dined here when they were in town, and Jessye Norman stayed while she was performing in San Diego. I highly recommend this place; I don't think you'll be disappointed.

Dining/Entertainment: The pretty dining room serves Mediterranean-California cuisine and three meals a day, with a cellist or guitarist on Friday and Saturday nights; there's dancing under the stars on Thursday nights in July and August. Tea and cocktails are served in La Sala, from which there is a great view of the hot-air balloons at sunset.

Services: 24-hour room service, complimentary morning paper and fresh orange juice, nightly turndown service, airport transportation from San Diego's Lindbergh Field, valet parking.

Facilities: Two cable TVs and VCRs in each suite; video rentals; in-room safes; two pools; three Jacuzzis; unlimited use of 18 hard-turf tennis courts, tennis clinics, and match arranging; regulation croquet court; golf privileges at four nearby private golf clubs; fitness room; bicycles; massage rooms.

ESCONDIDO

Best known as the home of the **Wild Animal Park** (described in chapter 7), Escondido is also the site of the **California Center for the Performing Arts,** an attractive 12-acre campus that includes two theaters, an art museum, a conference center, and a cafe. It's worth the 45-minute to 1-hour drive to Escondido (along Interstate 15 north to the Escondido exits) just to see the appealing postmodern architecture of this facility, which opened its doors in 1994. (To find out what's playing and for ticket information, call ☎ **760/738-4100.**)

This city of 125,000 is in the heart of a major agricultural area, so it's not surprising that the **Farmers' Market** held here on Tuesday afternoons is one of the county's best. The nearby **Welk Resort Center,** at 8860 Lawrence Welk Dr. (☎ **800/ 932-9355**) offers lodging, golf, tennis, and live theatrical entertainment. In total, North County is home to 36 golf courses (some are described in chapter 7). **Orfila Vineyards** is near the Wild Animal Park; for details, refer to "For Wine Lovers" in Section 7 of chapter 7. For shopping, **North County Fair,** at 272 E. Via Rancho Pkwy. (☎ **760/ 489-2332**), is a three-story, fully enclosed mall, with Nordstrom, Macy's, and other department stores, plus a food court and nearly 100 smaller shops and boutiques.

WHERE TO DINE

✪ 150 Grand Cafe

150 West Grand Ave. ☎ **760/738-6868.** Reservations recommended, especially for weekend nights. Main courses $7.50–$20. AE, DC, MC, V. Mon–Fri 11:30am–9pm, Sat 5–9:30pm. MODERN MULTIETHNIC.

What a treat to discover this delightful cafe on the main drag in downtown Escondido—an area I hadn't associated with fine dining. However, now I keep finding excuses to go to North County and 150 Grand Cafe, owned by English expatriates Cyril and Vicki Lucas. The bright, attractive decor feels like a cross between a conservatory and a library. Lunchtime favorites include grilled poblano chili (with Havarti cheese, roasted-tomato vinaigrette, tomatillos, cilantro, and red and blue tortilla strips) and the flash-grilled tuna salad (Hawaiian ahi, orange basmati, mixed greens, rice noodles, and sesame-ginger vinaigrette). Dinners include grilled filet mignon, forest-mushroom pasta, sautéed salmon, and roast game hen. There's indoor and outdoor seating.

PALOMAR MOUNTAIN

Palomar Observatory (☎ 760/742-2119) and its mammoth telescope have kept a silent vigil over the heavens since 1949. To get there from San Diego, take I-15 north to Highway 76 east, and turn left onto County Highway S6. Even if you don't want to inch your way to the top, drive the 3 miles to the lookout or just beyond it to the campground, grocery store, restaurant, and post office. Palomar Observatory's impressive dome is 135 feet high and 137 feet in diameter. The telescope itself has a single 200-inch mirror and weighs 530 tons. Now completely computerized, it has an approximate light range of more than a billion light years. Start your visit in the museum, which is open daily from 9am to 4pm (except December 24 and 25) and has a continuously running informative video that makes a walk up the hill to the observatory more meaningful. The observatory closes at 4pm, and you'll only be able to look at (not through) the mammoth telescope. Palomar is primarily a research facility. The museum and the observatory both have rest rooms. Try to visit the observatory in the morning; late in the day, you'll have the sun in your eyes coming back down the mountain.

For a downhill thrill, take the **Palomar Plunge** on a 21-speed mountain bike. From the top of Palomar Mountain to its base, you'll experience, courtesy of gravity, a 5,000-foot vertical drop stretched out over 16 miles. **Gravity Activated Sports,** P.O. Box 683, Pauma Valley, CA 92061 (☎ **800/985-4427** or 760/742-2294; fax

Select Spas

It's not too surprising that two premier spa retreats—the **Golden Door** and **Cal-a-Vie**—are discreetly tucked away in the hills of North County. After all, this is southern California, where looking good is an art form and year-round outdoor rest and relaxation are possible. It seems only natural that those yearning to get into shape would find their way here. And they do, from all over the world.

Spa goers receive unparalleled pampering, but they also work their buns off—or at least into shape. At the Golden Door, 39 guests follow their own personal schedule; everyone is encouraged to begin the day with an early-morning hike, followed by exercise classes, healthy meals, "mocktail" parties, and—the best part—massages. You'll feel renewed by the diet, physical exertion, and the spa's peaceful atmosphere. "Everyone leaves here happy," I was told; about three-quarters of the guests return.

Women are the primary clientele; the spa only sets aside 4 weeks for men and designates 2 weeks as "co-ed." And paradise isn't cheap: the all-inclusive rate is $4,500 a week during the winter, $4,000 during the summer. But aren't you worth it? A three-to-one staff ratio means someone is always available to do your bidding. (Rooms are cleaned every 2 hours.) For more information, write Golden door at P.O. Box 463077, Escondido, CA 92046-3077 (☎ **800/424-0777** or 760/744-5777; fax 760/744-5007).

Cal-a-Vie caters to 24 guests a week. Most weeks are co-ed, although one or two a month are set aside for women only. Like the Golden Door, the spa emphasizes enacting lifestyle changes and de-stressing, but Cal-a-Vie focuses more on European spa treatments—real sybaritic stuff—and less on the spiritual side. This spot is popular with celebrities, such as Angelica Huston, Julia Roberts, and Kathleen Turner. Oprah found Rosie here! If you could handle 16 spa treatments a week (including outdoor massages on private decks) in absolutely gorgeous surroundings, write Cal-a-Vie at 2249 Somerset Rd., Vista, CA 92084 (☎ **760/945-2055;** fax 760/630-0074). This pampering costs $4,350 a week; less during the summer.

If the Golden Door and Cal-a-Vie are out of your price range, you might consider **Rancho La Puerta,** located in Tecate, Mexico, just over the border from San Diego County. It's under the same ownership as the Golden Door, but because it's less expensive, its local moniker is "The Back Door." It's not as exclusive, but offers similar programs. To request a brochure, call ☎ **800/433-7565** or 619/744-4222.

Several resorts in the San Diego area also offer extensive spa facilities: **L'Auberge Del Mar Resort and Spa** and **La Costa Resort and Spa** (both described above), and **Le Meridien** in Coronado (described in chapter 5). If you're in town and want body work, I recommend my favorite massage therapist, **Linda Lowe** (☎ **619/454-6702**).

760/742-2293; Web site: **www.gasports.com**) supplies the mountain bike, helmet, gloves, lunch, souvenir photo, and T-shirt. This experience costs $80.

3 Temecula: Touring the Wineries

60 miles N of San Diego; 60 miles NW of Julian; 90 miles SE of Los Angeles

Located over the line in Riverside County, Temecula is known for its wineries and the excellent vintages they produce. The town's name (pronounced Te-*mec*-u-la) is a native American word meaning "where the sun shines through the mist." If you gaze out over the vineyards early in the morning or in the middle of the afternoon, the name still holds true. It's California's only West Coast town that still goes by its aboriginal name. Helen Hunt Jackson used the region as the setting for her novel *Ramona*, first published in 1884.

Temecula has a couple of unique claims to fame. Granite from its quarries (most of which closed down in 1915, when reinforced concrete became popular) constitutes most of San Francisco's street curbs. The last person sentenced to death by hanging in California was Temecula's blacksmith, John McNeil, who killed his wife in 1936.

When you turn onto Rancho California Road, all you'll see at first is new construction, but soon the vineyards come into view and the countryside turns natural again—a relief after the onslaught of progress, something relatively new to this area. Back in 1968, one vintner recalls, "If you heard a car come down Rancho California Road, you'd go to the window to see who could possibly be lost way out here."

Temecula's microclimate, which allows grapes to flourish, is due to a notch in the coastal mountains called Rainbow Gap, which lets breezes blow through from the ocean, 22 miles away. They result both in temperatures that are 8° to 10° cooler than on the coast and in a longer growing season; this lets grapes ripen more slowly. Most vineyards here are more than 1,400 feet above sea level.

Temecula is not as well known for its wines as Napa or Sonoma because those wine-producing regions have been at it for 100 years longer. Franciscan missionaries planted the first grapevines here in the early 1800s, but the land ended up being used primarily for cattle raising on the 87,000-acre Vail Ranch from 1904 until 1964, when the ranch was sold. Grapevines began to take root in the receptive soil again in 1968, and the first Temecula wines were produced in 1971.

ESSENTIALS

GETTING THERE   Drive north from San Diego on I-15 for 50 miles; when the Temecula Valley comes into view, it'll take your breath away. To reach the vineyards, head east on Rancho California Road.

VISITOR INFORMATION   For information on accommodations and maps and brochures on Old Town Temecula and the vineyards, contact the **Temecula Valley Chamber of Commerce,** 27450 Ynez Rd., Suite 104, Temecula, CA 92591 (☎ **909/676-5090**), or visit their home page at **www.temecula.org.** The **Temecula Valley Vintners Association,** Box 1601, Temecula, CA 92593-1601 (☎ **909/ 699-3626**), is another good source, especially about the vineyards.

The **area code** for Temecula is **909.**

TOURING THE WINERIES

Today there are 14 wineries in the region, most of them strung side by side for a couple of miles along Rancho California Road, producing white, red, and rosé wines. Most of them are not sold outside of California or the West, although some have made it as far as the White House.

Since the wineries in Temecula are smaller than their counterparts in northern California, and are mostly family-owned and -operated, you're more likely to get the chance to actually meet and talk with the vintners when you come to their property. However, don't expect a private tour—the wineries spill over with visitors on the weekends.

Harvest time is usually mid-August through September, and visitors are welcome then and year-round to tour, taste, and stock up. Most wineries in the area are closed New Year's Day, Easter, Thanksgiving Day, and Christmas Day.

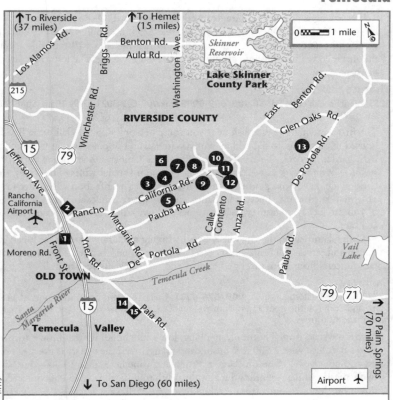

CALIFORNIA

Temecula • San Diego

Accommodations:
Butterfield Inn Motel **1**
Loma Vista **6**
Temecula Creek Inn **14**

Dining:
Baily Wine Country Cafe **2**
Cafe Champagne **5**
Temet Grill **15**

Wineries to Visit:
Callaway Vineyard & Winery **4**
Cilurzo Vineyard & Winery **12**
Maurice Carrie Winery **11**
Mount Palomar Winery **8**
Thornton Winery **5**

Other Wineries in Area:
Baily Vineyard & Winery **9**
Clos du Muriel Winery **7**
Filsinger Vineyard & Winery **13**
Hart Winery **3**
Temecula Creek Winery **10**

If bicycling is your thing, **Gravity Activated Sports,** P.O. Box 683, Pauma Valley, CA 92061 (☎ **800/985-4427** or 760/742-2294; fax 760/742-2293; Web site: **www.gasports.com**), offers a wine-country tour that includes a 10-mile ride around the area followed by a bus tour around the wineries for tasting. The tour costs $87.50 per person.

Thornton Winery

32575 Rancho California Rd. ☎ **909/699-0099.** Fax 909/699-3021. Daily 10am–5pm (tours Sat–Sun).

The first wine-making establishment you come to along Rancho California Road is housed in a striking stone building with a waterfall and sloping lawn in front and an herb garden in back. Today Thornton produces Culbertson sparkling wine, *à la méthode champenoise,* as well as Thornton premium varietal wines. The wines, sold nationwide, have been poured at the White House. The gift shop sells a nice range of wine-related items. There is a champagne bar where drinks are about $5 a glass, or you can pay $6 to taste two champagnes and two still wines. The bar opens daily at 11am.

Café Champagne, the vineyard's award-winning restaurant, is open for lunch and dinner and serves California cuisine (see "Where to Dine," below). The winery hosts jazz concerts from April through October and special events year-round.

Callaway

32720 Rancho California Rd. ☎ **909/676-4001.** Daily 10:30am–5pm; free tours at 11am, 1pm, and 3pm (on the hour 11am–4pm weekends). Closed New Year's Day, Easter, Thanksgiving, and Christmas.

Across the road from Thornton, in a long, low white building with brown trim, set in grounds lush with 2,500 rose bushes and orange trees, the winery is the area's oldest and now, at 720 acres, its largest. Producing wine here since 1974—nine labels in all, mostly whites—it offers the most in-depth tour. Each year 75,000 visitors look down on the operations from a raised, enclosed walkway. There's a $3 charge to sample four different wines; you get to keep the glass. The large gift shop features not only the Callaway Vintages, but also gift baskets, books on wine, aprons, cups, and T-shirts. A vine-covered picnic area overlooks the vineyards (if you didn't come prepared to dine alfresco, there's a market 4 miles down the road). Although the winery has foreign owners, its operation remains pure California.

Mount Palomar Winery

33820 Rancho California Rd. ☎ **909/676-5047.** Fax 909/694-5688. Daily 10am–5pm. Free tours 1:30 and 3:30pm weekdays; 11:30am, 1:30, and 3:30pm weekends; tasting of 4 wines of your choice costs $3, including the souvenir glass.

Turn off the main road and follow the blacktop up and over the hill to this 105-acre vineyard and its visitor center. Mount Palomar's Riesling and chardonnay are particularly popular, along with their port and cream sherry. The sherry is aged by the Spanish method, in old brandy barrels set out in the sun for 24 to 30 months. One of the region's first vineyards, Mount Palomar has continued its innovative style by introducing two new labels: The Castelletto label features the classic Italian varieties Sangiovese and Cortese, and the Rey Sol label has Mediterranean varietals like Syrah- and Rhone-style blends.

Ribbons won in wine competitions over the years are proudly displayed on the walls. Outside, 60 tables are available for picnicking, some on a spot overlooking the property belonging to the vineyard. A shop runs a full-service deli Friday through Sunday, and deli snacks are always available. Tasting of four wines of your choice costs $2, including the souvenir glass. From the winery, you can gaze out at Mount

San Jacinto and, behind it, Mount San Gorgonio, southern California's highest mountain. John Poole opened the winery in 1975, and his eldest son, Peter, runs it. Try to come before 1pm on weekends, when people may stand five deep for tastings, and be sure to heed the quotation in the tasting room: *"Donde el vino entra, la verdad sale"* ("Where wine enters, truth departs").

Cilurzo Vineyard & Winery
41220 Calle Contento (just off Rancho California Rd.). ☎ **909/676-5250.** Fax 909/676-7458. Daily 9:30am–4:45pm.

In some LA circles, Vince Cilurzo may be better known as the man who was the lighting director for the TV game show *Jeopardy!* for many years (he still does so a few days a week; he also lit the Lawrence Welk Show for many years), but out in Temecula he's known as a vintner who established his 52-acre vineyard in 1968 and started producing wines in 1978. One of the most popular Cilurzo labels is the Petite Syrah, which, Vince claims, can be served with anything from tomato sauce to curry. The winery also produces a nouveau and a late harvest version of the Petite Syrah, along with a number of other wines. Unlike many other Temecula wineries, this one has no bar for tastings; instead, visitors sit in chairs and Vince Cilurzo or his wife, Audrey, serves them. A tasting of five or six wines costs $1, refundable with a purchase. Photos on the tasting room's back wall capture moments from Vince's star-studded career. A picnic area overlooks the pond.

Maurice Carrie
34225 Rancho California Rd. ☎ **909/676-1711.** Daily 10am–5pm.

It's the last of the wineries on Rancho California Road, off to your right. You can't miss the large two-story pseudo-Southern building with veranda and gazebo—a "Victorian farmhouse," Maurice Van Roekel likes to call it. She and her husband, Budd, came here to retire, but soon were producing red and white wines instead. They've named four wines after their grandchildren. The property has a wine boutique, a resident cat called Butterscotch, and a lovely oak bar trimmed with black and white tiles that draws a good afternoon crowd. The boutique sells wine and champagne glasses and insulated wine coolers, among other items. A deli section carries juice, crackers, and cold wine. Tastings are available.

EXPLORING OLD TOWN TEMECULA

A wonderful, eccentric counterpoint to the vineyards is the old part of the city of Temecula, preserved as it was in the 1890s—western storefronts and all. It lies 4 miles west of the vineyards off Rancho California Road, stretches along six short blocks, and has a reputation as an antique-hunter's haven.

Park at the south end of town near the Swing Inn Café or Butterfield Plaza and walk north along Main Street to Sixth Street and back, going up one side of the street and back on the other. Take time to read the plaques on the old buildings along the way. Be forewarned that Temecula has become a traffic-clogged town, and you will hear the drone of cars most everywhere, even on the golf course.

One of my favorite spots in town, partly for the name, is the **Swing Inn Café,** at 28676 Front St., (☎ **909/676-2321**), where a sign claims that the cafe's been in existence since 1927. I asked my waitress if that was true. "Look around," she said. "Some of our customers have been here that long."

At Front and Sixth streets, turn right and walk a short block to **Sam Hicks Park,** home to the **"They Passed This Way" Monument** and the Old St. Catherine's Church, which dates from the early 1920s and is now part of the **Temecula Valley Museum** (☎ 909/676-0021). The museum houses native American artifacts from the area that are more than 1,000 years old, along with memorabilia from 1846 to the 1940s, and a model of the town from 1914. The museum is open Wednesday through Sunday from 11am to 4pm and by appointment.

Cross Front Street and walk back down the west side of the street. At Front and Sixth streets is the **Chaparral Antique Mall,** with more than 70 dealers under one roof (☎ **909/676-0070**). Down at Front and Main streets stands the **First National Bank,** which was built in 1912 and managed to stay open during the Great Depression, gaining it the nickname the "Pawn Shop." The bank finally closed in 1941, and the building now houses a Mexican restaurant. For many years, its second floor was the town's community center and dance hall.

Nearby are two plunderable antique malls: **Morgan's Antiques,** 42049 Main St. (☎ **909/676-2722**), in a brick building dating from 1891 that for 60 years was Burnham's Store, the mainstay of local ranchers, and beside it, the **Temecula Trading Post,** 42081 Main St. (☎ **909/676-5759**). Across the street stands the Old Welty/Temecula Hotel, built in 1882, the year the railroad came to Temecula; it burned and was rebuilt in 1891 and now is a private residence. Check out the store beside it, **Country Seller and Friends,** 42050 Main St. (☎ **909/676-2322**), which sells furniture and antiques.

At the southwest corner of Main and Front streets, the **Welty Building,** which dates from the 1880s, now houses a deli but used to be a gym where Jack Dempsey worked out.

OUTDOOR PURSUITS IN TEMECULA

In addition to wine tasting, area activities include hot-air balloon rides over the vineyards, an unforgettable sight. One company, which has been around for about 20 years, is **Sunrise Balloons** (☎ **800/548-9912**). Proprietor Dan Glick also offers horse-drawn carriage rides through the vineyards.

For an outing in more than 7,000 acres of unspoiled terrain, take I-15 north to Clinton Keith Road and drive west for about 5 miles to get to the **Santa Rosa Plateau Ecological Reserve,** 22115 Tenaja Rd., Murrieta, owned and maintained by the **Nature Conservancy** (☎ **909/677-6951** or 909/699-1856). Here, walking trails, coyotes, hawks, migrating birds, and maybe even an eagle or two await you.

WHERE TO STAY

Butterfield Inn Motel

28718 Front St., Temecula, CA 92390. ☎ **909/676-4833.** Fax 909/676-2019. 39 rms. A/C TV TEL. Weekdays $40–$43 double; weekends $45–$55 double. Extra person $5. AE, DISC, MC, V. Take I-15 north to Rancho California Rd. west to Front St.

Within walking distance of Old Town Temecula shops, the motel (not really an inn) has an Old West facade, a small, unheated outdoor pool, and a Jacuzzi. There's complimentary coffee in the lobby in the morning. It's easy to imagine the Butterfield stagecoach pulling up here any moment.

Loma Vista

33350 La Serena Way, Temecula, CA 92591. ☎ **909/676-7047.** Fax 909/676-0077. 6 rms. A/C. $95–$135 double; $75–$115 midweek. Rates include full champagne breakfast. DISC, MC, V. Take I-15 to Rancho California Rd. east; inn is on left just beyond Callaway vineyard.

Betty and Dick Ryan came here from Los Angeles in 1988 and designed and built this tiled-roof mission-style house for their bed-and-breakfast inn. Perfectly named, it sits on a hill (*loma* in Spanish) overlooking the best vista around. From the living room, you can see the Callaway vineyard and the Santa Ana Mountains. All guest rooms have full private baths; four have private wisteria-covered balconies. Favorite balconied rooms are Sauvignon Blanc, with Southwestern furnishings made of white pine and a four-poster queen-size bed; and Fumé Blanc, in California garden style with white wicker. Besides complimentary fruit and a decanter of sherry in each room, free wine and cheese are served by the fire at 6pm. A spa bubbles away on the back patio, while the front patio, a great place just to while away the hours, has a fire pit. The property is a real oasis, with 85 rosebushes, ranunculas, daisies, Australian tea bushes, and 325 grapefruit trees. The Ryans—Betty actually runs the operation and does all the cooking—are both from Montana. The resident dog is a Dalmatian named Casey. Old Town Temecula is 5 miles away.

✪ Temecula Creek Inn

44501 Rainbow Canyon Rd., Temecula, CA 92592. ☎ **800/962-7335** or 909/694-1000. Fax 909/676-3422. 70 rms (56 nonsmoking), 10 junior suites. A/C MINIBAR TV TEL. Sun–Thurs $126 double; from $150 junior suite. Fri–Sat $145 double; $175 junior suite. Golf and wine-country packages available. AE, DC, DISC, MC, V. From San Diego, take I-15 north to exit 79 (Indio); turn right off the exit ramp and proceed to Pala Rd.; turn right, go over a little bridge, then take an immediate right onto Rainbow Canyon Rd.; entrance to inn is $^1/_2$ mile from here and well marked.

This small resort is more a country lodge than an inn, its inviting lobby replete with adobe walls, leather couch, native American artifacts, and fireplace. Rooms in five two-story understated buildings all have restful views, as well as custom-designed native American–inspired furnishings that creatively combine art, muted colors, and textures. Junior suites are oversize corner rooms with sitting areas, in-room safes, two balconies, and floor-to-ceiling windows. The TV is hidden away quite cleverly (under a piece of sculpture), and you'll luxuriate in down pillows, unless you're allergic. Magnolia trees line the walkway from the resort's lobby to the restaurant. There are no porters, but you can drive up close to many of the rooms.

Dining/Entertainment: The Temet Grill (see "Where to Dine," below) is outstanding; breakfast, lunch, dinner, and Sunday brunch are offered. There is live music nightly in the lounge adjoining the restaurant. Food and cocktail service is available poolside.

Services: Laundry/dry cleaning, complimentary newspaper in lobby.

Facilities: Outdoor pool, barbecue under live oaks, 27 holes of golf, driving range, volleyball, croquet, two tennis courts, golf-and-tennis pro shop, meeting rooms, hair dryer and magnifying mirror in baths, coffee and tea in room (including beans and a grinder), in-room safe, cribs.

WHERE TO DINE

Baily Wine Country Cafe

27644 Ynez Rd., (at Rancho California Rd.) in the Albertson's shopping center. ☎**909/ 676-9567.** Reservations recommended, especially on weekends. Lunch main courses $8–$11; dinner main courses $13–$22. AE, CB, DC, MC, V. Mon–Thurs 11am–2:30pm and 5–9pm, Fri 11am–2:30pm and 5–9:30pm, Sat 11am–9:30pm, Sunday 11am–9pm. CALIFORNIA/ CONTINENTAL.

Baily's has the largest selection of Temecula Valley wines anywhere, including those from the Baily family's own winery on Rancho California Road. To show them off to best advantage, the cafe's chef has concocted some mouth-watering dishes, which change every few months. Consider such appetizers as crab cakes with roasted red–bell-pepper sauce and mixed greens, Caesar salad with shaved Parmesan cheese, and fresh mixed greens with balsamic shallot vinaigrette. At lunch, try the penne with roasted garlic, fresh vegetables, and tomato sauce made chunky with Italian sausage;

Southwestern-style grilled cheese sandwich with cilantro (a regional prize winner); and grilled chicken piccata salad with mixed greens and lemon-caper vinaigrette. Dinner favorites include Southwestern pork tenderloin with garlic mashed potatoes; salmon Wellington with cucumber-and-papaya relish and fresh vegetables; and chicken ravioli in a basil pesto. Finish off the meal with Carol Baily's white-chocolate cheesecake, a top choice with local diners. If you're in luck, the Baily family, which is always in evidence at the cafe, will be hosting one of its celebrated "Dinners in the Wine Cellar." Smoking is allowed on the patio but not inside the restaurant. They can provide picnics to go with 24-hours notice. The restaurant is to your right and up the hill after you enter the shopping center.

✪ Café Champagne

Thornton Winery, 32575 Rancho California Rd. ☎ **909/699-0088.** Reservations recommended. Main courses $13–$21. AE, DC, MC, V. Daily 11am–9pm. CALIFORNIA.

The toast of the Temecula wine country, this bistro and cafe features tasty dishes specially created to be served with nine Thornton champagnes. The wine list also features other Temecula and California labels. The lunch and dinner menus, California cuisine at its best, feature appetizers like soup du jour, warm brie en croûte with honey-walnut sauce, crab-and-shrimp strudel, and smoked salmon carpaccio. Among the entrees are angel-hair pasta primavera or angel-hair seafood pasta, mesquite-grilled tuna, and baked pecan chicken. The list of mesquite-grilled entrees expands at dinner, and at lunch tempting lighter fare includes hearty salads and sandwiches filled with mesquite-grilled hamburger, steak, or chicken. The setting, overlooking the vineyard, is sublime. It's a small place, so do reserve ahead. If you want really good food, you're going to like it here.

Temet Grill

In the Temecula Creek Inn, 44501 Rainbow Canyon Rd. ☎ **909/676-5631.** E-mail temeculacreekinn@jcresorts.com. Reservations recommended. Main courses $15.50–$21. AE, CB, DC, DISC, MC, V. Mon–Sat 6:30am–10pm, Sun 6am–10pm. FRENCH WINE COUNTRY.

The Temet Grill is outstanding, from the service to the California wine-country cuisine to the view beyond the dramatic window wall. The very attractive dining room has five striking chandeliers, native American artifacts in glass cases, and floor-to-ceiling picture windows overlooking the golf course. The menu changes frequently, with house specialties like grilled tortilla pizza or grilled chilies rellenos with chipotle salsa. Main courses might include roasted sea bass in a five-spice crust, sautéed or grilled chicken breast with beer mustard and chipotle hollandaise, or grilled swordfish or steak. All the dishes are creatively presented. The wine list emphasizes California vintages, along with some from Oregon and Washington and a few French champagnes.

TEMECULA AFTER DARK

Any time of year, for a fun evening out in Old Town Temecula, indulge in a little bit of country-western dancing at **The Midnight Roundup,** 28721 Front St., opposite the Butterfield Inn (☎ **909/694-5686**). This may be California's biggest saloon/dance hall, with 4,000 square feet incorporating dance areas for two-steppers, swing dancers, and line dancers. There's room left for eight pool tables; tables and chairs; and two impressive bars, one 110 feet long and the other 60 feet long. It's open Tuesday through Sunday from 6pm until the crowd goes home, with dance lessons given on Tuesday and Thursday nights. Live bands are on hand from 8:30pm until 2am Thursday through Saturday nights, when there is a $5 cover; otherwise, there's a DJ. Devotees range in age from the minimum of 21 to 80-plus, most decked out in western garb; weekends are crowded. The entrance is at the back of the building.

4 Disneyland & Other Anaheim Area Attractions

by Stephanie Avnet

160 miles N of San Diego

The sleepy Orange County town of Anaheim grew up around Disneyland, the West's most famous theme park. Now, even beyond this Happiest Place on Earth, the city and its neighboring communities are kid-central: Otherwise unspectacular, sprawling suburbs have become a playground of family-oriented hotels, restaurants, and unabashedly tourist-oriented attractions. Among the nearby draws are Knott's Berry Farm, another family-oriented theme park, in nearby Buena Park. At the other end of the scale is the Richard Nixon Library and Birthplace, a surprisingly compelling presidential library and museum, just 7 miles northeast of Disneyland in Yorba Linda.

ESSENTIALS

GETTING THERE   From downtown San Diego, take I-5 north to the Harbor Boulevard exit and turn left. The main entrance will be one-quarter mile ahead on the right. The drive from downtown San Diego takes approximately 90 minutes.

Eight **Amtrak** trains go to Anaheim daily from San Diego. The one-way fare is $17 and the trip takes about 2 hours. Amtrak also offers 1-day and 5-day excursion packages. For an additional $45.00, the 1-day package includes round-trip shuttle service from the train station to Disneyland and admission fees. For an additional $75.00, you can extend your stay with the 5-day package, which includes admission for 5 days and shuttle service to the train station. To make reservations and for schedule information, call ☎ **800/USA-RAIL.**

VISITOR INFORMATION   The **Anaheim/Orange County Visitor and Convention Bureau,** at 800 W. Katella Ave. (P.O. Box 4270), Anaheim, CA 92803 (☎ **714/999-8999**), can fill you in on area activities and shopping shuttles. It's located just inside the Convention Center (across the street from Disneyland), next to the dramatic cantilevered arena, and welcomes visitors Monday to Friday from 8:30am to 5:30pm. The **Buena Park Convention and Visitors Office,** 6280 Manchester Blvd., Suite 103 (☎ **800/541-3953** or 714/562-3560), will provide specialized information on its area, including Knott's Berry Farm.

DISNEYLAND

Disney was the originator of the mega–theme park. Opened in 1955, Disneyland remains unsurpassed. Despite constant threats from pretenders to the crown, Disneyland and its sibling park, Walt Disney World outside Orlando, Florida, remain the kings of the theme parks. At no other park is fantasy elevated to an art form. Nowhere else is as fresh and fantastic every time you walk through the gates, whether you're 6 or 60—and no matter how many times you've done it before. There's nothing like Disney Magic.

The park stays on the cutting edge by continually updating and expanding, while still maintaining the hallmarks that make it the world's top amusement park (a term coined by Walt Disney himself). Look for the most recent Disney additions during your visit—1995's Indiana Jones Adventure is a high-tech thrill that's not to be missed, no matter how long the wait. It was "lights out" in 1996 for the beloved Main Street Electrical Parade's 24-year run; Light Magic, a new nighttime spectacular featuring enchanted pixies and larger-than-life fiber-optic and video light displays, premiered in its place in 1997. Also look for live-action musical extravaganzas based on Disney's most recent animated features: *Pocahontas, The Hunchback of Notre Dame,* and *Hercules.*

And keep your eyes open as Disney prepares to round the century mark—work has already begun on a new, separate sister park and great big hotel/resort that will debut in 2001 adjacent to Disneyland. Until then, related construction obstructions are likely to add time and frustration to your park experience, so be prepared.

ADMISSION, HOURS & INFORMATION   Admission to the park, including unlimited rides and all festivities and entertainment, is $36 for adults and children over 11, $32 for seniors 60 and over, and $26 for children 3 to 11; children under 3 enter free. Parking is $6. Also, 2- and 3-day passes are available; in addition, some area accommodations offer lodging packages that include one or more days' park admission.

Disneyland is open every day of the year, but operating hours vary, so we recommend that you call for information that applies to the specific day(s) of your visit (☎ **714/781-4565** or 213/626-8605, ext. 4565). Generally speaking, the park is open from 9 or 10am to 6 or 7pm on weekdays, fall through spring; and from 8 or 9am to midnight or 1am on weekends, holidays, and during winter, spring, or summer vacation periods.

If you've never been to Disneyland before and would like to get a copy of their *Souvenir Guide* to orient yourself to the park before you go, write to **Disneyland Guest Relations,** P.O. Box 3232, Anaheim, CA 92803. Or pick up a copy of *The Unofficial Guide to Disneyland* (Macmillan Travel) at your local bookstore.

DISNEY TIPS   Disneyland is busiest from mid-June to mid-September and on weekends and school holidays year-round. Peak hours are from noon to 5pm; visit the most popular rides before and after these hours, and you'll cut your waiting times substantially. If you plan on arriving during a busy time, purchase your tickets in advance and get a jump on the crowds at the ticket counters.

Many visitors tackle Disneyland systematically, beginning at the entrance and working their way clockwise around the park. But a better plan of attack is to arrive early and run to the most popular rides first—the Indiana Jones Adventure, Star Tours, Space Mountain, Big Thunder Mountain Railroad, Splash Mountain, the Haunted Mansion, and Pirates of the Caribbean. Lines for these rides can last an hour or more in the middle of the day.

If you're going to stay in Anaheim, you might want to consider staying at the Disneyland Hotel. Hotel guests get to enter the park early almost every day and enjoy the major rides before the lines form. The amount of time varies from day to day, but usually you can enter 1½ hours early. Call ahead to check the schedule for your specific day.

Disneyland's attendance falls dramatically during the winter, so the park offers discounted (about 25% off) admission to southern California residents who may purchase up to six tickets per zip-code verification. If you'll be visiting the park with someone who lives here, be sure to take advantage of this money-saving opportunity.

TOURING THE PARK

The Disneyland complex is divided into several themed "lands," each of which has a number of rides and attractions that are, more or less, related to that land's theme.

Main Street U.S.A., at the park's entrance, is a cinematic version of turn-of-the-century small-town America. This whitewashed Rockwellian fantasy is lined with gift shops, candy stores, a soda fountain, and a silent theater that continuously runs early Mickey Mouse films. You'll find the practical things you might need here too, such as stroller rentals and storage lockers. Because there are no rides here, it's best to tour Main Street during the middle of the afternoon, when lines for rides are longest, and in the evening, when you can rest your feet in the theater that features "Great

Moments with Mr. Lincoln," a patriotic (and Audio-Animatronic) look at America's 16th president. There's always something happening on Main Street; stop in at the information booth to the left of the main entrance for a schedule of the day's events.

You might start your day by circumnavigating the park by train. An authentic 19th-century steam engine pulls open-air cars around the park's perimeter. Board at the Main Street Depot and take a complete turn around the park or disembark at any one of the lands.

Adventureland is inspired by the most exotic regions of Asia, Africa, India, and the South Pacific. There are several popular rides here. This is where you'll find the Swiss Family Treehouse. On the Jungle Cruise, passengers board a large authentic-looking Mississippi River paddleboat and float along an Amazon-like river. En route, the boat is threatened by Audio-Animatronic wild animals and hostile natives, while a tour guide entertains with a running patter. A spear's-throw away is the Enchanted Tiki Room, one of the most sedate attractions in Adventureland. Inside, you can sit down and watch a 20-minute musical comedy featuring electronically animated tropical birds, flowers, and "tiki gods."

The Indiana Jones Adventure is Adventureland's newest ride. Based on the Steven Spielberg series of films, this ride takes adventurers into the Temple of the Forbidden Eye, in joltingly realistic all-terrain vehicles. Riders follow Indy and experience the perils of bubbling lava pits, whizzing arrows, fire-breathing serpents, collapsing bridges, and the familiar cinematic tumbling boulder (this effect is *very* realistic in the front seats!). Disney "Imagineers" reached new heights with the design of this ride's line which—take my word for it—has so much detail throughout its twisting path that 30 minutes or more simply flies by.

New Orleans Square, a large, grassy, gas-lamp–dotted green, is home to the Haunted Mansion, the most high-tech ghost house we've ever seen. The spookiness has been toned down so kids won't get nightmares, and the events inside are as funny as they are scary. Even more fanciful is Pirates of the Caribbean, one of Disneyland's most popular rides. Here, visitors float on boats through mock underground caves, entering an enchanting world of swashbuckling, rum-running, and buried treasure. Even in the middle of the afternoon you can dine by the cool moonlight and to the sound of crickets in the Blue Bayou Restaurant, the best eatery in the land.

Critter Country is supposed to be an ode to the backwoods—a sort of Frontierland without those pesky settlers. Little kids like to sing along with the Audio-Animatronic critters in the musical Country Bear Jamboree show. Older kids and grownups head straight for Splash Mountain, one of the largest water flume rides in the world. Loosely based on the Disney movie *Song of the South,* the ride is lined with about 100 characters who won't stop singing "Zip-A-Dee-Doo-Dah." Be prepared to get wet, especially if someone sizable is in the front seat of your log-shaped boat.

Frontierland gets its inspiration from 19th-century America. It's full of dense "forests" and broad "rivers" inhabited by hearty-looking (but, luckily, not-smelling) "pioneers." You can take a raft to Tom Sawyer's Island, a do-it-yourself play island with balancing rocks, caves, and a rope bridge, and board the Big Thunder Mountain Railroad, a runaway roller coaster that races through a deserted 1870s gold mine. You'll also find a petting zoo and an Abe Lincoln–style log cabin here; both are great for exploring with the little ones.

On Saturday, Sunday, holidays, and vacation periods, head to Frontierland's Rivers of America after dark to see the FANTASMIC! show—a mix of magic, music, live performers, and sensational special effects. Just as he did in *The Sorcerer's Apprentice,* Mickey Mouse appears and uses his magical powers to create giant water fountains, enormous flowers, and fantasy creatures. There's plenty of pyrotechnics, lasers, and

Disneyland

Big Thunder Mountain
Circlevision
Haunted Mansion
Indiana Jones Adventure
It's A Small World
Jungle Cruise
King Arthur Carousel
Matterhorn Bobsleds

Pirates of the Caribbean
Space Mountain
Splash Mountain
Star Tours
Submarine Voyage
Swiss Family Treehouse
Tom Sawyer Island

Frontierland's
Rivers of
America

Frontierland

Critter
Country

New Orleans
Square

Adventureland

Disneyland Hotel

Picnic
Area

Group Sales

Ticket Booths

Disabled
Parking

1-0853

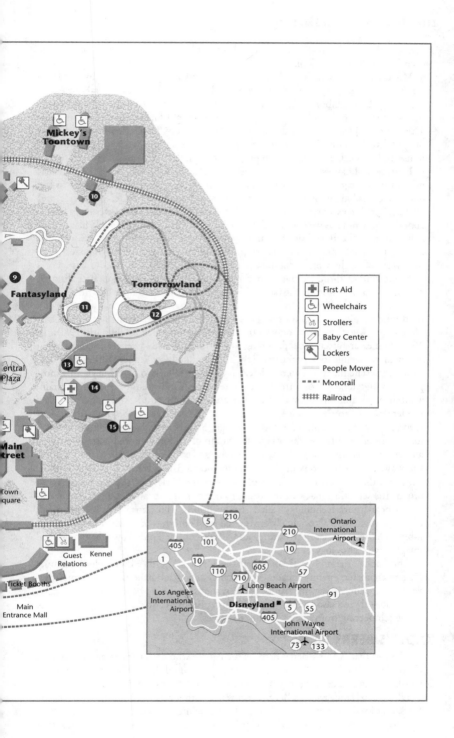

Mickey's
Toontown

10

9
Fantasyland

11

Tomorrowland

12

Central
Plaza

13

14

Main
Street

15

Town
Square

	First Aid
	Wheelchairs
	Strollers
	Baby Center
	Lockers
	People Mover
	Monorail
	Railroad

Guest   Kennel
Relations

Ticket Booths

Main
Entrance Mall

210
5   210
Ontario
International
Airport

405   101
10
1   10
110   710   605   57
Los Angeles   Long Beach Airport
International
Airport   Disneyland   5   55   91
405
John Wayne
International Airport
73   133

fog, as well as a 45-foot-tall dragon that breathes fire and sets the water of the Rivers of America aflame. Cool!

Mickey's Toontown is a colorful, wacky, whimsical world inspired by the *Roger Rabbit* films. This is a gag-filled land populated by toons. There are several rides here, including Roger Rabbit's CarToonSpin, but these take a back seat to Toontown itself—a trippy smile-inducing world without a straight line or right angle in sight. This is a great place to talk with Mickey, Minnie, Goofy, Roger Rabbit, and the rest of your favorite toons. You can even visit their "houses" here. Mickey's red-shingled house and movie barn is filled with props from some of his greatest cartoons.

Fantasyland has a storybook theme and is the catch-all "land" for all the stuff that doesn't quite seem to fit anywhere else. Most of the rides here are geared to the under-6 set, including the King Arthur Carousel, Dumbo the Flying Elephant ride, and the Casey Jr. Circus Train, but some, like Mr. Toad's Wild Ride and Peter Pan's Flight, appeal to grownups as well. You'll also find Alice in Wonderland, Snow White's Scary Adventures, Pinocchio's Daring Journey, and more in Fantasyland. The most lauded attraction is It's a Small World, a slow-moving indoor river ride through a saccharine nightmare of all the world's children singing the song everybody loves to hate. For a different kind of thrill, try the Matterhorn Bobsleds, a zippy roller coaster through chilled caverns and drifting fog banks. It's one of the park's most popular rides.

Tomorrowland, conceived as an optimistic look at the future, has always had a hard time keeping a jump on real advances. 1955's "Rocket to the Moon" became "Mission to Mars" in 1975, only to be a dated laughingstock by the early 1980s. In 1997, Disney architects are redesigning Tomorrowland with a vengeance, employing an angular, metallic look popularized by futurists like Jules Verne. During the transformation, scheduled to be completed in Spring 1998, two of Disneyland's most popular attractions in Tomorrowland will remain up and running; Space Mountain, a pitch-black indoor roller coaster that assaults your equilibrium and ears, is a modern cousin to the classic coaster experience. Star Tours, the original Disney/George Lucas joint venture, is a 40-passenger StarSpeeder that encounters a spaceload of misadventures on the way to the Moon of Endor, achieved with wired seats and video effects (not for the queasy); the line can last an hour or more, but it's worth the wait. New attractions in the works include a 3-D adventure called "Honey, I Shrunk the Audience," which promises, using a variety of theatrical effects, to impart the sensation that you've shrunk to thumbnail size; and an interactive pavilion of near-future technology called "Innoventions." This attraction sounds much closer to what old Walt originally envisioned for Tomorrowland, when he created exhibits like the "House of the Future" and "Bathroom of Tomorrow" that showcased imaginative technology of the day.

The "lands" themselves are only half the adventure. Other joys include roaming Disney characters, penny arcades, restaurants and snack bars galore, summer fireworks, mariachi and ragtime bands, parades, shops, marching bands, and much more. Oh, yeah—there's also the storybook Sleeping Beauty Castle. . . . Can you spot the evil witch peering from one of the top windows?

KNOTT'S BERRY FARM

Cynics say that Knott's Berry Farm is for people who aren't smart enough to find Disneyland. Well, there's no doubt that visitors should tour Disney first, but it's worth staying in a hotel nearby so you can play at Knott's during your stay.

Like Disneyland, Knott's Berry Farm is not without its historical merit. Rudolph Boysen crossed a loganberry with a raspberry, calling the resulting hybrid the "boysenberry." In 1933, Buena Park farmer Walter Knott planted the boysenberry, thus

Disney Dossier

Believe it or not, the Happiest Place on Earth keeps more than a few skeletons—as well as some just plain interesting facts—in its closet. Did you know that:

- Disneyland was carved out of orange groves, and the original plans called for carefully chosen individual trees to be left standing and included in the park's landscaping. On groundbreaking day, July 21, 1954, each tree in the orchard was marked with a ribbon—red to be cut and green to be spared. But the bulldozer operator went through and mowed down *every* tree indiscriminately . . . no one had foreseen his color-blindness.

- Disneyland designers utilized forced perspective in the construction of many of the park's structures to give the illusion of height and dramatic proportions while keeping the park a manageable size. The buildings on **Main Street U.S.A.,** for example, are actually 90% scale on the first floor, 80% on the second, and so forth. The stones on **Sleeping Beauty Castle** are carved in diminishing scale from the bottom to the top, giving it the illusion of towering height.

- The faces of the **Pirates of the Caribbean** were modeled after some of the early staff of Walt Disney Imagineering, who also lent their names to the second-floor "businesses" along Main Street U.S.A.

- Walt Disney maintained two apartments inside Disneyland. His private apartment above the **Town Square Fire Station** has been kept just as it was when he lived there.

- The elaborately carved horses on Fantasyland's **King Arthur Carousel** are between 100 and 120 years old; Walt Disney found them lying neglected in storage at Coney Island in New York, and brought them home to be carefully cleaned and restored.

- **It's a Small World** was touted at its opening as "mingling the waters of the oceans and seas around the world with Small World's Seven Seaways." This was more than a publicity hoax—records from that time show such charges as $21.86 for a shipment of seawater from the Caribbean.

- The peaceful demeanor of Disneyland was broken during the summer of 1970 by a group of radical Vietnam protesters who invaded the park. They seized **Tom Sawyer Island** and raised the Viet Cong flag over the fort before being expelled by riot specialists.

- **Indiana Jones: Temple of the Forbidden Eye,** Disneyland's newest thrill ride, won't be experienced the same way by any two groups of riders. Like a sophisticated computer game, the course is programmed with so many variables in the action that there are 160,000 possible combinations of events.

- After the 24-year run of the enormously popular **Main Street Electrical Parade** ended in 1996, 700,000 of the floats' light bulbs were sold, at $10 a piece, with the benefits going to several local charities.

launching Knott's berry farm on 10 acres of leased land. When things got tough during the Great Depression, Mrs. Knott set up a roadside stand, selling pies, preserves, and home-cooked chicken dinners. Within a year she was selling 90 meals a day. Lines became so long that Walter decided to create an Old West Ghost Town as a diversion for waiting customers.

The Knott family now owns the farm that surrounds the world-famous Chicken Dinner Restaurant, an eatery serving over a million fried meals a year. And Knott's

Berry Farm is the nation's third-most-attended family entertainment complex (after the two Disney parks, of course).

During the last half of October, locals flock to Knott's Berry Farm. Why? Because the entire park is revamped as "Knott's *Scary* Farm"—the ordinary attractions are made spooky and haunted, every grassy area is transformed into a graveyard or gallows, and even the already-scary rides get special surprise extras, like costumed ghouls who grab your arm in the middle of a roller-coaster ride!

GETTING THERE   Knott's Berry Farm is located at 8039 Beach Blvd. in Buena Park. It's about a 5-minute ride north on I-5 from Disneyland. From I-5 or Calif. 91, exit south onto Beach Boulevard. The park is located about half a mile south of Calif. 91.

ADMISSION, HOURS & INFORMATION   Admission to the park, including unlimited access to all rides, shows, and attractions, is $29 for adults and children 12 and over, $19 for seniors 60 and over and children 3 to 11, and free for children under 3. Admission is $14 for everyone after 4pm. Like Disneyland, Knott's offers discounted admission during the off-season for southern California residents, so if you're bringing local friends or family members along, be sure to take advantage of the bargain. Also like Disneyland, Knott's Berry Farm's hours vary from week to week, so you should call about the day you plan to visit. Generally speaking, the park is open during the summer daily from 9am to midnight. The rest of the year, it opens at 10am and closes at 6 or 8pm, except Saturday when it stays open till 10pm. Knott's is closed Christmas Day. Special hours and prices are in effect during Knott's Scary Farm in late October.

For recorded information, call ☎ 714/220-5200.

TOURING THE PARK

Knott's Berry Farm still maintains its original Old West motif. It's divided into five "Old Time Adventures" areas:

Old West Ghost Town, the original attraction, is a collection of refurbished 19th-century buildings that have been relocated from actual deserted Old West towns. Here, you can pan for gold, ride aboard an authentic stagecoach, ride rickety train cars through the Calico Mine, get held up aboard the Denver and Rio Grande Calico Railroad, and hiss at the villain during a melodrama in the Birdcage Theater.

Fiesta Village has a south-of-the-border theme that means festive markets, strolling mariachis, and wild rides like Montezooma's Revenge and Jaguar!, a roller coaster that includes two heart-in-the-mouth drops and a loop that turns you upside down.

The Roaring '20s Amusement Area contains Sky Tower, a parachute jump/drop with a 20-story free-fall. Other white-knuckle rides include XK-1, an excellent flight simulator "piloted" by the riders; and Boomerang, a state-of-the-art roller coaster that turns riders upside down six times in less than a minute. Kingdom of the Dinosaurs features extremely realistic *Jurassic Park*–like creatures. It's quite a thrill, but it may scare the little kids.

Wild Water Wilderness is a $10-million, 3½-acre attraction styled like a turn-of-the-century California wilderness park. The top ride here is a white-water adventure called Bigfoot Rapids, featuring a long stretch of artificial rapids; it's the longest ride of its kind in the world.

Camp Snoopy will probably be the youngsters' favorite area. It's meant to re-create a wilderness camp in the picturesque High Sierra. Its 6 rustic acres are the playgrounds of Charles Schulz's beloved beagle and his pals, Charlie Brown and Lucy, who greet guests and pose for pictures. The rides here, including Beary Tales Playhouse, are tailor-made for the 6-and-under set.

Thunder Falls contains Mystery Lodge, a truly amazing high-tech, trick-of-the-eye attraction based on the legends of local native Americans. Don't miss this wonderful theater piece.

The Boardwalk is Knott's newest themed area, presented as a salute to southern California's beach culture—it's main attraction is Windjammer, a wind-whipping dual roller coaster originally intended to evoke the flips and glides of windsurfing, but often advertised as a twister tornado.

Stage shows and special activities are scheduled throughout the day. Pick up a schedule at the ticket booth.

ATTRACTIONS BEYOND THE THEME PARKS

Crystal Cathedral

12141 Lewis St., Garden Grove. ☎ **714/971-4000.**

This angular, mirror-sheathed church (think of the movie *Superman*'s Fortress of Solitude), otherwise known as the Garden Grove Community Church, is a shocking architectural oddity, with nine-story-high doors and a vast, open interior that's shaped like a four-pointed star. Opened in 1980, it's the pulpit for televangelist Robert Schuller, who broadcasts sermons and hymns of praise on radio and television to an international audience of millions. Each Sunday an overflow crowd listens to the service blaring from loudspeakers into the parking lot. Annual Christmas and Easter pageants feature live animals, floating "angels," and other theatrics. A $5-million stainless-steel carillon, which began ringing in 1991, has prompted some of the cathedral's neighbors to complain that they want less joyful noise and more peace on earth.

Medieval Times Dinner and Tournament

7662 Beach Blvd., Buena Park. ☎ **800/899-6600** or 714/521-4740. Admission $34–$36 adults, $23 children 12 and under. Shows Mon–Thurs at 7pm, Fri at 6:30 and 8:45pm, Sat at 6 and 8:15pm, Sun at 5 and 7:15pm. Call for reservations (be sure to inquire about auto-club discounts).

Guests crowd around long wooden tables and enjoy a four-course banquet of roast chicken, ribs, herbed potatoes, and pastries—all eaten with your hands in medieval fashion, of course. More than 1,100 people can fit into the castle, where sword fights, jousting tournaments, and various feats of skill are performed by colorfully costumed actors, including fake knights on real horses. It's kind of ridiculous, but kids of all ages love it.

A word of warning: The horses (and horseplay) kick up lots of dirt, so if you have any allergies to dust or animal dander, keep an eye on the nearest exit.

Movieland Wax Museum

7711 Beach Blvd. (Calif. 39), Buena Park. ☎ **714/522-1155.** Admission $12.95 adults, $10.55 seniors, $6.95 children 4–11, free for children 3 and under. Daily 9am–7pm. Discount combination admission includes Ripley's Believe It Or Not! Museum (across the street).

At this goofy museum, located one block north of Knott's Berry Farm in Buena Park, you can see wax-molded figures of all your favorite film stars, from Bela Lugosi in *Dracula* and Marilyn Monroe in *Gentlemen Prefer Blondes* to Leslie Nielsen in the *Naked Gun* movies. "America's Sweetheart," Mary Pickford, dedicated the museum on May 4, 1962; it has risen steadily in popularity ever since, with new stars added yearly, taking their place next to the time-tested favorites. The museum was created by film addict Allen Parkinson, who saw to it that some of the most memorable scenes in motion pictures were re-created in exacting detail in wax. In the seemingly unrelated Chamber of Horrors, you almost expect the torture victims to scream "tourist trap!" Discount combination admission tickets include the **Ripley's Believe It**

Or Not! Museum across the street—grown-ups yawn but young kids marvel at the "astounding" facts presented in a sensational manner.

Richard Nixon Library and Birthplace

18001 Yorba Linda Blvd., Yorba Linda. ☎ **714/993-5075.** Fax 714/528-0544. Admission $5.95 adults, $3.95 seniors, $2 children 8–11, free for children 7 and under. Mon–Sat 10am–5pm, Sun 11am–5pm.

Although he was the most vilified U.S. president in modern history, there has always been a warm place in the hearts of Orange County locals for Richard Nixon. This presidential library, located in Nixon's boyhood town, celebrates the roots, life, and legacy of America's 37th president. The 9-acre site contains the modest farmhouse where Nixon was born, manicured flower gardens, a modern museum containing presidential archives, and the final resting place of both Nixon and his wife, Pat.

Displays include videos of the famous Nixon-Kennedy TV debates, an impressive life-size statuary summit of world leaders, gifts of state (including a gun from Elvis Presley), and exhibits on China and Russia. There's also an exhibit of the late Pat Nixon's sparkling First Lady gowns. There's a 12-foot-high graffiti-covered chunk of the Berlin Wall, symbolizing the defeat of Communism, but hardly a mention of Nixon's leading role in the anti-Communist "witch hunts" of the 1950s. There are exhibits on Vietnam, yet no mention of Nixon's illegal expansion of that war into neighboring Cambodia. Only the Watergate Gallery is relatively forthright, where visitors can listen to actual White House tapes and view a montage of the president's last day in the White House.

WHERE TO STAY
EXPENSIVE

✪ **Disneyland Hotel**
1150 W. Cerritos Ave. (west of the Disneyland parking lot), Anaheim, CA 92802. ☎ **714/778-6600.** Fax 714/965-6597. 1,136 rms, 62 suites. A/C MINIBAR TV TEL. $175–$270 double; from $425 suite. AE, MC, V. Parking $10.

The "Official Hotel of the Magic Kingdom," attached to Disneyland via a monorail system that runs right to the hotel, is the perfect place to stay if you're doing the park. You'll be able to return to your room anytime you need to during the day, whether it's to take a much-needed nap or to change your soaked shorts after your Splash Mountain Adventure. Best of all, hotel guests get to enter the park early almost every day and enjoy the major rides before the lines form. The amount of time varies from day to day, but usually you can enter 1 1/2 hours early. Call ahead to check the schedule for your specific day.

The theme hotel is a wild attraction unto itself. The rooms aren't fancy, but they're comfortably and attractively furnished like a good-quality business hotel. Many rooms feature framed reproductions of rare Disney conceptual art, and the Disney Channel is free on TV, naturally. The beautifully landscaped hotel is an all-inclusive resort, offering six restaurants, five cocktail lounges, every kind of service desk imaginable, a "wharf-side" bazaar, a walk-under waterfall, and even an artificial white-sand beach. The complex also includes the adjoining Pacific Hotel, which offers a Disney version of Asian tranquillity (including a fine and pricey Japanese restaurant.)

When you're planning your trip, inquire about multiday packages that allow you to take on the park at your own pace, and usually include free parking for the duration of your stay.

Dining/Entertainment: The best restaurant is Stromboli's, an Italian/American eatery that serves all the pasta staples. Kids love Goofy's Kitchen, where the family can enjoy breakfast and dinner with the Disney characters.

Services: Concierge, room service, laundry, shoe-shine, nightly turndown, baby-sitting, express checkout.

Facilities: Three large heated outdoor pools, complete health club, putting green, shuffleboard and croquet courts, sundeck, special children's programs, beauty salon, 20 shops and boutiques.

Sheraton Anaheim Hotel

1015 W. Ball Rd. (at I-5), Anaheim, CA 92802. ☎ **800/325-3535** or 714/778-1700. Fax 714/535-3889. 500 rms, 26 suites. A/C MINIBAR TV TEL. $170–$190 double; $290–$360 suite. AE, CB, DC, MC, V. Free parking; shuttle to Disneyland.

This hotel rises to the festive theme-park occasion with its fanciful English Tudor architecture, a castle that lures business conventions, Disney-bound families, and area high-school proms equally successfully. The public areas are quiet and elegant—intimate gardens with fountains and koi ponds, plush lobby and lounges—which can be a pleasing touch after a frantic day at the amusement park. The rooms are modern and unusually spacious, but otherwise not distinctive; a large swimming pool is located in the center of the complex, surrounded by attractive landscaping. Don't be put off by the high rack rates listed; rooms more commonly go for $100 to $130, even on busy summer weekends.

Dining/Entertainment: The Garden Court Bistro offers indoor and outdoor ambiance, while the California Deli is open from 6am to midnight and serves standard delicatessen fare. There's also a wood-and-tapestry cocktail lounge.

Services: Concierge, room service, laundry services, overnight shoe-shine, nightly turndown.

Facilities: Heated outdoor pool, sundeck, gift shop.

MODERATE

Anaheim Plaza Hotel

1700 S. Harbor Blvd., Anaheim, CA 92802. ☎ **800/228-1357** or 714/772-5900. Fax 714/772-8386. 300 rms and suites. A/C TV TEL. $79–$119 double; from $175 suite. AE, DC, DISC, MC, V. Free parking; shuttle to Disneyland.

You can easily cross the street to Disneyland's main gate, or you can take advantage of the Anaheim Plaza's free shuttle to the park. Once you return, you'll appreciate the way this 30-year-old hotel's clever design shuts out the noisy world. In fact, the seven two-story garden buildings remind me of 1960s Waikiki more than busy Anaheim. The Olympic-size heated outdoor pool and whirlpool are unfortunately surrounded by Astroturf, but the new management was halfway through a total room renovation in 1997, so there's always hope. They won't change a thing about the light-filled modern lobby, nor the friendly rates, which can often drop as low as $49. There's room service from the casual cafe in the lobby, plus valet service and coin-operated laundry.

Buena Park Hotel

7675 Crescent Ave. (at Grand), Buena Park, CA 90620. ☎ **800/422-4444** or 714/995-1111. Fax 714/828-8590. 350 rms and suites. A/C TV TEL. $99–$109 double; $175–$250 suite. AE, DC, DISC, MC, V. Free parking; shuttle to Disneyland.

Within easy walking distance of Knott's Berry Farm, the Buena Park Hotel also offers a free shuttle to Disneyland just 7 miles away. The pristine lobby has the look of a business-oriented hotel, and that it is. But vacationers can also benefit from the elevated level of service designed for the business traveler. Be sure to inquire about Executive Club rates as well as Knott's or Disneyland package deals. The rooms in the nine-story tower are tastefully decorated, and facilities and services include room service, a charming heated outdoor pool and spa, two restaurants and a 1950s/1960s dance club, and a rental-car desk.

Candy Cane Inn

1747 S. Harbor Blvd., Anaheim, CA 92802. ☎ **800/345-7057** or 714/774-5284. Fax 714/772-5462. 173 rms. A/C TV TEL. $74–$95 double. Rates include expanded continental breakfast. AE, DC, DISC, MC, V. Free parking; shuttle to Disneyland.

Take your standard U-shaped motel court with outdoor corridors, spruce it up with cobblestone drive- and walkways, old-time street lamps, and flowering vines engulfing the balconies of attractively painted rooms, and you have the Candy Cane. The face-lift worked, making this motel near Disneyland's main gate a real treat for the stylish bargain hunter. The guest rooms are decorated in bright floral motifs with comfortable furnishings, including queen beds and a separate dressing and vanity area. Complimentary breakfast is served in the courtyard, where you can also splash around in a heated pool, spa, or kids' wading pool.

Howard Johnson Hotel

1380 S. Harbor Blvd., Anaheim, CA 92802. ☎ **800/422-4228** or 714/776-6120. Fax 714/533-3578. 320 rms. A/C TV TEL. $74–$94 double. AE, CB, DC, DISC, MC, V. Free parking.

This hotel occupies an enviable location, directly opposite Disneyland, and a cute San Francisco trolley car runs to and from the park every 30 minutes. The rooms are divided among several low-profile buildings, all with balconies opening onto a central garden with two heated pools for adults and one for children. Garden paths lead under eucalyptus and olive trees to a splashing circular fountain. During the summer you can see the nightly fireworks display at Disneyland from the upper balconies of the park-side rooms. Try to avoid the rooms in the back buildings, for they get some freeway noise. Services and facilities include in-room movies and cable, room service from the attached Coco's Restaurant, gift shop, games room, laundry service plus coin-laundry room, airport shuttle, and family lodging/Disney admission packages. We think it's pretty classy for a HoJo's.

Inn at the Park

1855 S. Harbor Blvd. (south of Katella Ave.), Anaheim, CA 92802. ☎ **800/421-6662** or 714/750-1811. Fax 714/971-3626. 500 rms. A/C TV TEL. $150 double. AE, DC, DISC, MC, V. Parking $8; free shuttle to Disneyland.

Although the inn is in the Anaheim Convention Center Complex (across the street from Disneyland) and draws primarily a business crowd, there's much to appeal to the leisure traveler. The contemporary and comfortable rooms in the 12-story tower all have balconies overlooking either Disneyland or the hotel's luxurious pool area, which includes a large heated pool, deluxe spa, attractive sundeck, and snack/cocktail bar gazebo. The hotel offers guest laundry and valet, an activities desk, room service, and a gift shop, plus an Old West frontier-themed restaurant serving up steak and seafood plus a few colorful game selections.

Jolly Roger Hotel

640 W. Katella Ave. (west of Harbor Blvd.), Anaheim, CA 92802. ☎ **800/446-1555** or 714/772-7621. Fax 714/772-2308. 225 rms, 11 suites. A/C TV TEL. $75–$118 double; $98–$200 suite. AE, DC, DISC, MC, V. Free parking; shuttle to Disneyland.

The only thing still sporting a buccaneer theme here is the adjoining Jolly Roger Restaurant, and that's just fine. The comfortable but blandly furnished rooms are in either an older, two-story L-shaped motel or two newer five-story annexes. We prefer the older units for their quiet and also for the palm-shaded heated pool in the center of it all. Across the driveway is the swashbuckling restaurant where dinner will set you back a few doubloons. The all-day coffee shop is more reasonable, and there's nightly entertainment and dancing in the lounge. Conveniently located across the street from Disneyland, the Jolly Roger also has meeting and banquet rooms, plus a second pool, a spa, beauty salon, and gift shop.

INEXPENSIVE

Best Western Anaheim Stardust

1057 W. Ball Rd., Anaheim, CA 92802. ☎ **800/222-3639** or 714/774-7600. Fax 714/535-6953. 103 rms, 18 suites. A/C TV TEL. $70–$85 double; $105 family room. Rates include full breakfast. AE, DC, DISC, MC, V. Free parking.

Located on the back side of Disneyland, this modest hotel will appeal to the budget-conscious traveler who isn't willing to sacrifice everything. All rooms have a refrigerator and microwave, breakfast is served in a refurbished train dining car, and you can relax by the large outdoor heated pool and spa while doing wash in the laundry room. The extra-large family rooms will accommodate virtually any brood, and shuttles run regularly to the park.

Colony Inn

7800 Crescent Ave. (west of Beach Blvd.), Buena Park, CA 90620. ☎ **800/98-COLONY** or 714/527-2201. Fax 714/826-3826. 130 rms and suites. A/C TV TEL. $49–$98 double or suite. AE, MC, V. Free parking.

Although it's composed of two modest U-shaped motels, the recently refurbished Colony Inn has a lot to offer. It's the closest lodging to Knott's Berry Farm's south entrance and is just 10 minutes away from Disneyland. They cheerfully offer discount coupons for Knott's and other nearby attractions, as well as complimentary coffee and doughnuts to jump-start your morning. The rooms are spacious (doubles sleep up to four people, and suites sleep up to eight) and comfortably outfitted with conservatively styled furnishings. There are two pools, two wading pools for kids, two saunas, and a coin-operated laundry on the premises.

WHERE TO DINE

Inland Orange County isn't known for its restaurants, most of which are branches of reliable California or national chains you'll easily recognize. We've listed a few intriguing options, but if you're visiting the area just for the day, you'll probably eat inside the theme parks; there are plenty of restaurants to choose from at both Disneyland and Knott's Berry Farm. At Disneyland, in the Créole-themed **Blue Bayou,** you can sit under the stars inside the Pirates of the Caribbean ride—no matter what time of day it is. At Knott's, try the fried-chicken dinners and boysenberry pies at Mrs. Knott's historic **Chicken Dinner Restaurant.** For the most unusual dinner you've ever had with the kids, go to **Medieval Times** (see "Attractions Beyond the Theme Parks," above).

EXPENSIVE

Chanteclair

18912 MacArthur Blvd. (opposite John Wayne Airport), Irvine. ☎ **714/752-8001.** Reservations required. Main courses $15–$24. AE, CB, DC, MC, V. Mon–Fri 11am–3pm; Mon–Sat 6–11pm. CONTINENTAL/FRENCH.

Chanteclair is expensive and a little difficult to reach, but it's worth seeking out. Designed in the style of a provincial French inn, the rambling stucco structure is built around a central garden court and houses several dining and drinking areas, each with its own unique ambiance. The antique-furnished restaurant has five fireplaces. At lunch you might order grilled lamb chops with herb-and-garlic sauce, chicken-and-mushroom crepes, or Cajun charred ahi. Dinner is a worthwhile splurge that might begin with a lobster bisque with brandy or Beluga caviar with blinis. For a main dish, we recommend the rack of lamb with thyme sauce and roasted garlic.

Mr. Stox

1105 E. Katella Ave. (east of Harbor Blvd.), Anaheim. ☎ **714/634-2994.** Reservations recommended on weekends. Main courses $12–$23. AE, CB, DC, DISC, MC, V. Mon–Fri 11am–2:30pm and 5:30–10pm, Sat 5:30–10pm, Sun 5–9pm. AMERICAN.

Hearty steaks and fresh seafood are served in an early California manor-house setting here at Mr. Stox. Specialties include roast prime rib and mesquite-broiled fish, veal, and lamb. Chef Scott Raczek particularly excels at reduction sauces and innovative herbal preparations. Sandwiches and salads are also available. The homemade breads and desserts, such as chocolate-mousse cake, are unexpectedly good. Mr. Stox has an enormous and renowned wine cellar, and there's live entertainment nightly.

MODERATE

Felix Continental Cafe

36 Plaza Sq. (at the corner of Chapman and Glassell), Orange. ☎ **714/633-5842.** Reservations recommended for dinner. Main courses $6–$14. AE, DC, MC, V. Mon–Thurs 7am–9pm, Fri 7am–10pm, Sat 8am–10pm, Sun 8am–9pm. CUBAN/SPANISH.

If you like the re-created Main Street in the Magic Kingdom, then you'll love the historic 1886 town square in the city of Orange, on view from the cozy sidewalk tables outside the Felix Continental Cafe. Dining on traditional Cuban specialties and watching traffic spin around the magnificent fountain and rosebushes of the plaza evokes old Havana or Madrid rather than the cookie-cutter Orange County communities just blocks away. The food receives glowing praise from restaurant reviewers and loyal locals alike.

Peppers Restaurant and Nightclub

12361 Chapman Ave. (west of Harbor Blvd.), Garden Grove. ☎ **714/740-1333.** Reservations recommended on weekends. Main courses $9–$14. AE, CB, DC, DISC, MC, V. Mon–Thurs 11am–10pm, Fri–Sat 11am–11pm, Sun 10am–10pm. CALIFORNIA/MEXICAN.

This colorful Californian/Mexican–themed restaurant just south of Disneyland looks like a partying kind of place, and it doesn't disappoint. The varied menu features mesquite-broiled dishes and fresh seafood daily. Mexican specialties include lots of variations of tacos and burritos, but the grilled meats and fish are best, especially Pepper's signature King Fajitas with crab legs or lobster tails. Dancing is available nightly to top-40 hits starting at 9pm, and Monday nights a Mexican group plays live music. There's a free shuttle to and from six area hotels between 6pm and the nightclub closing time of 2am.

Renata's Caffè Italiano

227 E. Chapman Ave. (at Grand), Orange. ☎ **714/771-4740.** Reservations recommended for dinner. Main courses $8–$15. AE, DISC, MC, V. Mon–Thurs 11am–9pm, Fri 11am–10pm, Sat 4–10pm. ITALIAN.

Near Felix Cafe in the historic plaza district, owner Renata Cerchiari draws a steady stream of regulars with good if not great contemporary Italian specialties. We found the charming patio dining in this small-town atmosphere a welcome change from Orange County's frantic pace (particularly if you're staying by the amusement parks), and the wide selection of appetizers and pasta dishes more authentic and reasonably priced than anywhere else, although the creamy Caesar salad wins higher marks than the disappointing cannoli.

INEXPENSIVE

Belisle's Restaurant

12001 Harbor Blvd. (at Chapman), Garden Grove. ☎ **714/750-6560.** Main courses $3–$23. MC, V. Sun–Thurs 7am–midnight, Fri–Sat 7am–2am. AMERICAN.

Harvey Belisle's modest pink cottage has been doling out "Texas-size" portions of diner-style food since before Disneyland opened in 1955. This is the place to bring a ravenous football team or just your hollow-legged teenage boys. Portions are enormous; we can't say that enough, from the four-egg omelets accompanied by mountains of hash browns to the 12-ounce chicken-fried steak to a chocolate eclair the size of a log, we think Paul Bunyan would feel right at home here. Just say "fill 'er up!"

5 Julian: Apple Pies & More

60 miles NE of San Diego; 60 miles SE of Temecula; 35 miles W of Anza-Borrego Desert State Park

A trip to Julian (pop. 1,500) is a trip back in time. The old gold-mining town, now best known for its apples, has some good eateries and a handful of cute B&Bs, but its popularity is based on the fact that it provides a chance for city-weary folks to get away from it all. However, when it's sunny in San Diego, it may be snowing in Julian, perched at 4,235 feet above sea level.

People first ventured into these fertile hills in search of gold in the late 1860s; they discovered it in 1870 near where the Julian Hotel stands today, and 18 mines sprang up like mushrooms. During all the excitement, four cousins—all former Confederate soldiers from Georgia, two with the last name Julian—founded the town of Julian. The mines are estimated to have produced up to $13 million worth of gold in their day.

Before you leave, try Julian's apple pies; whether the best pies come from Mom's Pies or the Julian Pie Company is always a toss-up. It's best to sample all of them and decide for yourself.

ESSENTIALS

GETTING THERE   The 90-minute drive can be made via Highway 78 or I-8 to Highway 79. I suggest taking one route going and the other coming back. Highway 79 winds through scenic Rancho Cuyamaca State Park, while Highway 78 traverses open country and farmland. If you come by Highway 78, you'll pass the **Mission Santa Ysabel** (1812), where there is a tiny museum and a large native American cemetery that still serves as a place of worship, as well as **Dudley's Bakery,** 30218 Hwy. 78, (☎ **800/225-3348**), which is off to the left at the junction with Highway 79 and just 7 miles from Julian. The bakery, here since 1963, is known for miles around for its breads, from raisin-date-nut to jalapeño, and on weekends, 5,000 to 6,000 loaves come out of the ovens. Dudley's also makes pastries and cookies, and it's open from 8am to 5pm Wednesday through Sunday. Across the street from Dudley's is **Once Upon a Time,** a cute shop selling antiques and gifts.

Getting to Julian by public transportation is a relatively slow, but inexpensive, process. You start by taking the trolley from San Diego to the El Cajon Station, then catch the Northeast Rural bus to Julian. The bus runs in the afternoon Monday through Saturday only, and the one-way trip costs $2.50, including the trolley. You have to pay the bus driver in exact change (show your trolley stub and you pay only an additional $1). Try to reserve your seat at least 24 hours in advance; call

☎ **760/767-4BUS** (4281) between 7 and noon and 2 and 5pm Monday through Saturday, or leave a message on the answering machine.

VISITOR INFORMATION   Once in Julian, you'll need a car if you want to stay at one of the B&Bs that are located out of town. However, Main Street is only six blocks long, and some lodgings, shops, and local cafes are on it or a block away. Town maps and flyers for accommodations are available from the Town Hall on Main Street at Washington Street; public rest rooms are behind the Town Hall. There's no self-service laundry (so come prepared), but you'll find a post office, liquor store, and a few grocery stores. Shops are often closed on Monday and Tuesday. The town has a **24-hour hot line** (☎ 760/765-0707) to provide information on lodging, dining, shops, activities, upcoming events, weather, and road conditions. For a brochure on what to see and do in Julian, contact the **Julian Chamber of Commerce,** P.O. Box 413, Julian, CA 92036 (☎ **760/765-1857;** Web site: **icsol.com/west/julian**).

SPECIAL EVENTS   Special events include Julian's popular **fall apple harvest** held the entire month of October (it used to be only 1 weekend, but the traffic in town got way out of hand); the **annual wildflower show** lasts for a week in early May; and the **annual weed show,** a tradition since 1961, is usually held the last few weeks in August or the beginning of September. There's a **craft show** on weekends in November. If you arrive on the **Fourth of July,** count on participating in a community barbecue and seeing a quilt exhibition and parade. It's also fun to visit in December when activities include caroling and a living nativity pageant, and the town takes on a winter wonderland appearance. The first 2 weekends in December, the members of the **Julian Bed and Breakfast Guild** host open houses with complimentary refreshments.

TOURING THE TOWN

It's fun to learn about the town and surrounding area by visiting the **Julian Cider Mill** (☎ 760/765-1430), which moved into the center of town about 20 years ago when a service station moved out. The father-and-son team of Turk and Fred Slaughter run the place, an actual mill where you can see cider being made. Homemade peanut butter is ground on the premises too, and in the spring a glass-enclosed beehive bustles with activity. Because the town is relatively near to both desert and sea (either is within a $1^1/_2$-hour drive away), Julian honey is particularly good. It's hard not to feel like a kid in their store filled with jawbreakers, nuts, preserves, trail mix, and easy conversation around a potbellied stove. Fred Slaughter calls it "a hobby that got a bit out of hand."

On the right as you come into town is the **Julian Pioneer Museum** (☎ 760/765-0227), at Fourth and Washington streets, housed in an old brewery and open Tuesday through Sunday from 10am to 4pm from April through November, and weekends and holidays December through March. Here you can learn about some of the old-timers buried up the hill in the Haven of Rest Cemetery.

Near the museum, the **Julian Library** (☎ 760/765-0370), at Fourth and Washington streets, is housed in the old Witch Creek School (ca. 1888). The school closed in 1954, and in 1970 the building was cut in half and moved along a narrow two-lane road to this spot, as the photos in back by the stove attest. The library displays a model of the old school. It is open Tuesday through Saturday from 10am to 1pm and 2 to 5pm.

The **Eagle and High Peak Mines** (☎ 760/765-0036), six blocks from Main Street via C Street, still operate daily from 9am to 4pm, but only for educational reasons, since the gold is long gone. You can however, venture inside and explore the mines.

SHOPPING

It's fun to dart in and out of the little shops in Julian. My favorites are the **Julian Farms Antiques Shop,** 2818 Washington St. (☎ 760/765-0250), for gifts and patio accessories, and **Warm Hearth,** 2125 Main St. (☎ 760/785-1022), for gifts, cassettes (a must since local radio stations don't come in well), and wood-burning stoves, if you're in the market for one. **Applewood,** next door to Julian Farms Antiques, is also very good for gifts and antiques.

EXPLORING THE COUNTRYSIDE

If there's something about being in the country that makes you want to hop in the car and drive down one rural road after another, Julian is an ideal starting point. You'll pass rolling hills, country stores, rambling houses, and fruit stands, and come upon towns with names like Ramona, Ballena, and Wynola.

One of my favorite short drives is along the road that leads to the **Menghini Winery,** owned and run by Toni and Michael Menghini; it's 2 miles out on Farmer's Road (follow it west out of town until you see the winery sign, and then bear to the left down the hill). The winery is usually open Monday, Friday, Saturday, and Sunday from 10am to 4pm, daily in October and December, or call for an appointment (☎ 760/765-2072). The grapes come from Ramona and Temecula (see Section 3 of this chapter), and the local favorite wine is Julian Blossom. The tanks are right in the tasting room, and the wines are only sold locally, for $7 to $10 per bottle. You may enjoy your purchase right away in the picnic area in the apple orchard.

If you don't make it to the desert this trip, at least take a moment to gaze out at it and the Salton Sea from **Inspiration Point,** just 1¹/₂ miles south of Julian on Highway 79 opposite Pinecroft Park. **Lake Cuyamaca** (pronounced Kwee-yah-*mack*-ah), 10 miles south on Highway 79, offers boating, fishing (bass, trout, and crappie), and recreational-vehicle camping on a first-come, first-served basis. Its facilities are open from sunrise to sunset daily (☎ 760/765-0515 or 760/447-8123). There are motorboat and rowboat rentals, a 3¹/₂-mile hiking trail around the lake, and a charge for fishing ($4.50 for adults, $2.50 for children 8 to 15). A restaurant with a deck and adjoining store overlook the lake.

Back in Julian, **Country Carriages** (☎ 760/765-1471) will show you the sights and give you a spin down a country lane in a horse-drawn wagon for $20 per couple, or around the town for $5 per adult, $2 per child. It's a tradition for Julian locals to take a Christmas Eve carriage ride. Hop in from in front of, or kitty-corner to, the drugstore; the ride lasts a half hour.

The **Julian Bicycle Company,** off Main Street at 1897 Porter Lane, is actively involved in the Julian Flat Tire Festival, held in mid- or late April, as well as several other biking-related events. Contact them for specific information and dates (☎ 619/765-2200) or drop by Wednesday through Saturday from 10am to 5pm.

For a different way to tour, try **Llama Trek,** P.O. Box 2363, Julian (☎ 800/LAMAPAK [526-2725] or 760/765-1890; fax 760/765-1512; E-mail **llamatrek@wikiupbnb.com.**; Web site: http://www.wikiupbnb.com.). You'll lead the llama, which carries packs, for hikes to see rural neighborhoods, an historic gold mine, mountain and lake views, and apple orchards. Rates vary from $65 to $75 per person and include lunch. Overnight wilderness trips available.

Within 10 miles of Julian are numerous hiking trails that range from easy to challenging, many with spectacular views. **Volcan Mountain Preserve** is just over 3 miles long with a rise of 1,400 feet. Hikers are rewarded with a 360° view from the Salton Sea to forested mountains, and the Pacific Ocean. **William Heise County Park** has

8 miles of trails. The hikes range from a self-guided nature trail, a gentle trail leading through an incense cedar forest, to a moderate trail through canyon live oak, and a more vigorous trail that rewards hikers with a view of the desert. **Cuyamaca State Park** has over 100 miles of trials. If you want trail maps and hiking information, contact the Julian Chamber of Commerce (☎ **760/765-1857**), William Heise County Park (☎ **760/765-0650**), or Cuyamaca State Park (☎ **760/765-0755**).

WHERE TO STAY

Julian Farms Lodging

2818 Washington St. (P.O. Box 879), Julian, CA 92036. ☎ **760/765-0250.** 4 attached cottages and 1 cabin. TV. $69 double; $99 cabin. Extra person $5. AE, DC, MC, V.

As you drive into town, it's easy to pass right by this little place on the left. That would be a shame because the yellow cottages with blue shutters and a grape arbor in front make the perfect secret hideaway. Three of the cottages have a double bed and a daybed in a single room; one has two double beds in two rooms and is perfect for families. All have small private baths with showers, hot pots, country antiques, goose-down comforters, and a split of Julian Blossom wine. A nearby cabin has a queen bed and a sitting area. You can pick all the grapes you want and eat them in the vine-covered gazebo. It's just down the hill from Main Street, and there is a wonderful gift shop on the premises. Reserve 3 to 4 months in advance for weekends. Smoking is permitted outside only. Breakfast isn't served here, but a few cafes in town open early. This is a good choice for visitors without cars.

Julian Hotel

Main St. and B St. (P.O. Box 1856), Julian, CA 92036. ☎ **760/765-0201.** Fax 760/765-0201. 14 rms, 2 cottages. $72–$90 double with private bath, $82–$110 double with ensuite bath; $125–$160 cottage. Rates include full breakfast. AE, MC, V.

The Julian Hotel has been putting a roof over travelers' heads since the days when the Butterfield stagecoach stopped across the street. A potbellied stove still sits in the parlor, along with an upright piano that arrived here from Philadelphia via Cape Horn. The hotel's original owners, Albert and Margaret Robinson, were former slaves; their photograph hangs on the parlor wall. There are a dozen rooms in the original part of the house—with "necessary rooms" at the end of the hall—and each room is decorated in a variation of a Victorian theme. Another three rooms added off the front porch in 1920 have private baths as do two cottages. One of the cottages, the Honeymoon House, features a Franklin (freestanding) fireplace and an old-fashioned tub. The cottages book up to 2 months in advance. The hotel's generous breakfast menu includes apple-filled pancakes and omelets. Coffee, tea, cakes, and cookies are served in the parlor at 5pm. "O. J.," the resident parakeet, fills the lobby with happy chirps. This is a good choice for visitors who want to be in the thick of things on the main drag.

Orchard Hill Country Inn

2502 Washington St. at Second St. (P.O. Box 425), Julian, CA 92036-0425. ☎ **800/71-ORCHARD** [716-7242] or 760/765-1700. Fax 760/765-0290. 22 suites and rooms. A/C MINIBAR TV TEL. $140–$195 double. Extra person $25. 2-night minimum stay if including Fri or Sat. Deposit required. Midweek discounts available. Rates include breakfast and hors d'oeuvres. AE, MC, V.

Hosts Darrell and Pat Straube offer the most upscale lodging in Julian—a two-story lodge and four 1928 California Craftsman-style cottages situated on a hill with a panoramic view that includes the historic town site. Ten guest rooms, a guests-only dining room, and a "great room" with a massive stone fireplace are located in the lodge. Twelve suites are in cottages spread over 3 acres of grounds. All quarters feature attractive furnishings with plantation shutters and have private baths. Suite amenities include fireplaces, whirlpool tubs, wet bars, telephones, VCRs, books, videos, games, window seats and wraparound porches. Breakfast can be delivered to suite occupants.

BED & BREAKFASTS

For a small place, Julian is blessed with some outstanding accommodations, including bed-and-breakfasts, even some for people who prefer not to share their breakfast with other guests or their hosts. For a list and a description of nearly two dozen B&Bs, cabins, and other accommodations, contact the **Julian Bed and Breakfast Guild**, P.O. Box 1711, Julian, CA 92036 (☎ **760/765-1555** daily from 9am to 9pm; Web site: **www.julianbnbguild.com**). All members are within a few miles of the town center. In the meantime, consider these quite different possibilities, all up in the Pine Hills, a few miles south of town.

Artists' Loft

4811 Pine Ridge Ave. (P.O. Box 2408), Julian, CA 92036. ☎ **760/765-0765.** Web site: bnbcity.clever.net/inns/20038. 2 rms and 1 self-contained cabin. $115 Manzanita Room; $125 Gallery Room (including breakfast); $150 cabin (with breakfast ingredients). MC, V. Turn off Hwy. 78 1 mile west of Julian, and follow Pine Hills Rd. to Pine Ridge Ave.; then drive .8 mile. Look for the "M*A*S*H" truck in the front yard.

This peaceful place, set on a hilltop under whispering pines, appeals to those with an interest in art, nature, and ideas. Owners Nanessence and Chuck Kimball are artists and have fashioned a most creative abode for themselves and others. The rooms come with tree limbs and trunks recycled in clever ways, a wood-burning stove, a comfortable queen-size bed, a coffeemaker, a private bath, pine tables, good reading lights, and original artwork (that's for sale). The cabin offers a screened-in porch, king bed, full kitchen, wood-burning stove, and CD player with a supply of classical and New Age CDs.

Everything about this B&B reflects the local environment—including fresh flowers. The natural decor is conducive to cocooning. You can easily go for walks from here. There is a Japanese-style teahouse on the 5-acre property and a wood deck overlooking the fabulous view that stretches across San Diego County to the ocean. The courtyard is filled with Adirondack chairs and a table, an apricot tree and a peach-nectarine tree, and even a Ho-Ti garden Buddha. A love for all living things is readily apparent. Breakfast is memorable at the Artists' Loft for two reasons: Chuck is a fabulous cook—he hands you a menu with almost 20 items to choose from—and the conversation is always lively and engaging and lasts 2 or 3 hours. This is a nonsmoking place, inside and out.

Julian White House

3014 Blue Jay Dr. (P.O. Box 824), Julian, CA 92036. ☎ **800/WHT-HOUS** or 760/765-1764. E-mail marvin@electriciti.com. Web site: www.julian-whitehouse-bnb.com. 4 rms. $90–$135 double. Rates include breakfast and late-night sweets. MC, V. Turn off Hwy. 78 1 mile south of Julian, and follow Pine Hills Rd. for 2 miles, turn right onto Blue Jay, and right into their driveway.

This was the dream home of a contractor who put in a hand-worked curved staircase, molding, and woodwork; although it resembles an antebellum mansion, it was built in 1981. Mary and Alan Marvin, the helpful B&B hosts, are the second owners; and their family photographs, along with vintage clothing and Victorian furnishings, add a nice touch to the rooms. The old-fashioned small Blue Room, with a detached full bath, and the large honeymoon suite, with its four-poster queen-size bed and high-back bathtub, are especially popular. Three rooms (including these two) are upstairs; one is on the ground level. Guests love the peace and quiet here and can often be found lying in the double hammock under the towering pines in the backyard, communing with the deer that wander onto the property; stargazing from the back porch; reading, chatting, relaxing in the Jacuzzi; or playing backgammon and Trivial Pursuit by the sitting room's fireplace. It's a short walk from here through the woods to the Pine Hills Dinner Theatre, and Mary supplies flashlights for the walk back. William Heise Park is 2 miles away. Smoking is allowed outside only.

Random Oaks

3742 Pine Hills Rd. (P.O. Box 454), Julian, CA 92036. ☎ **800/BNB-4344** or 760/765-1094. Fax 760/765-0524. 2 cottages. $150–$160 Fri–Sun, with full breakfast; $125–$135 Mon–Thurs, with continental breakfast; $245 midweek special for 2 nights (Tues–Wed only), with a bottle of champagne on arrival, a 1-hour carriage ride, and continental breakfast. MC, V. Turn off Hwy. 78 1 mile west of Julian, and follow Pine Hills Rd. for 1.4 miles; turn right at the white fence.

Definitely a choice for seclusion-seeking honeymooners or anniversary celebrants, Random Oaks offers two cottages, each elegantly decorated and equipped with a wet bar, a small refrigerator, a microwave, games, books on tape, snuggle blankets, robes, hair dryers, and a private deck or patio with a Jacuzzi (no TV or telephone, thankfully). The English Squire Cottage has Queen Anne furniture, a separate sitting area, bay windows, a marble fireplace with a mahogany mantle dating from 1898, and a lush green carpet. The Victorian Garden Cottage has a period cherry bed, lovely bedside lamps, and a table beside a window. Breakfast is brought to each cottage. The owners, Shari and Gene Helsel, were in horse racing but now breed thoroughbreds. Random Oaks is set in 8 acres, with a small apple orchard in front.

Shadow Mountain Ranch

2771 Frisius Rd. (P.O. Box 791), Julian, CA 92036. ☎ **760/765-0323.** Fax 760/765-0323. Web site: bnbcity.clever.net/inns/20002. 1 rm in main house, 4 detached rms, 1 cottage (all with bath). TV. $90–$100 double; $100 cottage ($160 for 4 people). Rates include full breakfast and afternoon tea. MC, V. Turn off Hwy. 78 1 mile south of Julian onto Pine Hills Rd., follow it to Frisius and turn left; the ranch will be on the right.

This is one of the most unusual B&Bs I've ever seen, and owners Loretta and Jim Ketcherside have obviously had a lot of fun creating it. The Enchanted Cottage, the Gnome Home (a whimsical round room ideal for short people), and the Tree House (which lacks a tub or shower) all live up to their names. The western-theme Manzanita Cottage has two bedrooms, a full kitchen, living room, and a porch; and Grandma's Attic is a quaint choice. All rooms have coffee pots and TVs. Jim chalks up the creativity of the accommodations to the fact that he and Loretta grew up before TV. They have lived in the main house since 1970, and theirs was Julian's first B&B. Shadow Mountain Ranch, with eight head of cattle, is on 8 acres, with access to 20 more. Guests enjoy a great view over pine trees and pastures, as well as croquet, badminton, archery, horseshoes, an indoor 40-foot lap pool, and an outdoor Jacuzzi (robes for the pool are provided). The family-style breakfast for a dozen people is so enormous you'll have to go into training to eat it all. The philosophy of the ranch, Loretta points out, is, "It's all yours—except my bed." Book 6 months ahead for weekends—while some folks might consider this place kitsch, others come back time and time again. No one under 18 is allowed, and there's no smoking in the rooms.

CAMPING

Cuyamaca Rancho State Park is 11 miles from Julian, and a new camp store and interpretive center are located a mile from the entrance. It's another 2 miles to a little museum and park headquarters where you can stock up on maps, information, and even books to help you identify local flora and fauna. The park has more than 100 miles of trails, and you can see Mexico from Cuyamaca Peak (6,512 ft.).

Campsites are set in the midst of trees and scrubs; each one has a table and fire ring. Reserve a spot in **Paso Picacho** or **Green Valley Campground,** both with about 80 sites (☎ **800/444-PARK** for reservations; 760/765-0755 for park information only). The camping fee is $15 to $16 in summer, $12 off-season, or $5 for day use only. They book up fast on weekends from Easter to Thanksgiving, so plan ahead. Park headquarters is open Monday to Friday from 8am to 5pm.

WHERE TO DINE

Julian Cafe
Main St. ☎ **760/765-2712.** Menu items $2.50–$9. MC, V. Mon–Fri 8am–7:30pm, Sat–Sun 7am–8:30pm. AMERICAN.

A tasty, filling chicken pie is the specialty here; buy it at lunch for $6.95 or pay $8.95 for the full dinner. Mashed potatoes come the old-fashioned way, smothered in country gravy. Other home-cooked offerings include fried chicken, liver and onions, meatloaf dinner, and a hot vegetable plate. This is a good place to bring kids; the waitresses are friendly and service is quick, even when it's packed.

Julian Grille
2224 Main St. (at A St.). ☎ **760/765-0173.** Reservations required Fri–Sun. Main courses $12.95–$20.95. AE, MC, V. Daily 11am–3pm; Tues–Sun 5–9pm. AMERICAN.

Julian's fanciest restaurant is in a cozy cottage with an enclosed porch. The dining room, complete with a fireplace, has lace, floral, and dusty-rose touches that look especially pretty by candlelight. The extensive lunch menu features hearty open-faced sandwiches. Dinner appetizers include prime tickler, Baja shrimp cocktail, and smoked fish. Main courses take down-home recipes and give them a creative twist; among the offerings are smoked pork chops in apple sauce (the local favorite), shrimp scampi, tenderloin, filet and prime rib, fisherman's stew, and vegetarian casserole. Dishes come with soup or salad and potatoes; children's selections are available. Beer and wine are also served.

Kendall's Korner Cafe
Third and B sts. ☎ **760/765-1560.** Menu items $4.25–$6. No credit cards. Daily 6am–5pm. AMERICAN.

This little hilltop cafe is the place to catch up on local goings-on, even if you're not local. At lunch there's a soup-and-half-sandwich special for $4.25; they also have buffalo burgers, dinner specials, and takeout. It's a great place for early risers. Breakfast menu items include eggs, omelets, pancakes, ham, sausage, biscuits and gravy, doughnuts, and cereal. Sit inside or out on the porch.

Romano's Dodge House
2718 B St. (just south of Main). ☎ **760/765-1003.** Main courses $8.70–$14.60. No credit cards. Fri–Sat 11am–10pm (to 9pm in winter), Sun–Mon and Thurs 11am–9pm. ITALIAN.

In the historic Dodge House, this cozy place has a plank-and-beam ceiling, red-and-white tablecloths, artwork for sale, soft taped music, and a little saloon in the back. It serves individual pizzas at lunchtime only, for $5 to $6; otherwise, they're 13-inchers. All sandwiches are served with a side of pasta, and all full dinners (add a few more bucks to the main course prices) come with salad, vegetables, including great broccoli and unique candied red cabbage and carrots, and homemade bread. Sorry, no apple pie.

JULIAN AFTER DARK

You can mix culture with barbecue at the **Pine Hills Dinner Theater** on Friday and Saturday nights at **Pine Hills Lodge,** a few miles from Julian off Pine Hills Road (☎ 760/765-1100). The rustic lodge opened its doors on July 4, 1912; in 1980, Dave and Donna Goodman bought it and opened the 96-seat dinner theater, which has staged almost 70 productions, among them *I'm Not Rappaport* and *Last of the Red-Hot Lovers.* The dinner buffet of delicious baby-back pork ribs or barbecue chicken starts promptly at 7pm; give them 24-hours notice, and you can get a vegetarian plate. Show time is at 8pm, and the price for the dinner and the theater is $28.50; for the show alone, it's $14.50. The playhouse is boxing champ Jack Dempsey's former gym, built for Dempsey in 1926 when he was in training for his fight against Gene Tunney.

To hear some music—folk music or piano or maybe the strains of a hammered dulcimer—head out to the **Wynola Coffee Company** (☎ 760/765-2368), in a big red barn just over 3 miles south of town on Highway 78; it'll be on the left. The musicians are on hand only on Saturday night from 7pm, and people of all ages come out to this local hangout with its mismatched tables and chairs to hear them and indulge in dessert and coffee. The cover is about $3.

6 Anza-Borrego Desert State Park

90 miles NE of San Diego; 35 miles E of Julian

The sweeping 600,000-acre Anza-Borrego Desert State Park, the nation's largest contiguous state park, lies mostly within San Diego County, and getting here is as much fun as being here. From Julian, the first 20 minutes of the winding hour-long drive feel as if you're going straight downhill; in fact, it's a 7-mile-long drop called Banner Grade. A famous scene from the 1954 movie *The Long, Long Trailer* with Lucille Ball and Desi Arnaz was shot on the Banner Grade, and countless westerns have been filmed in the Anza-Borrego Desert.

The desert is home to fossils and rocks dating from 540 million years ago; human beings arrived only 10,000 years ago. The terrain ranges in elevation from 15 feet above sea level to more than 6,000 feet and incorporates dry lake beds, sandstone canyons, granite mountains, palm groves fed by year-round springs, and more than 600 kinds of desert plants. After the spring rains, thousands of wildflowers burst into bloom, transforming the desert into a brilliant palette of pink, lavender, red, orange, and yellow. A sense of timelessness pervades this landscape; travelers tend to slow down and take a long look around.

When planning a trip here, keep in mind that temperatures rise to as high as 115° in summer.

ESSENTIALS

GETTING THERE Anza-Borrego Desert State Park is about a 2-hour drive from San Diego: The fastest route is via I-15 north to the Poway exit, then Highway 78 east at Ramona, and continue to Julian and on to the desert. Highway 79 to county roads S2 and S22 will also get you there. Another option is to take I-8 out to Ocotillo and then take Highway S2 north and follow the Southern Overland Stage Route of 1849 (be sure to stop and notice the view at the Carrizo Badlands Overlook) to S3 east into Borrego Springs.

The **Northeast Rural** bus connects Julian and Borrego Springs (☎ 760/ 767-4BUS [4281]). There is no bus service out of San Diego to Borrego Springs, but you can get the Northeast Rural bus (see telephone number above) in Escondido or El Cajon (the San Diego Trolley connects with the El Cajon Station).

As we go to press, there's a rumor that flights from Palomar Airport will soon provide another form of transportation for desert-bound travelers. The phone number for the **Borrego Airport** is ☎ **760/767-7415.**

GETTING AROUND   You don't need a four-wheel–drive vehicle to tour the desert, but you do need to get off the main highways and onto the jeep trails. The Anza-Borrego Desert State Park Visitor Center (see below) will be able to tell you which jeep trails are in condition for two-wheel–drive vehicles. You can also call ☎ **760/767-ROAD** (7623) for information on Borrego Springs road conditions. There's a $5 fee per vehicle per day for a Back Country Permit which is required to camp or use the jeep trails in the park. You can also explore with Desert Jeep Tours (see below). The Ocotillo Wells area of the park has been set aside for off-road vehicles such as dune buggies and dirt bikes. To use the jeep trails, a vehicle has to be licensed for highway use.

Another good way to see the desert is to tour on a bicycle. Call **Carrizo Bikes** at ☎ **760/767-3872** and talk with Dan Cain (a true desert rat) about bike rentals and tours in the area.

ORIENTATION & VISITOR INFORMATION   In Borrego Springs, the Mall is on Palm Canyon Drive, the main drag, and Christmas Circle surrounds a grassy park at the entry to town. The **Anza-Borrego Desert State Park Visitor Center** lies just west of the town of Borrego Springs. It supplies information, maps, and two 15-minute audiovisual presentations; one on the desert's changing faces and the other on wildflowers. You can contact park headquarters at ☎ **760/767-4205** (or 760/767-4684 for recorded wildflower information in season); the Visitor Center is open October through May daily from 9am to 5pm and June through September weekends from 10am to 5pm. For information on lodging, including everything from budget and camping possibilities to resorts, as well as local eateries and activities, contact the **Borrego Springs Chamber of Commerce,** 622 Palm Canyon Dr., Borrego Springs, CA 92004 (☎ **760/767-5555;** Web site: **www.borregosprings.com**).

A SPECIAL EVENT   From mid-March to the beginning of April, the desert wildflowers and cacti are usually in bloom, a hands-down, all-out natural special event that's not to be missed. It's so incredible, there's a hot line to let you know exactly when the blossoms burst forth: ☎ **760/767-4684.**

EXPLORING THE DESERT

Remember when you're touring in this area, hydration is of paramount importance. Whether you're walking, cycling, or driving, always have a bottle of water at your side.

You can explore the desert's stark terrain via one of its trails or on a self-guided driving tour; the Visitor Center can supply maps. For starters, the **Borrego Palm Canyon self-guided hike** (1¹/₂ miles each way), which starts at the campgrounds near the Visitor Center, is beautiful, easy to get to, and easy to do, leading in about half an hour to a waterfall and massive fan palms. It's grand for photos early in the morning.

You can also take an organized tour of the desert, offered by **Desert Jeep Tours,** (☎ **888/373-6200** or 619/528-2241; E-mail **fia@ziplink.net;** Web site: **www. ziplink.net/~fia**). Led by Paul Ford ("Borrego Paul"), these tours go to the awesome view point at Font's Point where you can look out on the Badlands. This area was named by the early settlers because it was an impossible area for moving or grazing cattle. *Note:* Whether you tour with Paul Ford or on your own, don't miss the sunset view from Font's Point. Savvy travelers plan ahead and bring champagne and beach chairs to this nightly ritual. Paul tells his passengers about the history and geology of the area. Scorpion spotting is a favorite after-dark activity. Even if you aren't interested in insects, drive a little way out of town on S22 to admire the starry night sky at its best.

If you only have 1 day, a good day trip from San Diego would include driving over on one route, going to the Visitor Center, hiking to Palm Canyon, having a picnic, and driving back to San Diego via another route.

GOLF & BIKING

Golfers will be content on the 18-hole, par-72 championship golf course at **Ram's Hill Country Club.** The 6,886-yard course has seven artificial lakes (☎ 760/767-5124). For a thrilling 12-mile bicycle ride down Montezuma Valley Grade, try the **Desert Descent** offered by **Gravity Activated Sports,** P.O. Box 683, Pauma Valley, CA 92061 (☎ **800/985-4427** or 760/742-2294; fax 760/742-2293; Web site: **gasports.com**). See "Biking" in chapter 7.

WHERE TO STAY

Borrego Springs is a small place, but there are enough accommodations to suit all travel styles and budgets. Camping in the desert is a meditative experience, to be sure, but if you truly want to splurge, you can do that too.

La Casa del Zorro Desert Resort

3845 Yaqui Pass Rd., Borrego Springs, CA 92004. ☎ **800/824-1884** or 760/767-5323. Fax 760/767-5963. 4 rms, 54 suites, 19 casitas. A/C TV TEL. Jan 15–Apr 30, $115 double ($95 weekdays); from $185 suite ($140 weekdays); from $225 casita ($165 weekdays). May 1–31 and Oct 1–Jan 15, $110 double ($85 weekdays); from $150 suite ($100 weekdays); from $180 casitas ($125 weekdays). June 1–Sept 30 $95 double ($75 weekdays); from $105 suite ($80 weekdays); from $185 casita ($135 weekdays). Weekday rates do not apply on holidays. Extra person $10. Tennis, jazz, holiday, and other packages available. AE, CB, DC, DISC, MC, V.

This pocket of heaven on earth was built back in 1937, and the tamarind trees that were planted back then have grown up around it. Guests can choose from standard hotel rooms, suites, or one-, two-, or three-bedroom adobe casitas with tile roofs. All the casitas have a minifridge and microwave, some have a fireplace or pool, and each bedroom has a separate bath. If you come to this desert oasis during the week, you benefit from lowered room rates.

Dining/Entertainment: The Presidio and the Butterfield dining rooms serve breakfast, lunch, and dinner; a breakfast buffet is served poolside on Saturday and Sunday during summer, indoors the rest of the year. The Fox Den Lounge features live entertainment and dancing. Don't be caught off guard (as we were): Men are required to wear a jacket and a collared shirt at dinner October through May.

Services: Room service (9am to 11pm), bicycle rentals, massage therapy, child care and holiday kids' camp, in-room movies, VCR and movie rentals, free transportation to golf and the airport.

Facilities: Three pools and Jacuzzis, beauty shop, six championship tennis courts, pro shop, 9-hole putting green, horseshoes, Ping-Pong, volleyball, jogging trails, basketball, shuffleboard, a life-size chess set, shop, meeting rooms.

CAMPING

The park has two developed campgrounds. **Borrego Palm Canyon,** with 117 sites, is 2$\frac{1}{2}$ miles west of Borrego Springs and near the Visitor Center. Full hookups are available, and there's an easy hiking trail. **Tamarisk Grove,** at Highway 78 and county road S3, has 27 sites. Both have rest rooms with showers and a campfire program; reservations are a good idea. The park allows open camping along all of the trail routes. For more information check with the Visitor Center (☎ **760/767-4205**).

WHERE TO DINE

Kendall's Cafe

In the Mall, Borrego Springs. ☎ **760/767-3491.** Reservations not necessary. Lunch main courses $3.50–$7.95; dinner main courses $5.95–$10.95. MC, V. Daily Sept–May 6am–8pm; June–Aug Thurs–Mon 6am–8pm. COFFEE SHOP.

Here's an economical little spot to grab a quick bite. Emu burgers from the local emu and ostrich farm are the specialty of the house. Buffalo burgers and Mexican dishes are also popular. Dinner choices include pork chops and chicken-fried steak. They claim their apple pies are better than Julian's. Anything can be packed to go if you'd rather dine overlooking the desert.

7 Tijuana: Going South of the Border

16 miles S of San Diego

Like many large cities in developing nations, Tijuana is a mixture of new and old, rich and poor, modern and traditional. With almost 2.5 million people, it's the second-largest city on the west coast of North America (only Los Angeles is larger). The Mexico you may be expecting—charming town squares and churches, women in colorful, embroidered skirts and blouses, and bougainvillea spilling out of every orifice—is to be found in southern Baja California and even more so in the interior of the country in places such as San Miguel de Allende and Guanajuato (but that's another trip and a different guidebook). What you'll find in Tijuana is poverty (begging in the streets is commonplace), sanitary conditions that may make you nervous, and, surprisingly, a local populace that seems no more or less happy than their north-of-the-border counterparts. If you're spending a few days or more in Baja, please refer to the "Baja California: Exploring More of Mexico" section later in this chapter.

ESSENTIALS

GETTING THERE   If you plan to visit only Tijuana, I recommend leaving the car behind, as the traffic can be challenging. However, bus tours only give you several hours in Tijuana in the afternoon, so you miss evening activities. Another alternative is walking across the border; you can either park your car in one of the safe, long-term parking lots on the San Diego side for about $8 a day or take the San Diego Trolley to the border. Once you're in Tijuana, it's easier to get around by taxi than to fight the local drivers. Cab fares from the border to downtown Tijuana run about $5. If you plan to visit the Baja Peninsula south of Tijuana, I suggest driving.

By Car   Take I-5 south to the Mexican border at San Ysidro. The drive takes about a half hour.

Many car-rental companies in San Diego now allow their cars to be driven into Baja California, at least as far as Ensenada. **Avis** (☎ **619/231-7155**) and **Courtesy** (☎ **619/497-4800**) cars may be driven as far as the 28th parallel and Guerrero Negro, the dividing line that separates Baja into two states, North and South; **Bob Baker Ford** (☎ **619/297-5001**) and **Colonial Ford** (☎ **619/477-9344**) allow their cars to be driven the entire 1,000-mile stretch of the Baja Peninsula.

Keep in mind that if you drive in, you'll need Mexican auto insurance in addition to your own. You can get it in San Ysidro, just north of the border at the San Ysidro exit, from a car-rental agency in San Diego, or from a AAA office if you're a member.

By Trolley In downtown San Diego, hop aboard the bright-red trolley headed for San Ysidro and get off at the last, or San Ysidro, stop (it's nicknamed the Tijuana Trolley for good reason). From here just follow the signs to walk across the border. It's simple, quick, and inexpensive; the one-way trolley fare is $2.00. The last trolley leaving for San Ysidro departs downtown around midnight; the last returning trolley from San Ysidro is at 1am. On Saturdays, the trolley runs 24 hours.

By Bus **Mexicoach/Five Star Tours** (☎ 619/232-5049; fax 619/4575-3075) offers a $2 round-trip fare (children under 5 free) between the border parking lots and trolley stop and downtown Tijuana, with departures every 15 minutes; the Mexicoach stop is at the Tijuana Tourist Terminal at 1025 Av. Revolución (between Calles 6 and 7).

    Gray Line (☎ 619/491-0011) offers a tour to Tijuana for $26, $36 with lunch, with a drop-off in the middle of town; you can spend a few hours or all day. **San Diego Mini Tours** (☎ 619/477-8687) also offers a tour to Tijuana for $26.

GETTING AROUND If you've come to Tijuana on the San Diego Trolley or if you leave a car on the U.S. side of the border, you will walk through the border crossing. The first structure you'll see on your left is a **Visitor Information Center,** open daily from 9am to 7pm; ask for a copy of the *Baja Visitor* magazine and the *Baja Times*. From here, you can easily walk into the center of town or take a taxi.

    A taxi ride to most any destination in downtown Tijuana will cost about $5, but be sure to negotiate the price with the driver before you get in the cab. Local taxis, on the other hand, cost only 50¢ per person (American coins are accepted), which you pay when you disembark.

VISITOR INFORMATION Prior to your visit, you can write for information, brochures, and maps from the **Tijuana Convention & Visitors Bureau,** P.O. Box 434523, San Diego, CA 92143-4523. Another good idea is to contact **Baja California Tourism Information** (☎ 800/522-1516 in California, Arizona, or Nevada; 800/225-2786 in the rest of the U.S. and Canada; or 619/298-4105; E-mail **impamexicoinfo@worldnet.att.net**). These capable folks dispense information and make bookings throughout Baja California.

    In Tijuana, visit the **Tourist Information Center,** which is just across the border. It's open daily from 9am to 7pm (☎ 83-14-05; fax 84-77-82); E-mail **convistj@bbs.cincos.net**). If you call Tijuana from the United States, add **011-52-66** before the number for the international call.

    The **State Tourism Assistance Office,** near the Tourist Information Center on Avenida Revolución, handles any complaints or problems that visitors might have, such as an auto accident or a theft (☎ 88-05-55). The following countries have Consulate offices in Tijuana: the **United States** (☎ 81-74-00), **Canada** (☎ 84-04-61), and the **United Kingdom** (☎ 81-73-23 or 86-53-20).

    Cybernaughts can get a preview of events, restaurants, and more at **www.tijuana-net.com/tijuana.htm.**

    The city does not take time for an afternoon siesta; you'll always find shops and restaurants open, as well as people in the streets, which are safe for walking. (Observe the same precautions you would in any large city.) Most people who deal with the traveling public speak English, often very well. To maneuver around someone on a crowded street or in a shop, say *"con permiso"* (with permission).

CLIMATE & WEATHER Tijuana's climate is similar to San Diego's. Don't expect sweltering heat just because you're south of the border, and remember that the Pacific waters won't be much warmer than in San Diego. The first beaches you'll get to are about 15 miles south of Tijuana.

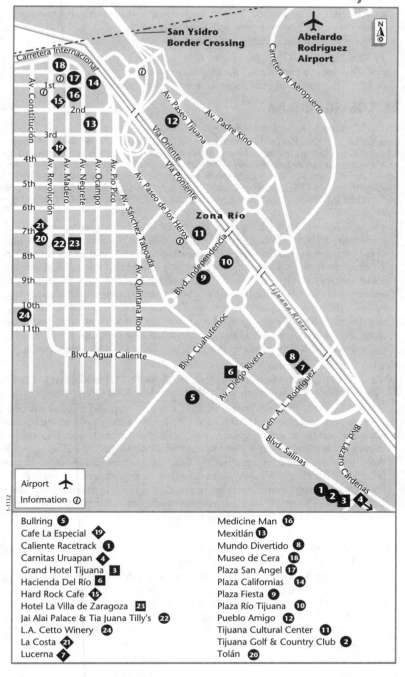

Tijuana

San Ysidro
Border Crossing

Abelardo
Rodríguez
Airport

Carretera Internacional

Av. Constitución

1st

2nd

3rd

4th

5th

6th

7th

8th

9th

10th

11th

Av. Revolución
Av. Madero
Av. Negrete
Av. Ocampo
Av. Pío Pico
Av. Sánchez Taboada
Av. Quintana Roo

Av. Paseo Tijuana
Vía Oriente
Vía Poniente
Av. Padre Kino
Av. Paseo de los Héros

Carretera Al Aeropuerto

Zona Río

Blvd. Independencia

Blvd. Cuahutemoc

Blvd. Agua Caliente

Av. Diego Rivera

Gen. A. L. Rodríguez

Blvd. Salinas

Blvd. Lázaro Cárdenas

Tijuana River

Airport ✈
Information ⓘ

1-1112

Bullring **5**	Medicine Man **16**
Cafe La Especial **19**	Mexitlán **13**
Caliente Racetrack **1**	Mundo Divertido **8**
Carnitas Uruapan **4**	Museo de Cera **18**
Grand Hotel Tijuana **3**	Plaza San Angel **17**
Hacienda Del Río **6**	Plaza Californias **14**
Hard Rock Cafe **15**	Plaza Fiesta **9**
Hotel La Villa de Zaragoza **23**	Plaza Río Tijuana **10**
Jai Alai Palace & Tia Juana Tilly's **22**	Pueblo Amigo **12**
L.A. Cetto Winery **24**	Tijuana Cultural Center **11**
La Costa **21**	Tijuana Golf & Country Club **2**
Lucerna **7**	Tolán **20**

237

CURRENCY You can visit Tijuana (or Rosarito and Ensenada, for that matter) without changing money because dollars are accepted everywhere and change is usually given in American currency and coins.

TAXES & TIPPING A sales tax of 10%, called an IVA, is added to most bills, including those in restaurants. This does not represent the tip; the bill will read *"IVA incluído,"* but you should add about 15% for the tip if the service warrants.

EXPLORING TIJUANA

Cava de Vinos L. A. Cetto (L. A. Cetto Winery)

Calle Cañon Johnson 2108 (at Av. Constitución Sur), Col. Hidalgo. ☎ **85-30-31.** Admission $2 for tour and tastings (for those 18 and older only; those 17 or younger are admitted free with an adult but cannot taste the wines), $3 with souvenir wine glass. Shop and tours, Mon-Sat 9:30am–6:30pm. Bus: Check if the shuttle bus from Revolución between Calles 4 and 5 is running. By foot: Take Revolución to Calle 10, turn right and continue 1 block, then turn left and proceed 1¹/₂ blocks. By car: Take Revolución to Calle 9, then an immediate left and continue for 2 blocks.

The striking building is shaped like a wine barrel, and the red-oak facade is actually made from old barrels in an inspired bit of recycling. In the entrance stand a couple of old wine presses that Don Angel Cetto used back in 1928 in the early days of production. His family still runs the winery, which opened this impressive visitor center in 1993. L. A. Cetto bottles both red and white wines, some of them award winners, including Petite Sirah, Nebbiolo, and cabernet sauvignon. The grapes come from the fertile Guadalupe Valley between Tecate and Ensenada. Visitors see a video that describes the 12 Cetto wines and the foods they complement. Most bottles cost about $5; the special reserves a little more than $10. The company also produces tequila, brandy, and olive oil, all for sale here. MasterCard and Visa are accepted.

Centro Cultural Tijuana (Cultural Center)

Av. Paseo de los Héroes and Avenida Mina, Zona Río. ☎ **84-11-11.** Museum free; OMNIMAX, $2.75 adults, $2 children 2 and over, free for children under 2. Daily 8am–8pm.

Opened in 1982, Tijuana's busy Cultural Center is comprised of three entities: a museum with changing exhibits downstairs, primarily of contemporary Mexican artists, and a permanent exhibit upstairs, with clothing and artifacts from Mexican prehistory to its colonial era; a planetarium and OMNIMAX theater with regular showings of *Pueblo del Sol* (People of the Sun), an excellent film about the culture, beauty, and diversity of Mexico, with a daily show in English; and a performing arts center, where a large theater hosts international performers in drama, opera, dance, and symphony. The museum has a restaurant and a store selling books (in Spanish) at a discount. It's less than a mile from the border crossing.

Mexitlán

8901 Calle 2 (Av. Benito Juárez) near Ocampo, Zona Centro. ☎ **38-41-01.** Admission $1.25 adults, 75¢ children under 12. Wed–Sun 9am–7pm.

Here, in the space of a full city block, you can see exquisitely detailed models of Mexico's finest buildings, ruins, churches, plazas, and villages. From the pyramids of Tenochtitlán to the charming plazas of Taxco, all the models are built to scale, illuminated, and animated. A favorite is Mexico City's University Stadium as it looked during the closing ceremonies of the 1968 Olympics, complete with spectators all doing "the wave." The park also includes shops, cafes, and restaurants, as well as free parking.

Mundo Divertido (Family Entertainment Center)

2578 José Ma. Velasco (at Av. Paseo de los Héroes), Zona Río. ☎ **34-32-14** or 34-32-15. Free admission; prices vary for rides and other activities. Daily noon–9pm. Follow Av. Paseo de los Héroes to José M. Velasco; it's a block from the statue of Abraham Lincoln.

Kids will love an outing to Fun World, where they'll find everything from bumper boats and cars to miniature golf to a small roller coaster. Many attractions are outdoors.

Museo de Cera (Wax Museum of Tijuana)

8281 Calle 1 (at Calle Madero, a block from Av. Revolución), Zona Centro. ☎ **88-24-78.** Admission $1. Daily 10am–7pm.

One of Latin America's few wax museums, it opened in Tijuana in 1993; if you're walking across the border and into town, you'll pass it on your way to Avenida Revolución and the Visitor Information Center, which is a block away. Sixty figures, faithfully rendered, await you, many of them such key players from Mexican history as Moctezuma, Pancho Villa, Emilio Zapata, Father Hidalgo, the reviled Porfirio Díaz, and Lazaro Cardenas, who abolished gambling in Mexico in the 1920s and 1930s. Fr. Junípero Serra, João Rodrigues Cabrilho (Juan Rodrígues Cabrillo), and Father Kino, who played a large part in San Diego's history, are also included; Mahatma Gandhi, Marilyn Monroe, Michael Jackson, Whoopi Goldberg, and the infamous Freddy Krueger of *Nightmare on Elm Street* fame have been thrown in for good measure. Texts are in Spanish and English.

SPECTATOR SPORTS & OUTDOOR PURSUITS

Tijuana is a major spectator-sports center. At its **Caliente Fronton Palace** (Jai Alai Palace), at Avenida Revolución between Calle 7 and 8 (☎ **85-25-24**), at least a dozen action-packed games are played Thursday through Tuesday, starting at 7:30pm. The ornate, colorful entrance has three arched doorways fronted by tall palms, a fountain, and a statue of a player atop a globe. During a game of jai alai, which is like high-speed racquetball, one opponent is pitted against another, and the ball travels faster than 100 miles per hour; you can bet on who you think will win, place, or show— or simply sit back and enjoy the fast-paced excitement.

Caliente Racetrack, on Bulevar Agua Caliente (☎ **81-78-11** in Tijuana; 619/ 231-1910 in San Diego), is the scene of greyhound races. The dogs run daily at 7:45pm and on Saturday and Sunday at 2pm.

Bullfights are held in two rings (**Toreo de Tijuana**) from April through September, Sundays at 4pm. They feature matadors from Mexico and Spain, and tickets start at $7.35. The downtown ring is at 100 Bulevar Agua Caliente, not far from the twin towers of the Grant Hotel Tijuana. The Bullring by the Sea is located on the coast south of the city.

A fairly well-kept secret is Tijuana's fairways, at the **Tijuana Golf and Country Club,** also on Bulevar Agua Caliente, even closer to the Grand Hotel Tijuana (☎ **81-78-55**). Greens fees are $25 on weekdays and $35 on weekends, with cart and club rentals available. The course dates from the 1920s. There is a restaurant on the premises. Open daily from 7am to 8pm.

SHOPPING

Tijuana's biggest attraction is shopping—ask any of the 44 million people who cross the border each year to do it. They come to take advantage of the reasonable prices on liquor and other items, such as guayabera shirts—embroidered men's cotton shirts that are extremely cool and comfortable and so acceptable and attractive that Mexican businessmen often wear them to work.

American currency is fully accepted here and as far south as Ensenada. (If you plan to buy silver jewelry, wait and do it there.) You'll even get back nickels and dimes in change, and you can bring up to $400 in merchandise back across the border duty-free.

Tijuana's shops are strung out along Avenida Revolución, the old downtown tourist strip with its perpetual carnival atmosphere. Off this well-beaten but colorful track, there are fine, modern shopping centers, such as the **Plaza Río Tijuana.** Here, more than on Avenida Revolución, you can observe the "real" Tijuana, where the locals shop and stroll.

Avenida Revolución is lined with shops, stalls (where you can bargain), vendors hawking their wares, eateries, and burros festooned with garlands and sombreros, just waiting to be photographed with you. Many visitors think that this is all there is to Tijuana, and they come away disappointed. But, don't fret, there's more than this.

Begin your Tijuana shopping experience browsing, as most newcomers to Tijuana do, along Avenida Revolución. As you stroll down it, you'll notice a mixture of modern and traditional shops. **Le Drug Store,** with its sleek glass facade at Revolución and Calle 4, sells perfumes, cosmetics, and leather bags. It has a cafe and rest rooms and accepts American Express and Visa.

Between Calles 4 and 5 stands the old **Hotel Caesar** (home of the original Caesar's salad), whose faded elegance recalls a bygone era. During the bullfight season, the matadors still headquarter here. In the lobby you can see, lovingly preserved, the "suits of lights" worn by some of Spain's and Mexico's most famous bullfighters, and along the stairwell, a photograph gallery commemorates their glory. Steps away from the commercial clatter of Avenida Revolución, this quiet oasis evokes one of Mexico's most romantic traditions.

To try your hand at bargaining, stroll through **Pasaje Sonia,** on Revolución between Calles 5 and 6. At 735 Revolución, **Hand Art** is an excellent source of hand-embroidered linens and clothing from the Mexican mainland.

At Revolución and Calle 7, across from the Jai Alai Palace, **Tolán** is the best place in Tijuana to shop for craft items. In six rooms, you'll discover clothing, wall hangings, glassware, and tin work. My favorites are the clay-and-tin *arboles de la vida* (trees of life) from Metepec and Puebla, the blue glassware from Guadalajara, and the tin Christmas ornaments from Oaxaca. There's something here for every pocketbook.

A block from Tolán, at the corner of Calle 7 and Avenida Madero, is a little shopping center with a **Ralph Lauren** shop, a linen shop, and stores selling beachwear, sportswear, and evening wear. One block beyond Tolán, on the opposite side of Revolución, is **Sanborn's,** a Mexico City tradition expanded to Tijuana. It contains a modern pharmacy, restaurant, bookstore, and souvenir shop all under one roof.

SHOPPING CENTERS

Plaza Californias and Plaza San Angel   You'll find this shopping center with both shops and street vendors just after you cross the border and take the pedestrian bridge over the now-dusty bed of the Tijuana River. As you make your way from here toward the Tourist Information Center, you'll see another little shopping center called Plaza San Angel, on Calle 1 between Avenidas Negrete and Madero.

Plaza Fiesta   Kitty-corner to the Cultural Center, at Avenida Paseo de los Héroes and Avenida Independencia, Plaza Fiesta has many colorful cafes in colonial Mexican style featuring international cuisines, among them Spanish and Italian, and **Harry's Bar** for Mexican food. Next door is **Plaza del Zapato,** two levels of nothing but shoe stores. However, one renegade store squeaked in called **La Herradura de Oro,** which sells cowboy and horse gear, and it's fun for browsing or window shopping.

Plaza Río Tijuana   There are excellent buys on French perfume, Italian leather, and liquor in the Plaza Río Tijuana shopping center, a cab ride away from Avenida

Revolución and across the street from the Cultural Center. Try **Importaciones Sara** for imported perfumes (they have another store on Revolución), and the huge **Comercial Mexicana** for an enormous variety of liquor at bargain prices. A cross between a modern supermarket and an open-air mercado, Comercial Mexicana delights the senses with displays of colorful chilies, exotic fruits, and fresh cheeses (which you're invited to sample). Next door, **Suzett** bakery makes irresistible pastries and breads. When your feet and your spirit need a rest, sip a free cup of their wonderful Mexican hot chocolate and munch on a fresh roll while watching couples, families, and young professionals stream by.

WHERE TO STAY

When calculating room rates, always remember that hotel rates in Tijuana are subject to a 12% tax.

Grand Hotel Tijuana

Agua Caliente 4500, Tijuana. ☎ **800/GRANDTJ**, or ☎ 81-70-00 in Tijuana. Fax 85-18-37. 422 rms and suites. A/C TV TEL. $81 double; from $150 suite. AE, DC, MC, V. Free underground parking.

You can see the 25-story twin towers of the Grand Hotel Tijuana when you come into town (one tower contains offices, the other, this hotel). It's part of the Aguacaliente Complex right beside the Tijuana Country Club and very near the racetrack.

Dining/Entertainment: Restaurant Las Torres offers Mexican food Monday through Saturday from noon to 5pm. For international fare, The Bistro, complete with piano music, is open for dinner from 6pm to midnight. The Plaza Café is open 24 hours. There's continuous music in the lobby bar from noon to 2am.

Services: 24-hour room service, laundry/dry cleaning.

Facilities: Concierge level (called Fiesta Grand Club) on top four floors, heated pool, tennis courts, sauna, Jacuzzi, meeting rooms, access to golf course, travel agency.

Hotel Hacienda Del Río

Bl. General Sánchez Taboada 10606, Tijuana, Zona Río. ☎ **800/522-1516** in Calif., Ariz., and Nev.; 800/225-2786 elsewhere in the U.S.; 84-86-44 in Tijuana; or 619/298-4105 in Calif. Fax 84-86-20. 130 rms, 4 suites. A/C TV TEL. $53 double; from $59 suite. Children under 12 stay free in parents' room. MC, V.

Just a block from Avenida Paseo de los Héroes, Hacienda del Río is a modern three-story property, which opened in August 1989. Rooms on the second and third floors have tubs in the bathrooms; there are showers in the first-floor rooms. Suites have separate living rooms and vanities and marble-tiled baths. Recliners, tables, and umbrellas surround the hotel pool. The restaurant is open for breakfast, lunch, and dinner. Facilities include a hotel shop and meeting room.

Hotel La Villa de Zaragoza

Av. Madero 1120, Tijuana, Zona Centro. ☎ **85-18-32**. Fax 85-18-37 in Tijuana. 66 rms and suites. A/C TV TEL. $42.85 double; $61.70 suite. Extra person $5.35. Rates include tax. MC, V. Free parking.

Situated downtown behind the Jai Alai Palace, this is your best bet for convenience sake if you don't have a car and are on a budget. Rooms have furnishings that are worn but clean, tiled showers, and separate vanities. Courtyard rooms are the quietest, but other rooms are larger. There is no extra charge for local telephone calls. The hotel has a casual restaurant and a somewhat more formal bar. There is room service from 7am to 11pm, and laundry service is available. There's hotel security at night. Reserve 2 weeks in advance for weekends.

Lucerna

Av. Paseo de los Héroes 10902, Zona Río, Tijuana. ☎ **800/522-1516** in Calif., Ariz., and Nev.; 800/225-2786 elsewhere in the U.S.; 33-39-00 in Tijuana; or 619/298-4105 in Calif. Fax 619/294-7366. 163 rms, 5 suites. TV TEL. $85 double; $88 suite, AE, DC, MC, V.

This striking property, with a courtyard fountain, has a friendly, attentive staff. The pretty rooms have either balconies or brick patios. A French restaurant in the hotel serves dinner from 8 to 11pm, as well as Saturday and Sunday brunch; there are two bars, one of them featuring piano music nightly. In summer, there are cookouts around the pool, and room service is available from 7am to 11pm. Car-rental and laundry service are also offered.

WHERE TO DINE
EXPENSIVE

La Costa

Calle 7, no. 150 (just off Av. Revolución), Zona Centro. ☎ **85-84-94.** Fax 85-31-24. E-mail fpedrin@bbs.cincos.net. Main courses $11–$22. MC, V. Daily 10am–midnight. MEXICAN-STYLE SEAFOOD.

Fish gets top billing here, starting with the hearty seafood soup. There are combination platters of half a grilled lobster, stuffed shrimp, and baked shrimp; fish fillet stuffed with seafood and cheese; and several abalone dishes.

Tour de France

Gobernador Ibarra 252 (on the old road to Ensenada between the Palacio Azteca Hotel and Motel La Sierra), Col. America. ☎ **81-75-42.** Fax 81-75-42. Web site: www.tijuananet.com/restaurant/tdfrance. Reservations recommended. Main courses (including soup and salad) $18–$21; MC, V. Mon–Thurs 8am–10:30pm, Fri–Sat 8am–11:30pm. FRENCH.

Martín San Román, the chef and co-owner of Tour de France, was sous-chef at San Diego's famous Westgate hotel and then went on to open the top-class Marius restaurant in the Meridian hotel in Coronado. His loyal clientele has followed him from San Diego, and he has acquired new devotees in Tijuana. It's worth a trip to Tijuana just to sample Martín's pâtés or his escargots; and the vegetables, prepared and presented with the flair of an artist, all come fresh from local Ensenada farms. The wine list is extensive and international, and the atmosphere is as fine as the food.

MODERATE

Hard Rock Cafe

520 Av. Revolución (between Calles 1 and 2), Zona Centro. ☎ **85-02-06.** Menu items $5–$10. MC, V. Daily 11am–2am. AMERICAN/MEXICAN.

Here's proof of Tijuana's modernity: its own Hard Rock Cafe, complete with burgers and fries and, of course, the usual T-shirts and other merchandise. But this place, which is popular with families at lunchtime, also makes a bow to Mexico on its menu, with fajitas, nachos, and guacamole. Daily specials include the catch of the day. There's live music Thursday through Sunday evenings. It's conveniently located near the Tourist Information Center.

Tia Juana Tilly's

Av. Revolución 701 (at Calle 7), Zona Centro. ☎ **85-60-24.** Main courses $8–$12. AE, MC, V. Daily 11am–11pm. Courtesy parking available behind Jai Alai. MEXICAN.

Centrally situated beside the Jai Alai Palace, this lively spot features all manner of Mexican fare, including chicken and beef dishes and combination plates.

INEXPENSIVE

Cafe La Especial

Av. Revolución 718 (at the foot of the stairway to Gómez Arcade), Zona Centro. ☎ **85-66-54.**
Menu items $3–$12. Daily 9am–10pm. MEXICAN.

For as many years as anyone can remember, La Especial has been a favorite refuge
from the commotion of Avenida Revolución. The food is dependably fresh and well
prepared, and the beer is always cold. Served with fresh, warm tortillas, the *carne asada*
(grilled steak) is particularly delicious; the cheese enchiladas are the best in town at
any price. Traditional Mexican breakfasts are available all day.

Carnitas Uruapan

Bd. Díaz Ordáz 12650 (across from Plaza Pacífica), La Mesa. ☎ **81-61-81.** Menu items $2.50–
$8. No credit cards. Daily 7am–3am. MEXICAN.

Going to Carnitas Uruapan, 1 1/2 blocks from the racetrack, is like attending a Mexican family celebration. You sit at brightly painted long tables, often with other
groups, while strolling mariachis and bustling waiters and waitresses contribute to
a fiesta atmosphere. The only dish to order here is *carnitas:* succulent chunks of pork
served family-style with Mexican beans, hot sauce, and fresh cilantro, all of which
gets rolled up in a warm tortilla to create an incomparable treat. Half a kilo (about
1 lb.) of carnitas, plenty for two people, costs about $12 and comes with all the
trimmings.

TIJUANA AFTER DARK

Tijuana has several lively discos, and perhaps the most popular is **Baby Rock
Discoteca,** 1482 Diego Rivera, Zona Río (☎ 34-24-04), (an obvious cousin to
Acapulco's lively Baby O), which features everything from jungle rock to hard rock.
It's located in the Zona Río, close to the Guadalajara Grill restaurant.

A recent addition to Tijuana's nightlife has been the proliferation of "sports bars,"
cheerful watering holes featuring satellite wagering from all over the United States,
as well as from Tijuana's Caliente track. The most popular of these bars cluster in
Pueblo Amigo, Via Oriente and Paseo Tijuana in the Zona Río, a new center designed to resemble a colonial Mexican village. Even if you don't bet on the horses,
you can soak up the atmosphere. Two of the town's hottest discos, **Rodeo de Media Noche** (☎ 82-49-67) and **Señor Frogs** (☎ 82-49-62), are also in Pueblo
Amigo, as well as **La Tablita de Tony** (☎ 82-81-11), an Argentinean restaurant.
Pueblo Amigo is conveniently located less than 2 miles from the border: a short taxi
ride or—during daylight hours—a pleasant walk.

8   Baja California: Exploring More of Mexico

If you have a car, you can easily venture into Baja California for a getaway of a few
days. Since 1991, American car-rental companies have allowed their cars to be driven
into Baja. **Avis** (☎ 619/231-7155) and many other car-rental companies let their
cars go as far south as the 28th parallel, the dividing line between the states of Baja
North and Baja South. **Bob Baker Ford** allows its cars to be driven the entire 1,000-
mile stretch of the Baja peninsula (☎ 619/297-5001). Many other companies offer rentals to Baja as well, so do a little comparison shopping before you sign a rental
agreement. Whether you drive your own car or a rented one, you'll need Mexican
auto insurance in addition to your own; it's available at the border in San Ysidro or
through the car-rental companies.

It takes relatively little time to cross the international border in Tijuana, but be prepared for a delay of an hour or more on your return to San Diego; if you take local buses down the Baja coast, which is possible, the delays come en route rather than at the border.

You can also visit Rosarito and Ensenada through a tour. **San Diego Mini Tours** (☎ **619/477-8687**) makes daily trips.

VISITOR INFORMATION   The best source of information is **Baja California Tourism Information** (☎ **800/522-1516** in Calif., Ariz., or Nev.; 800/225-2786 in the rest of the U.S. and Canada; or ☎ 619/298-4105). This office provides advice and makes hotel reservations throughout Baja California. You can also contact the **Secretaria de Turismo** of Baja California, P.O. Box 2448, Chula Vista, CA 91912 (☎ **81-94-92;** fax 81-95-79).

A SUGGESTED ITINERARY   Begin your trip in Tijuana with an afternoon and maybe an overnight stay that includes watching some fast-paced jai alai (see "Spectator Sports & Outdoor Pursuits," in section 7 for in-depth information), then head down the coast to the seaside town of Rosarito Beach, and then on to Puerto Nuevo and Ensenada.

Two roads run between the largest and third-largest cities in Baja: the scenic, coast-hugging toll road (marked *cuota*) and the free but slower-going public road (marked *libre*). I strongly recommend starting out on the toll road, but use the free road along Rosarito Beach so that you can pull on and off easily to shop and look at the view. Pick up the toll road again at Puerto Nuevo for the remainder of the trip to Ensenada. Even if you don't plan to drive as far as Ensenada, at least go to an overlook on the toll road called El Mirador, and slightly beyond it, because the drive is spectacular and shouldn't be missed. To get to El Mirador, take the exit south of Baja Mar.

ROSARITO BEACH

The main draw in Rosarito Beach, which is 36 miles south of San Diego and 20 miles south of Tijuana, is the **Rosarito Beach Hotel,** the Hotel del Coronado of Mexico. The hotel came first, and the town of Rosarito Beach, which now numbers 90,000 inhabitants, followed. And so did celebrities and heads of state. Paulette Goddard and Burgess Meredith were married here, and in 1955 Prince Ali Khan and actress Rita Hayworth brought an entourage of 24 and took over all the hotel's bungalows for several weeks. Telephone calls to Rosarito Beach from the United States are international calls, and you need to add **011-52-661** before the number. In front of Plaza Quinta in Rosarito Beach, you'll find the **tourist information kiosk,** open weekdays from 10am to 4pm, weekends from 10am to 5pm; English is spoken (☎ **2-03-96**).

Sleepy Rosarito Beach has caught the attention of Hollywood. *Titanic,* an enormous project costing $170 million, was filmed here from September 1996 to March 1997 in a state-of-the-art production facility. An 800-foot-long Titanic replica was constructed, and many local citizens served as extras in the movie. The "ship" remains on the set, and there are rumors that Hollywood plans to use it in other upcoming productions.

SHOPPING

Interiores Los Ríos is in Rosarito Beach at Avenida Benito Juárez 25500. Owned by transplanted Californians David Lugo and JoAnne Hutsel, who have made this their home since 1954, the shop is filled with colonial Mexican furniture, accessories, and folk art. The furniture is mainly of pine or alder, stained or hand-painted, and it can be custom-made and delivered anyplace in the United States, Canada, or Europe. Pieces include chests, tables, chairs, armoires, hutches, and headboards. Prices tend to be high, but the quality is excellent, and you're likely to find folk art from

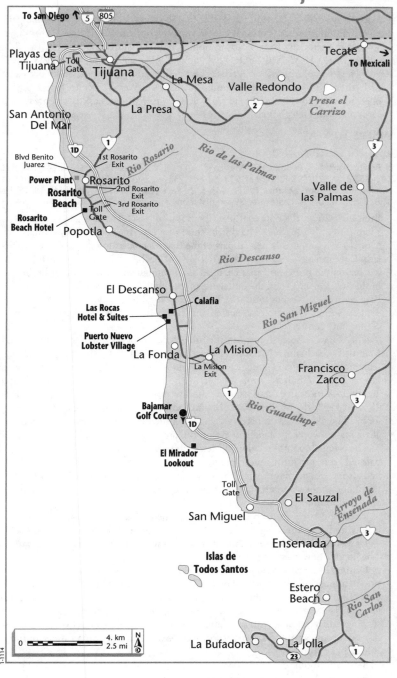

Baja California

To San Diego ↑ 5 805

Playas de Tijuana

Toll Gate

Tijuana

La Mesa

Valle Redondo

Tecate

→ To Mexicali

2

Presa el Carrizo

San Antonio Del Mar

La Presa

1D

1

Blvd Benito Juarez

1st Rosarito Exit

Rio Rosario

Rio de las Palmas

3

Power Plant

Rosarito

2nd Rosarito Exit

Valle de las Palmas

Rosarito Beach

3rd Rosarito Exit

Rosarito Beach Hotel

Toll Gate

Popotla

Rio Descanso

El Descanso

Calafia

Las Rocas Hotel & Suites

Rio San Miguel

Puerto Nuevo Lobster Village

La Fonda

La Mision

La Mision Exit

Francisco Zarco

1

3

Bajamar Golf Course

1D

Rio Guadalupe

El Mirador Lookout

Toll Gate

El Sauzal

Arroyo de Ensenada

San Miguel

3

Ensenada

Islas de Todos Santos

Estero Beach

Rio San Carlos

0   4. km   2.5 mi

N

La Bufadora

La Jolla

23

1

1-1114

245

Michoacán, Oaxaca, Nayaut, or Puebla on the sale rack. There are also some paintings. The shop accepts personal checks (with identification), traveler's checks, and Visa. It is open daily from 10am to 6pm. Contact them at ☎ **2-16-51** (fax 2-30-44), or write 416 W. San Ysidro Blvd., Suite L-714, San Ysidro, CA 92173.

If you love colorful Mexican fabrics and designs, drop by Nelda Stoke's fun shop, **El Último Tango,** south of Interiores Los Ríos on Avenida Benito Juárez. They're open Monday through Saturday from 9:30am to 5:30pm; cash is accepted, credit cards aren't (no telephone).

WHERE TO STAY

Rosarito Beach Hotel

Bl. Benito Juárez #31, Rosarito, B.C. Mexico (P.O. Box 430145, San Diego, CA 92143). ☎ **800/ 343-8582** or 619/498-8230. Fax 011/52-661-21176. E-mail reserv@telnor.net. Web site: www.rosaritohtl.com. 275 rms. TV TEL. $69–$129 Sept–June, $89–$139 July–Aug and U.S. holidays. 2 children under 12 stay free in parents' room. Packages available. MC, V. Free parking.

Built in 1926 on the Baja coastline, the Rosarito Beach Hotel began as a small, 12-room inn with a big bar. The dream child of a Los Angeles attorney named Jacob Morris Danziger, this hotel was part of the Baja scene that lured Americans, particularly Californians, away from the strict laws of Prohibition with legal drinking and betting on the horses. All that changed soon enough with the repeal of Prohibition in the States in 1933 and the outlawing of gambling in Mexico in 1935. Of the three Baja resorts of that era, only the Rosarito Beach Hotel would survive as a hotel; Tijuana's Agua Caliente disappeared and Ensenada's Riviera del Pacífico became a community center.

The Rosarito Beach resort, on the other hand, expanded under the direction of Manuel Barbachano, a Mexican businessman credited with bringing electricity and television to Tijuana, Tecate, Ensenada, and Mexicali. In 1937 the present owner, Hugo Torres Chabert, took over, and the hotel was remodeled by a Belgian architect—tiles, murals, and painted rafters were added generously throughout. From 1937 to 1939, the Mexican artist Matias Santoyo created the striking murals in the lobby. The old man with his dog depicted in the mural on the south wall was actually a mason who kept a vigilant eye on the progress of the artist.

The original rooms, in colonial Mexican decor with white stucco walls and hand-painted trim, are most inviting. They have beamed, painted ceilings, two double beds (some rooms have queen- or king-size beds), tiled baths with showers, TVs, telephones, tables and chairs, and heaters. Only the rooms in the new tower have air-conditioning.

The hotel entry features a welcoming stained-glass depiction of a Latin beach beauty and a sign reading POR ESTA PUERTA PASAN LAS MUJERES MAS HERMOSAS DEL MUNDO ("Through this doorway pass the most beautiful women in the world"). The hotel is now quite popular with families.

Dining/Entertainment: Chabert's Steakhouse serves steaks and international cuisine in a mansion built by the Torres-Chabert family in 1926. It's open daily from 4 to 11pm in summer; weekends only off-season. The Azteca Restaurant serves breakfast, lunch, dinner, and Sunday buffet brunch, and there's an ocean-side bar. The striking Sala Mexicana, with tiles, murals, and painted ceiling, has live music on Friday, Saturday, and Sunday nights, as well as a Fiesta Mexicana dinner buffet on Friday and Saturday.

Services: Room service (7:30am to 10pm).

Facilities: Fully equipped European-style spa in elegant mansion; sauna, Jacuzzi, gym, aerobics classes ($10 charge); pool with a slide; Olympic-size pool trimmed in tiles; minigolf; gym, racquetball and tennis courts; playground overlooking the beach; nonsmoking rooms; meeting rooms; shopping arcade on the property.

WHERE TO DINE

While in Rosarito Beach, you may want to try **Chabert's** (elegant, French) or the more casual **Azteca Restaurant,** both in the Rosarito Beach Hotel, or outside the hotel, the nearby **Cazuela del Mole** for chicken enchiladas with mole sauce and *caldo de pollo* (chicken broth), **Ortega's** for lobster (unless you plan to drive south to Puerto Nuevo; see below), and, across the street from it, the tiny **Tacos Meno** for delicious fish tacos. All of these places are conveniently located on the main street, Avenida Benito Juárez.

Bibi's Bakery, in Plaza Quinta, has good pastries and bread.

ROSARITA BEACH AFTER DARK

Because the legal drinking age in Baja is 18, the under-21 crowd from southern California tends to flock across the border on Friday and Saturday nights. The most popular spot in town is **Papas and Beer,** a relaxed come-as-you-are–type club on the beach, a block north of the Rosarito Beach Hotel. Even for those young in spirit only, it's great fun, with open-air tables and a bar surrounding a sand volleyball court. Music, dancing, and volleyball games go on simultaneously, and the camaraderie is contagious. The cover charge varies depending upon the season, the crowd, and the mood of the staff. The **Salon Méxican** in the Rosarito Beach Hotel itself attracts a slightly more mature crowd, with live music on Friday, Saturday, and Sunday nights.

EN ROUTE FROM ROSARITO TO ENSENADA

The toll-free road south from Rosarito Beach passes numerous stands selling pottery, as well as new homes, beachfront condos, and resort hotels. About 6 miles south, at km 35.5, on the right, stands **Calafia Ocean Resort** (☎ **2-15-81**) a restaurant/bar on Descanso Bay. Here tables rest on terraces created from the cliff overlooking the sea, and the breathtaking view is not to be missed. This is a great spot for dining and dancing.

About a mile farther south, also on the right, an arched entryway will come into view, inviting you to **Puerto Nuevo,** a real treat if you're a lobster lover because that's the only thing you'll find on the menu in the dozens of eateries in this tiny seacoast community. About 40 years ago, the local fishermen's wives began to serve lobster in their kitchens, and a tradition was born. Baja lobster is available year-round (fresh from September to March); a filling meal of lobster with beans, rice, tortillas, and fresh limes and salsa costs about $10, or more, depending on the size of the lobster. Of the many dining choices in this *colonia,* my friends and I always eat at the place right across from the tiny chapel. There isn't a name on the outside, but the last time I was there it was painted blue. Don't expect to be handed a menu; everyone has the same thing. Do watch Maria and her helpers make the tortillas. Be prepared to wait for a table on weekends.

WHERE TO STAY

Hotel Las Rocas

Km 37.5 Free Road (P.O. Box 8851, Chula Vista, CA 91912-8851). ☎ and fax **2-21-40.** 48 rms, 26 suites. TV TEL. May–Sept, from $75 double; from $115 suite. Oct–Apr, from $55 double; from $89 suite. Senior discounts; packages available. AE, DC, MC, V. Take the 2nd Rosarito exit off the toll road, then drive 6 miles south; or follow the free road south from Rosarito; it'll be on the right.

Six miles south of Rosarito, on the free road, stands the striking Las Rocas, designed by the internationally known architect José Orozco. The lagoonlike swimming pool, poolside bar, and two Jacuzzis carved into rocks emphasize the hotel's dramatic setting on a cliff overlooking the Pacific Ocean. The suites and rooms all have ocean views and private terraces. The suites also feature an enormous sunken tiled shower, fireplace, wet bar, refrigerator, microwave, and coffeemaker. Add a tennis court, restaurant, cozy piano bar, and nearby tide pools to explore, and you have one of Baja's most romantic hideaways.

Dining/Entertainment: Colorful Café Carnaval is open for breakfast and lunch from 7:30am to 3pm and has a terrace for outdoor dining. Pretty Restaurante El Meson serves Mexican and European cuisine from 3 to 10pm; Bar Olé, off the main lobby, often has piano music. Under a thatched roof, Bar La Palapa serves drinks during the day overlooking the pool and the Pacific.

Services: Room service, *Los Angeles Times* and *San Diego Union-Tribune* for sale in lobby, satellite TV.

Facilities: Outdoor pool and two Jacuzzis are open from 8am to 10pm, tennis court, gift shop.

FARTHER SOUTH

Continuing south on the free road, you will soon come to a Moorish-looking building set back from the road, at km 51, which is actually **Café Americana,** run by the Piazza family from Los Angeles, who after years of vacationing here decided to put down roots. Popular for its 21 gourmet pizzas, including traditional cheese and vegetarian, the restaurant, beautifully decorated inside, also serves meatless (and meaty) pasta dishes, lobster or chicken Alfredo, *lasagne al forno* (oven-baked), eggplant Parmesan, chicken marsala, and salads at moderate prices.

Just down the free road, at km 59, is a nostalgic favorite with authentic Mexican ambiance, **La Fonda,** both a restaurant and an oceanfront hotel clinging to a cliff about 25 miles north of Ensenada. It's been here since 1936 and is the perfect place for a secret getaway or a leisurely lunch or supper on the bougainvillea-covered terrace overlooking the Pacific. House specialties include black-bean soup, homemade tortillas, scalloped potatoes, spit-roasted suckling wild piglet, and fresh spring lamb. Sunday brunch, from 10am to 3:30pm, is particularly popular, and San Diegans sometimes drive south just to enjoy it and go for a stroll on the beach, accessible via a cliff-side walkway, afterward. The rooms at La Fonda are basic, with few amenities, but the location is terrific; if you stay, request one of the new rooms.

At La Fonda, you can pick up the toll road once more to drive the remaining 28 miles along the coast to Ensenada—or at least 10 or so more miles to a fantastic lookout or a beachside campground. The free road also continues to Ensenada, but it heads inland, winding through vineyards, citrus groves, and farmland, circumventing the dramatic view; an occasional roadside stand sells cold drinks, snacks, and homemade local cheeses.

Eight miles along this stretch of the toll road, you pass **Baja Mar Golf Course and Resort** where there is a championship 27-hole golf course. About a mile beyond it, at km 84 you'll find ✪ **El Mirador,** a lookout over the dramatic sweep of Todos Santos Bay and the graceful curve of the Baja coastline. It was said the lookout, which has an excellent Mexican restaurant and bar (☎ **1-03-78**), shops, and a little playground for children, was built to keep Americans from running their cars off the cliff here to collect the insurance.

A few miles farther south on the toll road, you'll come to a sign for **Salsipuedes Bay** (the name means "leave if you can"). The dramatic scenery along the drive ends here, so you can take the exit if you want to turn around and head north again; or if you plan to do some camping, head down the near mile-long, rutted road to **Salsipuedes Campground,** set under olive trees on a cliff. Each campsite has a fire ring and costs $5 a day (day use is also $5). There's a natural rock tub with hot-spring water at the campground and some basic cottages that rent for $30 a day. There is no easy access to the beach, known for its good surfing, from the campground.

Ensenada, with its shops, restaurants, and winery, is another 15 miles away.

ENSENADA

Ensenada, 84 miles south of San Diego and 68 miles south of Tijuana, is a pretty town surrounded by sheltering mountains; it's about 40 minutes from Rosarito, and it's the kind of place that loves a celebration. Most any time you choose to visit, the city is festive—be it for a bicycle race or a seafood festival.

There are a couple of **tourist information** offices in Ensenada. The **Tourist & Conventions Visitors Bureau** located at the northern entrance to town, on your right at the beginning of Bulevar Lazaro Cardenas, known also as Bulevar Costero, is open Monday through Friday from 9am to 7pm and Saturday and Sunday from 10am to 2pm. Eight blocks south you'll find the **State Secretary of Tourism** at Bulevar Lazaro Cardenas No. 1477, Government Building, (☎ **61-72-30-22;** fax 61-72-30-81), which is open Monday through Friday from 9am to 7pm, Saturday from 10am to 3pm, and Sunday from 10am to 2pm. Both offices have extended hours on U.S. holidays. **Taxis** park along López Mateos.

Note: Telephone calls to Ensenada from the United States are international calls, and you need to add **011-52-617** before the number.

EXPLORING ENSENADA

Compared to Tijuana's Avenida Revolución, with its jumble of activity and street vendors constantly hawking their merchandise, Ensenada's main drag, **Avenida López Mateos,** is cool, calm, and collected. No bargaining goes on in the stores, but the merchandise, which is of good quality and variety, is reasonably priced. You'll find leather goods, textiles, fashions, and handcrafted Mexican jewelry.

Among the outstanding shops in town are **Galería Sterling,** López Mateos 851, for crafts and silver jewelry; **Tesoros del Mar,** López Mateos 871, for shells galore and shell jewelry; **Artesanias Castillo,** López Mateos 656, for leather and high-quality designs in silver jewelry for which Mexico has justifiably become famous; and **Tannery South,** López Mateos 675, for leather products. From the shopping street, it's easy to stroll down to the **pier** where the fishing boats go out; munch on some fish tacos sold at the stands. You can also arrange fishing trips here.

You won't be in town long before you hear the name **"Houssong."** It's the local honky-tonk cantina, at the northern end of town off López Mateos at Avenida Ruiz 113, and it's been around since 1892. Sawdust covers the floor, and local musicians are liable to be serenading anyone who sits at a table instead of at the bar. Don't expect glamour, or even doors on the stalls in the women's room. The place is open daily from 10am to 2am.

If you linger too long at Houssong's, you might need to pay a visit to the **Medicine Man** pharmacy, on López Mateos at Castillo, conveniently open daily from 9am to 8:30pm (☎ **8-31-54**). A block away, at López Mateos and Blancarte, is one of the best restaurants in Mexico, **El Rey Sol,** which features French cuisine. It was founded in 1947 by Baja-born, Cordon Bleu–trained Virginia Geffroy (see "Where to Dine," below).

A local Ensenada attraction, **La Bufadora,** a blowhole, sends water spouting 75 feet into the air. The name means "the snort," and if you go at high tide, you'll see why. It's 16 miles south of town on Route 1 at the tip of Punta Banda.

Wine lovers can tour **Santo Tomas Winery,** Baja's oldest winery, established in 1888, now with a production of about 100,000 cases a year. It offers daily bilingual tours and wine tastings with cheese and bread. The cost is $2.50 per person. There is now a restaurant in one of the aging rooms of the winery, called **La Embotelladora Vieja.** It serves Mediterranean-style cuisine, with an emphasis on local ingredients, and wines from Baja, Chile, and Europe. The winery is centrally located at the northern end of town, at Avenida Miramar 666 between Calle 6 and Calle 7 (☎ **8-33-33** for general information).

WHERE TO STAY

While most visitors to this part of Baja tend to stay at the large waterfront properties along Rosarito Beach, some do stay in town. The following hotels in downtown Ensenada are within easy walking distance of the shops and restaurants along López Mateos.

Remember that in Mexico a single- or double-room rate has nothing to do with people, just beds: a single room has one bed, a double has two, and you pay accordingly.

San Nicolas Resort Hotel

Avenidas López Mateos and Guadalupe, Ensenada (P.O. Box 437060, San Ysidro, CA 92073-7060). ☎ **800/522-1516** or 619/298-4105 in Calif.; 800/225-2786 elsewhere in the U.S.; 52/617-61901 in Mexico. Fax 90-617-64-930. 143 rms, 7 suites. AC TV TEL. $58–$88 double; from $130 suite. Extra person $10. MC, V. Free parking.

This cheerful place glows with color, from the green trim of its roof to the bright green, red, and blue of the carpeting in its hallways. Rooms have balconies, most facing the Olympic-size pool lined with palms and beach chairs. Courtyard rooms, with high, wood-beamed ceilings, are particularly quiet, except for the relaxing sounds of a waterfall wafting in the window. Hallways on the second and third floors are unique and Spanish in style. Suites are large, lovely, and made for romance, with dimmer switches and large mirrors everywhere; the split-level La Condesa suite has a huge raised Jacuzzi and two living rooms.

Dining/Entertainment: Choose from a restaurant, cocktail lounge, and discotheque.

Services: Room service (7am to 11pm), complimentary margarita at the bar upon arrival.

Facilities: Two pools, Jacuzzi, beauty salon, gift shop, travel agency.

Villa Fontana Hotel—Days Inn

Av. López Mateos 1050, Ensenada, Mexico. ☎ **800/422-8204** in Calif., Ariz., and Nev., or 52/617-83434. 62 rms, 4 junior suites. Summer, $52 double, $80 suite. Rates are higher on holidays, lower in winter. Rates include continental breakfast but do not include tax. AE, MC, V. Free parking.

This pretty downtown hotel is peach-colored, with gray-and-white trim and gabled roofs. Rooms continue the color theme; baths, usually with showers, rather than tubs, are on the small side. Some second-story rooms have balconies and A-frame ceilings with rafters. Since the hotel is right on the main street, rooms in the back tend to be quieter. There's a second-story patio and a small pool.

WHERE TO DINE

El Charro

Av. López Mateos 475 (between Ruiz and Gastellum). ☎ **8-38-81.** Menu items $5–$12; $20 for lobster. No credit cards. Daily 11am–2am. MEXICAN.

You'll recognize El Charro by its front windows: Whole chickens rotate slowly on the rotisserie in one, while a woman makes tortillas in the other. This little place has been here since 1956 and looks it, with charred walls and a ceiling made of split logs. The simple fare consists of such dishes as half a roasted chicken with fries and tortillas or carne asada with soup, guacamole, and tortillas. Giant piñatas hang from the walls above the concrete floor. Kids are welcome; they'll think they're on a picnic. Wine and beer are served, and beer is cheaper than soda.

✪ El Rey Sol

Av. López Mateos 1000 (at Blancarte). ☎ **8-17-33.** Reservations recommended for weekends. Main courses $12–$32. AE, MC, V. Daily 7:30am–10:30pm. FRENCH/MEXICAN.

Its name means the "Sun King," and the restaurant is housed in a building that is red, white, and blue on the outside and country French on the inside. Waiters wear white jackets, and tables are covered with white-and-blue linen cloths. All the ingredients in the dishes served here are fresh, many of them grown on the family farm of the restaurant's founder, Virginia "Pepita" Geffroy. Her family carries on the tradition of fine food, service, and ambiance that she began in 1947. Appetizers include escargots, house pâté, and *"almejas El Rey Sol"* (broiled fresh clams with melted cheese). Main courses feature fish and seafood—manta ray in black butter sauce; medaillons topped with capers and a white-wine sauce; trout amandine; and baby clams steamed in butter, white wine, and cilantro. There are some meat and Mexican dishes, such as chicken chipotle (half a chicken cooked with brandy, port wine, chipotle chilies, and cream). Lunch is a good value: Along with your main course, you get homemade soup or green salad, vegetables, bread and butter, plus sorbet to clear the palate. You can choose from a French, American, or Mexican breakfast, or enjoy cappuccino and pastries in its pretty, European-style tearoom.

Appendix: Useful Toll-free Numbers & Web Sites

A Major Hotel & Motel Chains

Best Western International
☎ 800/528-1234 in North America
☎ 800/528-2222 TDD

Clarion Hotels
☎ 800/CLARION in the continental U.S. and Canada
☎ 800/228-3323 TDD
www.hotelchoice.com/cgi-bin/res/webres?clarion.html

Comfort Inns
☎ 800/228-5150 in the continental U.S. and Canada
☎ 800/228-3323 TDD
www.hotelchoice.com/cgi-bin/res/webres?comfort.html

Courtyard by Marriott
☎ 800/321-2211 in the continental U.S. and Canada
☎ 800/228-7014 TDD
www.courtyard.com/

Days Inn
☎ 800/325-2525 in the continental U.S. and Canada
☎ 800/325-3297 TDD
www.daysinn.com/daysinn.html

Doubletree Hotels
☎ 800/222-TREE

Econo Lodges
☎ 800/55-ECONO in the continental U.S. and Canada
☎ 800/228-3323 TDD
www.hotelchoice.com/cgi-bin/res/webres?econo.html

Embassy Suites
☎ 800/362-2779 in the continental U.S. and Canada
☎ 800/458-4708 TDD
www.embassy-suites.com/

Fairfield Inns by Marriott
☎ 800/228-2800
www.marriott.com/fairfieldinn/

Hampton Inns
☎ 800/HAMPTON in the continental U.S. and Canada
☎ 800/451-HTDD TDD
www.hampton-inn.com/

Hilton Hotels Corporation
☎ 800/HILTONS in the continental U.S. and Canada
☎ 800/368-1133 TDD
www.hilton.com

Holiday Inn
☎ 800/HOLIDAY in the continental U.S. and Canada
☎ 800/238-5544 TDD
www.holiday-inn.com/

Howard Johnson
☎ 800/654-2000 in the continental U.S. and Canada
☎ 800/654-8442 TDD
www.hojo.com/hojo.html

ITT Sheraton
☎ 800/325-3535 in the continental U.S. and Canada
☎ 800/325-1717 TDD

La Quinta Motor Inns
☎ 800/531-5900 in the continental U.S. and Canada
☎ 800/426-3101 TDD

Marriott Hotels
☎ 800/228-9290 in the continental U.S. and Canada
☎ 800/228-7014 TDD
www.marriott.com/

Motel 6
☎ 800/4-MOTEL6 in the continental U.S. and Canada

Omni Hotels
☎ 800/843-6664 in the continental U.S. and Canada

Quality Inns
☎ 800/228-5151 in the continental U.S. and Canada
☎ 800/228-3323 TDD
www.hotelchoice.com/cgi-bin/res/webres?quality.html

Radisson Hotels International
☎ 800/333-3333 in the continental U.S. and Canada

Ramada Inns
☎ 800/2-RAMADA in the continental U.S. and Canada
www.ramada.com/ramada.html

Red Carpet Inns
☎ 800/251-1962

Red Lion Hotels and Inns
☎ 800/547-8010 in the continental U.S. and Canada

Red Roof Inns
☎ 800/843-7663 in the continental U.S. and Canada
☎ 800/843-9999 TDD
www.redroof.com

Residence Inn by Marriott
☎ 800/331-3131 in the continental U.S. and Canada
☎ 800/228-7014 TDD
www.marriott.com/

Rodeway Inns
☎ 800/228-2000 in the continental U.S. and Canada
☎ 800/228-3323 TDD
www.hotelchoice.com/cgi-bin/res/webres?rodeway.html

Super 8 Motels
☎ 800/800-8000 in the continental U.S. and Canada
☎ 800/533-6634 TDD
www.super8motels.com/super8.html

Travelodge
☎ 800/255-3050 in the continental U.S. and Canada

Vagabond Hotels
☎ 800/522-1555

B Car-Rental Agencies

Advantage Rent-A-Car
☎ 800/777-5500 in the continental U.S. and Canada

Alamo Rent A Car
☎ 800/327-9633 in the continental U.S. and Canada
www.goalamo.com/

Avis
☎ 800/331-1212 in the continental U.S.
☎ 800/TRY-AVIS in Canada
☎ 800/331-2323 TDD
www.avis/com/

Budget Rent A Car
☎ 800/527-0700 in the continental U.S. and Canada
☎ 800/826-5510 TDD

Dollar Rent A Car
☎ 800/800-4000 in the continental U.S. and Canada

Enterprise Rent-A-Car
☎ 800/325-8007 in the continental U.S. and Canada

Hertz
☎ 800/654-3131 in the continental U.S. and Canada
☎ 800/654-2280 TDD

National Car Rental
☎ 800/CAR-RENT in the continental U.S. and Canada
☎ 800/328-6323 TDD
www.nationalcar.com/index.html

Payless
☎ 800/PAYLESS

Rent-A-Wreck
☎ 800/535-1391

Sears
☎ 800/527-0770

Thrifty Rent-A-Car
☎ 800/367-2277 in the continental U.S. and Canada
☎ 800/358-5856 TDD

Value Rent-A-Car
☎ 800/327-2501 in the continental U.S. and Canada
www.go-value.com/

C Airlines

Aeromexico
☎ 800/237-6639

Alaska Airlines
☎ 800/426-0333 in the U.S. and Canada

American Airlines
☎ 800/433-7300 in the continental U.S. and western Canada
☎ 800/543-1586 TDD
www.americanair.com/aa_home/aa_home.htm

America West
☎ 800/235-9292 in the continental U.S. and Canada

Continental Airlines
☎ 800/525-0280 in the continental U.S.
☎ 800/343-9195 TDD
www.flycontinental.com:80/index.html

Delta Air Lines
☎ 800/221-1212 in the continental U.S.
☎ 800/831-4488 TDD
www.delta-air.com/index.html

Northwest Airlines
☎ 800/225-2525 in the continental U.S. and Canada
www.nwa.com/

Southwest Airlines
☎ 800/435-9792 in the continental U.S. and Canada
www.iflyswa.com

TWA
☎ 800/221-2000 in the continental U.S.
www2.twa.com/TWA/Airlines/home/home.htm

United Airlines
☎ 800/241-6522 in the continental U.S. and Canada
www.ual.com/

US Airways
☎ 800/428-4322 in the continental U.S. and Canada
www.usair.com/

Index

See also separate Accommodations and Dining indexes, below.

ACCOMMODATIONS

RESTAURANTS

UP TO **$100.00 OFF**

Save up to $ \00 off when you buy
your airline ticke~ ~ Travel Discounters.

Call 1-800-355-1065 an~   ~e FRO in order to
receive the discount. See rev~   ~or discount prices.

May not be used in conjunction with a~   ~t or promotion.
Offer valid through 12/31/99. Coupon ~   ~re than once.

$5.00 Off Per Night

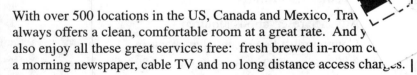

With over 500 locations in the US, Canada and Mexico, Tra~
always offers a clean, comfortable room at a great rate. And y~
also enjoy all these great services free: fresh brewed in-room c~
a morning newspaper, cable TV and no long distance access char~s.

And if you present this certificate upon check-in, we'll take $5.00
off the regular room rate for each night of your stay at a Travelodge
location. It just makes sense to stay with us and save.

For reservations, call **1-800-578-7878** or your travel agent
and ask for the 5CPN discount.

Savings are subject to certain restrictions and availability. Good for domestic and international travel that originates in the U.S. Valid for flights on most airlines worldwide.

Minimum Ticket Price	Save
$200.00	$25.00
$250.00	$50.00
$350.00	$75.00
$450.00	$100.00

Terms and Conditions

1. Advance reservations required.
2. Coupon must be presented at check-in.
3. Coupon cannot be combined with any other special offers, discounted rates.
4. Subject to availability.
5. No photocopies allowed.

For reservations, call **1-800-578-7878** or your travel agent and ask for the 5CPN discount.

FROMMER'S COMPLETE TRAVEL GUIDES
(Comprehensive guides to destinations around the world, with selections in all price ranges—from deluxe to budget)

Acapulco, Ixtapa & Zihuatenejo
Alaska
Amsterdam
Arizona
Atlanta
Australia
Austria
Bahamas
Barcelona, Madrid & Seville
Belgium, Holland & Luxembourg
Bermuda
Boston
Budapest & the Best of Hungary
California
Canada
Cancún, Cozumel & the Yucatán
Cape Cod, Nantucket & Martha's Vineyard
Caribbean
Caribbean Cruises & Ports of Call
Caribbean Ports of Call
Carolinas & Georgia
Chicago
Colorado
Costa Rica
Denver, Boulder & Colorado Springs
England

Europe
Florida
France
Germany
Greece
Hawaii
Hong Kong
Honolulu, Waikiki & Oahu
Ireland
Israel
Italy
Jamaica & Barbados
Japan
Las Vegas
London
Los Angeles
Maryland & Delaware
Maui
Mexico
Miami & the Keys
Montana & Wyoming
Montréal & Québec City
Munich & the Bavarian Alps
Nashville & Memphis
Nepal
New England
New Mexico
New Orleans
New York City
Northern New England
Nova Scotia, New Brunswick & Prince Edward Island
Paris

Philadelphia & the Amish Country
Portugal
Prague & the Best of the Czech Republic
Provence & the Riviera
Puerto Rico
Rome
San Antonio & Austin
San Diego
San Francisco
Santa Fe, Taos & Albuquerque
Scandinavia
Scotland
Seattle & Portland
South Pacific
Spain
Switzerland
Thailand
Tokyo
Toronto
Tuscany & Umbria
U.S.A.
Utah
Vancouver & Victoria
Vienna & the Danube Valley
Virgin Islands
Virginia
Walt Disney World & Orlando
Washington, D.C.
Washington & Oregon

FROMMER'S DOLLAR-A-DAY BUDGET GUIDES
(The ultimate guides to low-cost travel)

Australia from $50 a Day
Berlin from $50 a Day
California from $60 a Day
Caribbean from $60 a Day
Costa Rica & Belize from $35 a Day
England from $60 a Day
Europe from $50 a Day
Florida from $50 a Day
Greece from $50 a Day
Hawaii from $60 a Day

India from $40 a Day
Ireland from $45 a Day
Israel from $45 a Day
Italy from $50 a Day
London from $60 a Day
Mexico from $35 a Day
New York from $75 a Day
New Zealand from $50 a Day
Paris from $70 a Day
San Francisco from $60 a Day
Washington, D.C., from $50 a Day

FROMMER'S PORTABLE GUIDES
(Pocket-size guides for travelers who want everything in a nutshell)

Charleston & Savannah	New Orleans	San Francisco
Dublin	Puerto Vallarta,	Venice
Las Vegas	Manzanillo &	Washington, D.C.
Maine Coast	Guadalajara	

FROMMER'S FAMILY GUIDES
(The complete guides for successful family vacations)

California with Kids	New York City with Kids	Washington, D.C.,
Los Angeles with Kids	San Francisco with Kids	with Kids

FROMMER'S AMERICA ON WHEELS
(Everything you need for a successful road trip, including full-color road maps and ratings for every hotel)

California & Nevada	Mid-Atlantic	South-Central States
Florida	New England & New York	& Texas
Great Lake States &	Northwest & Great Plains	Southeast
Midwest		Southwest

FROMMER'S WALKING TOURS
(Memorable neighborhood strolls through the world's great cities)

London	San Francisco	Venice
New York	Spain's Favorite Cities	Washington, D.C.
Paris	Tokyo	

SPECIAL-INTEREST TITLES

Arthur Frommer's Branson!
Arthur Frommer's New World of Travel
The Civil War Trust's Official Guide to
 the Civil War Discovery Trail
Frommer's America's 100 Best-Loved
 State Parks
Frommer's Caribbean Hideaways
Frommer's Complete Hostel Vacation Guide
 to England, Scotland & Wales
Frommer's Europe's Greatest
 Driving Tours
Frommer's Food Lover's Companion
 to France
Frommer's Food Lover's Companion to Italy

New York Times Weekends
Outside Magazine's Adventure Guide
 to New England
Outside Magazine's Adventure Guide
 to Northern California
Outside Magazine's Adventure Guide
 to the Pacific Northwest
Outside Magazine's Guide
 to Family Vacations
Places Rated Almanac
Retirement Places Rated
Wonderful Weekends from NYC
Wonderful Weekends from San Francisco

FROMMER'S IRREVERENT GUIDES
(Wickedly honest guides for sophisticated travelers)

Amsterdam	Manhattan	Paris	U.S. Virgin Islands
Chicago	Miami	San Francisco	Walt Disney World
London	New Orleans	Santa Fe	Washington, D.C.

UNOFFICIAL GUIDES
(Get the unbiased truth from these candid, value-conscious guides)

Atlanta	The Great Smoky	Miami & the Keys	Walt Disney World
Branson, Missouri	& Blue Ridge	Mini-Mickey	Walt Disney World
Chicago	Mountains	New Orleans	Companion
Cruises	Las Vegas	Skiing in the West	Washington, D.C.
Disneyland			

BAEDEKER

(With four-color photographs and a free pull-out map)

Amsterdam	Crete	Lisbon	Scandinavia
Athens	Florence	London	Scotland
Austria	Florida	Mexico	Singapore
Bali	Germany	New York	South Africa
Belgium	Great Britain	New Zealand	Spain
Berlin	Greece	Paris	Switzerland
Brazil	Greek Islands	Portugal	Thailand
Budapest	Hawaii	Prague	Tokyo
California	Hong Kong	Provence	Turkish Coast
Canada	Ireland	Rome	Tuscany
Caribbean	Israel	San Francisco	Venice
China	Italy	St. Petersburg	Vienna
Copenhagen			

FROMMER'S BY NIGHT GUIDES

(The series for those who know that life begins after dark)

Amsterdam	Los Angeles	Manhattan	Paris
Chicago	Madrid	Miami	Prague
Las Vegas	& Barcelona	New Orleans	San Francisco
London			Washington, D.C.

FROMMER'S BEST BEACH VACATIONS

(The top places to sun, stroll, shop, stay, play, party, and swim, with ratings for each beach)

California	Florida	Mid-Atlantic
Carolinas & Georgia	Hawaii	New England

FROMMER'S BED & BREAKFAST GUIDES

(Selective guides with four-color photos and full descriptions of the best inns in each region)

California	Mid-Atlantic	The Rockies
Caribbean	New England	Southeast
Great American Cities	Pacific Northwest	Southwest
Hawaii		

FROMMER'S DRIVING TOURS

(Four-color photos and detailed maps outlining spectacular scenic driving routes)

America	California	Ireland	Scotland
Australia	Florida	Italy	Spain
Austria	France	New England	Switzerland
Britain	Germany	Scandinavia	Western Europe

FROMMER'S BORN TO SHOP

(The ultimate guides for travelers who love to shop)

Caribbean Ports	Great Britain	London	New York
of Call	Hong Kong	Mexico	Paris
France	Italy	New Egnland	

TRAVEL & LEISURE GUIDES

(Sophisticated pocket-size guides for discriminating travelers)

Amsterdam	Hong Kong	New York	San Francisco
Boston	London	Paris	Washington, D.C.